# MAPPING SADDLEWORTH
## Volume II

# MAPPING SADDLEWORTH

*Volume II*
*Manuscript Maps of the Parish 1625 - 1822*

Edited by

Mike Buckley, David Harrison, Victor Khadem,
Alan Petford and John Widdall

Saddleworth Historical Society

Uppermill

2010

Published by
The Saddleworth Historical Society, Uppermill, Saddleworth, Yorkshire, England.
www.saddleworth-historical society.org.uk

ISBN  0 904982 12 2

Text in Baskerville Old Face 12pt.
Printed by The Amadeus Press, Ezra House, West 26 Business Park, Cleckheaton,
Yorkshire.  BD19 4TQ

# FOREWORD

The production of this volume has involved a talented and dedicated team. The editors wish to place on record their gratitude for the substantial assistance rendered by many people. We are grateful to Alan Schofield for undertaking so many of the administrative aspects of the project and to Jason Harrison and Neil Barrow for their advice and assistance throughout its preparation. Thanks also go to Neville Ingrey for proof reading the text. Peter Fox, Victor Khadem, Mike Buckley, Alan Schofield, and Jean Sanders are responsible for producing the keys to the maps and Jean has taken the lead in the cover design. As for the editors, Mike Buckley recreated the 1822 Township map, David Harrison produced the 1808-12 Denshaw Moor Enclosure maps, the 1766 Giles Shaw Estate map, the 1779 John Buckley Estate maps and the 1625 Quick Moor map. John Widdall produced the 1770 James Farrer Estate map and Harrop Edge Enclosure map. John's experience was invaluable in the finer points of digital processing. Alan Petford, Victor Khadem and Mike Buckley wrote the text.

The Saddleworth Historical Society Archive has the original much faded and decayed 1822 Vestry Map and, with the permission of Oldham Local Studies and Archives to use the copy made in 1863, it has been possible to recreate the map for publication. The 1766 Giles Shaw Estate map, the 1770 James Farrar Estate map and the 1808-12 Harrop Edge Enclosure maps were generous donations to the Society's and Saddleworth Museum's archives. We are indebted to Bolton Public Library for permission to reproduce the Denshaw Moor Enclosure maps from the Albinson Collection and to The Greater Manchester County Record Office (with Manchester Archives), for the 1779 John Buckley Estate maps. The 1755 version of the 1625 Quick Moor map was prepared for us to copy by Sandy Haynes, the Archivist to the Mrs. Bissill's Marriage Settlement Collection housed at Enville Hall Estate, Stourbridge, Staffordshire, and we are grateful to them for permission to reproduce it here. Our thanks also go to Chetham's Library, Manchester, for permission to reproduce the Ollerenshaw Map in Figure 1 and to the Greater Manchester Archaeological Unit for the aerial view of Denshaw Moor in Figure 5.

Mike Buckley
David Harrison
Victor Khadem
Alan Petford
John Widdall

# CONTENTS

# INTRODUCTION

As the age of cartography dawned, Saddleworth was to be found on the margins of maps. Christopher Saxton depicted Saddleworth in his atlas of 1579, not only on the map of Yorkshire but also at the edges of his maps of Lancashire, Cheshire and Derbyshire. When John Speed published revisions of Saxton's maps in his *Theatre of the Empire of Great Britain* of 1611, Saddleworth appeared additionally at the edge of the new West Riding map.[1]

Through the medium of printed maps, cartography entered public consciousness. We can see this in a sketch map of the river Mersey and its tributaries that Edward Ollerenshaw drew in his copy of Holinshed's Chronicles late in the sixteenth century. (see Figure 1).[2] At first sight this map might appear rather crude but it is actually drawn to scale and the points of the compass are clearly indicated. Saxton's maps of Cheshire, Lancashire, Yorkshire and Derbyshire in his *Atlas of the Counties of England and Wales*, published in 1579, were almost certainly his source. Ollerenshaw made extensive annotations in his copy of Holinshed and at the end of the volume noted that he had finished reading it in August 1588, writing, 'historia hec est lecta 24 Augusti 1588'.[3] Interestingly, Ollerenshaw has added 'Saddleworthe frithe', placing it, rather vaguely, at the eastern extremity of the map. Here is an example of an educated man using maps to aid his understanding of the region and perhaps to advance his antiquarian studies. Ollerenshaw used the term 'Saddleworthe frithe' because Holinshed had used it in describing the course of the river Tame. Edward Ollerenshaw typifies that educated gentry interest in maps which would, in the next century, fuel the demand for printed county maps and which, at a more local level, was one of the motives behind the creation of estate maps, three examples of which are printed in the present collection. These maps celebrate ownership, are visually pleasing and could be useful administrative tools.

But there are many other motives for the creation of maps. Disputes are productive of documents. In many cases maps were created as part of the legal process and this is certainly the case with the map associated with the division of Quick Moor in 1625, a map that played its part in the settlement of a long-running conflict over one of the more potentially lucrative commons in Saddleworth. Equally this map was a useful administrative tool in dividing up the area and it played a significant role in the creation of the new landscape. Just how significant can be gauged by the fact that a new map had to

---

[1] These were not, perhaps, quite the earliest occasions when Saddleworth appeared on a map. There is the enigmatic *Map of the Boundaries of Holmfirth* that purports to date from the reign of Henry V (1413-1422). A brief discussion of this map is to be found in R.A. Skelton and P.D.A. Harvey, *Local Maps and Plans from Medieval England*, Oxford, The Clarendon Press, 1986, pp. 351-352. Perhaps the best copy is in the archives of the Yorkshire Archaeological Society, Leeds, MD 225/ Map 17. This map marks all the townships adjacent to the Graveship of Holme, including Saddleworth. It also shows *Rimmond pit* on the western boundary, probably because the Graveship of Holme was claiming that their territory extended as far west as this, a claim not finally refuted until the nineteenth century. See M. Buckley, D. Harrison and A. Petford, *Mapping Saddleworth*, Vol. I, Uppermill, Saddleworth Historical Society, 2007, p. 7.

[2] This map is drawn at the end of Ralph Holinshed, *The Historie of Irelande from the first inhabitation thereof, unto the year 1509...* which is bound up with volume one of R. Holinshed, *The Chronicles of England Scotland and Ireland*, London, Harrison, 1577, in Chetham's Library, Manchester. Little is known about Edward Ollerenshaw.

[3] *ibid.* p. 115.

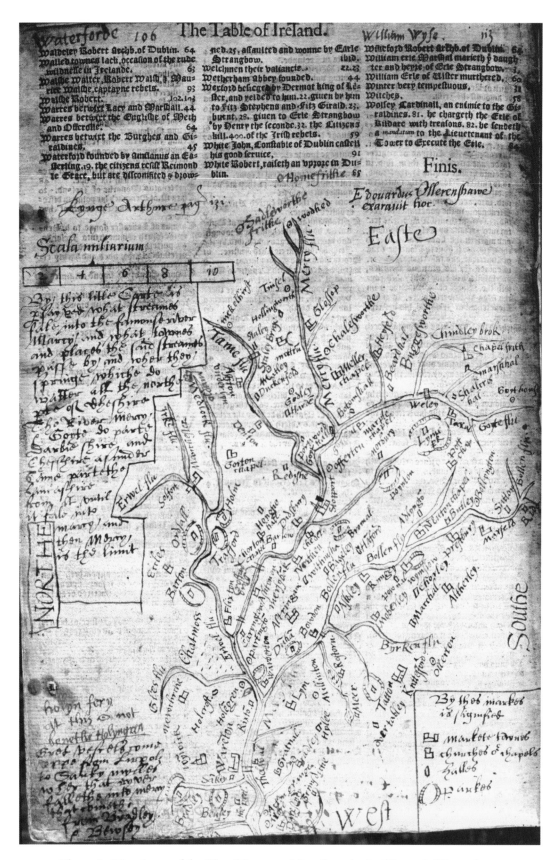

Figure 1.  Map drawn of the River Mersey and its tributaries by Edmund Ollerenshaw
in his copy of Holinshed's *Historie of Irelande*, c.1588.

be created in 1755 when more intensive exploitation of the area was contemplated and uncertainty arose as to boundaries of the original division.

Included in the present volume are two sets of maps produced as a consequence of the process of Parliamentary enclosure. These are good examples of maps produced by a parliamentary and legal process, which at the same time played an important part in the creation of new landscapes. They illustrate the important truth that maps not only record landscapes; they can sometimes create them. But we need to view them critically; for not all the features depicted so confidently on maps actually appeared on the ground. For instance not every road, nor every boundary shown on the Denshaw Moor maps was created. Comparison with other maps and a close examination of the landscape itself are essential if we are to understand and interpret maps as historical documents.

The final map, the Vestry Map of 1822, differs in many respects from all other maps in this collection. It is a map of record, intended for the simple practical purpose of facilitating a re-rating of the township. It is at once the most detailed and least decorative of the maps in the collection. It is also the only map not published here in facsimile. Such is the flawed state of the surviving manuscripts that this map has had to be painstakingly reconstructed from a variety of sources.[4]

The troubled history of the creation of the Vestry Map that was finally finished in 1822, raises the question of how the maps included in the present collection were made. Most were the creation of a single surveyor, or, in one or two cases, a small group of surveyors. Even the ambitious Vestry Map never seems to have had more than four professional surveyors working on it at any one time. The magnitude of their task is evident when we compare this low level of manpower to the teams of Ordnance surveyors who, less than thirty years later, were employed to cover the district at a scale of six inches to the mile. Of the tools of those who surveyed Saddleworth we know little; probably the land chain and plain table were the mainstay of their equipment. In 1766 John Lees specifically indicated that his map of Giles Shaw's estate had been measured by Gunter's Chain and he drew it up at a scale of three chains to an inch.[5] Significantly, on all maps, the scale is expressed in chains per inch. In all but the Quick Moor map the chain was the statute chain that is, in fact, Gunter's chain. Interestingly, the scale of the Quick Moor map is given in Lancashire chains.[6] Clearly local units of areal measure still had currency in the later years of the eighteenth century; witness the fact that Ralph Wood's survey of John Buckley's estates gave their extent in Cheshire and Lancashire units as well as in statute measure.[7]

As to the surveyors themselves, five are named on the maps and documentary evidence allows us to name a further four who worked on the Vestry Map at various times. Out of these nine named surveyors three are definitely Saddleworth residents. The earliest

---

[4] The details of reconstruction are given on page 168 below.

[5] Gunter's Chain was introduced by Edmund Gunter (1581-1626). Like the majority of contemporary chains it was twenty-two yards or four poles long; what made it popular was its division into 100 links, each measuring 7.92 inches. C. Singer et al (editors), *A History of Technology*, Vol. 3, Oxford, The Clarendon Press, 1957, p. 542.

[6] A Lancashire Chain measured seven poles, as opposed to a Statute Chain which contains four poles, E.H. Smith, 'Lancashire Long Measure', *Transactions of the Historic Society of Lancashire and Cheshire*, Vol. CX for 1958, Liverpool, The Historic Society of Lancashire and Cheshire, 1959, pp. 1-14.

[7] For these measures see page 97 below.

of these was John Lees who produced both the map for Giles Shaw and the original version of James Farrar's map of 1770. Lees was followed by Joel Hawkyard, Joseph Hesslegreave and Joseph Shaw. It says much for the extent to which cartography had become an indispensable feature of life that there was sufficient employment for these men. It should be remembered that much of their work involved the measurement and valuing of land but not necessarily the production of maps. Surveyors from outside the district who were employed at various times included John Tinker the creator of the 1755 version of the Quick Moor map, who may have come from Salford; John Albinson of Bolton who drew the maps for the Denshaw Moor enclosure; James Monk of Atherton in Lancashire and John Johnson who may be the same man who drew a map of Marsden in 1801.[8]

During the period covered by the maps in this book, Saddleworth was a West Riding township in the Lancashire parish of Rochdale. The township, which was sometimes known by the name of Saddleworth cum Quick or simply Quick, was divided into four Meres: Friarmere, Lordsmere, Shawmere and Quickmere. The township was coterminous with the chapelry and, in spite of many instances of Saddleworth being called a parish even in official documents such as the Enclosure Act, it did not achieve parochial status until 1869.

---

[8] Survey of the Township of Marsden in the Parish of Almondbury in the County of York. Survey'd in the Year of Our Lord 1801 by John Johnson, Surveyor, KC 500, West Yorkshire Archive Service (Kirklees). Hereafter West Yorkshire Archive Service is abbreviated to WYAS, the district office being indicated in brackets. John Johnson may be well the West Riding surveyor active between 1791 and 1830 and who is referred to in S. Bendall (editor), *Dictionary of Land Surveyors and Local Map-Makers of Great Britain and Ireland 1530-1850,* Second Edition, Vol. 1, London, The British Library, 1997, p. 279.

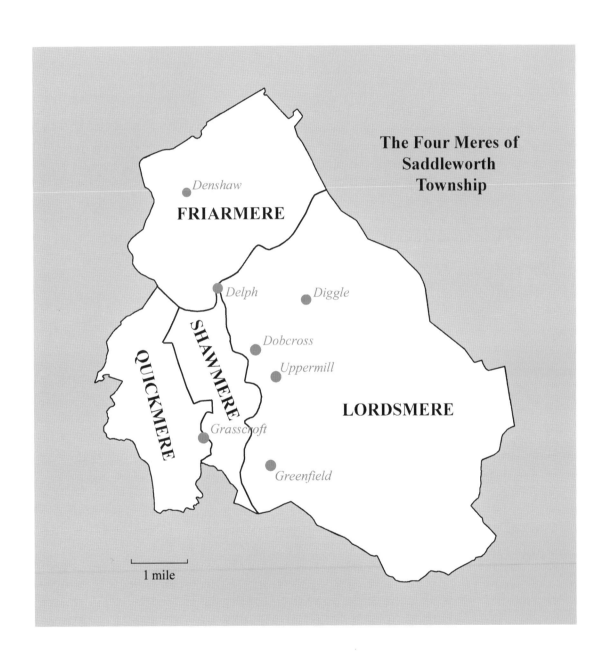

Denshaw

FRIARMERE

The Four Meres of
Saddleworth
Township

Delph

Diggle

SHAWMERE

QUICKMERE

Dobcross

Uppermill

LORDSMERE

Grasscroft

Greenfield

1 mile

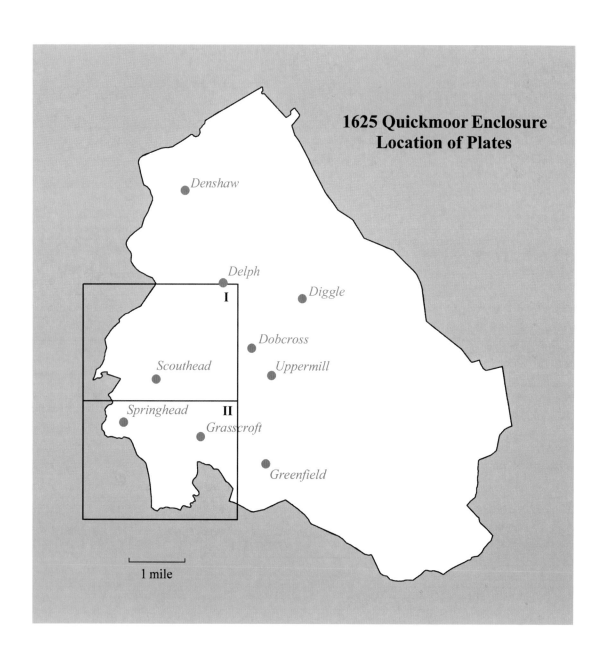

**1625 Quickmoor Enclosure
Location of Plates**

Denshaw

Delph

**I**

Diggle

Dobcross

Scouthead

Uppermill

Springhead

**II**

Grasscroft

Greenfield

1 mile

# A MAP OF QUICK EDGE, WHARMTON, HIGH MOOR AND BADGER EDGE, 1625

| | |
|---|---|
| *Location:* | Enville Hall Estate, Stourbridge, Staffordshire, Mrs. Bissill's Marriage Settlement Collection |
| *Date of Survey:* | 1625 |
| *Surveyor:* | Unknown |
| *Date of Map:* | 1755 |
| *Map Maker:* | John Tinker |
| *Material:* | Parchment |
| *Size of Original:* | 27" x 33½" |
| *Scale of Original:* | 1" : 5 Lancashire Chains (approximately 12½" : 1 mile) |
| *Scale of Reproduction:* | approximately 6⅓" : 1 mile |

As the population of Saddleworth expanded during the sixteenth century, the demand for new tenements and land increased. The commons, which covered vast tracts of open moorland, had been hitherto unprofitably granted to the use of tenants for pasturing animals, digging turf for fuel and quarrying small amounts of stone. Gradually however, the total area available for cultivation grew as a result of both large-scale, planned schemes, such as the enclosure of Castleshaw Moor, and relatively small encroachments of fields and cottages upon the lower lying wastes. The process of enclosure in most of Saddleworth appears to have been largely a consensual one. Tenants anxious to extend their tenements would agree with the lord of the manor upon a specific area to enclose. The lord of the manor would then appoint his steward to oversee the process of enclosure.[1] However, Quick Moor proved to be somewhat more controversial. Having operated as an autonomous sub-manor since the early medieval period, Quickmere and its associated commons were not under the direct control of the lord of the manor of Saddleworth. By the seventeenth century there were three main claimants to the lordship of Quick. These claimants were the Booths of Dunham Massey and the Leghs of High Legh, two powerful Cheshire families, and the Ramsdens of Longley Hall in Almondbury, who had purchased an estate in Quickmere in 1606.[2] In addition, by virtue of being lord of the manor of Saddleworth, Sir John Ramsden attempted to counter the claims of both the Booths and Leghs by arguing he was chief lord of the whole Township of Saddleworth including Quickmere and therefore sole claimant to the commons.

The complexity of the claims, coupled with the determination of each of the absentee landlords to extract the most advantageous settlement, meant that there were several cases brought both in the Court of Chancery and the Common Pleas. Dame Elizabeth Booth and her son Sir George seem to have pushed the case for enclosure most vigorously, bringing a case against Sir John Ramsden in respect of their claim to the commons in November 1622 . Lady Booth complained that 'by reason of her great age and many infirmities of body' and because of her residence in Bath 'for these ffouretie

---

[1] A letter from three Saddleworth tenants to William Ramsden in 1616 describes the process of Wrigley Maralew's enclosures and some of its attendant problems. This letter was attached to the Large Account Book of William Ramsden, DD/RA/M 4a, WYAS (Kirklees), but is now missing. A copy is in the possession of the authors.

[2] 'Seeing Through a Glass Darkly, An Outline of the Early History of Saddleworth', M. Buckley, *Saddleworth Historical Society Bulletin*, Vol. 39, No. 2, Summer 2009, p. 33.

yeres last part or thereabouts', she was unable to visit her Saddleworth estate.[3] Despite her absence, the estate appears to have been well managed. Since the 1570s her officers had been granting permission in Quickmere for:

> *divers houses of stone and covered in slate to the number of ten at least to*
> *be erected and divers enclosures to be made in great quantities.*[4]

Indeed, her officers pulled down the cottages and enclosures of Robert Mayall, Edmund Taylor and Rowland Dixon because they had not obtained her licence. When Lady Booth's bailiff, Nicholas Walker, arrived at Dixon's cottage (which is depicted on the map, see Plate I) it was reported by his son William that there were:

> *then a wife and seven children in it who made a pittifull crye and*
> *lamantacion when the same was pullinge downe they did for that cause*
> *forbeare to pull downe the rest thereof for that tyme whereuppon this*
> *deponent at the intreatie of the said Rowland Dixon did write a letter to*
> *intreate the said Ladie Bouth that the said cottage might by her license and*
> *with her consent stand and continue.*[5]

The letter appears to have so moved Lady Booth that she gave permission for the cottage to be rebuilt and:

> *gave tymber growinge upon divers partes of Sr George Bouthes land to the*
> *said Dixon towards the erectinge of the said cottage.*[6]

Sir John Ramsden was unwilling to let the Booths' exploitation of the commons go unchecked. In the wake of the court cases, which may never have reached a resolution, meetings were held between the three claimants in the period from August to October of 1624.[7] A formula for dividing the wastes was eventually agreed upon, which ultimately favoured Ramsden, going some way to recognise his claim to be chief lord (for which there was minimal evidence). For Quick Moor Ramsden was granted a quarter share in recognition of his chief lordship whilst he was entitled to a further three sixteenths for the land his father had purchased in 1606. Sir George Booth was to have six sixteenths, whilst Thomas Legh was allocated three sixteenths. Separate formulae were applied to Quick Edge and the Strines. After the main negotiations had ended, claims of commoners on Quick Moor were addressed. A meeting was arranged for 8th March 1625, at which Ramsden proposed:

> *Both to dispatch the inferiour Charterers & Commoners, and also to conferre*
> *with the better sort, touching their rights.*[8]

Ramsden was as ruthless with the commoners as he had been in asserting his rights against Booth and Legh. He was confident that he could bring to the meeting sufficient deeds and evidences as would quash some of the 'Claymes on Quick commons'.[9] The Buckleys, as sole charterers of Grasscroft, were given the Grasscroft chartership which is shown on the map. This was possibly in return for Robert Buckley's willingness to

---

[3] Boothe v Ramsden, C 3/334/6, The National Archives (hereafter TNA).

[4] *loc. cit.*

[5] *loc. cit.*

[6] *loc. cit.*

[7] Cornwall-Legh MS., 1053a-c, John Rylands University Library, Manchester.

[8] Cornwall-Legh MS., 1056f, John Rylands University Library, Manchester.

[9] *loc. cit.*

serve as a significant witness for Ramsden in the Chancery case. Other of the 'better sort' to whom concessions were made included Mr. Cudworth of Oldham, for his freehold tenement of Crawshaw, and the Asshetons of Chadderton, as charterers of Greenacres and Palden. Despite agreements being reached further delays were encountered:

> *by reason of the extremetye of the season being so cold....and also that by reason of the snowe coveringe all the wastes, so as they cannot decerne the good ground from the bad.*[10]

The final division appears to have been completed by 10th May 1625.[11]

Over the following century all three principal landholders sold significant portions of their newly enclosed land to tenants. Meanwhile the highest and least profitable lands, particularly on Wharmton, were left largely unenclosed and only vaguely distinguished on the ground. As a result of this lack of clearly defined boundaries, a fresh dispute arose between William Farrar, successor to the Ramsdens as lord of the manor, and George, Earl of Warrington, the descendant of Sir George Booth. When the members of the Court Baron representing Farrar met with the Earl of Warrington's bailiffs on 19th June 1755, some of the 'antient Mears' could not be found.[12] Therefore another meeting was called on the 24th June. At this meeting the differences between the two parties were resolved by Mr. John Tinker of Ashton and Mr. John Lees of Saddleworth, 'Two Juditious Surveors Indifferently Chosen by the said parties', who measured the land as 'ye Maps Laid it out'.[13] It seems to have been as a result of this dispute that John Tinker produced his map, which he described as being 'Transcribed From the most correct plans in June 1755' (see Plate II).

Whether Tinker's map was a direct copy of a map of 1625, or whether it was a compilation from a number of different sources remains unclear. The fact that the strips of land originally allocated to Booth bear the name of the Earl of Warrington, a title which the family only acquired in 1690, shows that at least some elements of the copy were not faithful to the original. In addition, there appears to be considerable confusion surrounding Mr. Legh's portions, with many acreages left unrecorded and one whole strip omitted at the bottom of Quick Edge. It is possible to account for these discrepancies if it is accepted that Tinker's map was an attempt to make a composite of three different original maps, which in 1625 had been given to each of the three landholders. Each map may have only recorded the strips relating to the landholder in question. The numerous references in 1755 to 'plans' and 'maps' in the plural, imply there was more than one, whilst the uncertainty surrounding Legh's portions could be explained by the fact that the 1755 dispute was between the inheritors of the Booth and Ramsden portions. Legh's land had long since been sold to individual tenants and therefore the deeds along with any associated maps and plans may well have been lost or not been readily available in 1755.

It is difficult to say with any certainty how much stylistic influence the original map or maps had on Tinker's copy. However, it seems reasonable to suggest that the main

---

[10] Cornwall-Legh MS., 1056f, John Rylands University Library, Manchester.

[11] Abraham Lees Book, L 29, Box 9, Greater Manchester County Archives (with Manchester Archives).

[12] Saddleworth Court Roll, 1755, Wentworth-Woolley Papers, Box 8/5, Special Collections [MS] Deposit 1946/1, Brotherton Library, University of Leeds. The reference to the 'antient Mears' comes from the Court Roll for 3rd June 1756 in the same collection.

[13] *loc. cit.*

cartouche, some of the lettering and the depictions of cottages and houses replicate an earlier style. It may also be significant that the scale of the map uses Lancashire Chains and was presumably originally measured in this unit. The Lancashire Chain had been largely superseded by Gunter's Chain which was in common use by eighteenth century surveyors. The employment of different units of measurement may well lie at the root of discrepancies that have been observed in different documents when they state the acreages allocated to each claimant. In addition, there is evidence of faulty arithmetic in the compilation of the total acreages which appear in the cartouche.

The map bears witness to the growing pressure for enclosure of the wastes and commons in the Pennines during the seventeenth century. Contrary to many of the other early piecemeal enclosures in Saddleworth, Quick Moor represented an opportunity for the major landholders to undertake a large-scale systematic project which would yield significant returns. The map lays out a plan which ultimately led to a radical alteration of a large proportion of the Saddleworth landscape. Its impact can be clearly discerned not only on the Vestry Map of 1822 and the first edition six inch Ordnance Survey map but also on the landscape today. It is eloquent of a level of influence on the landscape that Saddleworth's absentee landlords would rarely enjoy again.

Figure 2. Highmoor. A landscape of geometric enclosures created
by the seventeenth century surveyors.

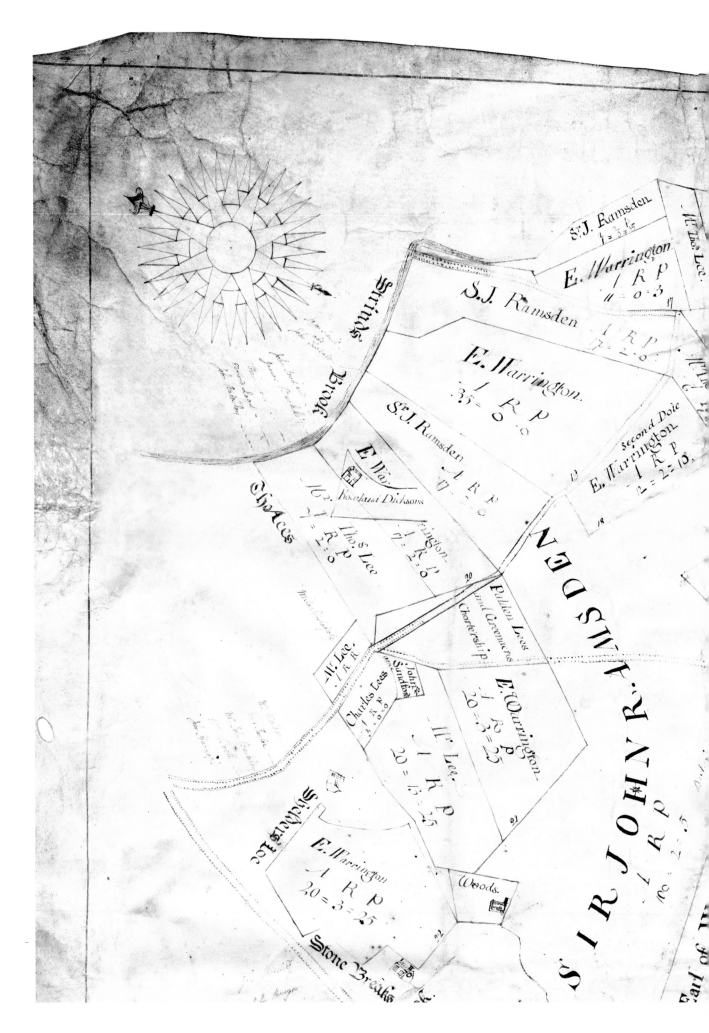

Sr. J. Ramsden
4=3=34

E. Warrington
A R P
11 = 0=3    17

Mr. Thos. Lee

S. J. Ramsden
A R P
7=2=0

E. Warrington.
A R P
35 = 0=0

Second Dole
E. Warrington
A R P
2 = 2= 15

18

Sr. J. Ramsden
A R P

Spring Brook

E. War
162.        Roseland Dicksons
A R P
7 = 2 = 0

Thos. Lee
A R P
2=2=0

rington
A R P
7 = 2= 0

Threes

Pullen Lees
and Greenacres
Chartership.

90

S I R   J O H N   R A M S D E N

E. Warrington
A R P
20=3=25

Mr. Lee.
A R R

Charles Lees
A R P
4 =0=0

John &
Sandton

Mr. Lee.
A R P
20 = 13 = 25

91

Sidders Lee

E. Warrington
A R P
20 = 3 = 25

Woods.

A R P
10 = 2 = 5

Stone Breaks

Earl of W

12

Plate I

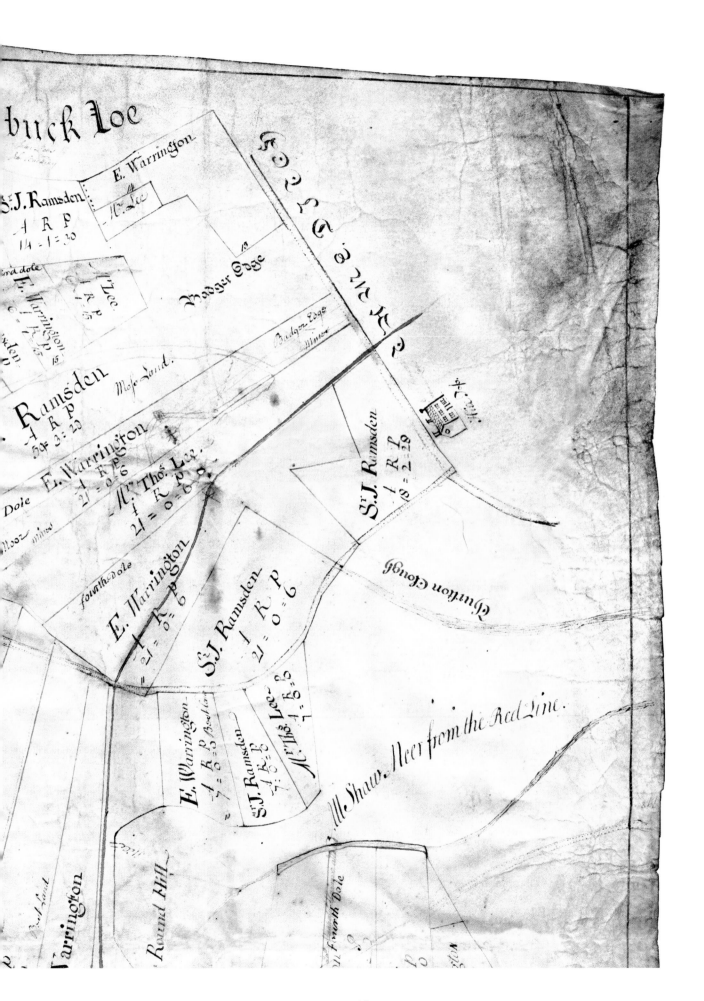

E. Warrington
A R P
20 = 3 = 25

Stone Breaks

Wood Brook

Woods.

S I R J O

George Earl

Load Hill

Grotton Head

S.J. Ramsden
A R P
13 = 2 = 12

All Quick Meer from the Red Line

Mr Cudworth
A R P
2 = 3 = 7

E. Warrington
A R P
3 = 1 = 3

S.J. Ramsden

Thorn Lee

Mr Lee

Grass Croft Chortens
A R P
1 = 0 = 0

Lydgate

St J. Ramsden
A R P
13 = 3 = 37

Mr Lee
A R P
12 = 3 = 1

E. Warrington
A R P
21 = 1 = 8

Mr Brightland

Sr John Ramsden
A R P
16 = 0 = 20

Hay Croft

Brook bottom

Parish

Part of Ashton

Quick Edge Top

Quick

A MAP
High moor, an
in the County o
the year 1625.
Earl of Warri
Mr Thomas Lee

To Geo
To Si
To

Exclusive of Wa

This
Transcribed
from the most correct plans
in June 1755.
By J. Tinker

Plate II

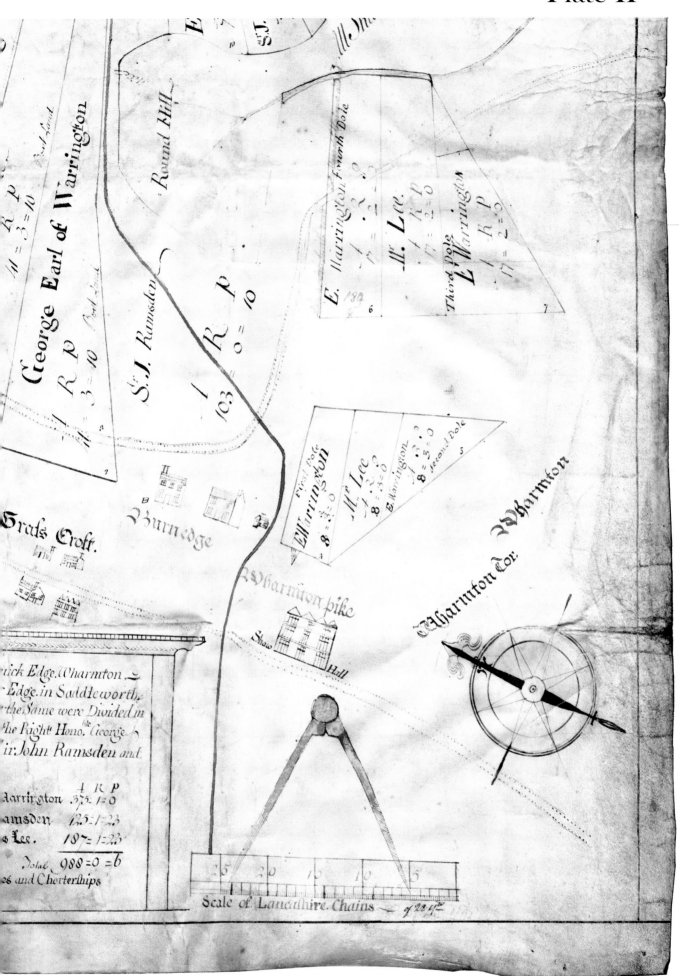

Scale of Lancashire Chains — of 22 y[ds]

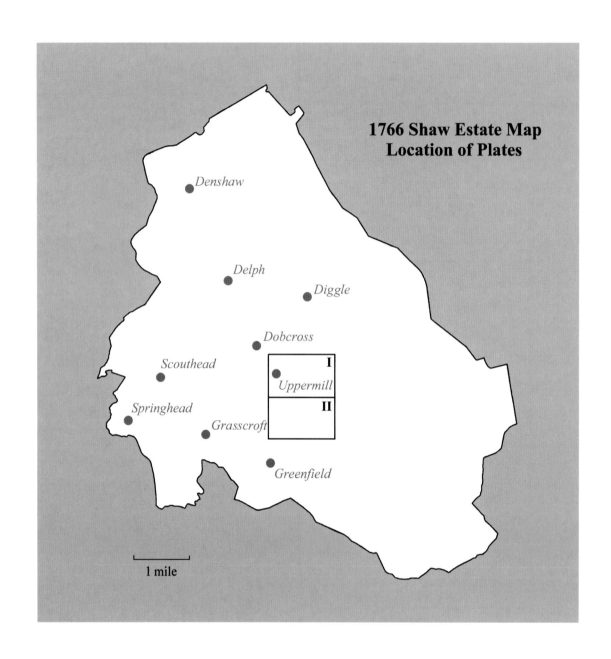

1766 Shaw Estate Map
Location of Plates

Denshaw

Delph

Diggle

Dobcross

Scouthead

Uppermill

I

II

Springhead

Grasscroft

Greenfield

1 mile

16

# A MAP OF MR. GILES SHAW'S ESTATES, TO WIT, FURLANE, CARR-BARN AND UPPER-MILL, 1766

| | |
|---|---|
| *Location:* | Saddleworth Historical Society Archives, H/GS/HOW 39a |
| *Date of Survey:* | 1766 |
| *Surveyor:* | John Lees |
| *Material:* | Paper |
| *Size of Original:* | 20½" x 25¼" |
| *Scale of Original:* | 1" : 3 Chains (26⅔" : 1 mile). |
| *Scale of Reproduction:* | approximately 20" : 1 mile |

Estate maps can have many functions. They can be an administrative tool, a legal record, a means to raise a mortgage or a record of possession. Why Giles Shaw chose to have this map made in 1766 is not known but it is typical of estate maps in that it is decorative as well as practical, indeed the decoration must have taken as much time to draw as the measured details of the land depicted.

Giles Shaw was an important Saddleworth freeholder; and as such would have been styled yeoman. As a yeoman, his title and status positioned him above his neighbours, the leasehold tenants of the manor, and entitled him to vote in national elections. The Shaws had leased the farm at Uppermill from the sixteenth century at least and all three properties depicted on the map had been purchased in the troubled civil war period from the then lord of the manor, Sir John Ramsden and his widow.[1] Giles Shaw lived at Furlane and was responsible for rebuilding the house in 1750; his name and that of his wife are carved on the lintel above the door. Although Giles Shaw was not living in Uppermill when this map was made, his eldest son, Thomas, was later to make it his home.[2]

In order to understand the three properties shown on the map, reference should be made to the Vestry Map of 1822, which shows them in their context. On that map the Furlane estate is numbered 145, the Carr-barn estate 181 and the Upper-Mill estate 189.

Shaw's map is perhaps of most interest for its depiction of his property in Uppermill. It should be borne in mind that it only shows Giles Shaw's land but nevertheless it is clear that in 1766 Uppermill consisted of little more than two farmsteads and the Upper Mill (not named but at the northern edge of the Lee field, a name preserved in the present Lee Street). Evidence that this map has, at some time, been used as an administrative tool is to be found in the faint pencil lines on the Uppermill estate which show the line of the Standedge to Oldham turnpike road, the act for which was passed in 1792 and which had reached Uppermill by 1794.[3]

The surveyor, John Lees, was a prolific map maker and surveyor in Saddleworth in the late eighteenth century, his most significant work being the manor survey of 1770.[4]

---

[1] Deeds copied by the Enclosure Commissioner, c.1810, H/EA/19, p. 15, Saddleworth Historical Society Archives, Saddleworth Museum, Uppermill (hereafter SHS).

[2] The property was later to be gothicised by George Shaw (1810-1876), great-grandson of Giles Shaw.

[3] B. Barnes, *Passage Through Time*, Uppermill, SHS, 1981, p. 44.

[4] See pages 23-4 below.

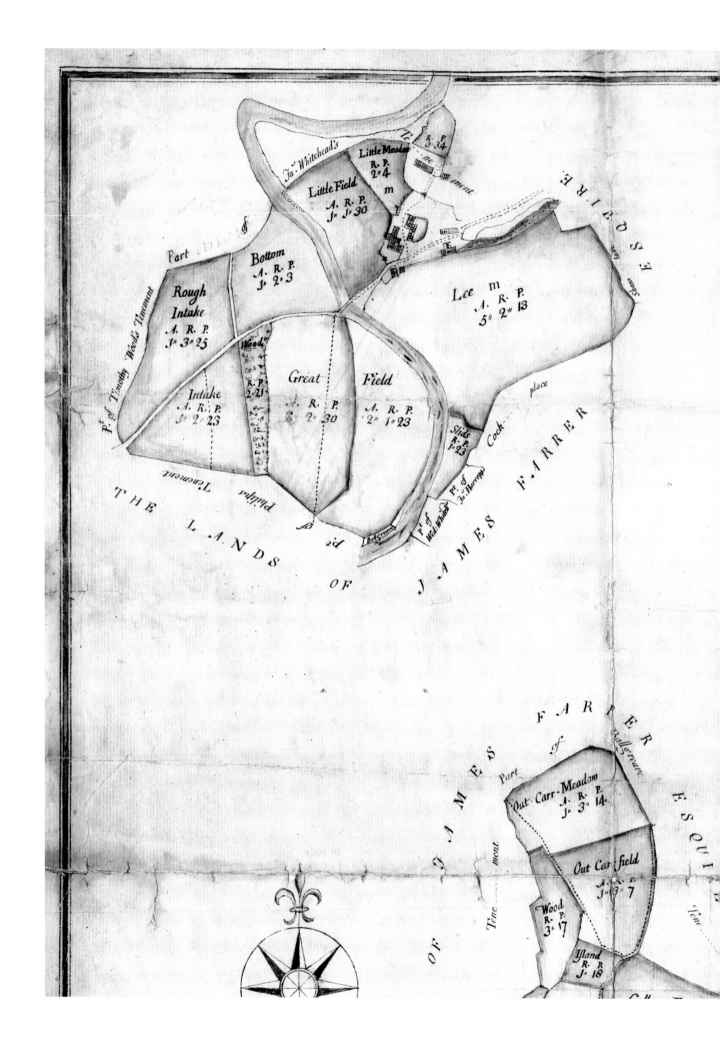

Ja.s Whitehead's

Little Meadow
R. P.
2ʳ 4

R P.
3 34

Little Field
A. R. P.
Jⁿ Jⁿ 30

m

Part

Bottom
A. R. P.
Jⁿ 2 3

Rough
Intake
A. R. P.
Jⁿ 3ʳ 25

Pᵗ of Timothy Woods Tenement

Wood

R. P.
2ʳ 21

Intake
A. R. P.
Jⁿ 2ʳ 23

Great
R. P.
2ʳ 30

Field
A. R. P.
2ʳ 1 23

Lee   m
A. R. P.
5ⁿ 2ⁿ 13

place

Slids
R. P.
1ʳ 23

Cock-

Pᵗ of
Ja. Harropi

Ballycross

Pᵗ of
Wid. Whale's

Philip's Tenement

Pᵗ of

THE   LANDS   OF   JAMES   FARRER

F A R R E R   E S Q U I R E

F A R R E R   of   Ballgreave   E S Q U I R

Part

Out Carr-Meadow
A. R. P.
Jⁿ 3ʳ 14

Tene        ment

Out Car field
A. R. P.
Jⁿ 3ʳ 7

J A M E S   of

Wood
R. P.
3ʳ 17

Island
R. P.
Jⁿ 18

Tene

O F

Plate I

# A MAP of Mr. GILES SHAW'S

Estates, to wit, Furlane Carrbarn and Upper-Mill

all within Saddleworth in the WEST RIDING

of the County of YORK. Measured by John Lees 1766.

| Furlane | A. | R. | P. |
|---|---|---|---|
| Housing Garden &c | | | 34 |
| Lowmost Croft | 1 | 3 | 15 |
| Middlemost Croft | 1 | 2 | |
| Uppermost Croft | 1 | 2 | 33 |
| Tunstead | 2 | 2 | 4 |
| Park | | | 39 |
| Little Meadow m | 1 | | 33 |
| Upper Meadow m | | 3 | 31 |
| Lower Meadow m | 1 | 1 | 11 |
| Greave Meadow m | 1 | 1 | 24 |
| Great Field | 2 | 3 | 9 |
| Ax | 2 | | 9 |
| | 17 | 3 | 2 |

| Carr-barn. | A. | R. | P. |
|---|---|---|---|
| Marled-earth | 2 | 1 | 33 |
| Rie-earth | 1 | 0 | 36 |
| Golbron Foot | 2 | 0 | 34 |
| | | 0 | 22 |
| Carr house Green m | 1 | 2 | 20 |
| Bent-Carr m | 2 | 0 | 5 |
| Long Carr | 3 | 0 | 31 |
| Wood | | 3 | 17 |
| Island | | 1 | 19 |
| Out-Carr field | 1 | 3 | 7 |
| Out-Carr-Meadow | 1 | 3 | 14 |
| | 17 | 3 | 27 |

| Upper-Mill. | A. | R. | P. |
|---|---|---|---|
| Housing Garden &c | | | 14 |
| The Jree m | 5 | 2 | 13 |
| Sinks | | 1 | 23 |
| Great field { 2 1 23 / 2 2 30 } | 5 | | 13 |
| The Wood | | 2 | 21 |
| Intake | 1 | 2 | 23 |
| Rough Intake | 1 | 3 | 25 |
| Bottom | 1 | 2 | 3 |
| Little Field | 1 | 1 | 30 |

19

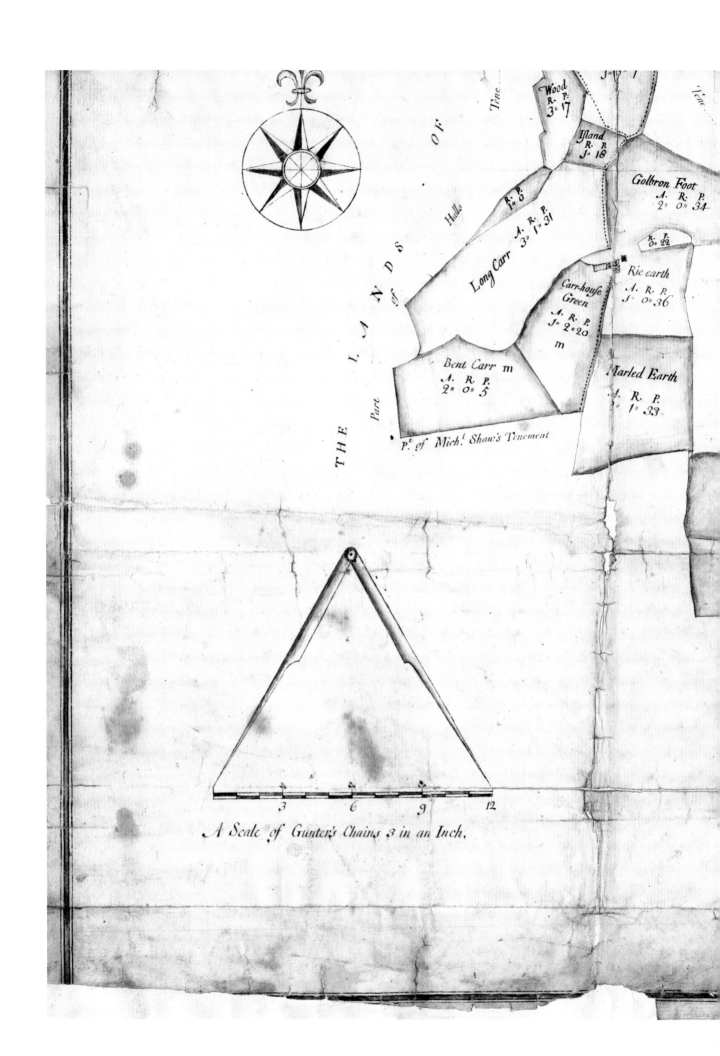

THE LANDS OF

Part of

Halls

Tene...

Wood
R. P.
3ᵃ 17

Island
R. P.
Jᵃ 18

Golbron Foot
A. R. P.
2ⁿ 0ⁿ 34

A. P.
1ⁿ 0

Long Carr A. R. P.
3ⁿ 1ⁿ 31

R. P.
0ⁿ 22

Rie earth
A. R. P.
Jⁿ 0ⁿ 36

Carr-house
Green
A. R. P.
Jⁿ 2ⁿ 20
m

Bent Carr m
A. R. P.
2ⁿ 0ⁿ 5

Marled Earth
A. R. P.
ⁿ 1ⁿ 33

Pᵗ of Michˡ Shaw's Tenement

3        6        9        12

A Scale of Gunter's Chains 3 in an Inch.

Plate II

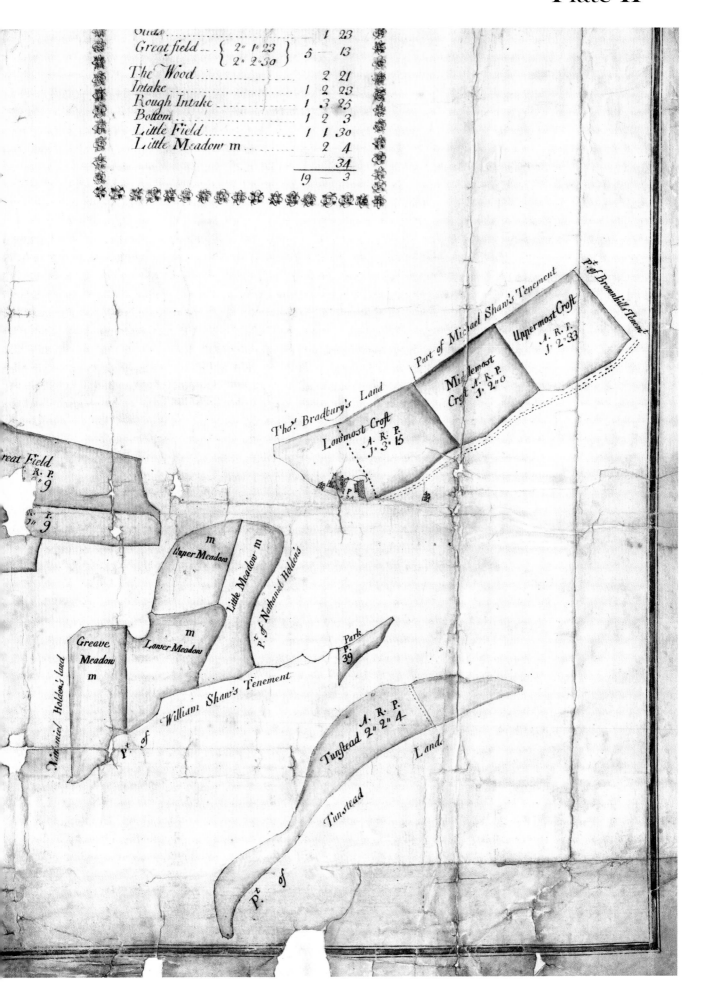

| | | | |
|---|---|---|---|
| Ends | | 1 | 23 |
| Great field ... { 2" 1" 23 } { 2" 2" 30 } | 5 | — | 13 |
| The Wood | | 2 | 21 |
| Intake | 1 | 2 | 23 |
| Rough Intake | 1 | 3 | 25 |
| Bottom | 1 | 2 | 3 |
| Little Field | 1 | 1 | 30 |
| Little Meadow m | | 2 | 4 |
| | | | 34 |
| | 19 | — | 3 |

Pt. of Michael Shaw's Tenement

Pt. of Broomhills Tenement

Uppermost Croft
A. R. P.
1 . 2 " 33

Middlemost Croft A. R. P. 1 . 2 " 0

Tho.s Bradbury's Land

Lowmost Croft
A. R. P.
1 . 3 . 15

reat Field
R. P.
9

F.
9

m
Upper Meadow

m

Little Meadow m

Pt. of Nathaniel Holden's

Greave Meadow m

m
Lower Meadow

Nathaniel Holden's land

Pt. of

William Shaw's Tenement

Park
P.
39

A. R. P.
Tunstead 2 " 2 " 4
Land.

Pt. of
Tunstead

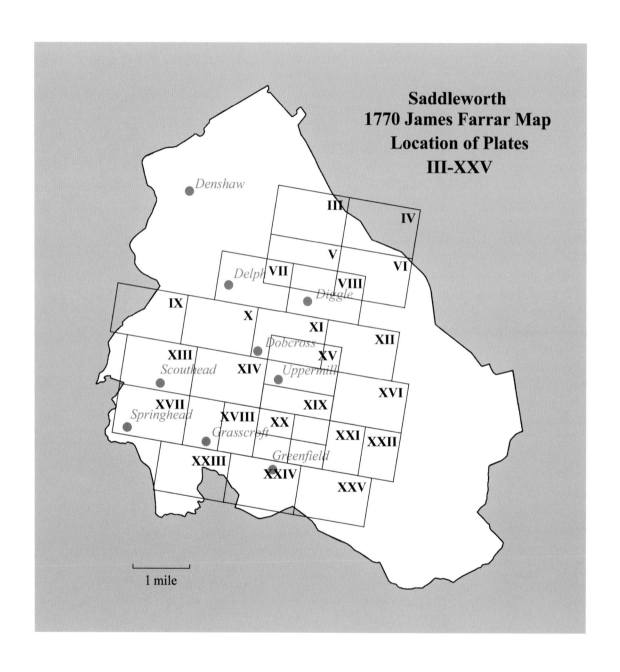

**Saddleworth**
**1770 James Farrar Map**
**Location of Plates**
**III-XXV**

Denshaw

III

IV

V

VI

Delph VII VIII

Diggle

IX X XI XII

Dobcross

XIII XV

Scouthead XIV Uppermill

XVI

XVII XIX

Springhead XVIII XX

Grasscroft XXI XXII

Greenfield

XXIII XXIV XXV

1 mile

# MAP OF THE INCLOSURES IN THE PARISH OF SADDLEWORTH BELONGING TO JAMES FARRAR ESQ., 1770

| | |
|---|---|
| *Location:* | Saddleworth Museum Archives, |
| | Map: M/BYR 6 |
| | Key: M/BYR 1 |
| *Date of Survey:* | 1770 |
| *Surveyor:* | John Lees |
| *Date of Copy* | 1825 |
| *Copied by:* | Joel Hawkyard |
| *Material:* | Parchment |
| *Size of Original:* | 57" x 63" |
| *Scale of Original:* | 1" : 6 Chains (13⅓" : 1 mile) |
| *Scale of Reproduction:* | 1" : 6 Chains (13⅓" : 1 mile) |

By the latter half of the eighteenth century the amount of land held by the lords of the manor was greater than at any time since the early medieval period. Although nominal chief rents were still received for freehold land, it was the leasehold properties which were of most concern to James Farrar as lord of the manor. These provided a substantial income to Farrar, an income that had grown in value through the course of the eighteenth century with the shift away from the customary rents of earlier times. It was therefore only these tenements which were depicted on the map of 1770. The circumstances of the map's creation are unknown, but it may have been drawn up in conjunction with one of the many mortgages Farrar made on the manor before its eventual sale in 1791.

The Farrars had purchased the manor of Saddleworth from the Ramsdens in 1656.[1] As a result they directly held the bulk of Lordsmere, though medieval freeholds, such as Tunstead and Fernlee were excluded, as were those lands that Sir John Ramsden had sold to tenants in 1636.[2] Purchases from the Radcliffes of Ordsall in 1604 and 1611 meant the whole of Shawmere was integrated into the manor and remained so in 1770.[3] In Quickmere, the Farrars also still held some of the strips allocated to Ramsden as part of the 1625 division, whilst the estate centred on Lydgate and Quick had been part of the manor since 1606.[4] Friarmere is totally unrepresented on Farrar's map. Having been granted to the Cistercian monks of Roche Abbey in the thirteenth century and subsequently sold by the Crown at the Dissolution, James Farrar held no lands in Friarmere, nor drew any chief rents there.

The surveyor, John Lees was the grandson of John Lees, who was minister of Saddleworth from 1663 until his death in 1712. Having vacated the parsonage on the arrival of the new incumbent, Joseph Beighton, the Lees family moved to nearby Banktop. This estate is numbered 77 on the map and accompanying 'Survey Book of Saddleworth' which provides the key (see page 83 below). Nothing is known about John Lees' education, though his grandfather's attendance at Manchester Grammar

---

[1] 'Seeing Through a Glass Darkly, An Outline of the Early History of Saddleworth', M. Buckley, *Saddleworth Historical Society Bulletin*, Vol. 39, No. 2, Summer 2009, p. 34.

[2] *ibid.* pp. 33-4.

[3] *ibid.* p. 33.

[4] *loc. cit.*

School, might suggest he was schooled there. James Farrar's choice of John Lees as surveyor is unsurprising as he had been acting as his agent in Saddleworth from the mid-eighteenth century. In 1755 he was chosen by Farrar to settle a dispute with the Earl of Warrington over enclosures on Wharmton, and memoranda on manorial chief rentals from the 1770s indicate Lees was borrowing the documents to make copies for his own record.[5] The scope of his activities as land agent and surveyor extended beyond his work for Farrar to include being employed by a number of landowners resident in Saddleworth. He produced the map of Giles Shaw's freehold estates in 1766 and acted as land agent in the auction of the Coatmans Estate in 1774[6]. He also served as an arbitrator in the private enclosure award for land at Thurston Clough in 1772.[7] However, during the 1740s and 50s the parish registers suggest his primary occupation was as a fustian weaver, indicating that the dual economy, important to so many Pennine parishes, could include more specialised professions as well as the conventional combination of agriculture and the textile industry.[8] Despite sharing the same surname and profession, it would appear he was unrelated to James Lees of Knotthill who worked as a surveyor for the proprietors of the manor in the 1790s.[9]

The map produced in this volume is a copy made by Joel Hawkyard in 1825. It is difficult to ascertain why Hawkyard reproduced the map, though it was possibly made for the proprietors of the manor during the enclosure of Saddleworth Moor in order to further evidence their claims to common rights. The fact that Hawkyard's copy was formerly in the possession of the Buckleys of Hollyville, who held a significant share in the manor and were active in its administration supports this contention. In 1791 the original map may have been held locally, for the Leeds surveyor, Jonathan Teale, copied parts of it when surveying the Greenfield sheep walk for John Whitehead.[10] Ultimately however, like so many other evidences relating to the manor, the map may have been retained by the Farrars at Barnburgh Grange[11]. Their reticence to pass their Saddleworth evidences to the proprietors of the manor after 1791 seems to have stemmed from their desire to persist in claiming residual manorial rights well into the nineteenth century.

---

[5] Saddleworth Court Roll 1755, Box 8/5 Wentworth-Woolley Papers, MS Deposit 1946/1, Brotherton Library, University of Leeds and Saddleworth Chief Rent Roll, Box 8/6, Wentworth-Woolley Papers, MS Deposit 1946/1, Brotherton Library, University of Leeds.

[6] *The Manchester Mercury*, October 11th 1774.

[7] An Award About the Commons on Thurston Clough and Green Leach, L 29, Box 9, Greater Manchester County Record Office (with Manchester Archives).

[8] J. Radcliffe (editor), *The Parish Registers of St. Chad, Saddleworth, 1613-1751*, Uppermill, printed for the editor, 1887, p. 51 *et seq.*

[9] James Farrar died in 1791 and, as directed in his will, the Trustees auctioned the bulk of his Saddleworth estates in April 1791. The remainder of the estates and the manorial rights were sold in August 1792 to a consortium of thirty one landholders and businessmen, who became the proprietors of the manor. See A.J. Petford, 'The Process of Enclosure in Saddleworth, 1625-1834', *Transactions of the Lancashire and Cheshire Antiquarian Society*, Manchester, printed for the society, Vol. 84, 1987, pp. 95-97.

[10] A Plan of the Estate Situate in Saddleworth belonging to Mr. John Whitehead, The Byrom Collection, M/BYR/2, Saddleworth Museum Archives, Saddleworth Museum, Uppermill (hereafter SMA).

[11] So few deeds were held in Saddleworth that the Enclosure Commissioner, Ralph Fletcher, had to send representatives to Barnburgh Grange to make a 'Search for any papers or Evidences that may be found there relating to Saddleworth Manor' in order to assist with his work in settling the township boundary. Enclosure Commissioner's Minute Book, p. 204, H/EA 4, SHS.

The key accompanying the map which bears the title 'Survey Book of Saddleworth', names all Farrar's tenants and the estates which they occupied. Field names and sizes are given as are descriptions of all the buildings on each estate. Being drawn up before the majority of Saddleworth's hamlets were substantially rebuilt and extended at the end of the eighteenth century, the key illustrates the state of the building stock of the manor where there is little extant architectural evidence. There are frequent references to buildings in a ruinous state and even at this late date a number of buildings retained their thatched roofs. In this context it is perhaps not surprising that many Saddleworth buildings show evidence of extensive reconstruction towards the end of the eighteenth century. As well as dwellinghouses outbuildings are also recorded. Among these are turf cotes, an indication that for many at this period turf or peat from the common moorlands was still an important source of fuel.

Dating the key is not simple. Clearly the starting point for the compilation of the key was the 1770 map, but as can be seen many entries record the position in 1789. Care should be exercised when using this document. Perhaps the copy we have was written up by Joel Hawkyard in 1825, and in doing so, he may have combined the original key with later annotations. However, the numerical ordering of the key was not a creation of 1770, but drawn from an earlier system whereby tenants were listed in alphabetical order. This practice was continued when drawing up the key in 1770, though the sequence was not updated. Thus, when a new tenant with a different surname took up a lease, the key was not revised by inserting his name in the correct alphabetical order. Rather, the tenement retained its old position in the sequence. This explains the occasional illogicality of the text as printed.

In the reproduction of the map that follows, Plate I shows the whole map and provides a useful reminder that this is very much a map of James Farrar's manor of Saddleworth and as such deliberately omits the freehold properties which were not in his hands. Plate II shows the elaborate cartouche executed by Joel Hawkyard for this copy of John Lees's original map which is currently untraced.

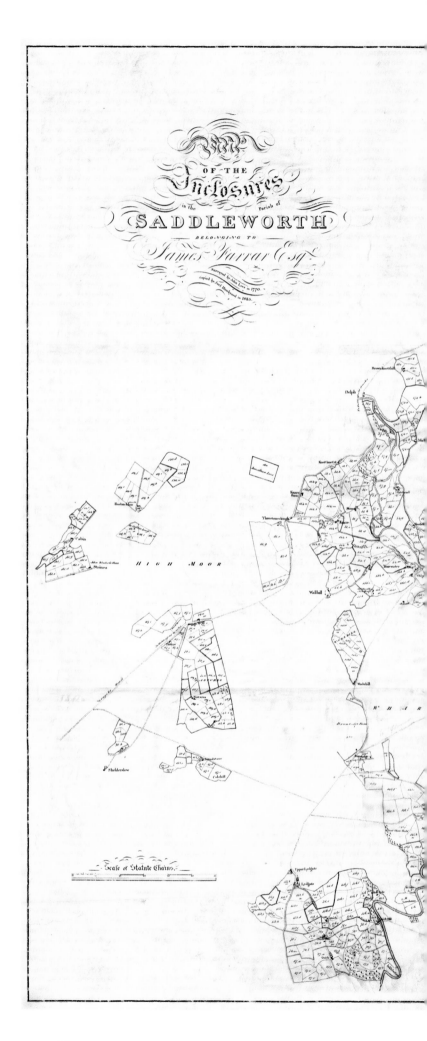

MAP
OF THE
Inclosures
in the        Parish of
SADDLEWORTH
BELONGING TO
James Farrar Esqr.

Surveyed by John Lees in 1770.
copied by Jno Bradford in 1825.

HIGH MOOR

Scale of Statute Chains

Plate I

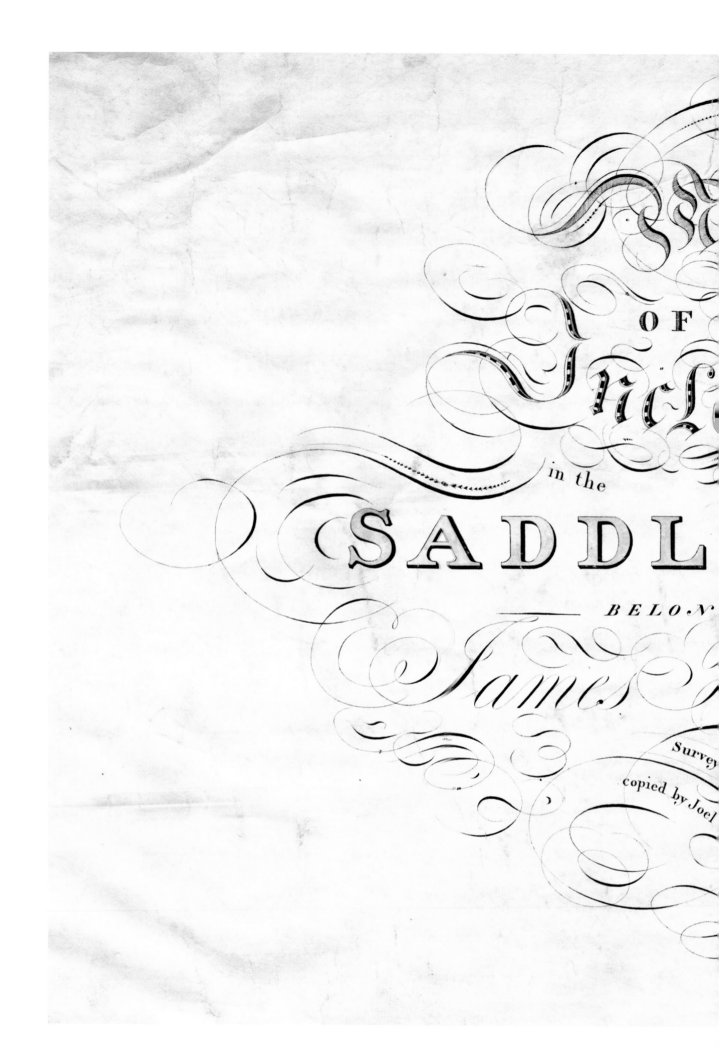

OF

in the

SADDL

BELON

James

Survey

copied by Joel

Plate II

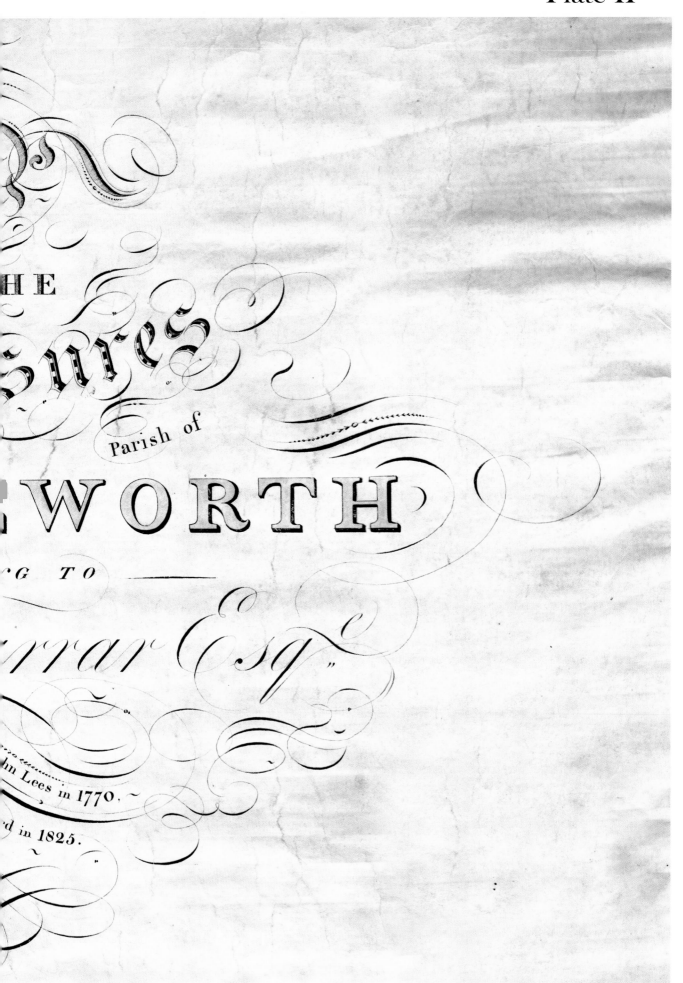

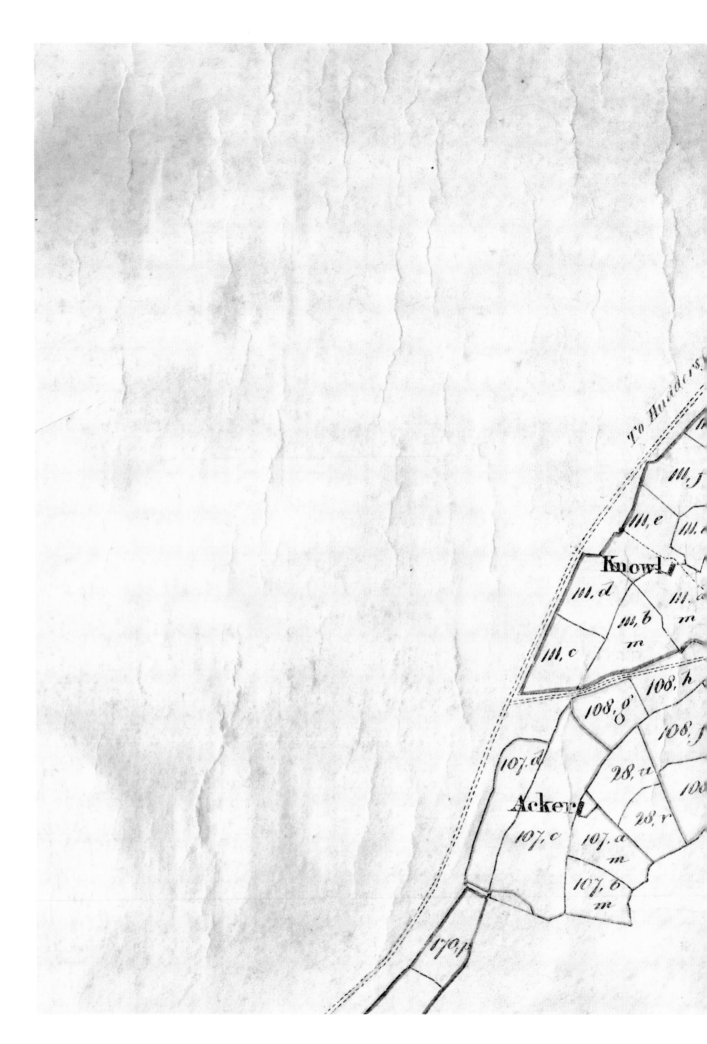

Plate III

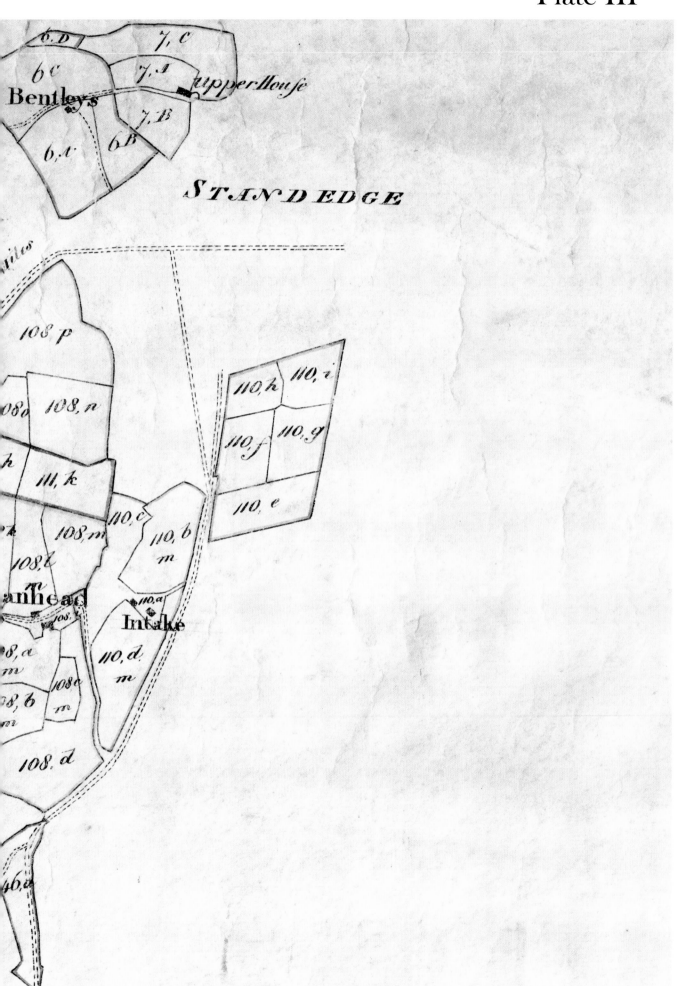

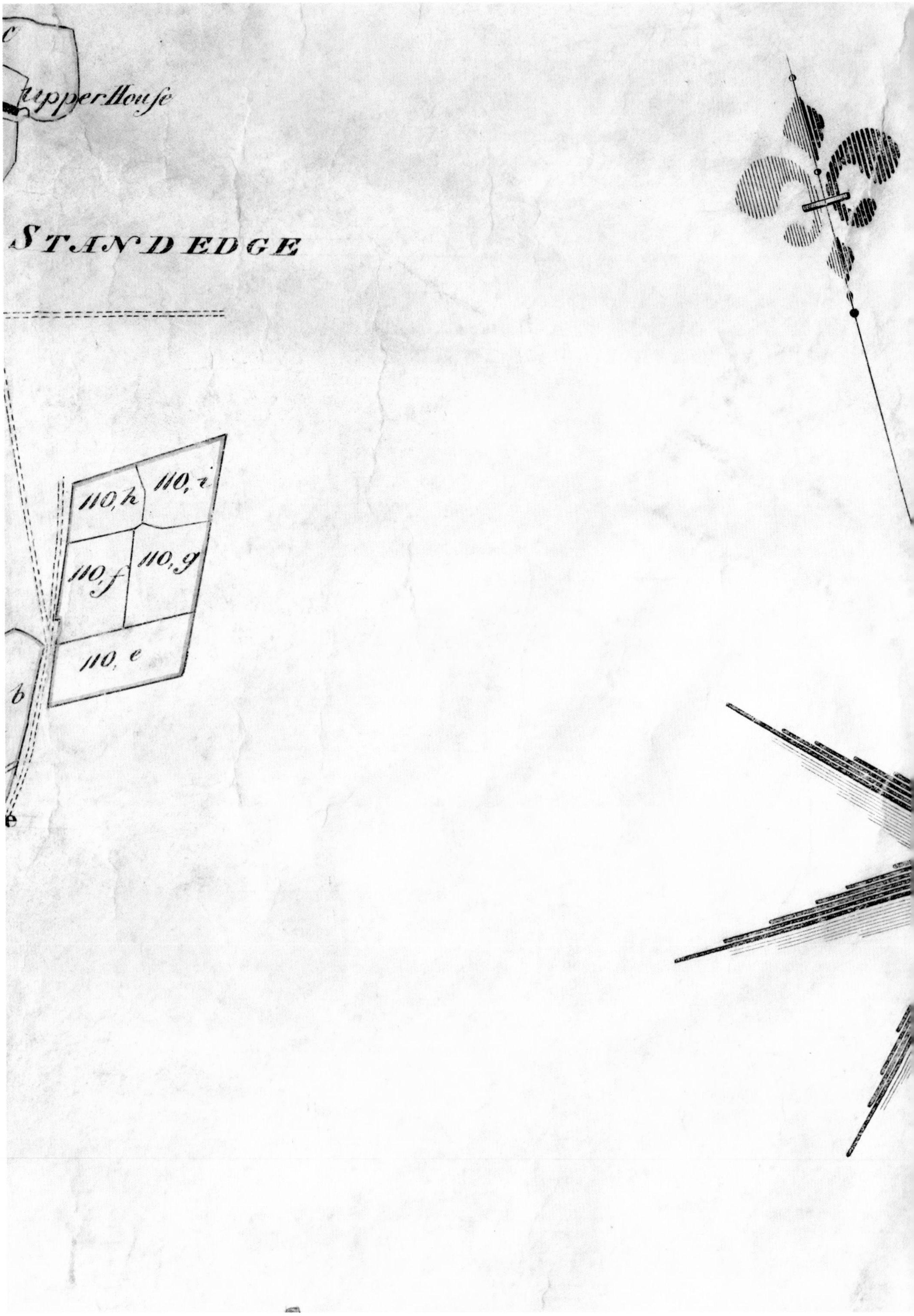

upperHouse

*STANDEDGE*

110, h     110, i

110, f     110, g

110, e

b

Plate IV

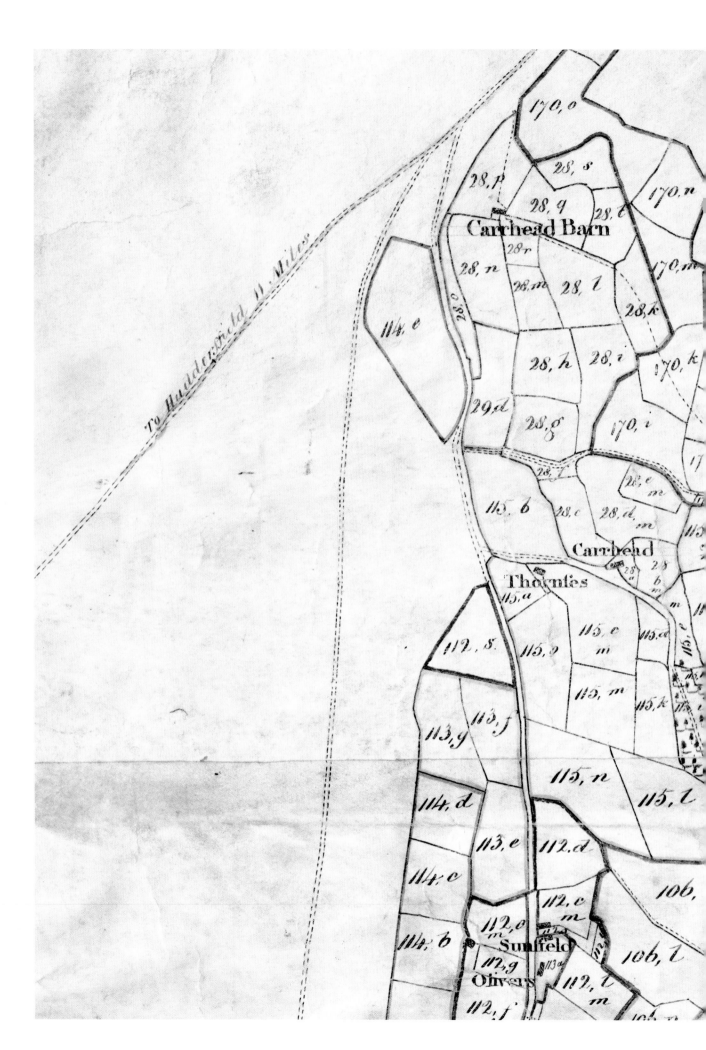

To Huddersfield 11 Miles

170, o

28, s

28, P

28, q          28, t          170, n

Carrhead Barn

28, r                        170, m

28, n      28, m    28, l

28, o                              28, k

114, e              28, h    28, i      170, k

29 d         28, g        170, i

28, f

28, e
m

115, b      28, c    28, d    115
m

Carrhead

Thornles          28
a        28
b
m

115, a                      m

112, s      115, g    115, e    115, d
m

115, m    115, k

113, f

113, g              115, n      115, l

114, d

113, e    112, d

114, c

112, c
m

114, b    112, o      106, l
m
Sunfield
112, g    113 a  106, l
Olivers          112, e
m

112, f

Plate V

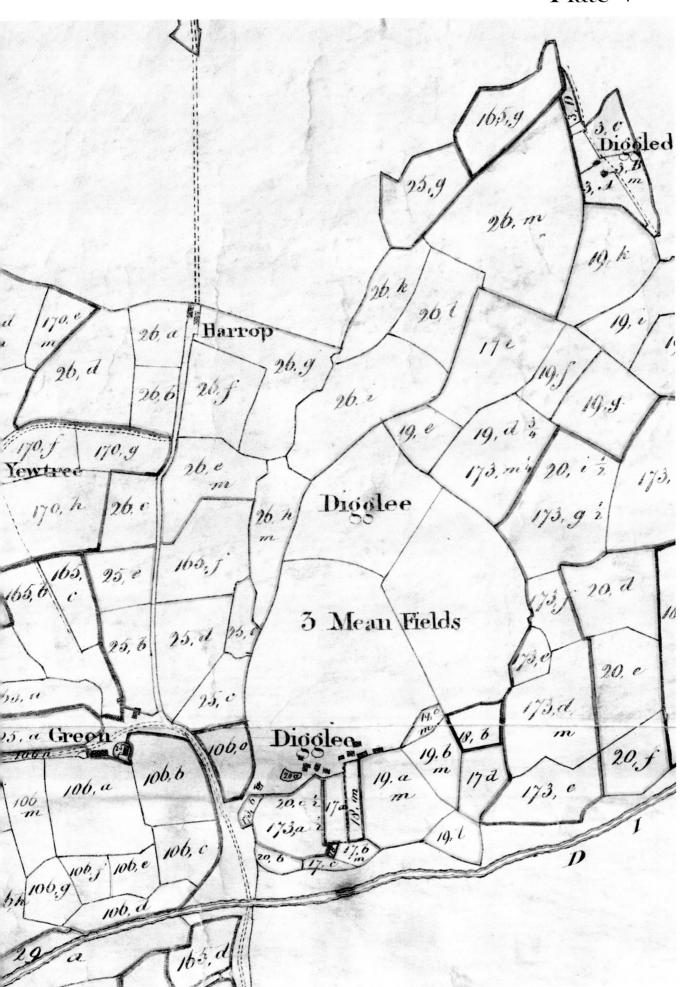

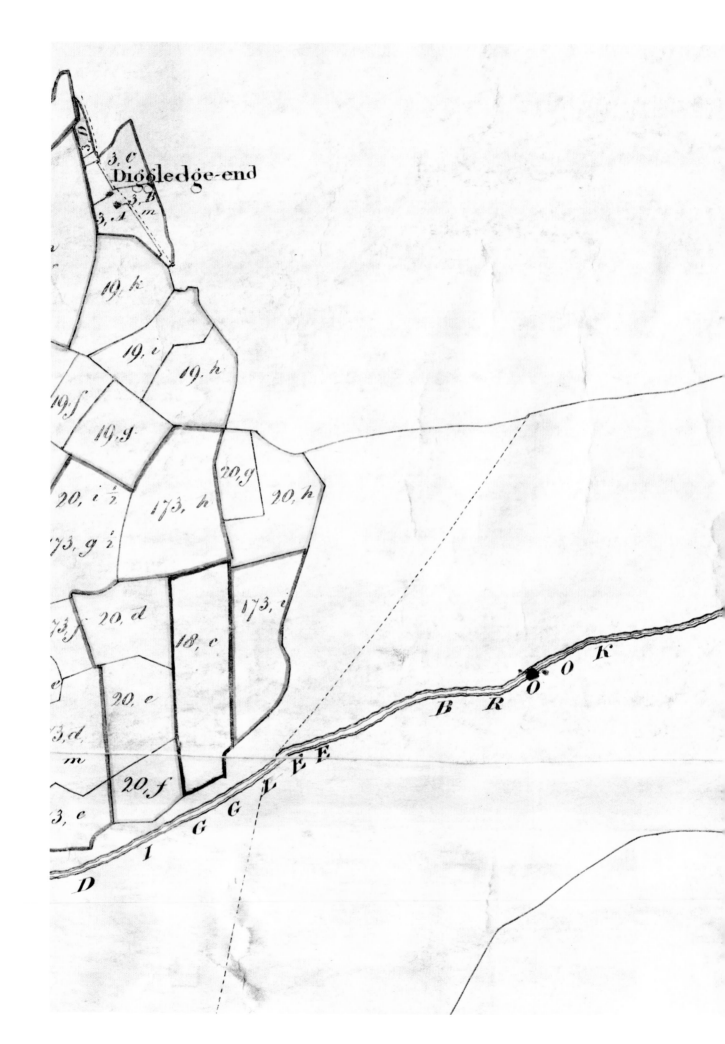

Diggledge-end

3, c

3, b

3, a    m

19, k

19, i

19, h

19, f

19, g

20, i ½

173, h

20, g

20, h

173, g i

173, i

20, d

18, c

173 f

20, e

173, d

m

173, e

20, f

D    I    G    G    L    E    E    B    R    O    O    K

36

Plate VI

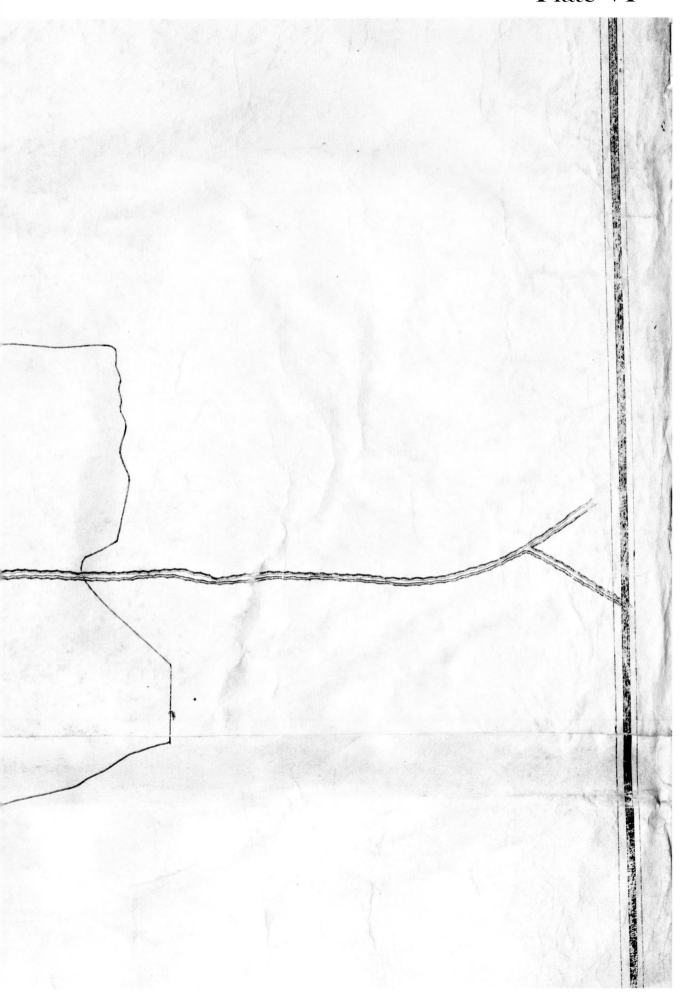

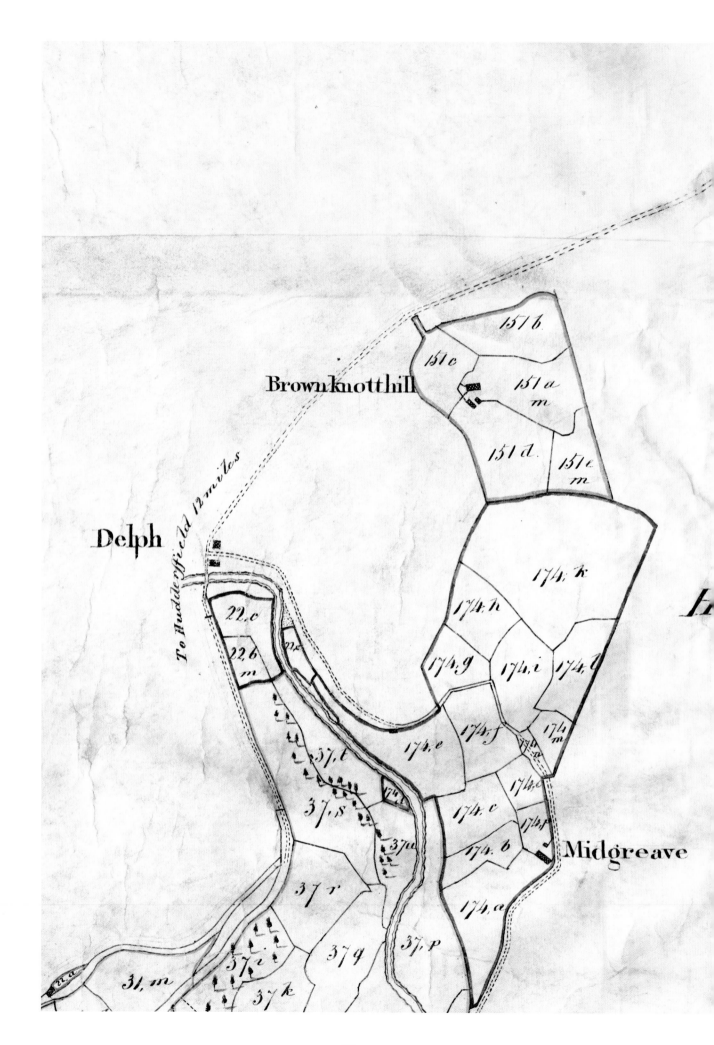

Brownknotthill

Delph

*To Huddersfield 12 miles*

Midgreave

151 b
151 c
151 a m
151 d
151 e m
174 k
174 h
174 g
174 i
174 ℓ
174 e
174 f
174 m
174 n
22 c
22 b m
37 t
37 s
174 d
174 c
174 g
174 f
174 b
37 u
37 r
174 a
37 q
37 p
31 m
37 c
37 k

Plate VII

114, b

112, c
m

112, c
m

Sunfield

112, g

Olivers

112, c
m

112, f

106, l

106, P

114, a

112, k

112, h

112, m
m

29, a

165, d

29, b

25, g
m

64, g

173, k
m

165, e

28, w

Lee

112, g

112, n
m

112, p

112, o
m

28, w

113, a

112, t
m

108, q
m

108, u

105, b
m

113, b
m

108
r

105, c

112, r

Leecrofs

65, i

173, l

28, y

108, t

105, a
m

64, f

65, g

James Rhodes
Cottage

65, b

65, d
m

David's Smithy

65, f

64, d

65, c
m

95, l
M

95, k
m

95, i

95, f

Ambroses

131, a

64, a
m

65, c

95, g
m

95, h

95, e

131, b

64, b

131, c

131, f

64, c
m

95, b

95, c

27, g

27, f

27, e
m

27, d

95, d

27, h

Mapslands

27, a

27, b
m

131, g

27, k

27, e

38, w

9, p

93, f

93, c

122, f

122, e

93, e

93, b

144, c

144, b

122, g
m

2, g

93, d

144, d

144, a

Plate VIII

BACK O'TH' LEE

Fairbanks

Runninghill

NNINGHILL

Runninghill head

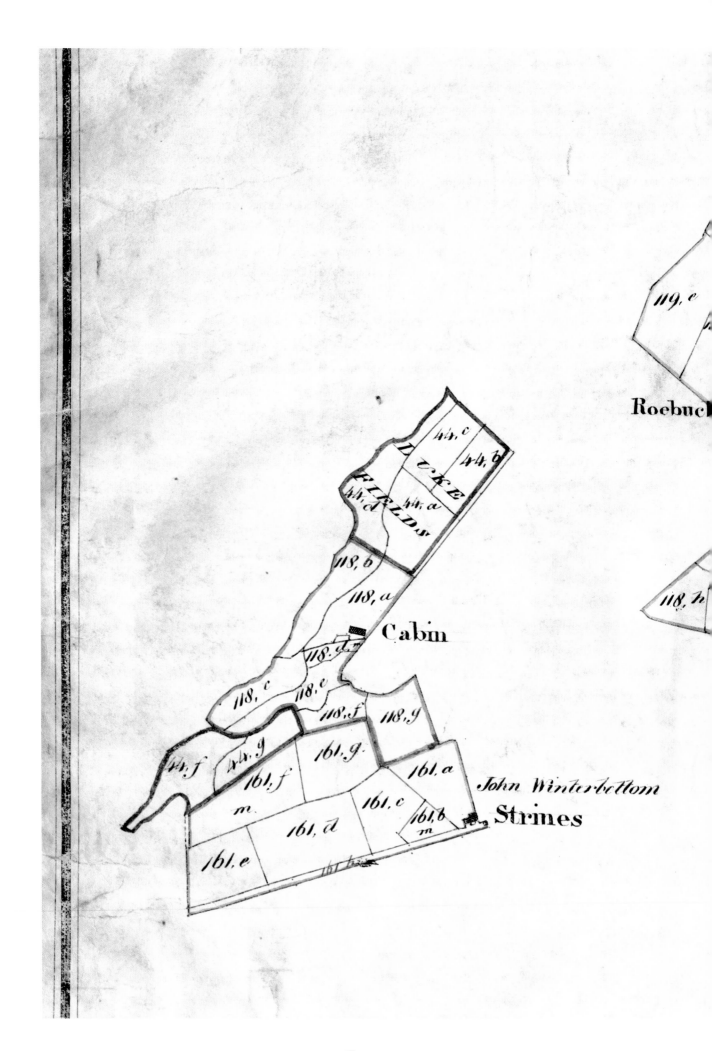

119, c

Roebuc

44, c

D U K E

44, b

F I E L D S

44, a

44, d

118, b

118, h

118, a

Cabin

118, d

118, c

118, e

118, f

118, g

44, f

44, g

161, g

161, f
m.

161, a

John Winterbottom

161, c

161, d

161, b
m.

Strines

161, e

161, b

Plate IX

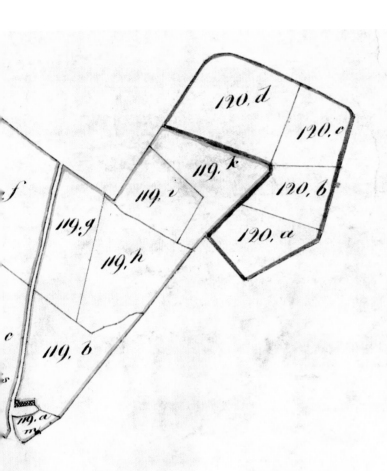

*H I G H    M O O R*

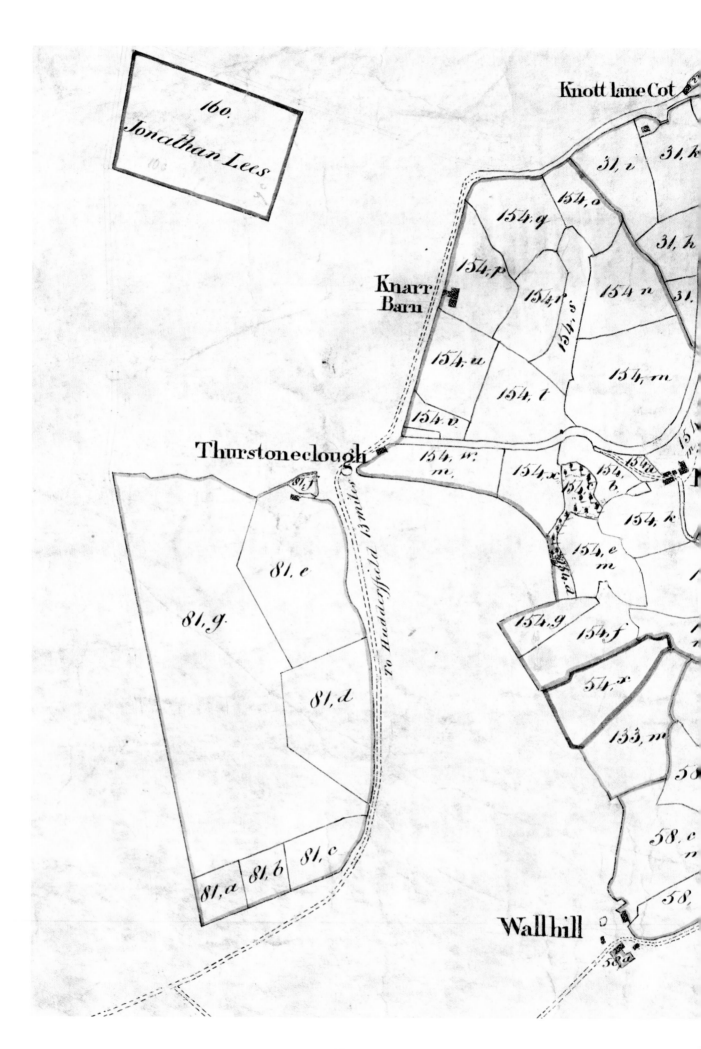

160.
Jonathan Lees

Knott Lane Cot

31, i
31, k
154, q
154, o
31, h
154, p
154, r
154, n
31,
Knarr
Barn
154, s
154, u
154, m
154, t
154
154, v

Thurstonclough
81, f
154, w, m,
154, x
154, b
154, a
81, e
154, k
154, e m
81, g
81, d
154, g
154, f
54, x
133, m
58,
81, c
58, c n
81, a   81, b
58,
Wall hill
58, a

44

Plate X

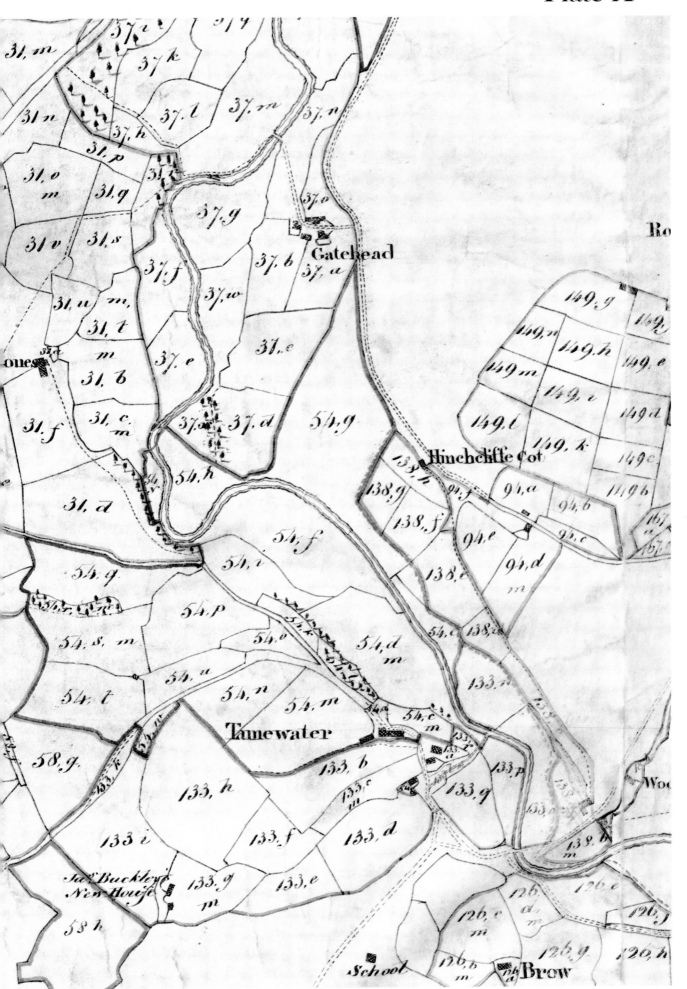

31, m

31 n

31, o
m

31 v    31, s

31, u m
31, t
m
31, b
31, f    31, c
m
31, d

37, e
37, k
37, l    37, m    37, n

37, o

37, g

37, b    37, a

Gatehead

37, w

31, e

54, g

37, c    37, d

54, h

149, g
149, n    149, h    149, e
149 m    149, c
149, t    149, d
149, k
Hinchcliffe Cot    149, c
138, h    94, f
138, g    94, a
138, f    94, b
94, e    94, c
138, e    94, d
m
94, d
m

54, f
54, i
54, p
54, s, m    54, o    54, d
m
54, u    54, n    54, m
54, t    Tamewater    54, a
54, c
m
133, a
54, e 138, a
133, m

58, g
133, b
133, c
m
133, h    133, p
133, q
133, i    133, f    133, d
138, b
m
Jas Buckley
New House    133, g    133, e
m
58 h    126, c
m
126, e
126, b    126, g    126, h
m
School    126, b    126    Brow
m    a

Ro

149

167
a
167

Woo

126
d,
m
126, f

45

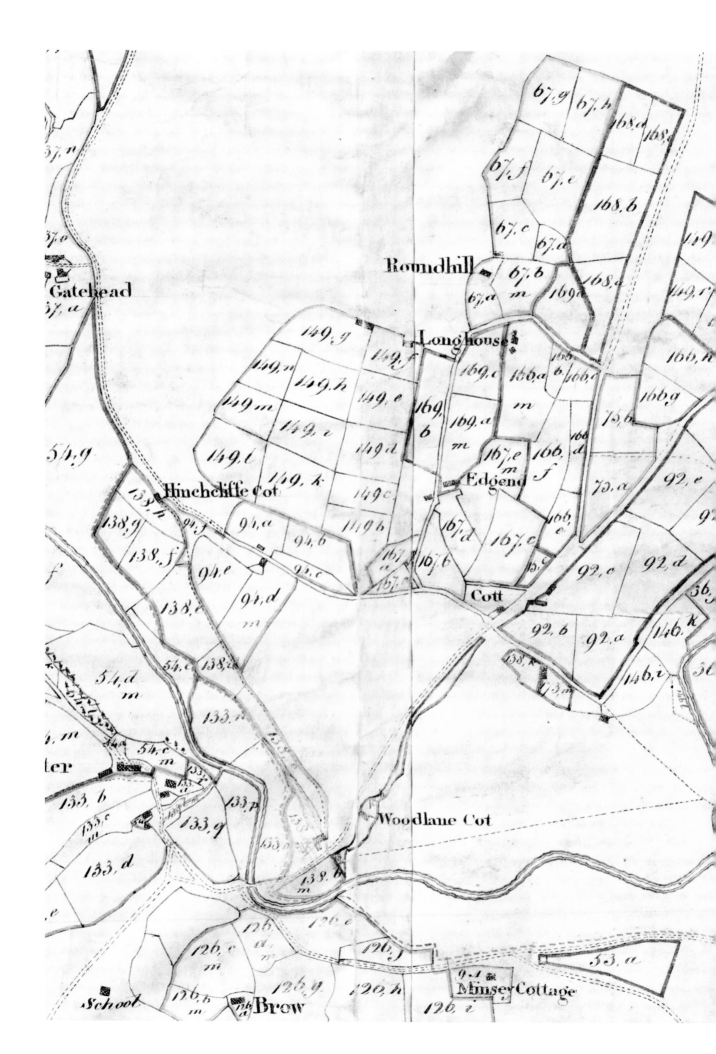

Gatehead

Roundhill

Longhouse

Hinchcliffe Cot

Edgend

Cott

Woodlane Cot

Minsey Cottage

School

Brow

46

Plate XI

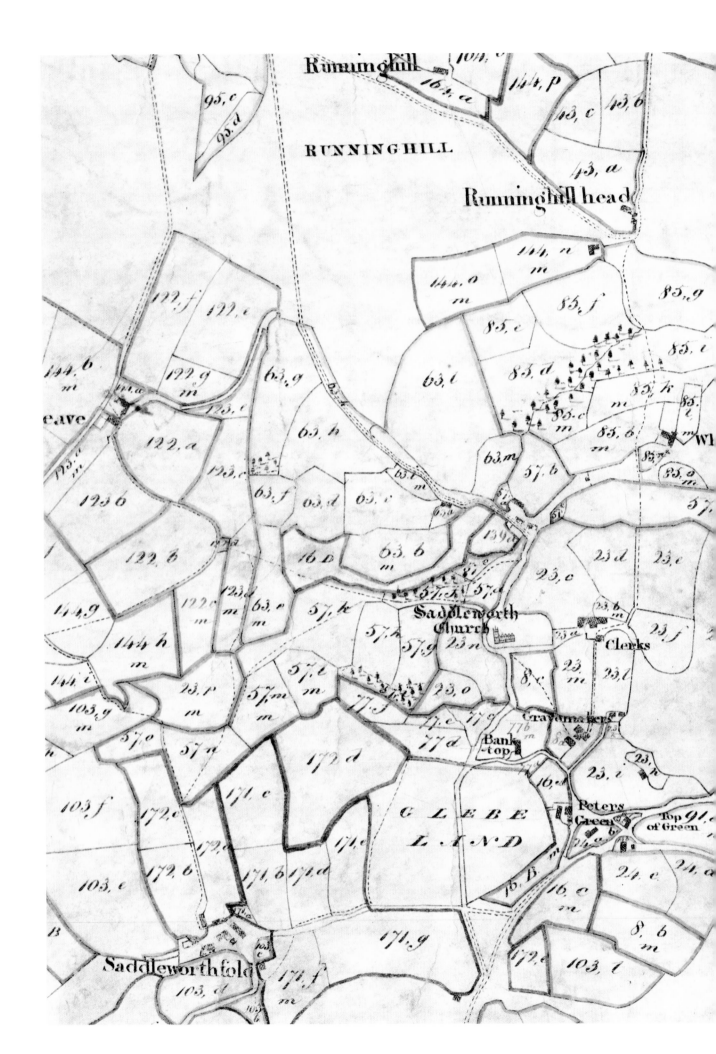

Plate XII

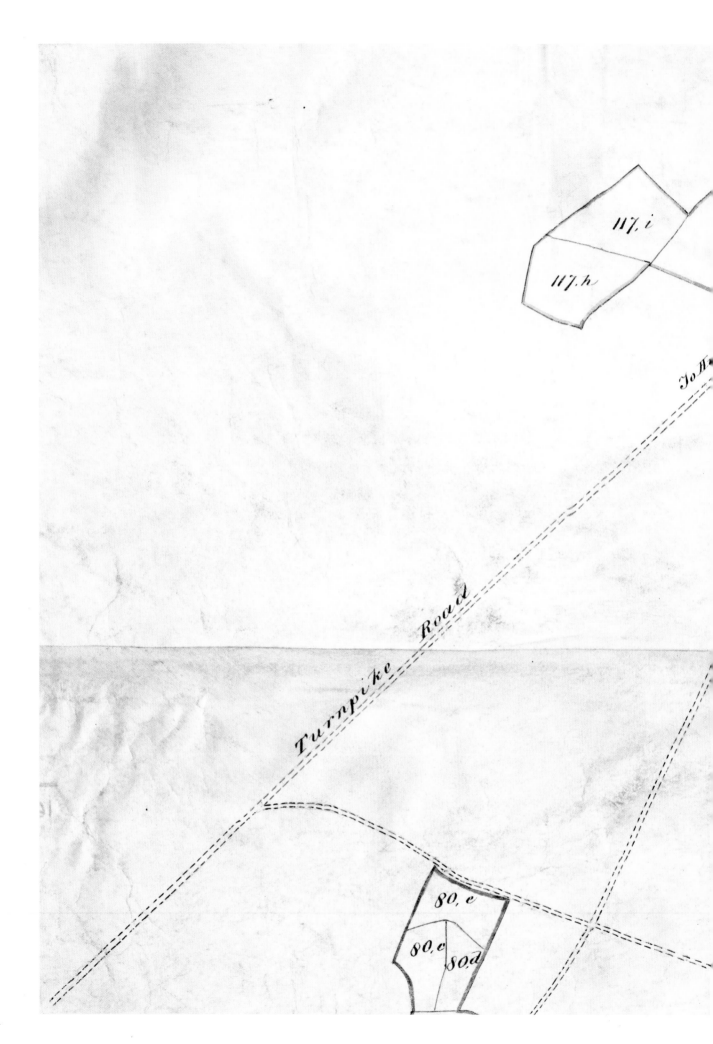

117, i

117, h

To H...

Turnpike Road

80, e

80, c 80, d

Plate XIII

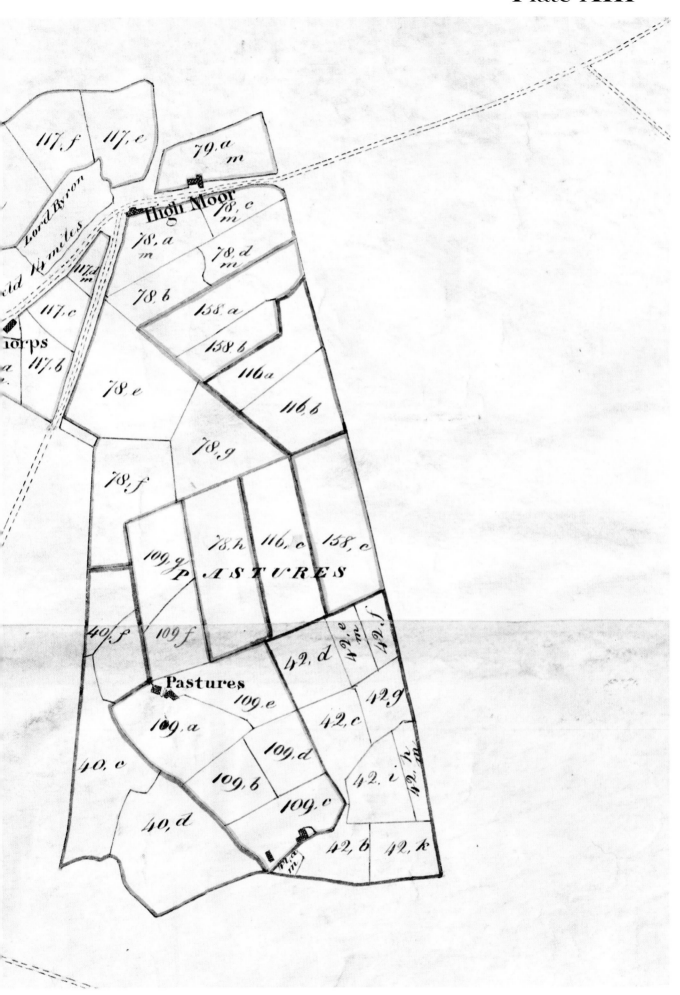

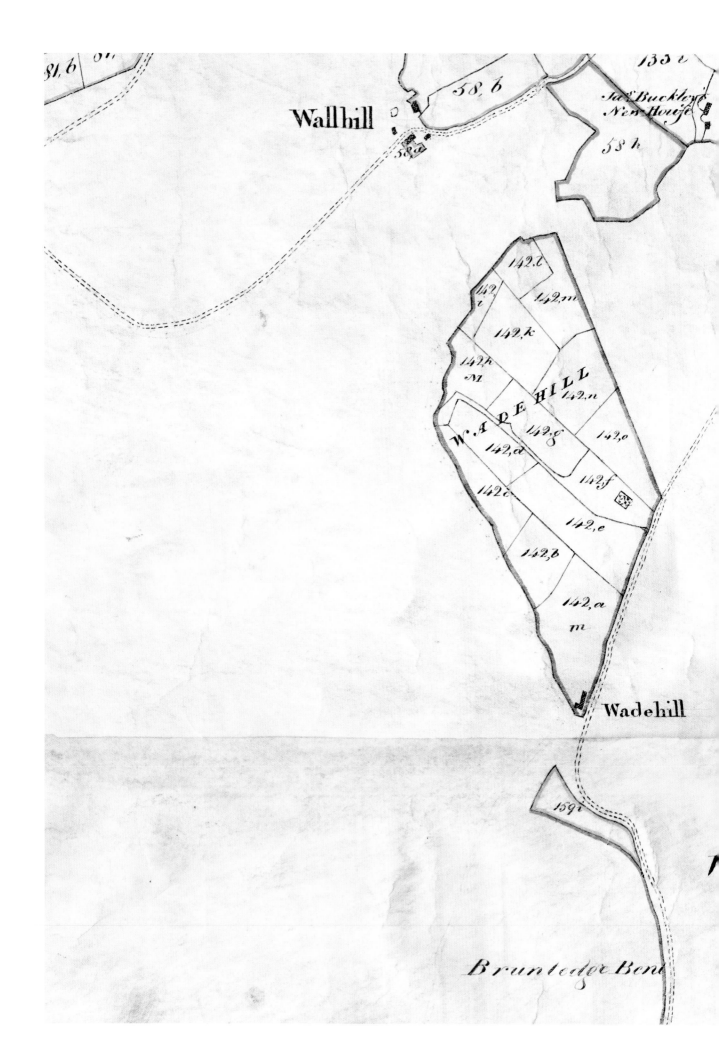

Wallbill

58, b

58 a

81, 6

135

Jas Buckley
New House

58 h

142, l

142 i

142, m

142, k

142 h
M

WADEHILL

142, n

142, g

142, o

142, d

142, f

142, c

142, e

142, b

142, a
m

Wadehill

159 i

Brunedge Bent

52

Plate XIV

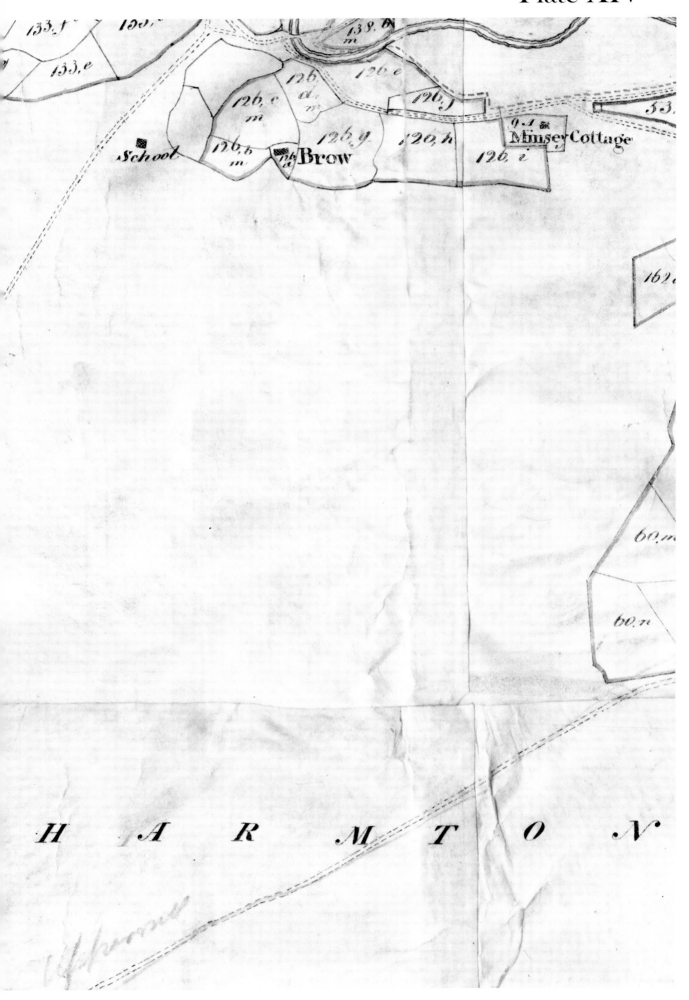

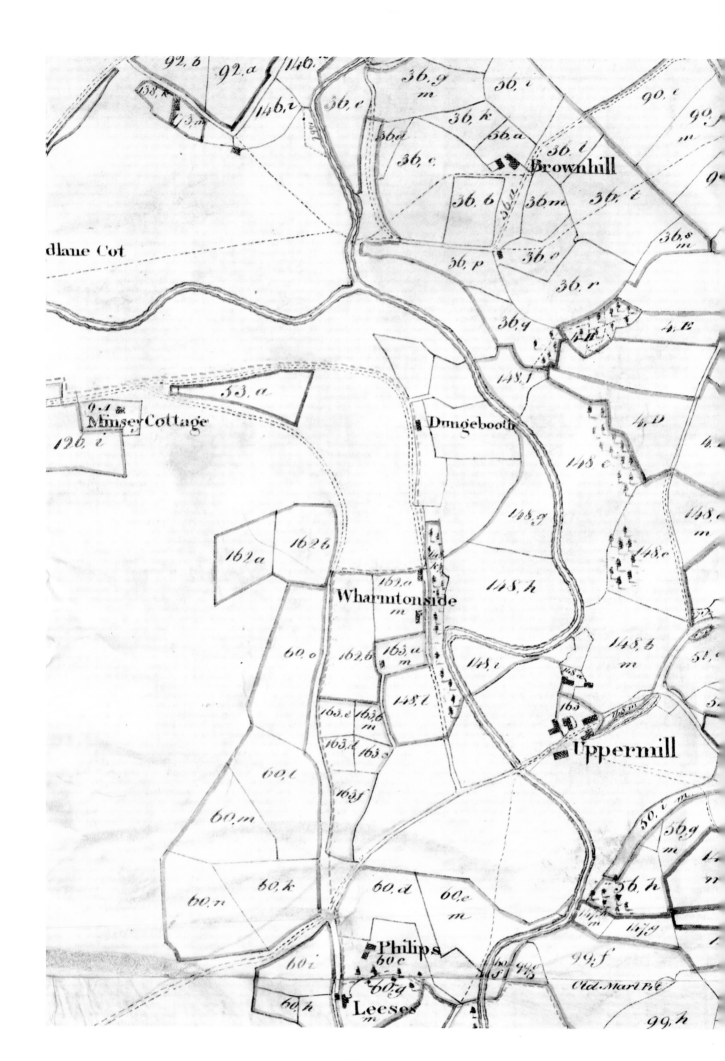

dlane Cot

92, b    92, a    146,    36, 9    36, i    90, c
138,                      m
146, i    36, e    36, k    90,
36, a    36, a    36, l    m
36, c    Brownhill
36, b    36, m    36, i
36, p    36, c    36, s
m
36, r
36, 4    4, E
148, f
9, A    53, a    Dungebooth    4, D
Minsey Cottage
126, i    148, c    4,
148, g
148, e
162 a    162 b    148, h    148,
m
148, c
162, a
Wharmtonside    148, b
m    m
60, o    162, b    163, a    148, i    148,
m    163    m
148, l    148, a
163, e    163, b    163
m
163, d    163
60, l    Uppermill
163, f    50, i    56, 9
m
60, m    56, h
n
60, k    60, d    60, e
m
60, n    m
Philips    99, f
60, c    99,
60, i    99    Old Marl Pit
60, 9    m    99, f
60, h    Leeses    99, h
m

54

Plate XV

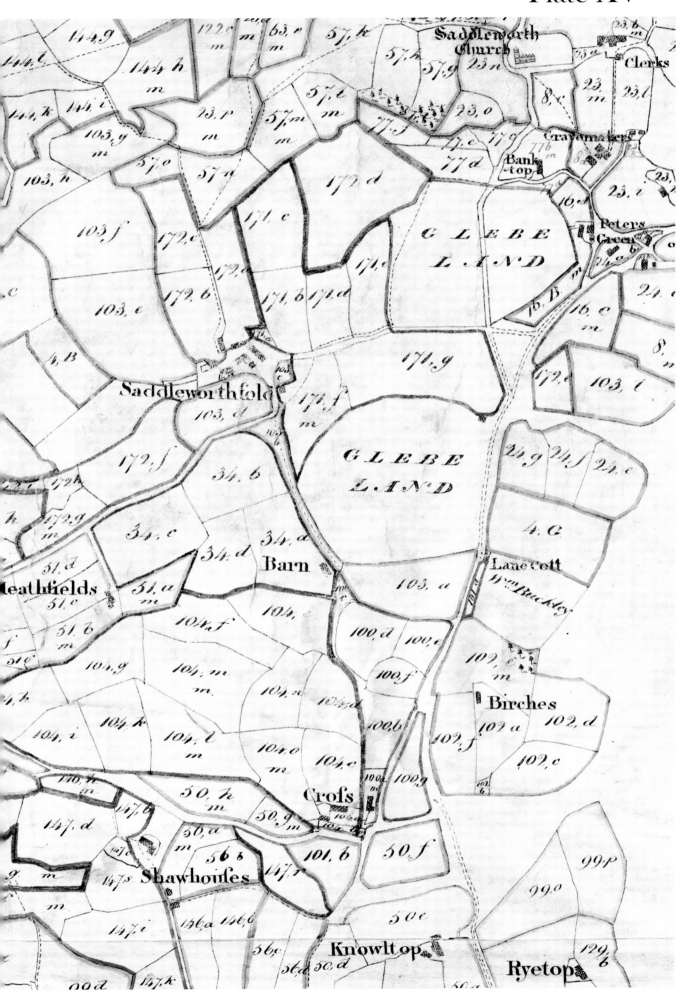

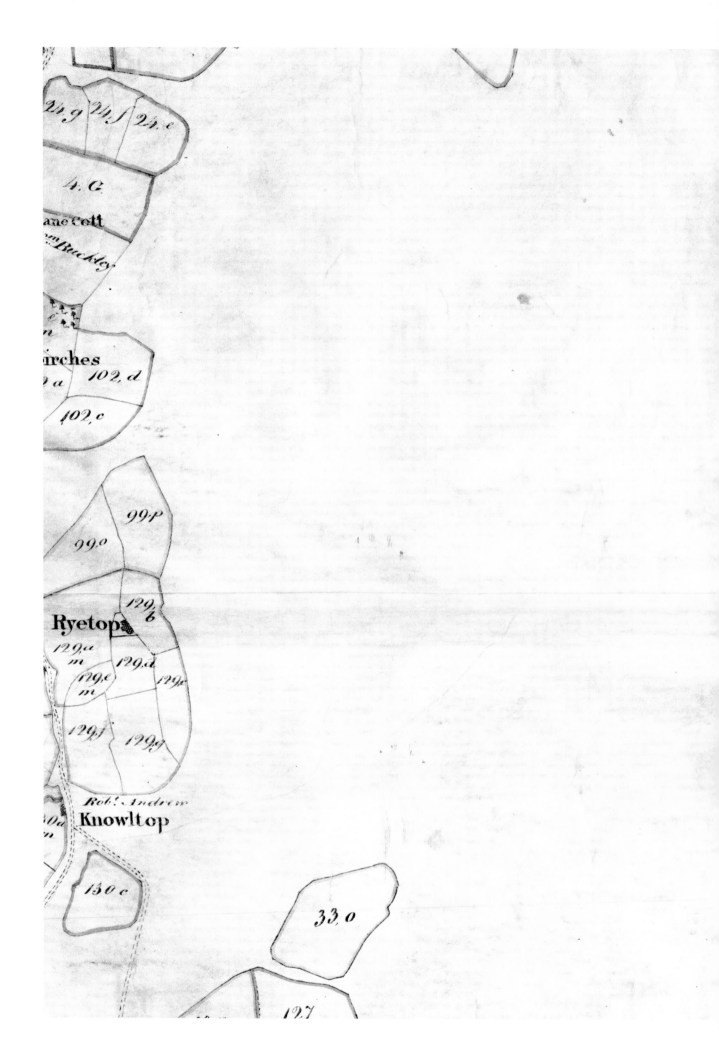

24.g 24.f 24.e

4.G

ane Cott

m Buckley

irches

a 102.d

102.c

99.P

99.o

129.b

Ryetop

129.a
m

129.e
m

129.d

129.c

129.f

129.g

Rob.t Andrew

Knowltop

130.a

130.c

33.o

127

Plate XVI

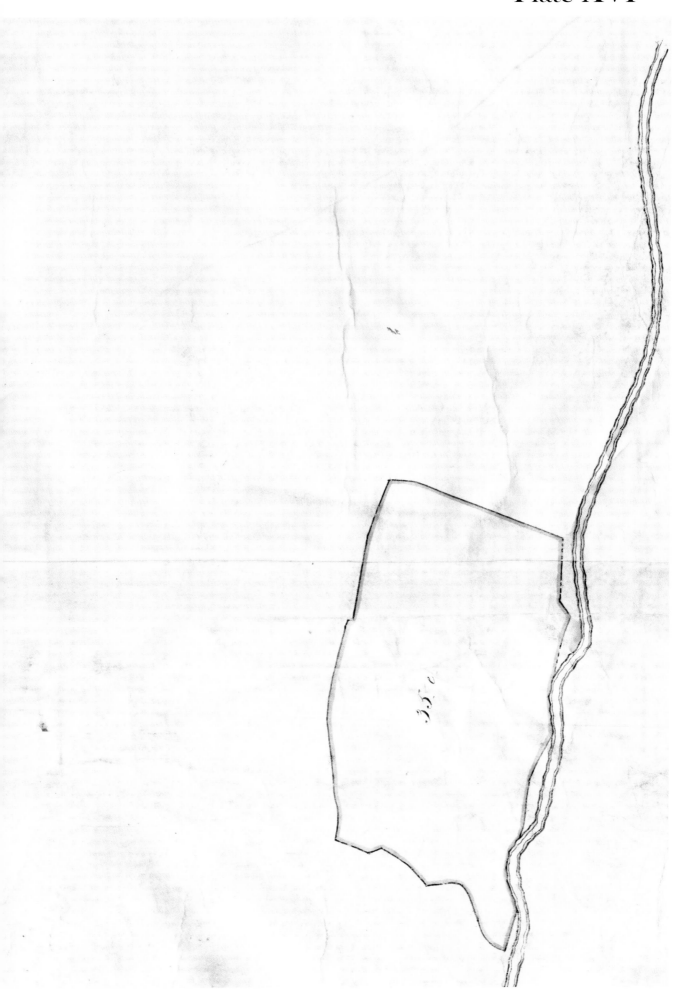

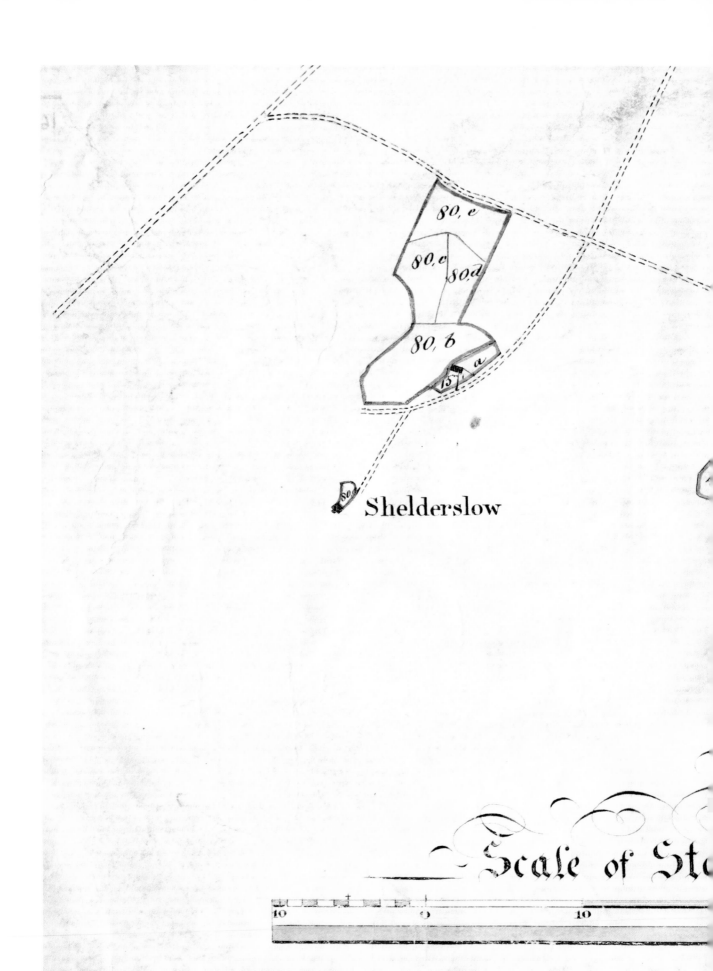

80, e

80, c

80d

80, b

a

15

80a

Shelderslow

Scale of St

10    0    10

Plate XVII

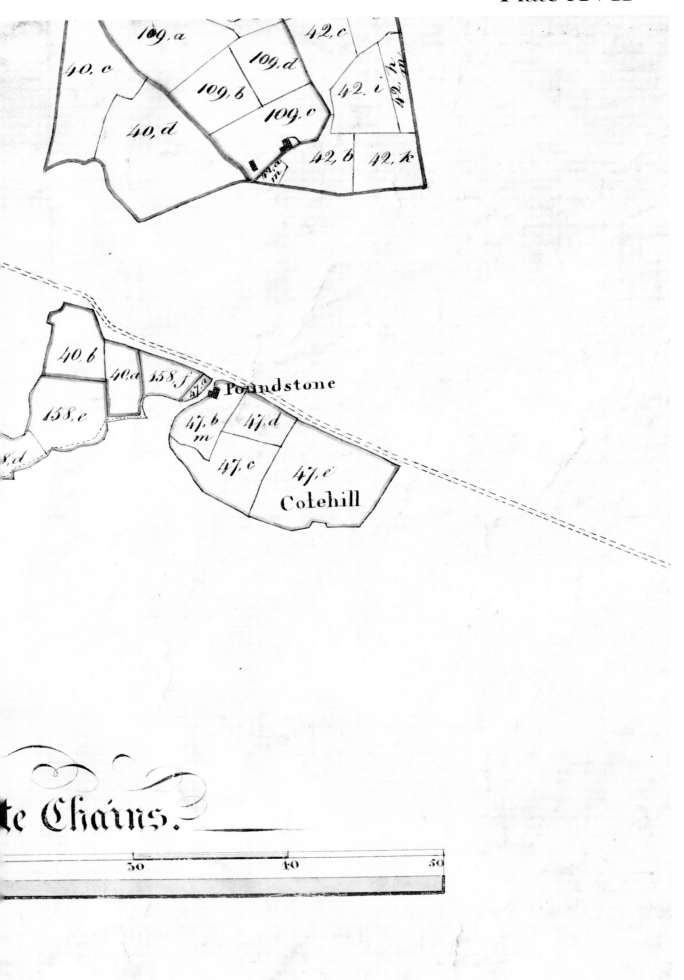

109, a

40, c

42, c

109, d

109, b

42, i

40, d

109, c

42, b    42, k

40, b

40, a    158, f

Poundstone

158, c

47, b m

47, d

47, c

47, e

Colehill

te Chains.

30        40        50

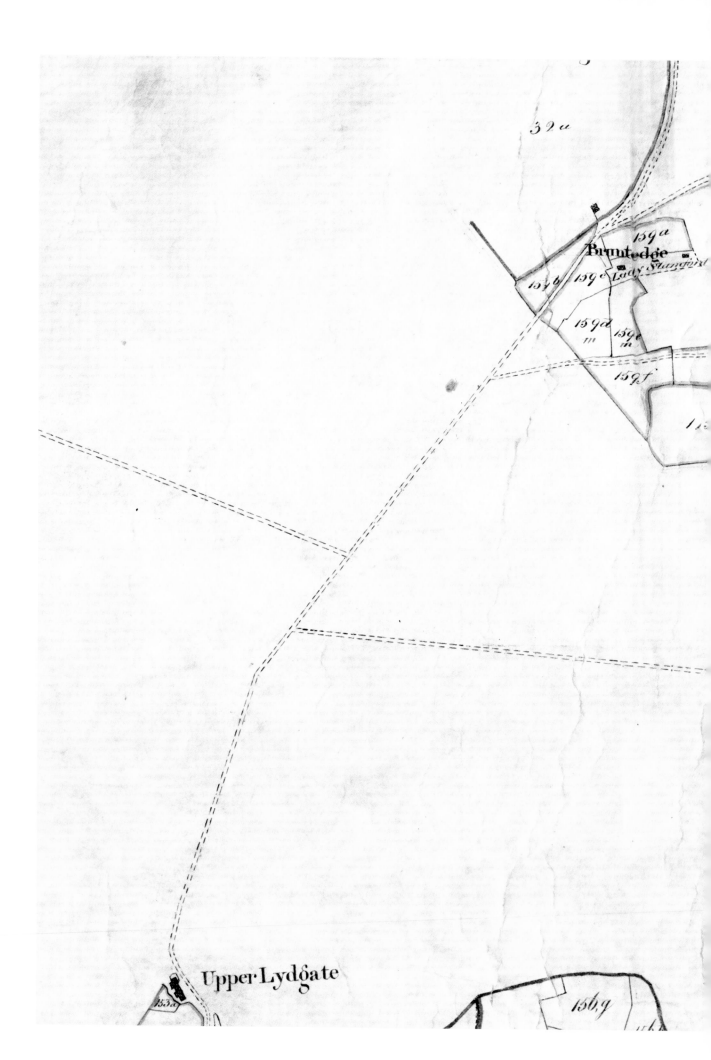

Plate XVIII

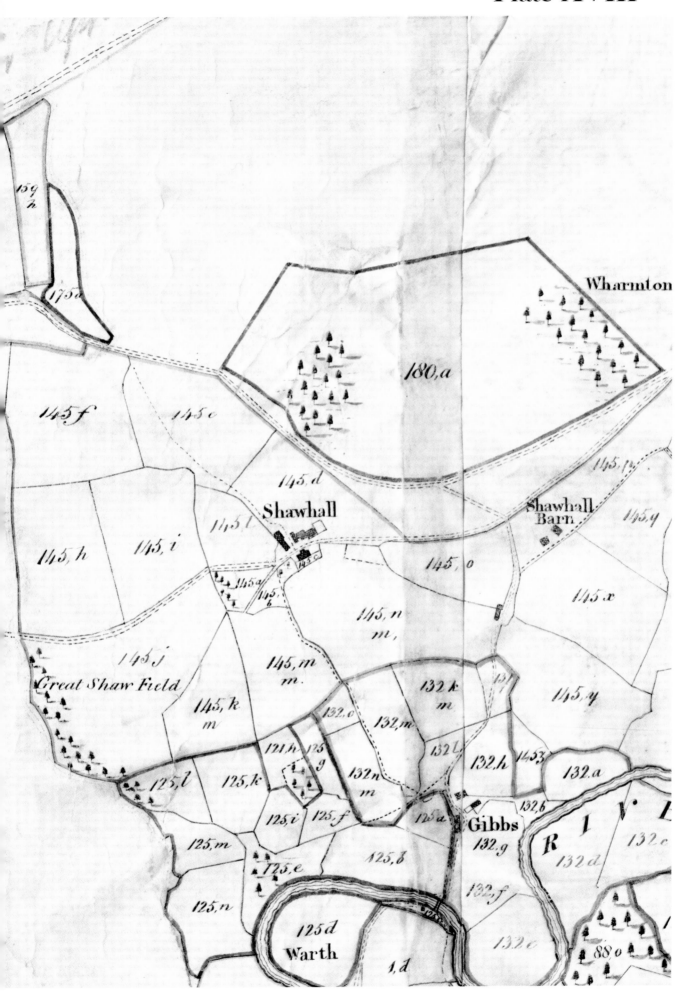

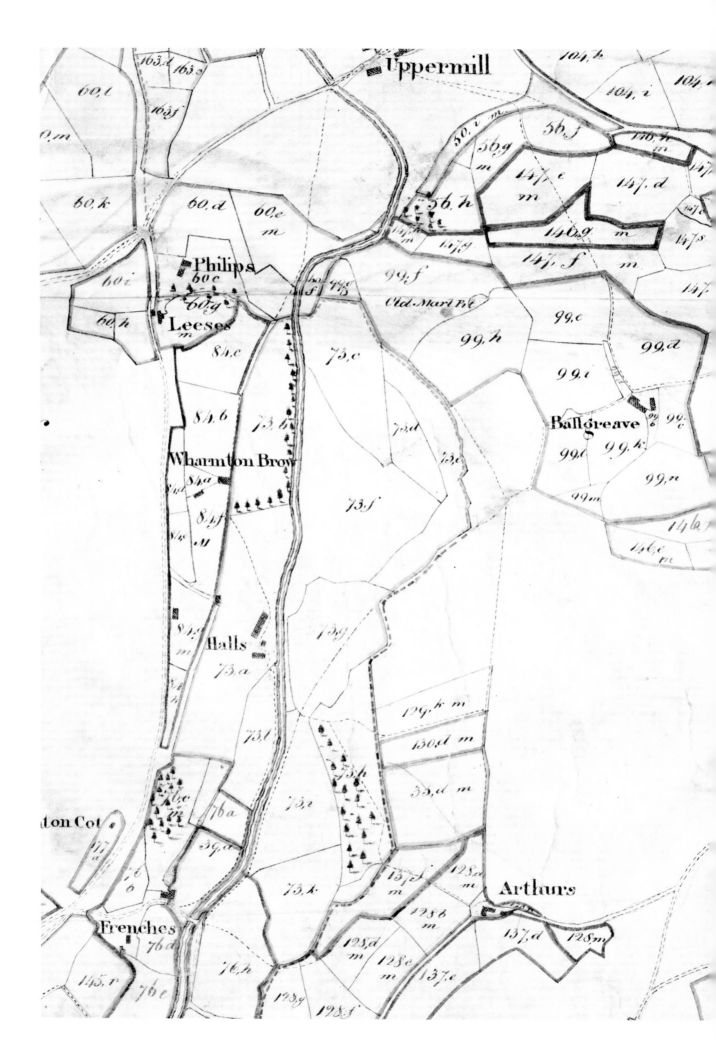

Uppermill

104, h    104, i    104,

163, d    163, e

60, l    163, f

0, m    50, i    m    56, f    146, k    m

60, k    60, d    60, e    56, g    m    147, e    147, d    147,

m    m

Philips    56, h    147, c

60, c    m    147, g    146, g    m    147, s

60, i    99, e    99, f    147, f    147

60, h    60, g    f    99    Old Marl Pit    m

Leeses    99, h    99, c    99, d

m    84, c    75, c    99, i

84, b    73, b    75, d    Ballgreave    99

Wharmton Brow    73, e    99, f    99, k

84, a    99, o    99, n

84, e    84, f    73, f    99, m

84, e    M    146, h

146, e    m

84, g    Halls    73, g

m    73, a    129, k m

130, d m

73, c    35, d m

76, c    76, a    73, h

m    on Cot    73, r

77    39, a    137, i    128, i

m    m    Arthurs

76    73, k    128, b

b    m

Frenches    128, d    128 m

76, d    m    128, c    137, d    128 m

145, r    76, h    m    137, e

76, e    128, g    128, f

62

Plate XIX

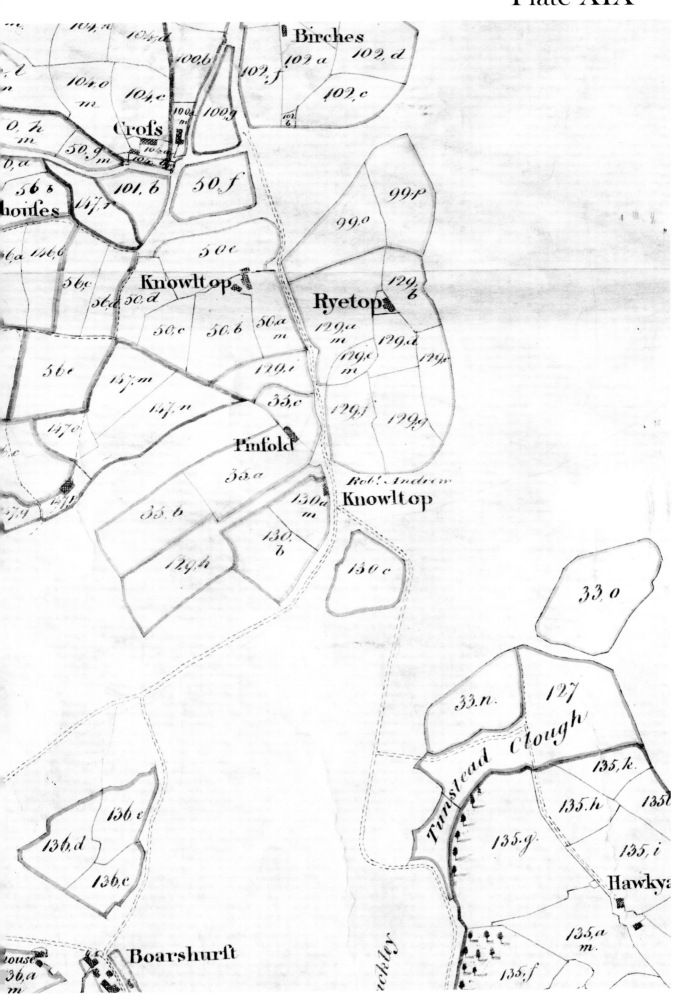

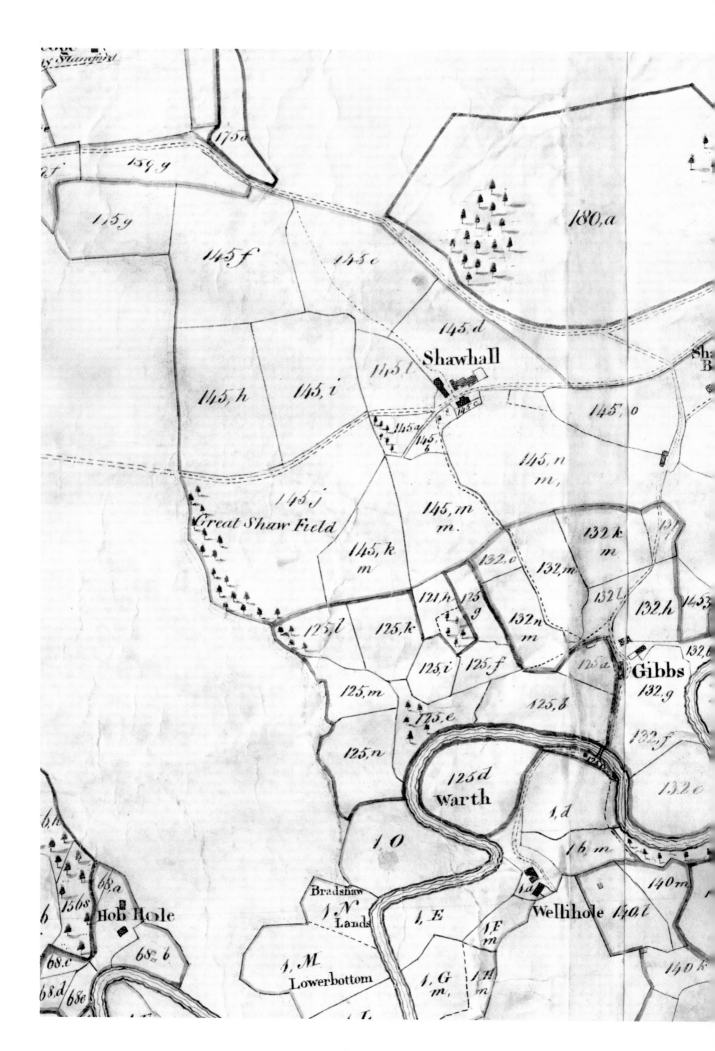

175 a

159 g

159

145 f

145 c

180, a

145, d

Shawhall

Sha
B

145 l

145 c

145, o

145, h

145, i

145 a

145 b

145, n
m,

145 j

145, m
m.

132 k
m

132

Great Shaw Field

145, k
m

132, o

132, m

132 l

132, h

145

121, h

125
g

125, l

125, k

132 n
m

125 a

Gibbs

132

125, i

125, f

132, g

132, f

125, m

125, b

132 c

125, e

125, n

125 d
Warth

1, d

1, O

1, b, m

140 m

6, h

Bradshaw

1 a

156 s

1, N
Lands

1, E

1, F
m

Wellihole 140 l

Hob Hole

68, a

68 c

1, M
Lowerbottom

1, G
m

1, H
m

140 k

68, b

68, d  68 e

64

Plate XX

136 e

136 d

136 c

hurs

128 m

Boarshurft

Lowhouse
136 b    136 a
m

4 B

33 p

Mr John Buckley

136 D

5 A

5 B

4 C

137 a

134 g

11 L

5 c

4 D
m

137 b
m

137 c
m

134 h

134 f

GREENFIELD RIVER

Nook Steer
Bridge

134 e r

12 H  Foot Way

12 G
m

12 I

Greenfield

11 C
m

Late Dr Buckley's Estate

12 F

12 E

12 C
m

12 D  Greenfield

Isaac Scholefield  11 B

12 A

Plate XXI

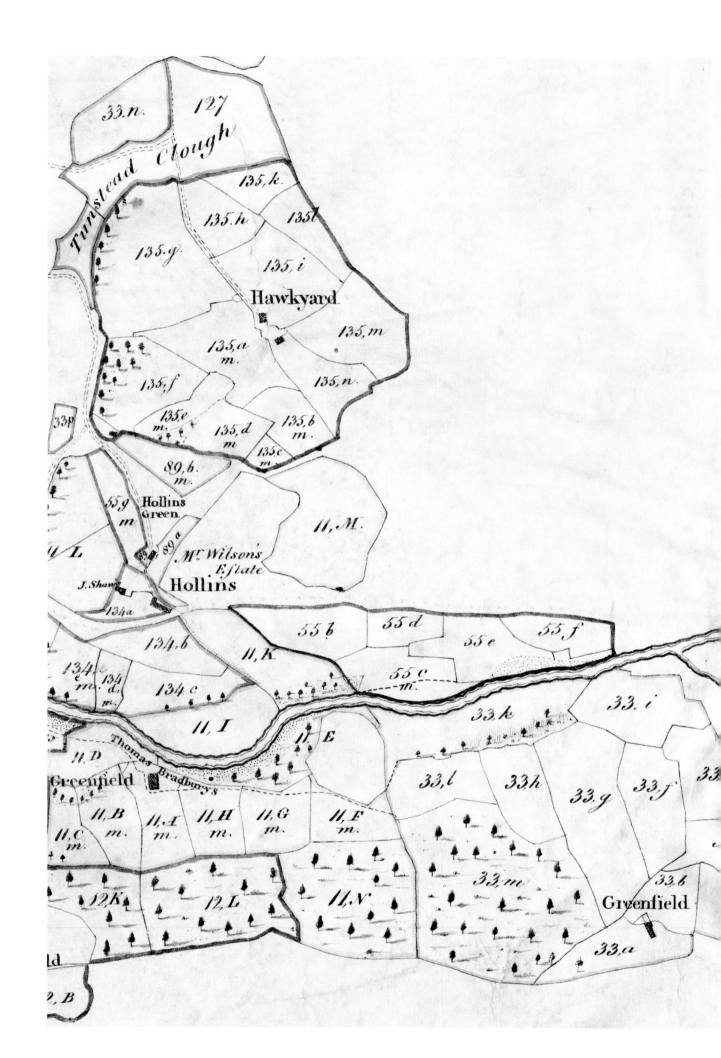

33.n.

127

Tunstead Clough

135, k.

135, h.

135 l

135. g.

135, i

Hawkyard

135, m

135, a
m.

135, n.

135, f

135e
m.

135, d
m

135, b
m.

135,c
m

33 f

89, b.
m.

55 g
m

Hollins
Green

89 a

11, M.

J. Shaw

Mr Wilson's
Estate

Hollins

11 L

134 a

134, b

11, K

55 b

55 d

55 e

55 f

134
e
m.

134
d.
m

134 c

55 c
m.

33. k

33. i

11, I

11, E

Thomas

11, D

33, l

33 h

33, g

33, f

33

Greenfield

Bradbury's

11, B
m.

11, A
m.

11, H
m.

11, G
m.

11, F
m.

11, C
m.

33, b

12 K

12, L

11, N.

33, m

Greenfield

33, a

ld

2, B

Plate XXII

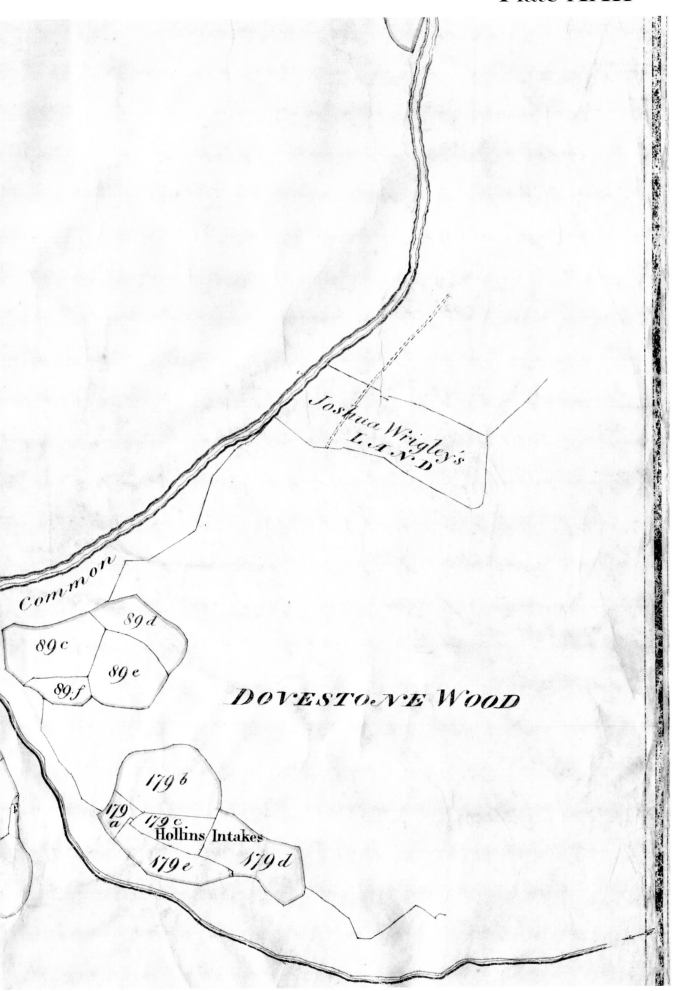

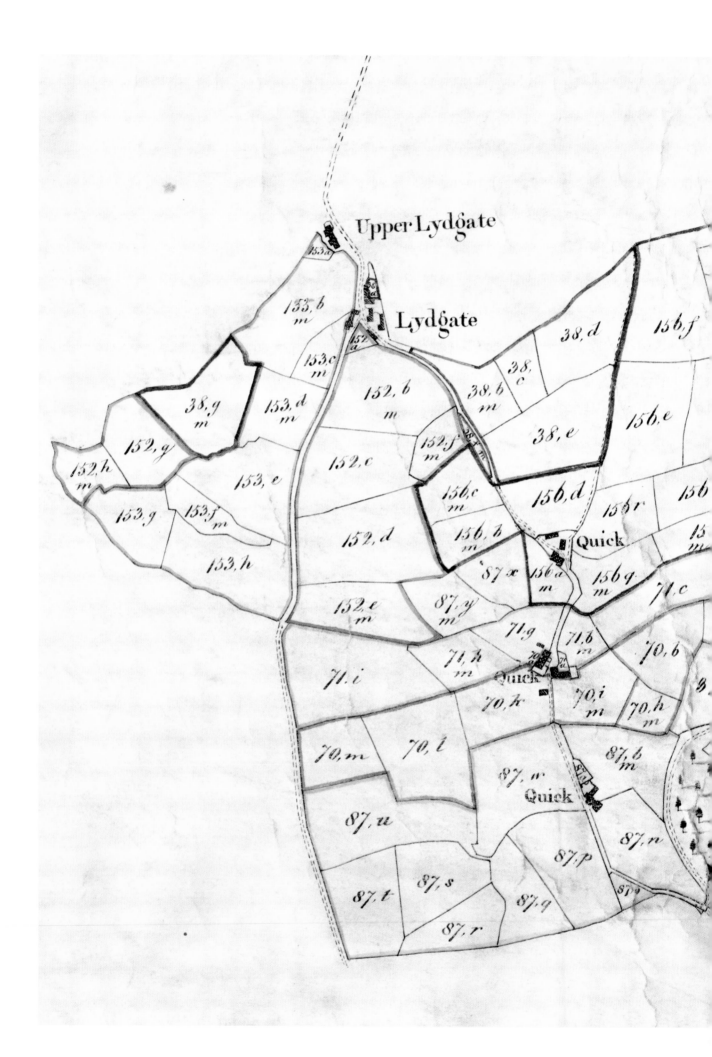

Upper Lydgate

Lydgate

153 a

153, b
m

153, c
m

153, d
m

38, g
m

152, g

152, h
m

153, g

153, f
m

153, e

153, h

152, a

152, b
m

152, c

152, d

152, e
m

152, f
m

38, b
m

38,
c

38, d

38, e

156, f

156, e

28, r
m

156, c
m

156, b
m

156, d

156 r

156

156
m

87 x

156 a
m

156 q
m

71, c

Quick

87, y
m

71, g

71, b
m

70, b

71, i

71, h
m

71
u

70, i
m

70, h
m

Quick

70, k

70, m

70, l

87, b
m

87, w

Quick

87, u

87, n

87, p

87, s

87, q

87, 9

87, t

87, r

70

Plate XXIII

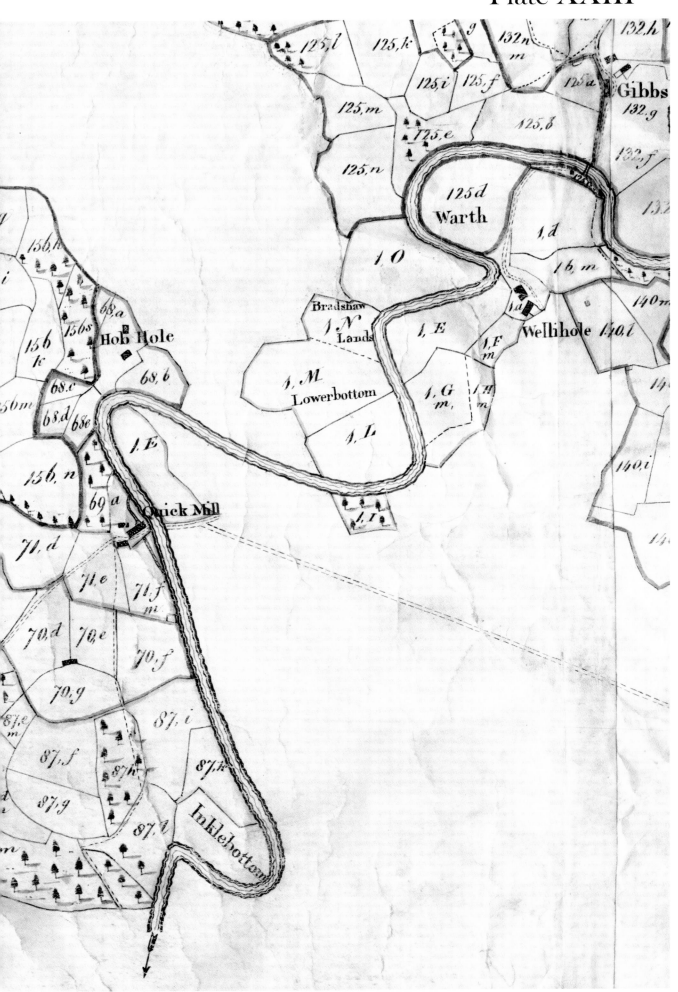

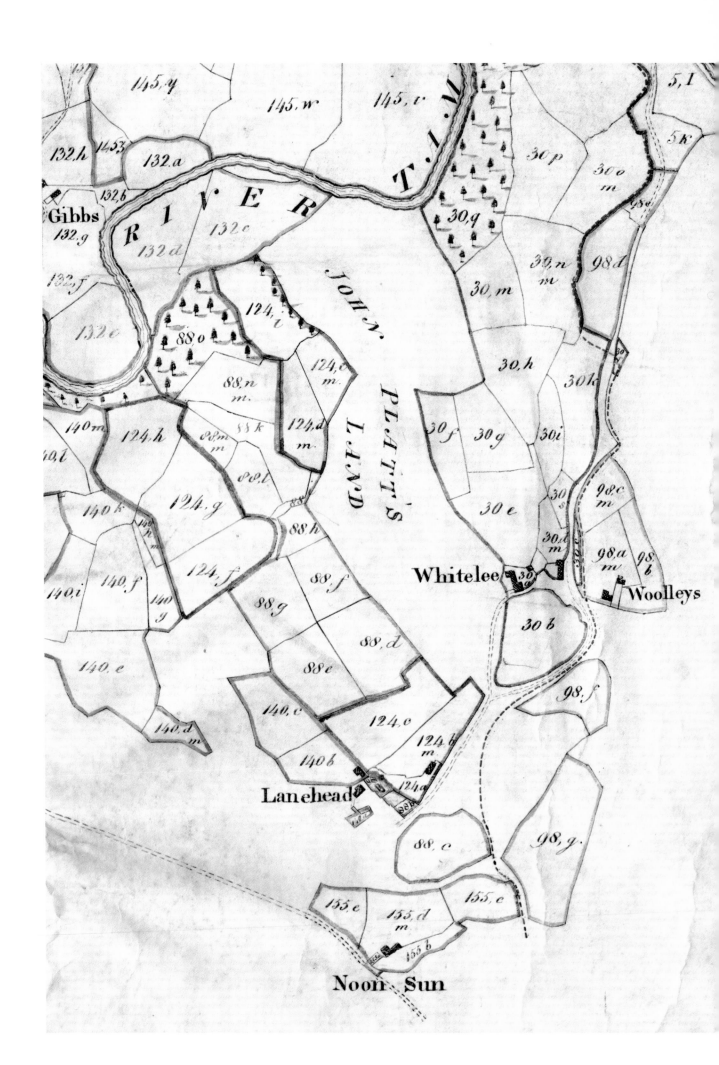

72

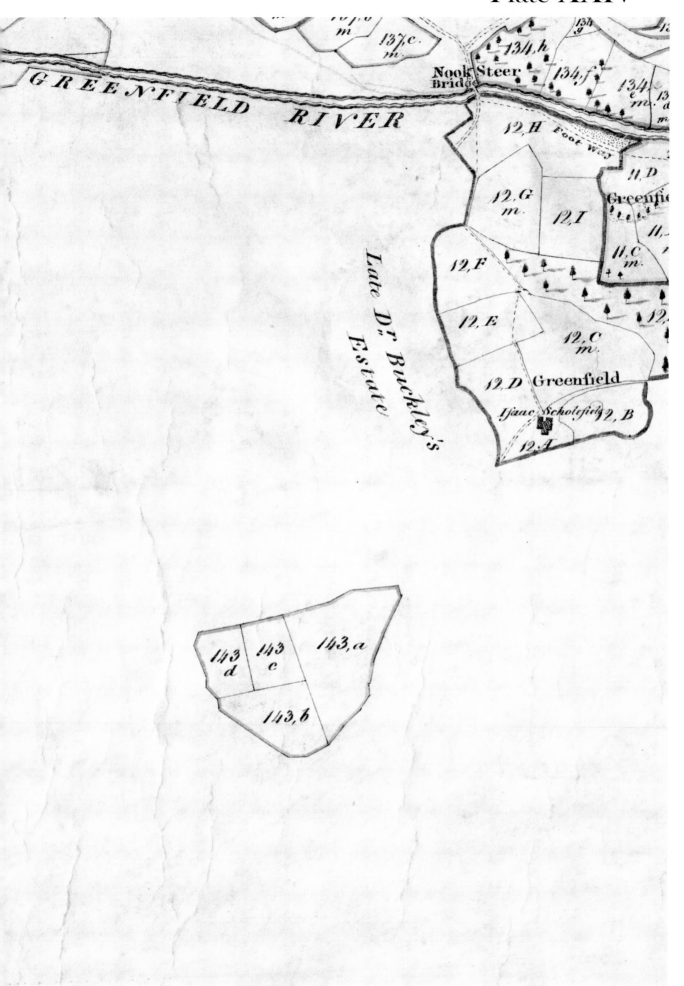

Plate XXIV

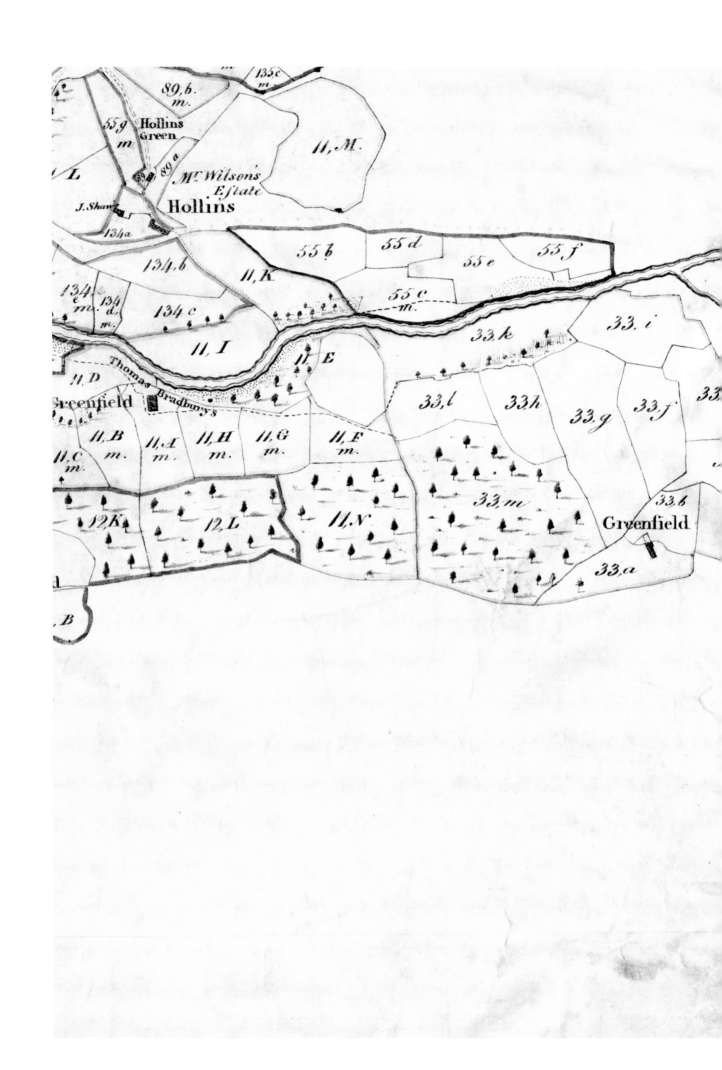

89,b.
m.

55,g    Hollins
m       Green

135,e
m.

11, M.

L

89,a
89

Mr Wilsons
Estate
Hollins

J. Shaw

134,a

134,b

11, K

55 b

55 d

55 e

55 f

134,e
m.

134,
d,
m.

134 e

11, I

55 c
m.

33, k

33. i

11, D

Thomas
Bradbury's

Greenfield

11, E

33, l

33,h

33, g

33, f

33

11, B
m.

11, A
m.

11, H
m.

11, G
m.

11, F
m.

33, m

33,b

Greenfield

11, C
m.

12,K

12, L

11, N

33, a

B

Plate XXV

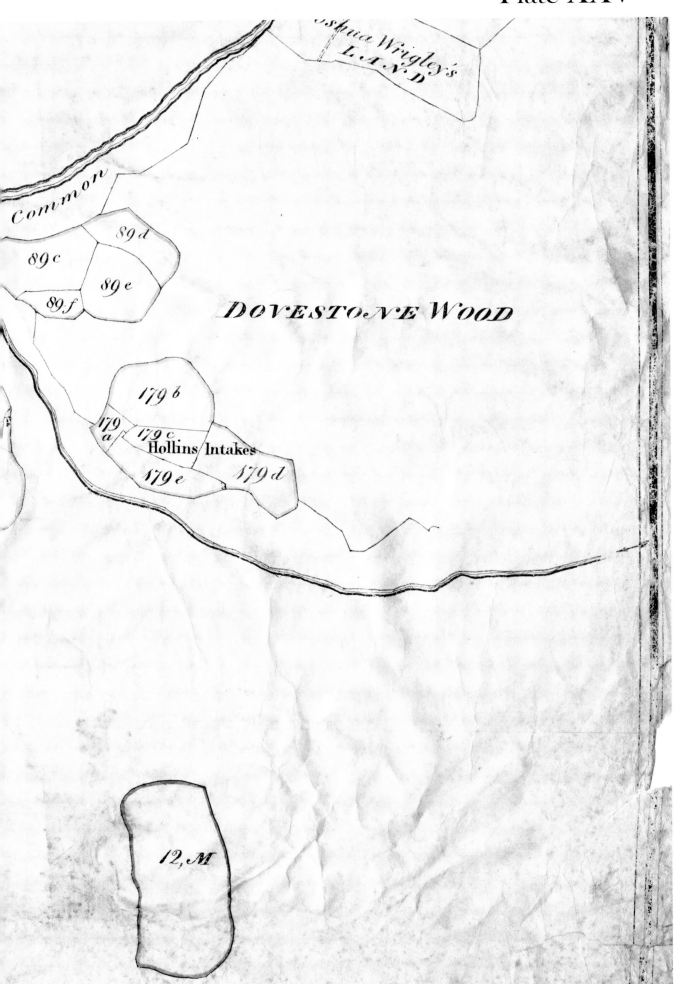

# SURVEY BOOK OF SADDLEWORTH

In 1789   John Scholefield and Brother

1  Alexander Scholefield  WELLIHOLE (S.M.)

| | | | A. | R. | P. |
|---|---|---|---|---|---|
| A. | Housing Fold &c | | 0 | 2 | 28 |
| B. | Marled Earth | M | 1 | 3 | 2 |
| C. | Shore (a Shrogg) | | 1 | 1 | 6 |
| D. | Bridgeing Field | | 2 | 3 | 27 |
| E. | Tenter Field | | 2 | 2 | 17 |
| F. | Little Meadow | M | 0 | 2 | 15 |
| G. | Barley Rood | M | 1 | 3 | 3 |
| H. | Long Meadow | M | 1 | 0 | 28 |
| I. | Meadow (a Shrogg) | | 0 | 3 | 20 |
| K. | Dodgehole | | 1 | 3 | 24 |
| L. | Warth | | 2 | 1 | 20 |
| M. | Lowerbottom } | | 5 | 0 | 10 |
| N. | Bradshaw Lands } | | | | |
| O. | Upperbottom | | 3 | 2 | 0 |
| | | | 26 | 2 | 0 |

In 1789   James Broadbent

3  Thomas Bradbury  Cott and Common (L.M.)

1 Dwelling house consisting of 2 Bays lately erected with one Bay of Outhousing adjoining thereto.

| | | A. | R. | P. |
|---|---|---|---|---|
| A | Meadow M divided into 2 parts | 1 | 0 | 20 |
| B | Stony Intake | 0 | 3 | 13 |
| C | New Field | 0 | 3 | 22 |
| D | New Croft | 0 | 1 | 19 |
| | | 3 | 0 | 34 |

In 1789   Philip

4  John Bentley  Boarshurst and Saddleworthfold (L.M.)

BOARSHURST

| | | | A. | R. | P. |
|---|---|---|---|---|---|
| A | House Barn and Garden | | 0 | 0 | 15 |
| B | Tenter Meadow | M | 2 | 1 | 8 |
| C | Further Field | | 3 | 2 | 6 |
| D | Little Meadow | M | 0 | 3 | 28 |
| E | Croft | M | 0 | 1 | 15 |
| | | | 7 | 0 | 32 |

SADDLEWORTHFOLD

| | | | A. | R. | P. |
|---|---|---|---|---|---|
| A | House and Garden | | 0 | 0 | 9 |
| B | Othwart | | 1 | 2 | 24 |
| C | Great Field | | 3 | 3 | 28 |
| D | Great Meadow | M | 2 | 2 | 30 |
| E | Little Meadow | M | 1 | 1 | 28 |
| F | Short Butts | | 1 | 3 | 19 |
| G | Intake | | 3 | 1 | 17 |
| H | Clough (a Shrogg) | | 0 | 2 | 7 |
| | | | 15 | 2 | 2 |
| | Brought down | | 7 | 0 | 32 |
| | | | 22 | 2 | 34 |

In 1789   Philip

5  John Bentley  LOWERHOUSE (L.M.)

| | | | A. | R. | P. |
|---|---|---|---|---|---|
| A | Pingot | | 1 | 0 | 7 |
| B | Blackearth | M | 1 | 1 | 13 |
| C | Bentend | | 2 | 2 | 32 |
| D | Frostylee | | 2 | 0 | 5 |
| E | Frostylee Meadow | | 0 | 3 | 26 |
| F | Knowl | | 0 | 2 | 14 |
| G | Waste | | 0 | 3 | 21 |
| H | Barley Butt | | 1 | 1 | 36 |
| I | Holm | | 2 | 1 | 22 |
| K | Shrogg | | 1 | 0 | 20 |
| | | | 14 | 1 | 36 |

In 1789   Abraham

6  John Bentley  BENTLEYS (L.M.)

| | | | A. | R. | P. |
|---|---|---|---|---|---|
| A | Meadow M with the Housing therein | | 2 | 3 | 36 |
| B | Old Meat | | 1 | 1 | 3 |
| C | Intake | | 3 | 0 | 33 |
| D | Croft | | 0 | 1 | 6 |
| | | | 7 | 2 | 38 |

7  James Bentley  UPPERHOUSE (L.M.)

| | | | A. | R. | P. |
|---|---|---|---|---|---|
| A | Upperside M with the Housing | | 1 | 0 | 39 |
| B | Lower Meadow | M | 1 | 1 | 23 |
| C | Rough | | 2 | 2 | 27 |
| | | | 5 | 1 | 9 |

In 1789   Widow

8  Michael Bottomley  GRAVEMAKERS (L.M.)

9 Bays of Housing & a Turf Cote all new Buildings except one Bay.

| | | | A. | R. | P. |
|---|---|---|---|---|---|
| A | Croft with the Housing therein as the same is divided into Gardens &c } | | 0 | 3 | 14 |
| B | Intake | M | 1 | 3 | 11 |
| | | | 2 | 2 | 25 |
| C | The Dial Field | | 1 | 0 | 13 |
| | | Total | 3 | 2 | 38 |

In 1789   Benjamin Brierley

9  John Bradbury  Minsey Cottage & Croft (S.M.)

Minsey Croft with an Old Cottage therein part of which hath been lately Repair'd.

| | | A. | R. | P. |
|---|---|---|---|---|
| A | Minsey Croft M with the Cottage therein | 0 | 3 | 27 |

In 1789   Thomas

10  John Bradbury  RUNNINGHILL (L.M.)

No Housing

| | | A. | R. | P. |
|---|---|---|---|---|
| A | The Rough | 7 | 1 | 15 |

In 1789   Robert

11  Executors Thomas Bradbury  GREENFIELD (L.M.)

A Good new built House and an Ancient Barn & Shippin in Good Repair

| | | | A. | R. | P. |
|---|---|---|---|---|---|
| A | Near Barn Meadow M wth. ye. Housing | | 2 | 0 | 23 |
| B | Lower Meadow | M | 2 | 0 | 22 |
| C | Bent | M | 1 | 0 | 28 |
| D | Lower Stannery | | 1 | 2 | 35 |
| E | Upper Stannery {2. 1. 2. / 2. 0. 29.} | | 4 | 1 | 31 |
| F | Upper Meadow | | 1 | 2 | 30 |
| G | Marled Earth | M | 1 | 3 | 4 |
| H | Farr Barn Meadow | M | 1 | 3 | 4 |
| I | Stannery | | 2 | 2 | 15 |
| K | Intake | | 3 | 0 | 15 |
| L | Timberty Carr (divided into two) | | 4 | 0 | 26 |
| M | Close | | 4 | 2 | 19 |
| N | Hey | | 6 | 1 | 0 |
| | | | 37 | 2 | 12 |

In 1789  Isaac Scholefield

12     James Ridgeway            **GREENFIELD (L.M.)**

A good House being 3 Bays with two Families therein, a good Barn & Shippen and an Out Isle.

|   |   |   | A. | R. | P. |
|---|---|---|---|---|---|
| A | Near Croft with the Housing | M | 1 | 0 | 36 |
| B | Farr Croft |   | 1 | 2 | 20 |
| C | Little end | M | 3 | 2 | 12 |
| D | Great end |   | 2 | 0 | 24 |
| E | Middlemost | C | 1 | 3 | 30 |
| F | Lowmostor New Ridd |   | 2 | 0 | 15 |
| G | Lower Meadow | M | 2 | 2 | 29 |
| H | Stannery |   | 3 | 1 | 36 |
| I | Upper Meadow | C | 2 | 0 | 26 |
| K | Near Hey |   | 4 | 2 | 38 |
| L | Farr Hey |   | 4 | 3 | 0 |
| M | Intake |   | 7 | 1 | 34 |
|   |   |   | 37 | 3 | 20 |

13     Extrs. Robt. Bradbury & Jno. Broadbent     **Top of Green (L.M.)**

2 Houses new built in Robert Bradbury & his Tenants Occupation. Also 1 Antient House in good repair & 1 New House in Nathaniel Broadbent & Tenants Occupation.

|   |   | A. | R. | P. |
|---|---|---|---|---|
| A | Croft and Garden with the Housing therein | 0 | 0 | 20 |
| B | Croft with the House therein | 0 | 0 | 22 |
| C | Intake | 1 | 1 | 22 |
|   |   | 1 | 2 | 24 |
| D | A croft adjoining the Slades | 0 | 0 | 10 |
|   |   | 1 | 2 | 34 |

14     Thomas Bradbury           **FAIRBANKS (L.M.)**

One good Dwelling House new Built one little Old House adjoining the same, a Barn & Shippen, also an Old Stable & Turfcote fallen down.

|   |   |   | A. | R. | P. |
|---|---|---|---|---|---|
| A | Housing Fold &c |   | 0 | 0 | 27 |
| B | Long Intake |   | 2 | 3 | 6 |
| C | New Intake |   | 2 | 2 | 30 |
| D | Upper little Intake |   | 0 | 1 | 35 |
| E | Lower little Intake |   | 0 | 1 | 33 |
| F | Great Intake |   | 3 | 0 | 9 |
| G | Uppermost Meadow | M | 1 | 1 | 15 |
| H | Middlemost Meadow | M | 1 | 2 | 18 |
| I | Blacklands | M | 2 | 0 | 24 |
| K | Lower Field |   | 1 | 3 | 0 |
| L | Lower Little Meadow | M | 0 | 2 | 30 |
| M | Back Intacke |   | 1 | 0 | 24 |
|   |   |   | 18 | 1 | 11 |

15     James Broadbent           **ABELS (L.M.)**

A very Old Cottage with a Cowhouse adjoining

|   |   |   | A. | R. | P. |
|---|---|---|---|---|---|
| A | Field at Door and Housing |   | 1 | 3 | 14 |
| B | Meadow | M | 1 | 1 | 14 |
| C | Tenterfield |   | 0 | 1 | 16 |
|   |   |   | 3 | 2 | 4 |

In 1789  James Buckley

16     John Bradbury           **PETERS (L.M.)**

Peters. 2 Dwelling Houses with a Barn & Shippen & Turfcote being 7 Bays in the whole all in Good repair

|   |   |   | A. | R. | P. |
|---|---|---|---|---|---|
| A | Housing Fold & Croft M adjoining |   | 0 | 3 | 4 |
| B | Long Croft | M | 0 | 3 | 23 |
| C | Meadow | M | 1 | 3 | 36 |
| D | Rushy Field |   | 2 | 0 | 36 |
|   |   |   | 5 | 3 | 19 |

**SLADES**

|   |   |   | A. | R. | P. |
|---|---|---|---|---|---|
| E | Black Piece |   | 9 | 0 | 22 |
| F | New piece |   | 11 | 2 | 18 |
| G | Great Meadow | M | 4 | 0 | 2 |
| H | Upper Meadow | M | 2 | 0 | 21 |
| I | Rough |   | 77 | 0 | 17 |
|   |   |   | 104 | 0 | 0 |

In 1789  Jonathan Rhodes

17     James Bradbury           **DIGGLEE (L.M.)**

3 Bays of building. 1 of them lately built by Joanthan Rhodes for a Dwelling House, the other 2 very Old.

|   |   |   | A. | R. | P. |
|---|---|---|---|---|---|
| A | Meadow | M | 0 | 2 | 29 |
| B | } 2 Crofts    0. 1. 8. } | M | 0 | 2 | 1 |
| C |    0. 0. 33. } |   |   |   |   |
| D | Marsh |   | 1 | 0 | 25 |
| E | Hey |   | 4 | 0 | 16 |
|   | In the mean fields |   | 1 | 2 | 38 |
|   |   |   | 8 | 0 | 29 |

In 1789  Jonathan Rhodes

18     John Bradbury           **DIGGLEE (L.M.)**

One Old Bay of Building very bad

|   |   |   | A. | R. | P. |
|---|---|---|---|---|---|
| A | Meadow | M | 0 | 2 | 14 |
|   | also James Bradburys Meadow |   | 0 | 0 | 6 |
|   | also a little Croft in ye Great Field |   | 0 | 0 | 3 |
| B | Marsh |   | 0 | 3 | 31 |
| C | Farr Marsh |   | 4 | 1 | 30 |
|   | In the mean Fields |   | 1 | 2 | 20 |
|   |   |   | 7 | 2 | 24 |

In 1789  James

19     Thomas Bradbury           **DIGGLEE (L.M.)**

4 Bays of antient building & 3 Bays of Outhousing in good repair being 7 Bays in Digglee & 3 Bays of old Building at Diggleedge

|   |   |   | A. | R. | P. |
|---|---|---|---|---|---|
| A | Nun Croft | M | 2 | 1 | 12 |
| B | Marsh | M | 1 | 0 | 30 |
| C | Croft | M | 0 | 1 | 8 |
| D | ¾ of Broadmeadow |   | 2 | 3 | 10 |
| E | Harlandhead | M | 1 | 0 | 27 |
| F | Newhey |   | 1 | 1 | 35 |
| G | Roughhey |   | 2 | 1 | 37 |
| H | Intake |   | 2 | 2 | 0 |
| I | Meadow |   | 1 | 3 | 30 |
| K | Intake |   | 3 | 0 | 21 |
|   | In the mean Fields |   | 4 | 2 | 7 |
|   |   |   | 24 | 0 | 17 |
| L | Washfold Green which they told me was taken out from the Back 'o th lee } |   | 0 | 3 | 13 |
|   |   |   | 24 | 3 | 30 |

In 1789  William

20     James Broadbent           **DIGGLEE (L.M.)**

6 Bays of Building, to wit, 2 very Old, 1 indifferent & 3 New Bays.

|   |   |   | A. | R. | P. |
|---|---|---|---|---|---|
| A | Tenter Croft |   | 0 | 0 | 34 |
| B | Park | M | 0 | 1 | 15 |
| C | ½ Meadow | M | 0 | 3 | 11 |
| D | Brun |   | 2 | 1 | 22 |
| E | Marsh |   | 2 | 2 | 20 |
| F | Marshbottom |   | 1 | 2 | 10 |
| G | New |   | 1 | 1 | 14 |
| H | Whorestones |   | 2 | 3 | 17 |
| I | ½ of rough broad Meadow |   | 2 | 1 | 13 |
|   | In the mean Fields |   | 6 | 2 | 16 |
|   |   |   | 20 | 3 | 26 |

In 1789  John Smith

21     James Broadbent           House in **ABELS (L.M.)**

A Housestead

A Housestead equal to 24 yds in Length & 12 yards in Breadth upon which a very good House is built, 9 perches.

22     Executors Henry Broadbent           Road & Knottylane Cott:

|   |   |   | A. | R. | P. |
|---|---|---|---|---|---|
| A | Cottage and Croft |   | 0 | 0 | 17 |
| B | Meadow | M | 0 | 3 | 1 |
| C | Road   {0. 2. 6. } {1. 1. 15.} |   | 1 | 3 | 21 |
|   |   |   | 2 | 2 | 39 |

| 22 | Henry Bentley | | | | |
| | **SADDLEWORTHFOLD** | | | | |

1789 vide 4th page

| | | | | | |
|---|---|---|---|---|---|
| | A good House consting of 2 Bays | | | | |
| | A new Barn and Shippen | | 0 | 0 | 6 |
| | Housing Garden &C | | 0 | 0 | 9 |
| | Othwart | | 1 | 2 | 24 |
| | Great Field | | 3 | 3 | 28 |
| | Short Butts | | 1 | 3 | 19 |
| | Great Meadow | M | 2 | 2 | 30 |
| | Little Meadow | M | 1 | 1 | 28 |
| | Clough (Shrogg) | | 0 | 2 | 7 |
| | Intake | | 3 | 1 | 17 |
| | | | 15 | 2 | 2 |

| 23 | James Broadbent | | | CLERK (L.M.) | |

An ancient House consisting of 3 or 4 Bays of Building also a new House being 2 Bays, with several Bays of Outhousing

| | | | | | |
|---|---|---|---|---|---|
| A | Housing Fold &c | | 0 | 1 | 13 |
| B | Backside | M | 0 | 0 | 38 |
| C | Meadow | M | 2 | 2 | 13 |
| D | Back Intake | | 1 | 2 | 32 |
| E | Farr Stony Intake | | 2 | 1 | 27 |
| F | Little Intake | | 1 | 1 | 20 |
| G | Great Intake | | 9 | 2 | 5 |
| H I | Walker Croft  (H, 0. 0. 23. / I, 2. 1. 20.) | M | 2 | 2 | 3 |
| K | Brigs Knowl | M | 0 | 0 | 26 |
| L | Croft | | 1 | 0 | 37 |
| M | Butt | | 1 | 1 | 2 |
| N | Church Green | | 1 | 3 | 31 |
| O | Bent | M | 0 | 2 | 32 |
| P | Redmires | M | 2 | 0 | 3 |
| | | | 28 | 0 | 2 |

| 24 | Robert Broadbent | | | GREEN (L.M.) | |

2 Bays of Building wherein 2 Families dwell

| | | | | | |
|---|---|---|---|---|---|
| A | Housing and Fold | | 0 | 0 | 19 |
| B | Croft | M | 0 | 1 | 30 |
| C | Lower Intake | M | 1 | 3 | 13 |
| D | Upper Intake | | 1 | 1 | 10 |
| E | Uppermost Greens | | 1 | 2 | 31 |
| F | Middlemost Greens | | 1 | 0 | 32 |
| G | Lowermost Greens | | 1 | 1 | 25 |
| | | | 8 | 0 | 0 |

In 1789 Wm. Broadbent & Hezekiah Shepperd

| 25 | Executors James Broadbent | | | GREEN (L.M.) | |

2 Dwelling Houses (being 2 Bays) lately built with several Bays of very old Thatch'd out Housing   0 0 4

| | | | A. | R. | P. |
|---|---|---|---|---|---|
| A | Meadow | M | 1 | 3 | 20 |
| B | Croft | | 1 | 2 | 19 |
| C | Old Lane Bank divided  (1. 2. 1 / 0. 2. 38) | | 2 | 0 | 39 |
| D | Lower Bank | | 2 | 2 | 31 |
| E | Long Gatehead | | 1 | 1 | 37 |
| F | Little Croft | | 0 | 0 | 12 |
| G | Backstone Intake | | 2 | 1 | 23 |
| | One half of Lee | M | 1 | 3 | 29 |
| | | | 14 | 1 | 14 |

In 1789 James Wrigley

| 26 | George Broadbents Executors | | | HARRUPP (L.M.) | |

3 Dwelling Houses wherein 4 Families reside, a good Barn & Shippen in Harropp & Outhousing at Cote

| | | | A. | R. | P. |
|---|---|---|---|---|---|
| | Housing | | 0 | 0 | 14 |
| A | Meadow | | 1 | 2 | 13 |
| B | Little Meadow | M | 1 | 0 | 26 |
| C | Little Calf hey | | 1 | 2 | 7 |
| D | Great Field | | 3 | 2 | 27 |
| E | Great Calf hey Meadow | M | 2 | 3 | 29 |
| F | Great Field | | 2 | 2 | 0 |
| G | Great Wood | | 4 | 0 | 13 |
| H | Littlehey | M | 3 | 1 | 37 |
| I | Rough Meadow | | 4 | 2 | 11 |
| K | Wood | | 1 | 3 | 6 |
| L | Cote Meadow | M | 2 | 2 | 0 |
| M | Intake as the same is divided | | 7 | 3 | 16 |
| | | | 37 | 2 | 39 |

| 27 | John Broadbent | | | MARSLANDS (L.M.) | |

5 Bays of Building in Good repair

| | | | A. | R. | P. |
|---|---|---|---|---|---|
| A | House and Garden | | 0 | 0 | 14 |
| B | Croft | M | 1 | 1 | 31 |
| C | Clod | | 0 | 0 | 35 |
| D | Great Field | | 1 | 2 | 32 |
| E | New Meadow | M | 1 | 3 | 27 |
| F | Long Field | | 2 | 0 | 30 |
| G | Tenterbank | | 1 | 0 | 10 |
| H | Steepbank | | 1 | 0 | 26 |
| I | Cote green | | 1 | 0 | 38 |
| K | Threenook | | 0 | 3 | 29 |
| | | | 10 | 1 | 32 |

| 28 | James Broadbent | | | CARRHEAD (L.M.) | |

2 Dwelling Houses being 5 bays with 3 Families therein, a Barn & Shippen 2 Bays, a Barn adjoining to his brother Ellas new built House, also 2 Bays for a House & 2 Bays for the Outhousing

| | | | A. | R. | P. |
|---|---|---|---|---|---|
| A | Housing and Field | | 0 | 1 | 5 |
| B | Meadow below the House | M | 0 | 3 | 37 |
| C | Field above the House | | 1 | 1 | 15 |
| D | Brownknowl | M | 2 | 0 | 22 |
| E | Lowerfold green | M | 0 | 3 | 19 |
| F | Redlane | | 0 | 1 | 34 |
| G | Milking Gap | | 1 | 2 | 9 |
| H | Limed Field | | 1 | 2 | 38 |
| I | Greenhill Meadow | | 2 | 0 | 24 |
| K | Rainy Clough | | 1 | 2 | 5 |
| L | New field | | 1 | 3 | 18 |
| M | Davy Field | | 1 | 0 | 17 |
| N | Hunterhill Field | | 2 | 2 | 7 |
| O | Long Field | | 0 | 3 | 16 |
| P | Roughend | | 1 | 3 | 22 |
| Q | Upper Meadow | M | 1 | 2 | 24 |
| R | Croft | M | 0 | 2 | 9 |
| S | Butts | | 1 | 0 | 19 |
| T | Lower Meadow | M | 1 | 1 | 17 |
| U V | Acker divided into 2  (U. 1. 2. 10 / V. 1. 0. 38) | | 2 | 3 | 8 |
| W | Lee Meadow | M | 2 | 0 | 18 |
| X | Waste at bottom of Lee Meadow | | 0 | 3 | 0 |
| Y | Upper Lee | | 2 | 3 | 29 |
| | | | 34 | 2 | 12 |
| * | Acker (divided into 2)  (1. 2. 10 / 1. 0. 38) | | 2 | 3 | 8 |
| | This is exchaned with John Rhodes Green for a meadow called Little Rough Meadow | | 30 | 2 | 0 |
| | Hunterhill Field | | 2 | 2 | 7 |
| | Rainy Clough | | 1 | 2 | 5 |
| | | | 34 | 2 | 12 |

In 1789

| 29 | James Broadbent and others. | | | Lee and Warth (L.M.) | |

No Housing a new Mill

| | | | A. | R. | P. |
|---|---|---|---|---|---|
| A | Warth | | 4 | 1 | 29 |
| B | Harry Lee | | 2 | 0 | 11 |
| C | Field at Bridge end | | 0 | 2 | 2 |
| D | Rough | | 2 | 0 | 1 |
| | | | 9 | 0 | 3 |

In 1789 George

| 30 | Executors Robt. Buckley | | | LANEHEAD (S.M.) | |

A Tolerable good House, and a good Barn & Shippen lately Built

| | | | A. | R. | P. |
|---|---|---|---|---|---|
| A | Housing Fold &c | | 0 | 1 | 2 |
| B | Croft | | 2 | 1 | 15 |
| C | Wheat Croft | | 0 | 0 | 30 |
| D | Turf cote Meadow | M | 0 | 2 | 27 |
| E | Field at Door | | 2 | 1 | 0 |
| F | Old Field | | 1 | 1 | 19 |

| | | | A. | R. | P. |
|---|---|---|---|---|---|
| G | Lower Field | | 2 | 0 | 6 |
| H | Hollin Shutt | | 2 | 1 | 5 |
| I | Clough Meadow | M | 0 | 3 | 27 |
| K | Lee | | 2 | 1 | 5 |
| L | Waste | | 0 | 1 | 14 |
| M | Sour Field | | 1 | 2 | 31 |
| N | Upper Meadow | M | 3 | 0 | 23 |
| O | Lower Meadow | M | 2 | 3 | 6 |
| P | New Field | | 2 | 3 | 23 |
| Q | Horsefall (a Shrogg) | | 7 | 0 | 12 |
| R | Clod | | 1 | 0 | 30 |
| S | | | 0 | 1 | 29 |
| | | | 34 | 0 | 34 |

**31     William Buckley     STONES (S.M.)**

| | | | A. | R. | P. |
|---|---|---|---|---|---|
| A | House and Garden | | 0 | 0 | 11 |
| B | Meadow under the House | M | 2 | 0 | 30 |
| C | Lowerwood Meadow | M | 1 | 2 | 18 |
| D | Lower Field   Shrogg {4. 0. 10 / 0. 2. 38} | | 4 | 3 | 8 |
| E | Upper Field | | 2 | 3 | 34 |
| F | Field at Door | | 2 | 3 | 20 |
| G | Hey | | 5 | 0 | 11 |
| H | New | | 1 | 1 | 17 |
| I | Heyhead Field | | 2 | 1 | 3 |
| K | Slack Field | | 2 | 3 | 26 |
| L | Kicknabwaste | | 1 | 1 | 27 |
| M | Higher Onefurr | | 2 | 2 | 1 |
| N | Lower Onefurr | | 1 | 1 | 29 |
| O | Great Meadow | M | 2 | 1 | 26 |
| P | Long Butts | | 1 | 0 | 11 |
| Q | Birches | | 0 | 3 | 7 |
| R | Clay butt | | 1 | 0 | 16 |
| S | Lower Longlands | | 1 | 2 | 10 |
| T | Calf Meadow | M | 1 | 1 | 12 |
| U | Smithy Croft | M | 1 | 0 | 20 |
| V | Upper Longlands | | 1 | 2 | 26 |
| W | Little Field | | 1 | 0 | 26 |
| | | | 43 | 2 | 29 |

**31     Benjn. Buckley     Housestead Assign'd to Mr. Jno. Harrop Junior**

In 1789   Mr. Hardman

**32     James Priestnal     BURNTEDGEBENT (S.M.)**

A House new Built by said James Priestnel.

| | | A. | R. | P. |
|---|---|---|---|---|
| A | House and Burntedgebent | 34 | 3 | 4 |

In 1789   Mr. John Bower

**33     James Buckley     Greenfield and Dovestonewood (L.M.)**

One ancient House Barn and Shippen in tolerable good repair

One House Barn and Shippen in tolerable good repair

| | | | | | |
|---|---|---|---|---|---|
| A | House and Green | | 2 | 1 | 10 |
| B | Old Intake | M | 1 | 2 | 3 |
| C | New Intake | | 2 | 3 | 25 |
| D | Upper Meadow | M | 2 | 2 | 8 |
| E | Lower Meadow | M | 2 | 1 | 11 |
| F | New hey | | 2 | 1 | 5 |
| G | Pit Marl'dearth | | 5 | 2 | 31 |
| H | Little Meadow | M | 2 | 0 | 30 |
| I | Lower Intake | | 2 | 3 | 28 |
| K | Stannery | | 4 | 3 | 20 |
| L | Lower Hey | | 2 | 0 | 18 |
| M | Wood Hey | | 10 | 3 | 18 |
| N | Cote Bank | | 2 | 0 | 30 |
| O | Pophas | | 3 | 2 | 12 |
| P | Croftend | | 0 | 1 | 35 |
| | | | 48 | 3 | 4 |
| | Dovestonewood | | 103 | 3 | 7 |
| | | | 152 | 2 | 11 |

**34     John Buckley     BARN (L.M.)**

A new House Shop and Outhousing being 5 Bays.

One Dwelling House of 2 Bays lately Built with 2 Bays of Outhousing & a Shop

| | | | A. | R. | P. |
|---|---|---|---|---|---|
| A | Meadow | M | 2 | 1 | 39 |
| B | Upper Field | | 2 | 1 | 8 |
| C | Lower Field | | 2 | 2 | 30 |
| D | Little Field | | 1 | 2 | 1 |
| | | | 8 | 3 | 38 |

| | | | | | |
|---|---|---|---|---|---|
| a | Backside M with the Garden | | 0 | 1 | 38 |
| b | Field at Door | | 1 | 1 | 4 |
| c | Lane | | 0 | 1 | 24 |
| d | Lower Field | | 1 | 1 | 34 |
| e | Meadow M | | 0 | 3 | 38 |
| f | Little Field | | 0 | 2 | 31 |
| g | Green | | 1 | 1 | 1 |

In 1789   James

**35     John Buckley     PINFOLD (L.M.)**

A Dwelling House being 2 Bays but indifferent Outhousing

An Ancient House with 2 or 3 Bays of very indifferent Outhousing

| | | | A. | R. | P. |
|---|---|---|---|---|---|
| A | Upper Field | | 2 | 2 | 27 |
| B | Lower Field | | 2 | 2 | 12 |
| C | Gindle | | 1 | 0 | 2 |
| D | Carr | M | 3 | 0 | 36 |
| E | Hey | | 31 | 2 | 32 |
| | | | 41 | 0 | 29 |

The Hey now let to Geo: Shaw

In 1789   Abraham Rhodes

**36     James Buckley     BROWNHILL (L.M.)**

One Dwelling House in Tolerable repair with an old Shippen adjoining & an old Barn at some distance

| | | | A. | R. | P. |
|---|---|---|---|---|---|
| A | Croft | M | 0 | 3 | 4 |
| B | New Ley | M | 1 | 1 | 30 |
| C | Old Ley | | 3 | 1 | 38 |
| D | Little black Bank | | 0 | 2 | 3 |
| E | Stonebottom | | 1 | 1 | 25 |
| F | Stonebottom Brow | | 1 | 0 | 7 |
| G | Slate Meadow | M | 1 | 3 | 12 |
| H | Black Bank {Black Bank 1. 1. 26. / Shrogg 0. 1. 22.} | | 1 | 3 | 8 |
| I | Well Field | | 1 | 3 | 24 |
| K | Middlemost meadow | M | 0 | 3 | 5 |
| L | Upper Brownhill | | 1 | 1 | 15 |
| M | Lambknowl | | 1 | 0 | 5 |
| N | Waste | | 0 | 2 | 5 |
| O | Brownhill | | 1 | 0 | 39 |
| P | Great Kiln Wood {1. 0. 23. | | 1 | 2 | 21 |
| Q | Little Kiln Wood {Shrogg 0. 1. 27.} | | 1 | 2 | 10 |
| R | Little Flatt | | 2 | 2 | 36 |
| S | Little Meadow | M | 0 | 3 | 30 |
| T | Great Flatt | | 3 | 3 | 13 |
| U | Milltowns | M | 3 | 1 | 23 |
| | | | 33 | 1 | 22 |

**37     James Buckley     GATEHEAD (S.M.)**

2 Good Houses, But very old Thatch'd Outhousing

| | | | A.. | R. | P. |
|---|---|---|---|---|---|
| A | Housing Fold &c | | 0 | 1 | 15 |
| B | Upper Meadow | M | 1 | 2 | 32 |
| C | Middlefield | | 2 | 1 | 22 |
| D | Furthermost Field | | 2 | 0 | 6 |
| E | {Oak Doles 1. 3. 1. | | | | |
| F | 1. 3. 20.} | | 3 | 2 | 21 |
| G | Wallbottom {2. 2. 12. / Shrogg 0. 1. 16.} | M | 2 | 3 | 28 |
| H | Trindle Carr | | 0 | 2 | 21 |
| I | Hollins | | 3 | 2 | 10 |
| K | Burnroad | | 1 | 3 | 16 |
| L | Cote Meadow | | 1 | 1 | 33 |
| M | Greenbottom | | 3 | 2 | 23 |
| N | Lower Green | | 1 | 3 | 15 |
| O | Upper Green | | 0 | 3 | 16 |
| P | Midgreave | M | 3 | 1 | 16 |
| Q | Stony road | | 2 | 2 | 22 |
| R | Highfield | | 2 | 3 | 37 |
| S | Backside o'th Highfield {2. 2. 17. / 1. 3. 7.} | | 4 | 1 | 24 |
| T | Upper Holm | | 2 | 1 | 3 |
| U | Lower Holm | | 1 | 2 | 7 |
| W | Little Wallbottom | | 1 | 2 | 25 |
| X | Fieldend | | 0 | 3 | 16 |
| | | | 47 | 3 | 33 |

38 Edmund Buckley LIDYATE (Q.M.)

| | | | A. | R. | P. |
|---|---|---|---|---|---|
| A | Housing Gardens &c | | 0 | 0 | 37 |
| B | Sevenacre Meadow | M | 1 | 2 | 19 |
| C | Little Sevenacre | | 1 | 0 | 7 |
| D | Lower Sevenacre | | 3 | 0 | 18 |
| E | Further Sevenacre | | 3 | 3 | 10 |
| F | Calf Croft | | 0 | 0 | 29 |
| G | Lower Meadow | M | 3 | 0 | 25 |
| | | | 13 | 0 | 25 |

N.B. The Calf Croft is (since ye measuring)
taken into the Turnpike Road

In 1789 Mr. Heginbottom & others

39 Mr. Joseph Lawton FRENCHES MILL (S.M.)

An Indifferent Dwelling House for the Miller to live in

| | | A. | R. | P. |
|---|---|---|---|---|
| A | Mill Clod & Waste | 1 | 2 | 6 |

In 1789 John Buckley part SHAWHALL (Q.M.)

40

No Housing

| | | | A. | R. | P. |
|---|---|---|---|---|---|
| A | Upper farside Brook | | 1 | 0 | 12 |
| B | Lower farside Brook | | 1 | 2 | 9 |
| C | Brownhill | | 4 | 0 | 28 |
| D | Rough Pasture | | 5 | 1 | 6 |
| E | Intake Meadow | M | 0 | 3 | 2 |
| F | Upper Fields | | 3 | 0 | 0 |
| | | | 15 | 3 | 17 |

Vide John Buckley's account of Land in No. 145

| | | A. | R. | P. |
|---|---|---|---|---|
| Bank | | 3 | 2 | 25 |
| Calf Croft | M | 1 | 2 | 2 |
| Round Meadow | | 3 | 3 | 29 |
| How Meadow (now divided into 2) | | 3 | 2 | 27 |
| Eller Croft | | 3 | 3 | 24 |
| Upper Flatt | | 6 | 1 | 25 |
| Lower Flatt | | 4 | 3 | 36 |
| Clod | | 0 | 1 | 14 |
| Marl'd Pitt Earth | | 5 | 2 | 0 |
| | | 33 | 3 | 22 |

41 Executors Jno. Buckley and 17 other Lessees COMMON (L.M.)

| | A. | R. | P. |
|---|---|---|---|
| Back oth'lee (inclos'd) | 221 | 0 | 0 |

42 Mr. Joseph Buckley STONEBREAKS (Q.M.)

| | | | A. | R. | P. |
|---|---|---|---|---|---|
| A | Little Meadow | M | 0 | 0 | 39 |
| B | Rough | | 1 | 2 | 27 |
| C | Lowermost Field | | 1 | 3 | 5 |
| D | Highmost Field | | 1 | 3 | 37 |
| E | New Meadow | M | 0 | 3 | 26 |
| F | Little Field | | 0 | 3 | 19 |
| G | Middlemost Field | | 1 | 1 | 17 |
| H | Stonesrake Meadow {H, 0. 3. 12.} | M | 2 | 1 | 16 |
| I | {I, 1. 2. 4.} | M | | | |
| K | New Field | | 1 | 2 | 29 |
| | | | 12 | 3 | 15 |

42 Ralph Bradbury part of Top of Green

In 1789 Thomas Bradbury

43 Nathaniel Broadbent RUNNINGHILL (L.M.)

An old House being 2 Bays very indifferent Outhousing a Tuf-Cote

| | | | A. | R. | P. |
|---|---|---|---|---|---|
| A | Croft | M | 2 | 3 | 12 |
| B | Long Field | | 1 | 1 | 8 |
| C | Round Field | | 1 | 0 | 6 |
| D | Lower Meadow | | 1 | 1 | 9 |
| E | Leetop | | 1 | 0 | 34 |
| | | | 7 | 2 | 29 |

44 Isaac Clegg LUKEFIELDS (Q.M.)

| | | A. | R. | P. |
|---|---|---|---|---|
| A B C D | Luke Fields | 6 | 3 | 8 |
| | Holes | 3 | 2 | 19 |
| | | 10 | 1 | 27 |

In 1789

44 Robert Broadbent Top of Green

In 1789

45 Abraham Rhodes CORN MILLS (L.M.)

The Mill and Kiln with one half of the fold commonly
called the Millpasture

| | A. | R. | P. |
|---|---|---|---|
| Half of ye Mill Fold ye whole being | 0 | 1 | 37 |

46 Peter Bradbury BROWNHILL (L.M.)

A Dwelling House & Cowhouse

| | | A. | R. | P. |
|---|---|---|---|---|
| A | Waste called Brownhill | 1 | 2 | 36 |

In 1789 Widow

47 George Dronsfield POUNDSTONE (Q.M.)

An old Cottage with an old Shippen for a Cow; about 3 Bays in the
whole

| | | | A. | R. | P. |
|---|---|---|---|---|---|
| A | Croft | M | 0 | 0 | 22 |
| B | Meadow | M | 1 | 1 | 6 |
| C D | Cotehills | | 2 | 3 | 29 |
| | | | 4 | 1 | 17 |

Also a Field formerly lett to Miles Mayal called

| | | | A. | R. | P. |
|---|---|---|---|---|---|
| E | Cotehill | | 4 | 0 | 28 |
| | Total | | 8 | 2 | 5 |

In 1789 John Buckley

48 Sand Mine on High Moor

49

In 1789 John & Wm. Radcliffe KNOWLTOP (L.M.)

50

One good new built House adjoining to Peter Greaves Barn, Built by
Jno. Broadbent alias Scholefd. all ye other being 4 Bays, 1 Slated & 3
Thatched

Very old Housing mostly Thatched

| | | | A. | R. | P. |
|---|---|---|---|---|---|
| | Housing Fold &c | | 0 | 0 | 14 |
| A | Upper Field | M | 1 | 1 | 1 |
| B | Stubble | | 2 | 0 | 29 |
| C | Upper Cotegreen | | 1 | 1 | 7 |
| D | Lower Cotegreen | | 1 | 1 | 14 |
| E | Barnend | | 2 | 1 | 24 |
| F | Intake | | 1 | 3 | 18 |
| G | Broadlane | M | 0 | 2 | 21 |
| H | Lower Broadlane | M | 1 | 2 | 6 |
| I | Cockplace | M | 1 | 1 | 18 |
| | | | 13 | 3 | 32 |

In 1789 John Platt

51 Garsides Executors HEATHFIELDS (L.M.)

2 Dwelling Houses

| | | | A. | R. | P. |
|---|---|---|---|---|---|
| A | Upper Meadow | M | 0 | 3 | 32 |
| B | Lower Meadow | M | 1 | 0 | 0 |
| C | Near Field with the Housing | | 1 | 0 | 37 |

| | | | A. | R. | P. |
|---|---|---|---|---|---|
| D | Farr Field | | 1 | 0 | 32 |
| E | Lower Field | | 2 | 2 | 12 |
| F | New Meadow | M | 0 | 3 | 3 |
| G | Little Meadow | M | 0 | 1 | 6 |
| H | Rails | | 0 | 3 | 24 |
| | | | 8 | 3 | 26 |

In 1789  Wm. Radcliffe

52  John Broadbent alias Scholefield

A Housestead in Peter Greaves' Farm.

53  Mr. James Harrop  LADCASTLE (S.M.)

| | | A. | R. | P. |
|---|---|---|---|---|
| A | New Field | 1 | 1 | 36 |

In 1789  Harrop Smith & Scholefd.

54  New Fulling Mill (S.M.)

| | | | A. | R. | P. |
|---|---|---|---|---|---|
| A | Housing Fold &c | | 0 | 1 | 5 |
| B | Old Kiln & Croft | | 0 | 0 | 14 |
| C | Bank laighen | M | 0 | 2 | 2 |
| D | Haybottom | M | 3 | 3 | 32 |
| E | Old Ridd | M | 0 | 3 | 2 |
| F | Upper Haybottom | | 4 | 0 | 33 |
| G | Rood | | 6 | 3 | 24 |
| H | Field end | | 1 | 3 | 30 |
| I | Thurstone butts | | 1 | 2 | 36 |
| K | Wood Meadow | | 0 | 1 | 28 |
| L | Wood | | 0 | 2 | 1 |
| M | Barnfield | | 3 | 3 | 10 |
| N | Wanegate head | | 2 | 1 | 12 |
| O | Waste | | 0 | 3 | 18 |
| P | New Meadow | M | 2 | 3 | 7 |
| Q | Shut | | 2 | 2 | 31 |
| R | Rumble Carr | M | | | |
| S | Cote Meadow | M | 2 | 3 | 34 |
| T | Carman Road | | 2 | 3 | 24 |
| U | Bank | | 1 | 0 | 34 |
| W | Rye Croft | | 0 | 1 | 11 |
| X | Maghey | Vide No. 154 | 2 | 2 | 1 |
| Y | Clod | | 0 | 1 | 10 |
| | | | 43 | 3 | 39 |

55  John Buckley  HOLLINS (L.M.)

A Dwelling House &1 old Shop adjoining (in each of which a family dwells) 1 old Barn & Shippen in bad repair

| | | | A. | R. | P. |
|---|---|---|---|---|---|
| A | House Garden &c | | 0 | 0 | 23 |
| B | Cockbank | | 2 | 1 | 19 |
| C | Nutbottom M | 1. 1. 4. / 0. 1. 2. | 1 | 2 | 6 |
| D | Middle Banks | | 1 | 0 | 10 |
| E | Middle Banks | | 1 | 3 | 5 |
| F | New Bank | | 1 | 2 | 7 |
| G | Cock Croft | M | 1 | 0 | 36 |
| | | | 9 | 2 | 26 |

56  James Harrop  SHAWS (L.M.)

An old Thatch'd House The whole about 23 or 24 yards in length of very old Housing

| | | | A. | R. | P. |
|---|---|---|---|---|---|
| | The Housing | | 0 | 0 | 5 |
| A | Gom Meadow | M | 0 | 3 | 23 |
| B | Sort Lands | | 1 | 1 | 39 |
| C | Lower Ley | | 1 | 1 | 35 |
| D | Upper Ley | | 1 | 1 | 10 |
| E | Eyebridge | | 2 | 3 | 16 |
| F | Dan road | | 1 | 0 | 32 |
| G | Calf Croft | M | 1 | 1 | 1 |
| H | Marledearth | M | 1 | 2 | 20 |
| | | | 12 | 0 | 21 |

In 1789  Ralph Royle

57  William Hawkyard  CLOUGHBOTTOM (L.M.)

2 Old Houses with the Outhousing adjoining being about 6 bays in the whole

| | | | A. | R. | P. |
|---|---|---|---|---|---|
| A | Dockcroft withe the Housing | | 0 | 0 | 26 |
| B | Croft | | 1 | 1 | 33 |
| C | Barley Croft | | 0 | 0 | 23 |
| D | Hollins | | 0 | 3 | 14 |
| E | Park | M | 0 | 1 | 9 |
| F | Waste | | 0 | 3 | 3 |
| G | Church bank | | 1 | 1 | 18 |
| H | Church bank | | 1 | 1 | 12 |
| I | Churchbank Wood (a Shrogg) | | 0 | 2 | 22 |
| K | Thistle Field | | 2 | 2 | 39 |
| L | Moss Meadow | M | 1 | 0 | 28 |
| M | Middlemost Meadow | M | 1 | 2 | 6 |
| N | Threenook | M | 1 | 3 | 19 |
| O | Foot | M | 0 | 2 | 32 |
| P | Intake | | 4 | 2 | 31 |
| | | | 19 | 2 | 35 |

58  John Hazelgreave  WALLHILL (S.M.)

A good Dwelling House with a Cowhouse adjoining also a Barn and Stable

| | | | A. | R. | P. |
|---|---|---|---|---|---|
| A | House Garden &c | | 0 | 0 | 15 |
| B | Acker | | 2 | 1 | 33 |
| C | Upper Meadow | M | 4 | 1 | 4 |
| D | Lower Meadow | M | 2 | 1 | 24 |
| E | Priest Field | | 4 | 0 | 26 |
| F | Lane | | 0 | 0 | 26 |
| G | Broadgate | | 1 | 0 | 13 |
| H | Sunside | | 5 | 0 | 0 |
| | | | 19 | 2 | 21 |

59  Widow Bradbury  New Barn at Runninghill (L.M.)

| | | | A. | R. | P. |
|---|---|---|---|---|---|
| Long Intake | 1. 3. 29. / 2. 1. 18. | M | 4 | 1 | 7 |
| Lamb Knowl | | | 1 | 3 | 32 |
| Little Wankin Clough | | M | 0 | 3 | 4 |
| Great Wankin Clough | | | 1 | 0 | 13 |
| | Total | | 8 | 0 | 16 |

These were Assign'd to Jonathan Bradbury, A New Barn & Shippen Built in ye Long Intake by the said Jonathan Bradbury

60  Executors James Mallalew  Dungebooth, Philips & Leeses (S.M.)

At Philips 3 or 4 Bays of Housing, at Leeses 3 Bays of very old Thatched Housing & a Turf Cote

DUNGEBOOTH

One good Dwelling House & Cow House lately Built, 3 Bays

| | | | A. | R. | P. |
|---|---|---|---|---|---|
| A | Meadow with the Housing | M | 1 | 0 | 12 |
| B | Pilling Field as ye same is divided | | 1 | 3 | 0 |

PHILIPS & LEESES

A tolerable good House with 2 Families & Outhousing at Philips & a very old Thatch'd House at Leeses

| | | | A. | R. | P. |
|---|---|---|---|---|---|
| C | Faugh with ye Housing therein | M | 1 | 3 | 27 |
| D | Old Wives Field | | 3 | 0 | 2 |
| E | Lower Meadow | M | 2 | 0 | 0 |
| F | Clod | | 0 | 1 | 19 |
| G | Lees Croft | M | 1 | 1 | 16 |
| H | Engines (3 small enclosures) | | 1 | 2 | 10 |
| I | Millstones Intake | | 1 | 2 | 1 |
| K | Intakes | 2. 2. 7. / 3. 1. 13. / 2. 3. 4. / 2. 3. 33. | 11 | 2 | 17 |
| L | | | | | |
| M | | | | | |
| N | | | | | |
| O | Two Acres | | 3 | 1 | 25 |
| | | | 29 | 2 | 9 |

61  Executors John Mallalieu  Dungebooth, Philips & Leeses

In 1789  Executors John

| | | | A. | R. | P. |
|---|---|---|---|---|---|
| 62 | Executors James Mallalew | LADCASTLE (L.M.) | | | |
| | No Housing | | | | |
| A | Ladcastle Intakes  { 1. 2. 17. | | 3 | 0 | 29 |
| B | { 1. 2. 22. | | | | |

In 1789

63  Robert Holden's Executors  CLOUGHBOTTOM (L.M.)

One Dwelling House and Barn & Shippen lately built by ye said Robert Holden

1 Bay for a Dwelling House & 2 Bays for Outhousing at High Stile, Also 2 Bays of Building in Cloughbottom by ye said Robt. Holden

| | | | A. | R. | P. |
|---|---|---|---|---|---|
| A | Housing and Croft | M | 0 | 1 | 4 |
| B | Bentmeadow | M | 1 | 2 | 25 |
| C | Cote Field | | 1 | 3 | 26 |
| D | Round Field | | 1 | 1 | 1 |
| E | Lower Calf Meadow | M | 1 | 2 | 0 |
| F | Rough Calf Meadow | M | 0 | 3 | 11 |
| G | Farr Heyhead | | 2 | 3 | 0 |
| H | Near Heyhead | | 2 | 3 | 4 |
| I | Upper Croft | M | 0 | 1 | 5 |
| K | High stile with the crofts | | 1 | 0 | 0 |
| L | Hill | | 5 | 1 | 4 |
| M | Coiting Green | M | 0 | 3 | 19 |
| | | | 20 | 1 | 19 |

In 1789  Paul

64  James Holden  DAVIDS SMITHY (L.M.)

One Dwelling House and Outhousing very old the whole being 4 Bays

| | | | A. | R. | P. |
|---|---|---|---|---|---|
| A | Little Meadow with ye Housing | M | 1 | 0 | 10 |
| B | Butt | | 2 | 1 | 0 |
| C | New Meadow | M | 1 | 3 | 4 |
| D | Croft | | 0 | 1 | 19 |
| E | Garden | | 0 | 0 | 4 |
| F | Intake | | 1 | 1 | 14 |
| G | Lee | | 2 | 2 | 13 |
| | | | 9 | 1 | 24 |

In 1789  James

65  Nathaniel Holden  DAVIDS SMITHY (L.M.)

5 Bays of good Building lately erected

| | | | A. | R. | P. |
|---|---|---|---|---|---|
| A | The Housing | | 0 | 0 | 5 |
| B | Nuning head | | 0 | 2 | 38 |
| C | Nuning | M | 1 | 2 | 18 |
| D | Nuning | M | 1 | 3 | 37 |
| E | Nuning bottom | | 1 | 0 | 20 |
| F | Owlers | | 0 | 2 | 29 |
| G | Crooked Nuning | | 2 | 0 | 14 |
| H | Little Nuning head | | 0 | 0 | 37 |
| I | Intake | | 1 | 1 | 24 |
| | | | 9 | 3 | 22 |

In 1789  George Hinchcliffe  Dodell Cottage in Walk mill Tenement

66

In 1789  Henry Winterbottom

67  Executors Thomas Kenworthy  ROUNDHILL (L.M.)

One Bay for a Dwelling House 2 Bays for Outhousing

| | | | A. | R. | P. |
|---|---|---|---|---|---|
| A | Bank with ye Housing therein | | 0 | 2 | 34 |
| B | Meadow | M | 1 | 0 | 8 |
| C | Lower Intake | | 1 | 0 | 8 |
| D | Little Meadow | M | 0 | 1 | 24 |
| E | Middlemost Field | | 1 | 3 | 32 |
| F | Upper Intake | | 1 | 1 | 12 |
| G | Acker | | 1 | 1 | 28 |
| H | Rushy Field | | 1 | 1 | 11 |
| | | | 9 | 0 | 37 |

68  Assignes John Kenworthy  HOBHOLE (Q.M.)
    Sold

| | | | A. | R. | P. |
|---|---|---|---|---|---|
| A | | | 1 | 1 | 29 |
| B | | | 1 | 0 | 8 |
| C | | | 0 | 1 | 24 |
| D | | | 0 | 1 | 38 |
| E | | | 0 | 1 | 37 |
| | | | 3 | 3 | 16 |

In 1789  Mrs.

69  William Kenworthy  FULLING MILL (Q.M.)

2 Dwelling Houses & Mill with 2 Wheels

| | | | A. | R. | P. |
|---|---|---|---|---|---|
| A | A Dwelling with 2 Fulling Mills adjoining it a Dyhouse, Cottage, Green & Shrogg | | 1 | 2 | 16 |

In 1789  Mrs.

70  William Kenworthy  NEAR QUICK (Q.M.)

Several Dwelling Houses Workhouses &c

| | | | A. | R. | P. |
|---|---|---|---|---|---|
| A | Housing | | 0 | 0 | 10 |
| B | Round Field | | 2 | 0 | 23 |
| C | Shortley | | 2 | 0 | 1 |
| D | Old Wood | | 2 | 0 | 9 |
| E | Thick Threelands | | 1 | 1 | 3 |
| F | Slade Meadow | M | 2 | 0 | 10 |
| G | Gibbknowl | | 1 | 2 | 36 |
| H | Lower Meadow | M | 0 | 3 | 38 |
| I | Well Meadow | M | 1 | 3 | 22 |
| K | Stove Field | | 2 | 1 | 36 |
| L | How Field | | 3 | 2 | 34 |
| M | Highlane | | 1 | 3 | 30 |
| | | | 22 | 1 | 12 |

In 1789  Mr. James Kenworthy  Waste & Water

71  William Kenworthy  QUICK or LOADHILLS (Q.M.)

| | | | A. | R. | P. |
|---|---|---|---|---|---|
| A | House and Garden | | 0 | 1 | 6 |
| B | Little Meadow | M | 1 | 0 | 1 |
| C | New Field | | 2 | 3 | 22 |
| D | Old Limed | | 2 | 0 | 22 |
| E | Tenter Field | | 1 | 1 | 38 |
| F | Mill Meadow | M | 1 | 1 | 18 |
| G | Barnbutt | | 1 | 1 | 7 |
| H | Upper Meadow | M | 1 | 2 | 23 |
| I | Great Hey | | 4 | 1 | 24 |
| | | | 16 | 2 | 1 |

In 1789  Mr. Hardman  House in Daubut Field

72  Jonathan Lawton  (L.M.)

| | | | A. | R. | P. |
|---|---|---|---|---|---|
| A | 2 very good Houses new Built with a Brewhouse, a Garden &c. | | 0 | 0 | 27 |

In 1789  Mr. Hardman

73  Mr. Joseph Lawton  HALLS (S.M.)

3 Dwelling Houses, a good Barn and Shippen

| | | | A. | R. | P. |
|---|---|---|---|---|---|
| | The Houseing Garden &c | | 0 | 2 | 0 |
| A | Bank (exclusive of the Housing) | | 6 | 1 | 24 |
| B | Kiln Meadow | M | 3 | 2 | 25 |
| C | Daff road | | 3 | 1 | 32 |
| D | New Meadow | | 1 | 1 | 29 |
| E | Wood | | 3 | 1 | 34 |
| F | Great Field | | 6 | 3 | 23 |
| G | Green | | 4 | 0 | 12 |
| H | Ramsbottom  { Shrogg  0. 2. 10. | | 5 | 1 | 28 |
| | { M  4. 3. 18. | | | | |
| I | Long Field | | 3 | 0 | 5 |
| K | Round Meadow | M | 2 | 2 | 30 |
| L | Wheat Lands | | 2 | 2 | 7 |
| | | | 43 | 2 | 9 |
| | 2 Little Fields at Dobcross to wit | | | | |
| M | Intake | | 0 | 1 | 20 |
| N | Upper part of Kiln Ditch or Garden | | 0 | 1 | 6 |
| | | | 44 | 0 | 35 |

| 74 | Joseph Lawton | | | Woodlane Cottage (L.M.) | | |
|---|---|---|---|---|---|---|
| | 3 or 4 Bays of ordinary Housing | | | | | |
| | | | | A. | R. | P. |
| A | An old Cottage Croft and Garden | | | 0 | 0 | 5 |

In 1789

| 75 | Joseph & Benjamin Lawton | | | DOBCROSS (L.M.) | | |
|---|---|---|---|---|---|---|
| | A very good new Built House with several other new Buildings | | | | | |
| | Several Bays of very good Housing at Dobcross lately Built | | | | | |
| A | Lower Intake | | | 1 | 1 | 32 |
| B | Upper Intake | | | 1 | 2 | 0 |
| | | | | 2 | 3 | 32 |

In 1789 Joseph & Philip

| 76 | Henry Buckley | | | FRENCHES (L.M.) | | |
|---|---|---|---|---|---|---|
| | 2 Bays of a good new Built House with 2 or 3 Bays of Outhousing very indifferent | | | | | |
| | | | | A. | R. | P. |
| A | Tenter brow with the Housing | | | 0 | 2 | 39 |
| B | Bank | | | 0 | 3 | 19 |
| C | Birches Meadow | Shrogg 0. 1. 37. } M 1. 2. 21. } | | 2 | 0 | 18 |
| D | Higher Meadow | | M | 1 | 0 | 10 |
| E | Lower Meadow | | M | 1 | 2 | 12 |
| F | Lower Field | | | 2 | 3 | 2 |
| G | Rushy Field | | | 2 | 3 | 5 |
| H | Upper Field | | | 3 | 0 | 33 |
| | | | | 15 | 0 | 18 |

| 77 | John Lees | | BANKTOP (L.M.) | | |
|---|---|---|---|---|---|
| | An ancient Dwelling House consisting of 2 Bays with 2 small Bays of Outhousing | | | | |
| | | | A. | R. | P. |
| A | Croft M and Garden | | 0 | 1 | 11 |
| B | Meadow M with ye Housing | | 1 | 0 | 15 |
| C | Owlers | | 0 | 3 | 4 |
| D | Bank | | 1 | 1 | 25 |
| E | Bankbottom | | 0 | 1 | 9 |
| F | Whams | | 0 | 3 | 30 |
| | | | 4 | 3 | 14 |

| 78 | John Lees | | HIGHMOOR (Q.M.) | | |
|---|---|---|---|---|---|
| | An Old House with very indifferent Outhousing, mostly thatched. | | | | |
| | 5 Bays of old Building | | | | |
| | | | A. | R. | P. |
| A | Lower Meadow | M | 2 | 0 | 35 |
| B | Little Field | | 1 | 2 | 25 |
| C | Farr Meadow | M | 1 | 0 | 4 |
| D | Upperend | M | 1 | 2 | 36 |
| E | Great New | | 5 | 0 | 6 |
| F | Sour New | | 3 | 0 | 35 |
| G | Rough | | 3 | 0 | 26 |
| H | Spring Pasture | | 4 | 0 | 28 |
| | | | 22 | 0 | 35 |

| 79 | John Lees | | HIGHMOOR (Q.M.) | | |
|---|---|---|---|---|---|
| | A very good Dwelling House with good Stabling &other Outhousing | | | | |
| | | | A. | R. | P. |
| A | Meadow | M | 2 | 1 | 30 |

| 80 | John Lees | | SHELDERSLOW (Q.M.) | | |
|---|---|---|---|---|---|
| | A Dwelling House being 2 Bays in bad repair, but no Outhousing | | | | |
| | | | A. | R. | P. |
| A | Croft at Door with ye House | | 0 | 0 | 26 |
| B | Meadow | M | 2 | 2 | 10 |
| C | Firwood Field | | 1 | 1 | 6 |
| D | Little Field | | 1 | 0 | 26 |
| E | Hodge Bank | | 1 | 3 | 2 |
| | | | 6 | 3 | 30 |

In 1789 Widow Greave

| 81 | James Lees | | THURSTONECLOUGH (S.M.) | | |
|---|---|---|---|---|---|
| | One little Cottage House | | | | |
| | A cottage erected therein | | | | |
| | | | A. | R. | P. |
| A } | | 0. 3. 31. } | | | |
| B } | 3 Fields | 0. 3. 28. } | 3 | 1 | 25 |
| C } | | 1. 2. 6. } | | | |
| D | Rough | | 4 | 1 | 22 |
| E | New Field | | 6 | 0 | 4 |
| F | Croft | | 0 | 0 | 22 |
| G | Great Rough | | 20 | 2 | 6 |
| | | | 34 | 1 | 39 |

| 82 | Jonathan Lees | | PART OF KNARR (S.M.) | | |
|---|---|---|---|---|---|
| | | | A. | R. | P. |
| P | Bent M with the Housing | | 2 | 0 | 17 |
| Q | Upper Thurstone | | 2 | 2 | 4 |
| R | Spout Field | | 2 | 0 | 24 |
| S | Upperhouse Meadow | M | 1 | 2 | 31 |
| T | Thurstone {2. 2. 31. } | | 5 | 0 | 11 |
| U | {2. 1. 20. } | | | | |
| V | Shutt | | 0 | 2 | 31 |
| W | Calf Pickle | M | 2 | 0 | 6 |
| X | Rough Calf Pickle | | 1 | 3 | 30 |
| | | | 18 | 0 | 34 |

N.B. The above Fields are to be found in the Map by the Letters annex'd to them in No. 154 James Winterbottom Knarr.

In 1789 Thomas Bradbury PART OF SLADES (L.M.)

| 83. | | | |
|---|---|---|---|
| | A. | R. | P. |
| Thomas Bradbury and others for Slades | 104 | 0 | 0 |

Hen: Whitehead

| 84 | Executors James Mallalew | | WHARMTONBROW (S.M.) | | |
|---|---|---|---|---|---|
| | One old Dwelling House Outhousing and 2 others lately built in the places where 2 old Cottages formerly stood the whole Occupied by 6 Families | | | | |
| | | | A. | R. | P. |
| A | Cotehead | | 0 | 1 | 14 |
| B | Near French Intake | | 2 | 0 | 17 |
| C | Further French Intake | | 1 | 3 | 1 |
| D } | | | | | |
| E } | Higher Intakes | | 1 | 1 | 8 |
| F | Meadow at Door | M | 1 | 1 | 36 |
| G | Brownhill Croft | M | 1 | 0 | 24 |
| H | New Intake | | 0 | 1 | 26 |
| | | | 8 | 2 | 6 |

In 1789 John

| 85 | George Mallalew | | WHICKENS (L.M.) | | |
|---|---|---|---|---|---|
| | 3 Bays of Building occupied by one Family a good Barn lately Built by Geo: Mallalew | | | | |
| | One Anceint Dwelling House with very good Outhousing. | | | | |
| | | | A. | R. | P. |
| | The Housing &c | | 0 | 0 | 24 |
| A | Barley Croft | M | 0 | 0 | 32 |
| B | Great Meadow | M | 2 | 1 | 0 |
| C | Little Meadow | M | 0 | 3 | 15 |
| D | Gorsybrow | | 2 | 3 | 7 |
| E | Littlehill | | 1 | 1 | 33 |
| F | Greathill | | 2 | 2 | 6 |
| G | Fimble Field | | 3 | 3 | 5 |
| H | Will Field | | 3 | 0 | 15 |
| I | Will Ridge | | 2 | 1 | 24 |
| K | Further Meadow | M | 1 | 2 | 23 |
| L | Back oth' House | M | 0 | 1 | 31 |
| M | Intake | | 6 | 2 | 0 |
| N | Intake enlarg'd out of the Common | | 0 | 2 | 19 |
| O | Croft | M | 0 | 1 | 16 |
| | | | 29 | 0 | 10 |

Also ye dotted Traingle (mostly in Will Field) was taken in at ye same time with the parcel N when ye fence was set over again.

86     Wm. Newton       Housestead Assign'd to Jas. Hollingworth

In 1789

87     John Nield & Mr. Cors. Kenworthy     QUICK (Q.M.)

A very good Newbuilt House with several Bays of Outhousing

| | | | A. | R. | P. |
|---|---|---|---|---|---|
| | Housing Fold &c. | | 0 | 0 | 27 |
| A | Calf Croft | M | 0 | 0 | 18 |
| B | Calf Hey | M | 2 | 2 | 35 |
| C | Stone Wall | | 1 | 3 | 31 |
| D | Calf Meadows | M $\left\{ \begin{array}{ccc} 1. & 2. & 7. \\ 0. & 1. & 29. \end{array} \right\}$ | | | |
| E | | | 1 | 3 | 36 |
| F | | | | | |
| G | Gibb Knowl | | 3 | 3 | 29 |
| H | Gibb Knowl Wood | | 1 | 2 | 34 |
| I | Inklebottom | M | 2 | 1 | 7 |
| K | Inklebottom | | 1 | 1 | 38 |
| L | Slades | | 2 | 0 | 26 |
| M | Wood with the 2 Enclosures of Wood | | 10 | 0 | 6 |
| N | Haining Field | | 2 | 1 | 27 |
| O | Bent | | 0 | 1 | 9 |
| P | Lower Hustead | | 3 | 0 | 36 |
| Q | Upper Hustead | | 2 | 0 | 7 |
| R | Bent | | 1 | 3 | 1 |
| S | Pitt Field | | 2 | 2 | 6 |
| T | Burnt Hill | | 2 | 3 | 28 |
| U | Cock Field | | 4 | 1 | 2 |
| W | Barn Field | | 3 | 3 | 36 |
| X | | | | | |
| Y | Kenworthy Meadows | M | 2 | 3 | 31 |
| | | | 54 | 3 | 30 |

In 1789

88     John Platt Executors     Shaw's LANEHEAD (S.M.)

A good House and Outhousing being Bays all lately built

| | | | A. | R. | P. |
|---|---|---|---|---|---|
| A | Housing Fold &c | | 0 | 0 | 30 |
| B | Upper Field | | 0 | 0 | 22 |
| C | Banks | | 1 | 3 | 36 |
| D | Hollow Field | | 2 | 0 | 17 |
| E | Fieldend | | 2 | 0 | 16 |
| F | Great Field $\left\{ \begin{array}{ccc} 1. & 2. & 1. \\ 1. & 3. & 21. \end{array} \right\}$ | | 3 | 1 | 22 |
| G | | | | | |
| H | Barley Spot | | 0 | 2 | 24 |
| I | Lane | | 0 | 0 | 26 |
| K | Hollow Meadow | M | 1 | 2 | 28 |
| L | Carr $\left\{ \begin{array}{ccc} 1. & 0. & 39. \\ 0. & 2. & 23. \end{array} \right\}$ | | 1 | 3 | 22 |
| M | | | | | |
| N | Broad Meadow | M | 2 | 0 | 19 |
| O | Wood | | 3 | 1 | 16 |
| | | | 19 | 2 | 38 |

89     James Platt     HOLLINS (L.M.)

A Dwelling House 2 Bays lately built and very old Outhousing

One Dwelling House new Built, a Barn & Shippen

| | | | A. | R. | P. |
|---|---|---|---|---|---|
| | House & Garden | | 0 | 0 | 12 |
| A | Croft M with the Stack yard | | 0 | 2 | 9 |
| B | Upper Meadow | M | 1 | 0 | 28 |
| C | Rough Intake | | 2 | 0 | 30 |
| D | Meadow | | 1 | 1 | 27 |
| E | Round Intake | | 1 | 2 | 37 |
| F | Little Intake | | 0 | 2 | 0 |
| | | | 7 | 2 | 23 |

In 1789   James Platt

90     John Platt's Executors     BUTTERWORTHS (L.M.)

A good Dwelling House being about 4 Bays new built a Barn & Shippen

A good Dwelling House consisting of about 4 Bays of Building & 4 Families dwell therein at present, Also a good Barn & Shippen

| | | | A. | R. | P. |
|---|---|---|---|---|---|
| | Housing Fold &c | | 0 | 0 | 13 |
| A | Croft | M | 0 | 3 | 4 |
| B | Othwart | M | 0 | 2 | 32 |
| C | Othwart | | 1 | 1 | 30 |
| D | Thistle Field | | 2 | 1 | 29 |
| E | Back oth' House | | 2 | 3 | 28 |
| F | Lower Field | | 2 | 1 | 8 |
| G | Great Meadow | M | 1 | 3 | 14 |
| H | Little Meadow | M | 0 | 3 | 8 |
| | | | 13 | 1 | 6 |

In 1789   Joseph Platt

91     Executors George Platt     PRIMROSEHILL (L.M.)

1 Dwelling House of 2 Bays & 2 Bays of Outhousing

A Dwelling House being 2 Bays with 2 small Bays of Outhousing

| | | | A. | R. | P. |
|---|---|---|---|---|---|
| A | Meadow | M | 1 | 3 | 13 |
| B | Whams | M | 0 | 1 | 39 |
| C | Lamblodge | | 0 | 0 | 36 |
| D | Lowmost Field | | 1 | 2 | 4 |
| E | Middlemost Field | | 1 | 3 | 30 |
| F | New Field | | 1 | 0 | 38 |
| G | Slack | | 1 | 1 | 32 |
| H | Intake | | 2 | 1 | 23 |
| | | | 11 | 0 | 15 |

92     Thomas Platt & Wm. Ken:     WOOLLROAD (L.M.)

2 Houses a Barn and Shippen being about 5 Bays

| | | | A. | R. | P. |
|---|---|---|---|---|---|
| A | Meadow | M | 2 | 2 | 23 |
| B | Near Intake | | 1 | 1 | 33 |
| C | Farr Intake | | 1 | 2 | 29 |
| D | Rake | | 2 | 0 | 24 |
| E | Upper Slack | | 2 | 0 | 32 |
| F | Lower Slack | | 1 | 2 | 29 |
| G | New Intake | | 5 | 3 | 0 |
| | | | 17 | 2 | 10 |

93     Thomas Platt     WOOLLROAD (L.M.)

One Bay of Building for a Dwelling House with 2 Bays of Outhousing & Garden

One Bay for a Dwelling House, with an Outisle for a porch & 2 Bays of Outhousing

| | | | A. | R. | P. |
|---|---|---|---|---|---|
| A | Tenter Croft | | 1 | 2 | 4 |
| B | Kiln Croft | M | 0 | 1 | 6 |
| C | Cote Green | | 2 | 0 | 23 |
| D | Lower Bank | | 1 | 1 | 32 |
| E | Upper Bank | | 1 | 0 | 32 |
| F | Rough Bank | | 0 | 3 | 38 |
| G | Birches | | 0 | 0 | 31 |
| | | | 7 | 3 | 17 |

94     Edmund Platt     PLATTLANE (L.M.)

One Dwelling House and Outhousing about 5 Bays

| | | | A. | R. | P. |
|---|---|---|---|---|---|
| | Housing & Fold | | 0 | 0 | 12 |
| A | Little Bank | | 0 | 3 | 18 |
| B | Great Bank | | 0 | 3 | 37 |
| C | Tenter Field | | 0 | 1 | 31 |
| D | Great Meadow | M | 1 | 2 | 19 |
| E | Sour Field | M | 1 | 1 | 0 |
| F | Long Meadow | M | 0 | 2 | 25 |
| G | Farr Field | | 1 | 0 | 10 |
| | | | 6 | 3 | 32 |

    Thos.

95     Edmund Platt     HOLLINGREAVE (L.M.)

| | | | A. | R. | P. |
|---|---|---|---|---|---|
| A | Housing Fold &c | | 0 | 0 | 19 |
| B | Waste | | 0 | 2 | 19 |
| C | Gorsey Heys $\left\{ \begin{array}{ccc} 1. & 3. & 36. \\ 1. & 2. & 31. \end{array} \right\}$ | | 3 | 2 | 27 |
| D | | | | | |
| F | Barn field | | 1 | 0 | 20 |
| G | Croft | M | 0 | 2 | 15 |
| H | Rood land | | 0 | 3 | 4 |
| I | Will Field | | 1 | 1 | 20 |
| K | Middlemost Meadow | M | 1 | 1 | 11 |
| L | Lowmost Meadow | M | 1 | 3 | 33 |
| | | | 11 | 2 | 8 |

96     George Shaw     PINFOLD HEY     In 1789

    No Housing

In 1789  John Lees

97  Executors James Radcliffe  COTTAGE (L.M.)

A cottage being 2 Bays and a small Garden adjoining it

In 1789  John Radcliffe

98  Alexander Radcliffe  WOOLLEYS (L.M.)

A Dwelling House with 2 Bays with but indifferent Outhousing

|   |   |   | A. | R. | P. |
|---|---|---|---|---|---|
|   | Housing & Fold |   | 0 | 0 | 16 |
| A | Upper Meadow | M | 1 | 2 | 18 |
| B | Little Croft |   | 1 | 0 | 26 |
| C | Lower Meadow | M | 1 | 0 | 33 |
| D | Lee |   | 2 | 1 | 8 |
| E | Leelane |   | 0 | 2 | 2 |
| F | Upper Croft |   | 1 | 2 | 15 |
| G | Back oth' Hill |   | 3 | 3 | 0 |
|   |   |   | 12 | 0 | 38 |

Wm. Radcliffe & Brother

99  Alexander Radcliffe  BALLGREAVE (L.M.)

1 Ancient Dwelling House & 1 New built very bad Outhousing being old & Thatched.

One old Dwelling House and one other new built, but very bad Outhousing

|   |   |   | A. | R. | P. |
|---|---|---|---|---|---|
| A | Housing Fold &c |   | 0 | 1 | 9 |
| B | Stackyard |   | 0 | 0 | 21 |
| D | Croft |   | 2 | 3 | 16 |
| E | Wetearth | M | 2 | 1 | 1 |
| F | Marledearth |   | 3 | 0 | 29 |
| G | Marledearth bottom |   | 0 | 2 | 10 |
| H | Great Meadow |   | 3 | 2 | 18 |
| I | New Meadow | M | 2 | 2 | 5 |
| K | Barn Field |   | 1 | 3 | 12 |
| L | Bent |   | 1 | 2 | 30 |
| M | Old Spout |   | 0 | 2 | 38 |
| N | Further Field with ye Croft above ye House |   | 3 | 0 | 19 |
| O }<br>P } | Intake |   | 4 | 3 | 28 |
|   |   |   | 27 | 2 | 36 |

100  William Radcliffe  CROSS (L.M.)

A Good Dwelling House of 2 Bays lately built, but indifferent Outhousing.

A Dwelling House lately built but indifferent Outhousing

|   |   |   | A. | R. | P. |
|---|---|---|---|---|---|
|   | Housing and Garden |   | 0 | 0 | 7 |
| A | Back side | M | 0 | 1 | 31 |
| B | Field at Door |   | 1 | 1 | 4 |
| C | Lane |   | 0 | 1 | 24 |
| D | Lower Field |   | 1 | 1 | 34 |
| E | Meadow | M | 0 | 3 | 38 |
| F | Little Field |   | 0 | 2 | 31 |
| G | Green |   | 1 | 1 | 1 |
|   |   |   | 6 | 2 | 10 |

In 1789  William & Wm. Radcliffe

101  William and Joshua Radcliffe  LANEHOUSE (L.M.)

A little old Cottage seemingly ready to fall

|   |   |   | A. | R. | P. |
|---|---|---|---|---|---|
| A | Cottage and Croft | M | 0 | 0 | 33 |
| B | Kiln Croft |   | 1 | 0 | 39 |
|   |   |   | 1 | 1 | 32 |

In 1789  William

102  Joshua Radcliffe  BIRCHES (L.M.)

A Dwelling House being 2 Bays with 2 Bays of Outhousing all lately Built

|   |   |   | A. | R. | P. |
|---|---|---|---|---|---|
| A }<br>B } | Little Field  { 1. 2. 4. }<br>{ 0. 0. 14. } |   | 1 | 2 | 18 |
| C }<br>D } | Intakes |   | 3 | 3 | 8 |
| E | Birches Meadow | M | 2 | 1 | 11 |
| F | Rough |   | 1 | 2 | 38 |
|   |   |   | 9 | 1 | 35 |

103  John Radcliffe  SADDLEWORTHFOLD (L.M.)

A Dwelling House being 3 Bays with about 3 Bays of Outhousing besides a Cote to lay Ashes in

|   |   |   | A. | R. | P. |
|---|---|---|---|---|---|
| A | Bardsley Wives |   | 2 | 2 | 16 |
| B | Lane |   | 0 | 3 | 22 |
| C | Laighen |   | 0 | 0 | 20 |
| D | Meadow below ye Fold | M | 1 | 3 | 27 |
| E | Near Field |   | 3 | 3 | 28 |
| F | Further Field |   | 3 | 2 | 14 |
| G | Broad Dole | M | 2 | 1 | 15 |
| H | Broad Dole foot |   | 1 | 3 | 4 |
| I | Intake |   | 2 | 3 | 20 |
|   |   |   | 20 | 0 | 6 |

In 1789  William Radcliffe & John Winterbottom

104  John & William Radcliffe  CROSS (L.M.)

One good Dwelling House consisting of 2 Bays, a good Barn & Shippen of 2 Bays built by ye said John & William's Father, 1 other built since & 1 other of 2 Bays new built by the said William

2 good Houses with several Bays of good Outhousing

|   |   |   | A. | R. | P. |
|---|---|---|---|---|---|
| A | Housing Fold &c |   | 0 | 1 | 1 |
| B | Orchard |   | 0 | 1 | 6 |
| C | Field at Door |   | 1 | 2 | 38 |
| D | Upper Further Field |   | 1 | 1 | 33 |
| E | Birchin Hey |   | 1 | 3 | 36 |
| F | Long Meadow |   | 2 | 0 | 19 |
| G | Slids |   | 2 | 0 | 3 |
| H | Rough Field |   | 2 | 0 | 39 |
| I }<br>K } | Butten road  { 1. 2. 17. }<br>{ 2. 0. 7. } |   | 3 | 2 | 24 |
| L | Wetearth | M | 2 | 3 | 6 |
| M | Great Meadow | M | 2 | 3 | 27 |
| N | Lower Farther Field |   | 1 | 3 | 0 |
| O | Lowerside of ye Field at Door | M | 1 | 3 | 1 |
|   |   |   | 24 | 3 | 33 |

In 1789  Samuel Broadbent

105  Jeremiah Rhodes & MB  LEECROSS (L.M.)

A House being 2 Bays with 2 Families therein lately built; the Outhousing old a Barn & Shippen

|   |   |   | A. | R. | P. |
|---|---|---|---|---|---|
| A | Meadow M with ye Housing |   | 2 | 2 | 22 |
| B | Croft | M | 0 | 2 | 33 |
| C | Lower Lee |   | 2 | 0 | 17 |
| D | John Wife of Green Intake |   | 1 | 0 | 4 |
| E | New Meadow |   | 1 | 0 | 10 |
| F | Bank |   | 0 | 2 | 32 |
|   |   |   | 8 | 0 | 38 |

106  John Rhodes  GREEN (L.M.)

2 Houses A good Barn & Shippen

|   |   |   | A. | R. | P. |
|---|---|---|---|---|---|
|   | Housing Garden &c |   | 0 | 0 | 24 |
| A | Lower Field | M | 3 | 2 | 27 |
| B | Kiln butts |   | 2 | 2 | 15 |
| C | Kiln Meadow |   | 1 | 2 | 35 |
| D | Warth |   | 1 | 1 | 30 |
| E | Meadow | M | 0 | 3 | 35 |
| F | Middlemost Meadow | M | 0 | 3 | 2 |
| G | Old Intak | M | 1 | 1 | 7 |
| H }<br>I } | Marled Earth  { 1. 3. 4. }<br>{ 1. 0. 18. } |   | 2 | 3 | 22 |
| K | Near Bank |   | 4 | 0 | 33 |
| L | Farr Bank |   | 3 | 3 | 28 |
| M | Strikeroad |   | 1 | 3 | 12 |
| N | Waste |   | 0 | 1 | 8 |
| O | Bank |   | 1 | 1 | 26 |
| P* | The little Rough Meadow |   | 1 | 1 | 26 |
|   |   |   | 28 | 2 | 10 |

*  This is exchanged with James Broadbent for 2 Rough Fields called the Acres

85

In 1789 James Rhodes

**107 John Rhodes Executors — ACKER (L.M.)**

One House Barn & Shippen

| | | | A. | R. | P. |
|---|---|---|---|---|---|
| | Housing Fold &c | | 0 | 0 | 11 |
| A | Great Acker | M | 1 | 2 | 36 |
| B | Little Acker | M | 1 | 1 | 8 |
| C | Bank | | 4 | 1 | 36 |
| D | New Field | | 1 | 3 | 24 |
| | | | 9 | 1 | 35 |

**108 Abraham Rhodes — DEANHEAD (L.M.)**

2 good new Houses with 4 Dwellings therein, a Shop, a good Barn and Shippen

| | | | A. | R. | P. |
|---|---|---|---|---|---|
| A | Great Meadow | M | 2 | 1 | 20 |
| B | Little Meadow | M | 1 | 1 | 8 |
| C | New Meadow | M | 0 | 2 | 24 |
| D | Bank | | 3 | 3 | 2 |
| E | Clay | | 2 | 2 | 9 |
| F | Acker | | 1 | 3 | 12 |
| G/H | Intakes {1. 1. 33. / 1. 1. 27.} | | 2 | 3 | 20 |
| I | Waste | | 0 | 1 | 27 |
| K | Ley | | 2 | 0 | 1 |
| L | Upper Meadow | M | 1 | 3 | 5 |
| M | Sheepfold | | 1 | 3 | 17 |
| N | Wimberlee Meadow | M | 2 | 1 | 22 |
| O | Hadden | | 0 | 3 | 27 |
| P | Wimberlee | | 4 | 1 | 0 |
| Q | Meadow | M | 2 | 2 | 12 |
| R | Croft | | 0 | 2 | 28 |
| S | Holme  at Wardlane | | 1 | 0 | 25 |
| T | | | | | |
| U | Lee | | 2 | 0 | 6 |
| | | | 35 | 1 | 25 |

In 1789 Abraham Rhodes Junior — Mill Housestead

**109 Abraham Rhodes — Part of Knights Pastures (Q.M.)**

4 Dwelling Houses with very good Outhousing all lately built

A good new House Barn and Shippen consisting of several Bays of Building 2 other new Houses

| | | | A. | R. | P. |
|---|---|---|---|---|---|
| | Housing &c | | 0 | 0 | 13 |
| A | Meadow | M | 3 | 0 | 8 |
| B | Lower Acre | | 1 | 3 | 3 |
| C | Stonerake | | 2 | 1 | 12 |
| D | Higher Acre | | 1 | 2 | 24 |
| E | Back oth' House | | 2 | 2 | 9 |
| F | Lower Black pasture | | 1 | 3 | 6 |
| G | Higher Black pasture | | 2 | 1 | 25 |
| | | | 15 | 2 | 20 |

**110 James Rhodes — INTAKE (L.M.)**

2 Houses in which 3 or 4 Families inhabit with several Bays of Outhousing

2 good Houses, (one of them new built) with 4 Families therein, a Barn & Shippen

| | | | A. | R. | P. |
|---|---|---|---|---|---|
| A | Housing, Fold Garden &c | | 0 | 1 | 15 |
| B | New | M | 2 | 0 | 39 |
| C | New Cloughs | | 2 | 0 | 0 |
| D | Meadow | M | 2 | 3 | 19 |
| E/F/G/H/I | Intakes {1. 3. 8. / 1. 2. 22. / 1. 1. 39. / 1. 0. 0. / 1. 0. 26.} | | 7 | 0 | 15 |
| | | | 14 | 2 | 8 |

**111 James Rhodes — KNOWL (L.M.)**

About 4 or 5 Bays of Housing

1 House with 2 Dwellings therein a Barn and Shippen in all 5 Bays

| | | | A. | R. | P. |
|---|---|---|---|---|---|
| A | Meadow (with ye Housing) | M | 2 | 1 | 1 |
| B | Intake Meadow | M | 1 | 3 | 5 |
| C/D | Great Intake {1. 2. 5. / 1. 3. 13.} | | 3 | 1 | 18 |
| E | Upper Field | | 1 | 3 | 23 |
| F | Great Wimberlee | M | 1 | 3 | 20 |
| G | Cross nook | | 1 | 0 | 18 |
| H | Brink | | 1 | 0 | 31 |
| I | Old Meat | | 1 | 0 | 9 |
| K | Little Wimberllee | | 2 | 1 | 13 |
| | | | 16 | 3 | 18 |

**112 Executors Thomas Rhodes — SUNFIELD (L.M.)**

| | | | A. | R. | P. |
|---|---|---|---|---|---|
| A | Housing Fold &c | | 0 | 0 | 15 |
| B | Calf Croft | | 0 | 0 | 27 |
| C | Croft | M | 1 | 0 | 24 |
| D | Back side | | 2 | 0 | 18 |
| E | New Field | | 1 | 1 | 0 |
| F/G | Barn Intake {1. 3. 31. / 0. 3. 9.} | M | 2 | 3 | 0 |
| H | Lower Bank | | 2 | 2 | 0 |
| K | Great Field | | 2 | 2 | 10 |
| L | New Meadow | M | 1 | 2 | 6 |
| M | Little Meadow | M | 1 | 1 | 1 |
| N | Great Meadow | M | 2 | 2 | 28 |
| O | Marled Earth | M | 1 | 0 | 12 |
| P | Kilnhole | M | 1 | 0 | 34 |
| Q | Long lee | | 2 | 1 | 31 |
| R | Littlelee | | 2 | 1 | 2 |
| S | Upper New | | 2 | 1 | 18 |
| T | Spirranlane meadow | M | 1 | 2 | 28 |
| | | | 29 | 0 | 14 |

**113 Executors Thomas Rhodes — Shaws or Olives (L.M.)**

2 Dwelling Houses with one Bay of Outhousing

| | | | A. | R. | P. |
|---|---|---|---|---|---|
| A | Croft M with the Housing | | 0 | 2 | 28 |
| B | Oliver Meadow | M | 2 | 1 | 31 |
| C | Weaky | | 0 | 0 | 28 |
| D | Little Moor | | 1 | 3 | 21 |
| E | Oliver Bank | | 2 | 2 | 10 |
| F | Oliver Lower New | | 2 | 0 | 11 |
| G | Oliver Upper New | | 2 | 0 | 37 |
| | | | 12 | 0 | 6 |
| H | Pingot | | 0 | 0 | 14 |
| | | | 12 | 0 | 20 |

**114 Thomas Rhodes Executors — COMMON (L.M.)**

| | | A. | R. | P. |
|---|---|---|---|---|
| A | Rough | 3 | 1 | 12 |
| B | Newbarn Intake | 1 | 3 | 25 |
| C | New Bank | 1 | 3 | 23 |
| D | Park | 1 | 3 | 0 |
| E | Hunterhill | 5 | 1 | 5 |
| | | 14 | 0 | 25 |

**115 James Rhodes — THORNSES (L.M.)**

One Dwelling House Barn and Shippen

| | | | A. | R. | P. |
|---|---|---|---|---|---|
| | The Housing | | 0 | 0 | 5 |
| A | Field above the House | | 0 | 3 | 38 |
| B | Intake | | 3 | 0 | 15 |
| C | Croft | M | 2 | 3 | 12 |
| D | Old Laighen | | 0 | 2 | 37 |
| E | Bank | M | 0 | 2 | 33 |
| F | Cote Meadow | M | 1 | 1 | 4 |
| G | Rough Meadow | M | 2 | 0 | 39 |
| H | Marledearth | M | 0 | 0 | 21 |
| I | Clough | | 1 | 2 | 14 |
| K | Holm | | 1 | 3 | 9 |
| L | Holt | | 3 | 1 | 0 |
| M | Quickrow | | 2 | 0 | 11 |
| N | Farr Field | | 4 | 0 | 0 |
| O | Pickhill | | 2 | 2 | 23 |
| | | | 27 | 1 | 21 |

| 116 | John Lees | | PASTURES (Q.M.) | | |
|---|---|---|---|---|---|
| | No Housing | | | | |
| A,B} | Lim'd Pastures | {2. 1. 36. / 2. 2. 4.} | 5 | 0 | 0 |
| C | Black Pasture | | 3 | 3 | 33 |
| | | | 8 | 3 | 33 |

In 1789  Isaac

| 117 | Jacob Savil | | THORPS (Q.M.) | | |
|---|---|---|---|---|---|
| | 3 or 4 Bays of tolerable good Housing | | | | |
| | | | A. | R. | P. |
| | Housing Fold &c | | 0 | 0 | 11 |
| A | Well Meadow | M | 1 | 0 | 36 |
| B | Great Meadow | M | 1 | 2 | 20 |
| C | Barn Field | | 1 | 0 | 24 |
| D | Little Meadow | M | 0 | 2 | 9 |
| E | Field above Carriers | | 2 | 1 | 22 |
| F | Middlemost Field | | 2 | 2 | 0 |
| G | Rough | | 5 | 0 | 16 |
| H,I} | New Fields | {2. 3. 33. / 2. 3. 18.} | 5 | 3 | 11 |
| | | | 20 | 1 | 29 |

In 1789  Peter

| 118 | Isaac Savil | | CABBIN (Q.M.) | | |
|---|---|---|---|---|---|
| | 3 or 4 Bays of Housing | | | | |
| | | | A. | R. | P. |
| A,B,C,D} | Six Acres | {1. 3. 34. / 1. 2. 34. / 1. 3. 33. / 4. 0. 10.} | | | |
| E | Two Acres | | 4 | 0 | 34 |
| F | Meadow | M | 2 | 1 | 26 |
| G,H} | Roughs | | 2 | 0 | 39 |
| | 3 or 4 Bays of Tolerable good Housing | | | | |
| | 2 Houses and Outhousing | | | | |
| A | Cabbin Hill | | 1 | 3 | 13 |
| B | Brow | | 1 | 1 | 10 |
| C | Lower Field | | 1 | 1 | 16 |
| D | Little Meadow | M | 0 | 1 | 20 |
| E | Meadow | M | 1 | 0 | 29 |
| F | Halfacre | | 0 | 3 | 17 |
| G | Acre | | 1 | 2 | 34 |
| H,I} | Roughs | | 2 | 0 | 39 |
| K | Meadow | M | 2 | 1 | 26 |
| L,M} | Two Acres | | 4 | 0 | 34 |
| | | | 17 | 1 | 38 |

In 1789  Joseph Savil & Brother

| 119 | James Savil | | ROEBUCKLOE (Q.M.) | | |
|---|---|---|---|---|---|
| | A good Dwelling House and Outhousing being 4 or 5 Bays of good Housing | | | | |
| | | | A. | R. | P. |
| | Housing &c. | | 0 | 0 | 15 |
| A | Little Meadow | M | 0 | 1 | 23 |
| B | Great Meadow | M | 3 | 0 | 10 |
| C | Bank | M | 3 | 1 | 4 |
| D,E} | Great Field | {1. 3. 25. / 3. 0. 28.} | 5 | 0 | 13 |
| F | North Nook | | 4 | 1 | 24 |
| G | Meadowhead | | 2 | 2 | 16 |
| H | Upper Meadow | | 3 | 2 | 24 |
| I,K} | Flake Field | | 4 | 1 | 27 |
| | | | 26 | 3 | 36 |

| 120 | John Savil | ROEBUCKLOE (Q.M.) | | |
|---|---|---|---|---|
| | No Housing | A. | R. | P. |
| A,B,C,D} | Six Axres  1. 3. 34. / 1. 2. 34. / 1. 3. 33. / 4. 0. 10. | 9 | 2 | 31 |

| 121 | Abraham Savil | Dicksons & Garlicks (Q.M.) |
|---|---|---|

In 1789  Widow

| 122 | James Scholefield | | HOLLINGREAVE (L.M.) | | |
|---|---|---|---|---|---|
| | One old House, a old Barn and Shippen the Roof of which has been lately Repair'd | | | | |
| | | | A. | R. | P. |
| | House and Garden | | 0 | 0 | 7 |
| A | Tenter Field | | 2 | 3 | 16 |
| B | Bank | | 3 | 2 | 4 |
| C | Lower Meadow | M | 1 | 2 | 28 |
| D | Top of Meadow | M | 0 | 0 | 11 |
| E | High Field | | 3 | 0 | 0 |
| F | Calf hey | | 3 | 1 | 9 |
| G | Little Meadow | M | 1 | 0 | 5 |
| | | | 15 | 2 | 0 |
| | Deduct Calf hey from ths Tenement & add it to Jno. Scholefields } | | 3 | 1 | 9 |
| | | | 12 | 0 | 31 |

| 123 | John Scholefield | | HOLLINGREAVE (L.M.) | | |
|---|---|---|---|---|---|
| | A very ancient House in indifferent repair, a Barn & Shippen whose Roof is in bad repair | | | | |
| | An old House Barn and Cowhouse | | | | |
| | | | A. | R. | P. |
| | House and Garden | | 0 | 0 | 10 |
| A | Barn Flatt Meadow | M | 1 | 0 | 6 |
| B | Barn Flatt | | 2 | 3 | 35 |
| C | Little Bank | | 2 | 1 | 11 |
| D | Lower Meadow | M | 1 | 2 | 38 |
| E | Little High Field | | 0 | 2 | 27 |
| | | | 8 | 3 | 7 |
| | Add ye Calf hey from page 122 | | 3 | 1 | 9 |
| | | | 12 | 0 | 16 |

| 124 | Joshua Platt | | LANEHEAD (S.M.) | | |
|---|---|---|---|---|---|
| | A new Dwelling House 1 Bay with 2 or three Bays of Outhousing very old | | | | |
| | | | A. | R. | P. |
| A | Nook with the Housing | | 0 | 1 | 34 |
| B | Meadow | M | 1 | 3 | 6 |
| C | Lower Field | | 3 | 0 | 6 |
| D | Broad Meadow | M | 1 | 2 | 16 |
| E | Little Meadow | M | 1 | 1 | 1 |
| F | Higher wood road | | 2 | 1 | 39 |
| G | Lowerwood road | | 3 | 0 | 39 |
| H | Carr | | 2 | 3 | 31 |
| I | Wood | | 2 | 1 | 11 |
| | | | 19 | 0 | 23 |

In 1789  James

| 125 | Alexander Scholefield | | GIBBS (S.M.) | | |
|---|---|---|---|---|---|
| | A good House Barn and Shippen | | | | |
| | | | A. | R. | P. |
| A | Croft M with ye Housing | | 0 | 3 | 32 |
| B | Millholme | | 3 | 0 | 11 |
| C | Clod | | 0 | 1 | 3 |
| D | Warth | | 2 | 3 | 5 |
| E | Sour Field | | 1 | 3 | 35 |
| F | Calf Meadow | M | 0 | 3 | 26 |
| G | Long Field | | 1 | 0 | 21 |
| H | Gibb Wood | | 1 | 0 | 27 |
| I | Round Field | | 1 | 0 | 38 |
| K | Broadmeadow | M | 2 | 0 | 31 |
| L | Further Meadow | | 1 | 3 | 15 |
| M | Little Field | | 1 | 2 | 29 |
| N | Marledearth | | 2 | 3 | 12 |
| | | | 22 | 0 | 5 |

### 126   Executors Robert Scholefield — Brow or Mow Walls (S.M.)

1 Old House & 1 new Built being about 5 Bays of Housing

|   |  |  | A. | R. | P. |
|---|---|---|---|---|---|
| A | Croft | | 0 | 0 | 39 |
| B | Butt | M | 0 | 3 | 16 |
| C | New Meadow | M | 1 | 2 | 33 |
| D | Old Meadow | M | 0 | 3 | 36 |
| E F | Mow Walls | | 2 | 0 | 12 |
| G | Old Intake | | 2 | 1 | 31 |
| H | Near New | | 2 | 0 | 8 |
| I | Farr New | | 2 | 0 | 31 |
|   |  |  | 12 | 2 | 6 |

### 127   Scholefd. Buckley & Bothomley — Tunstead Clough (L.M.)

No Housing

|  | A. | R. | P. |
|---|---|---|---|
| Tunstead Clough | 7 | 1 | 30 |

### 128   Joseph Scholefield — ARTHURS (L.M.)

One old House being 2 Bays – 2 or 3 Bays of old Thatched Outhousing
A Dwelling House, with very old Outhousing and Shop about 5 Bays in all

|   |  |  | A. | R. | P. |
|---|---|---|---|---|---|
|   | Housing Fold &c | | 0 | 0 | 12 |
| A | Carr | M | 1 | 0 | 0 |
| B | Tenter Meadow | M | 1 | 0 | 23 |
| C | Little Meadow | M | 1 | 1 | 6 |
| D | Great Meadow | M | 1 | 1 | 7 |
| E | Hole | | 0 | 2 | 5 |
| F | Rushy Field | | 2 | 0 | 8 |
| G | Knowl Stile | | 1 | 2 | 31 |
| H I | Wheels Field   {1. 3. 2. / 0. 0. 25.} | | 1 | 3 | 27 |
| K | Gladhill | | 2 | 2 | 13 |
| L | Owlers | | 0 | 1 | 23 |
| M | Rough | | 0 | 3 | 0 |
| N | Croft | | 0 | 0 | 8 |
|   |  |  | 14 | 3 | 3 |

### 129   Michael Shaw — RIETOP (L.M.)

An old Dwelling House and an old Barn and Shippen 4 or 5 Bays of very old Houseing mostly Thatched

|   |  |  | A. | R. | P. |
|---|---|---|---|---|---|
|   | Housing Fold &c | | 0 | 0 | 16 |
| A | Faugh | M | 2 | 3 | 39 |
| B | Back side | | 1 | 0 | 25 |
| C | Rough | | 1 | 0 | 23 |
| D | Near Rie | | 1 | 0 | 0 |
| E | Little Meadow | M | 0 | 2 | 12 |
| F | Green | | 1 | 3 | 34 |
| G | Farr Rie | | 2 | 0 | 27 |
| H | Will Field | | 3 | 0 | 20 |
| I | Intake | | 1 | 1 | 21 |
| K | Carr | M | 1 | 3 | 8 |
|   |  |  | 17 | 1 | 25 |

### 130   Robert Andrew — KNOWLTOP (L.M.)

A very old Cottage with a place to set a Cow in

|   |  |  |  | A. | R. | P. |
|---|---|---|---|---|---|---|
| A B | Brownhill Field   {1. 0. 31. / 2. 0. 14.} | M | | 3 | 1 | 5 |
| C | Readhead | | | 1 | 3 | 0 |
| D | Carr | M | | 1 | 1 | 22 |
|   |  |  |  | 6 | 1 | 27 |

### 131   John Sikes — AMBROSES (L.M.)

3 Bays of Good new Building

|   |  |  | A. | R. | P. |
|---|---|---|---|---|---|
| A | Upper Croft | M | 0 | 1 | 8 |
| B | Lower Croft | M | 0 | 3 | 17 |
| C | Long Croft | | 0 | 3 | 32 |
| D | Nabend | | 1 | 1 | 10 |
|   |  |  | 3 | 1 | 27 |

### 132   Shaws Executors now James Kenworthy — BARN (S.M.)

2 Good Houses lately Built one of which has 2 Families in, a good new built Barn and Shippen.  All built by the present Tenant.

|   |  |  | A. | R. | P. |
|---|---|---|---|---|---|
|   | Housing Fold &c | | 0 | 1 | 5 |
| A B | Millhill | | 1 | 2 | 35 |
| C | Further Field | | 3 | 1 | 37 |
| D | Near Field | | 3 | 1 | 0 |
| E | Mill Holme | | 2 | 2 | 16 |
| F | Near Mill Holme | | 1 | 2 | 6 |
| G | Green | | 1 | 3 | 15 |
| H | Back 'oth' House | M | 1 | 1 | 27 |
| I | Pingot | | 0 | 1 | 28 |
| K | Marled Earth | M | 2 | 1 | 22 |
| L | Three nook | | 1 | 0 | 16 |
| M | Preemhill | | 2 | 0 | 26 |
| N O | Parchmouth   {1. 3. 16. / 0. 2. 15.} | | 2 | 1 | 31 |
|   |  |  | 24 | 2 | 24 |

### 133   Executors James Buckley — TAMEWATER (S.M.)

One ancient Dwelling House with three or 4 Bays of outhousing also a good House & Outhousing being 4 or 5 Bays new built

One ancient House at Tamewater several Bays of Outhousing & 4 or 5 Bays of good Housing in the Husteads, new built, Also 1 new House or Warehouse in the Barnstead

|   |  |  | A. | R. | P. |
|---|---|---|---|---|---|
| A | Housing Fold &c | | 0 | 0 | 36 |
| B | Bank | | 2 | 0 | 39 |
| C | Kiln Meadow | M | 0 | 3 | 34 |
| D E | Intake | | 4 | 1 | 25 |
| F | Blakemeadow | M | 1 | 2 | 7 |
| G | Husteads M with ye new Housing | | 1 | 3 | 20 |
| H | Broadflatt | | 4 | 3 | 31 |
| I | Brownhill with the waste at Back'oth House | | 4 | 0 | 9 |
| K | Waste | | 0 | 1 | 29 |
| L | Backside | | 3 | 0 | 22 |
| M | Maghey | | 3 | 0 | 19 |
| N | Upperholme | | 1 | 2 | 14 |
| O | Longholme | M | 1 | 2 | 7 |
| P | Littleholme | M | 1 | 0 | 25 |
| Q | Road | M | 1 | 3 | 16 |
| R | Calf Croft & laighen | M | 0 | 0 | 30 |
|   |  |  | 33 | 1 | 3 |

### 134   James Shaw — HOLLINS (L.M.)

One Dwelling House 2 Bays, Barn & Shippen 2 Bays in tolerable good repair

One Dwelling House Barn and Shippen in tolerable good repair

|   |  |  | A. | R. | P. |
|---|---|---|---|---|---|
|   | Housing and Garden | | 0 | 0 | 7 |
| A | Croft | | 0 | 3 | 0 |
| B | Intake | | 1 | 3 | 6 |
| C | Marled Earth | | 1 | 3 | 30 |
| D | Little Meadow | M | 0 | 3 | 0 |
| E | Great Meadow | M | 1 | 2 | 8 |
| F | Leybutts | | 1 | 1 | 37 |
| G | Hole | | 0 | 0 | 36 |
| H | Knowl with the Shrogg | | 2 | 2 | 6 |
|   |  |  | 11 | 0 | 10 |

135 George Shaw — HAWKYARD (L.M.)

One good ancient Dwelling House and one very old House, a Barn, Shippen and Turfcote

| | | | A. | R. | P. |
|---|---|---|---|---|---|
| | Housing Fold &c | | 0 | 1 | 1 |
| A | Great Meadow | M | 3 | 1 | 24 |
| B | Calf hey | | 1 | 2 | 6 |
| C | Calf hey bottom | M | 0 | 1 | 31 |
| D | Calf hey Meadow | M | 1 | 1 | 24 |
| E | Croft Meadow M & Nursery | | 1 | 0 | 25 |
| F | Croft | | 2 | 2 | 14 |
| G | Great Field | | 5 | 3 | 20 |
| H, I | Upperfield {1. 2. 11. / 2. 3. 28.} | | 4 | 1 | 39 |
| K | Little Heath hey | | 1 | 1 | 24 |
| L | Long Heath hey | | 1 | 2 | 26 |
| M | Meadow head | | 2 | 3 | 21 |
| N | Turner hill | | 1 | 3 | 34 |
| | | | 29 | 0 | 9 |

In 1789 Robt. Buckley

136 William Shaw — LOWERHOUSE (L.M.)

One very old Dwelling House and one new built being 2 Bays with 2 Bays of Outhousing lately repaired

| | | | A. | R. | P. |
|---|---|---|---|---|---|
| | Housing and Garden | | 0 | 0 | 12 |
| A | Upper Field | M | 1 | 1 | 31 |
| B | Lower Field | | 2 | 0 | 1 |
| C | Upper Meadow | M | 1 | 0 | 20 |
| D | Lower Meadow | | 1 | 2 | 39 |
| E | Snipe Road | | 1 | 2 | 34 |
| | | | 8 | 0 | 17 |

In 1789 Hen: & James

137 Elizabeth Shaw — BOARSHURST (L.M.)

About 4 or 5 Bays of very old Thatched Housing in length about 23 yards

About 23 yards in length of old Thatched Housing

| | | | A. | R. | P. |
|---|---|---|---|---|---|
| | House and Gardens | | 0 | 0 | 9 |
| A | Intake | | 1 | 1 | 20 |
| B | Near Daubroad | M | 1 | 2 | 4 |
| C | Farr Daubroad | M | 1 | 1 | 28 |
| D | Hilltop | | 1 | 2 | 32 |
| E | Longlands | | 2 | 1 | 24 |
| F | Little Meadow | M | 1 | 2 | 20 |
| | | | 10 | 0 | 17 |

138 Samuel Heginbottom — DOBCROSS MILL (L.M.)

One Dwelling House with Outhousing a Fulling Mill with a Family dwelling in the Mill Chamber, also a Cottage in the Highmost bank, built by George Hinchcliffe

One ancient Dwelling House & Shippen also a Fulling Mill lately rebuilt with a Family dwelling in the Mill Chamber. Also a Cottage in the Highmost Bank built by George Hinchcliffe

| | | | A. | R. | P. |
|---|---|---|---|---|---|
| A | Upper Croft M and Housing | | 0 | 2 | 27 |
| B | Stonerow | M | 0 | 3 | 7 |
| C | Bank | | 1 | 1 | 13 |
| D | New Meadow | | 0 | 2 | 23 |
| E | Round Bank | | 1 | 2 | 18 |
| F, G | Rough {1. 0. 26. / 0. 3. 20.} | | 2 | 0 | 6 |
| H | Highmost Bank | | 0 | 3 | 22 |
| I* | Kiln Ditch | | 0 | 1 | 16 |
| K | Intake | | 0 | 1 | 24 |
| | | | 8 | 2 | 36 |

* This is now let to John Harrop See No. 185

In 1789 Robert Holden's

139 Michael Bottomley — SIKES COTTAGE (L.M.)

3 little bays of but indifferent housing

| | | | A. | R. | P. |
|---|---|---|---|---|---|
| A | Ward Croft | M | 0 | 2 | 1 |

In 1789 George

140 Executors Robert Scholefield — LANEHEAD (S.M.)

One Dwelling House consisting of several Bays in but indifferent repair, a good Barn and Shippen lately built

| | | | A. | R. | P. |
|---|---|---|---|---|---|
| A | Croft | | 0 | 0 | 23 |
| B | Well Meadow | M | 1 | 0 | 16 |
| C | Long Field | | 2 | 1 | 6 |
| D | Cowholes | M | 0 | 2 | 35 |
| E | Great Shawhurst | | 3 | 2 | 30 |
| F | Little Shawhurst | | 2 | 1 | 30 |
| G | Clough | | 0 | 3 | 26 |
| H | Clough Meadow | M | 0 | 1 | 6 |
| I | Top of Wood | | 1 | 2 | 22 |
| K | Little bank | | 1 | 0 | 10 |
| L | Cote Meadow | M | 2 | 0 | 35 |
| M | Cote Wood | | 1 | 1 | 22 |
| | | | 17 | 3 | 21 |

In 1789 George Buckley

141 Mrs. Whitehead — COTTAGE (L.M.)

5 or 6 Bays of Houseing lately built

142 Mr. Harropp and Buckleys — WADEHILL (S.M.)

A very good Dwelling House with good Outhousing all lately built
4 or 5 Bays of good new building

| | | | A. | R. | P. |
|---|---|---|---|---|---|
| A | Meadow M with ye Housing | | 3 | 0 | 1 |
| B | Little Acre | | 1 | 1 | 14 |
| C | Holme | | 1 | 1 | 25 |
| D | Lower Field | | 1 | 1 | 12 |
| E | Upper Field | | 2 | 2 | 9 |
| F | Waste with ye lane | | 1 | 3 | 1 |
| G | New Meadow | M | 1 | 1 | 36 |
| H | Slack Meadow | M | 1 | 1 | 26 |
| I | Little Bank | | 0 | 1 | 39 |
| K | Hanging Bank | | 1 | 3 | 8 |
| L | Croft | | 0 | 3 | 2 |
| M | New Field | | 1 | 2 | 14 |
| N | Slate Croft | | 1 | 3 | 18 |
| O | Poor Stubble | | 1 | 3 | 0 |
| | | | 22 | 2 | 5 |

In 1789 George Shaw

143 Executors Robt. Walker Scholefd. — WHITELEE (L.M.)

No Housing

| | | | A. | R. | P. |
|---|---|---|---|---|---|
| A, B, C, D | New Intake | Scholefield 4. 1. 7 / R. Walkers Executors or Assignes 4. 2. 21 | 8 | 3 | 28 |

In 1789 James Buckley

144 Martha Whewal — HOLINGREAVE (L.M.)

One new House, 2 other Houses, and 4 Families dwelling therein, very old Thatched Outhousing

| | | | A. | R. | P. |
|---|---|---|---|---|---|
| | Housing Garden and part of Fold* | | 0 | 0 | 20 |
| A | Croft** | | 0 | 1 | 12 |
| B | Meadow*** | M | 3 | 0 | 28 |
| C | Field under the Meadow | | 4 | 0 | 23 |
| D | Lower Field | | 2 | 2 | 8 |
| E | Upper Field | | 3 | 3 | 7 |

| | | | | A. | R. | P. |
|---|---|---|---|---|---|---|
| F }<br>G } | Upper Riefield | [2. 2. 20.]<br>[1. 3. 33.] | | 4 | 2 | 13 |
| H | Upper Meadow | | M | 2 | 1 | 29 |
| I }<br>K } | Lower Meadow | [0. 2. 30.]<br>[1. 0. 29.] | M | 1 | 3 | 19 |
| L }<br>M } | Lower Riefield | [1. 3. 9.]<br>[1. 3. 3.] | | 3 | 2 | 12 |
| | | | | 26 | 2 | 11 |

\*     To be divided equally
\*\*    To be divided as agreed
\*\*\*   [Fields C - M have 'Jas. Buckley' written against them]

vide     The following in ye Occupation of Jonathan Bradbury a new Barn and
No. 59   Shippen built by the said Jonathan

| | | | | | | |
|---|---|---|---|---|---|---|
| N }<br>O } | Long Intake | [1. 3. 29.]<br>[2. 1. 18.] | M | 4 | 1 | 7 |
| P | Lamb Knowl | | | 1 | 3 | 32 |
| Q | Little Wankin Clough | | M | 0 | 3 | 4 |
| R | Great Wankin Clough | | | 1 | 0 | 13 |
| | | | | 8 | 0 | 16 |
| | | Brought down | | 26 | 2 | 11 |
| | | Total of M. Whewal's Tenement | | 34 | 2 | 27 |

---

**145**     Mrs. Whitehead    R. Whitehead      SHAWHALL (S.M.)

5 Families at Shawhall and 2 new Houses in ye Bank

| | | | | A. | R. | P. |
|---|---|---|---|---|---|---|
| A | Plantation | | | 0 | 2 | 6 |
| B | Marled Earth Head | | M | 0 | 1 | 33 |
| C | Orchard | | | 0 | 0 | 31 |
| D | Wood Close | | | 4 | 2 | 24 |
| E | Rye Croft | | | 4 | 3 | 29 |
| F | Barn Field | | | 6 | 2 | 25 |
| G | Brownedge Meadow | | | 3 | 3 | 8 |
| H | Farr Shaw Field | | | 5 | 2 | 18 |
| I | Near Shaw Field | | | 5 | 2 | 4 |
| J | Great Shaw Field & Shrogg | | | 9 | 3 | 5 |
| K | Rawgreaves | | M | 3 | 2 | 11 |
| L | Hen Croft | | | 1 | 3 | 12 |
| M | Marled Earth | | M | 3 | 2 | 2 |
| N | Bent | | M | 7 | 3 | 9 |
| O | Ridding | | | 2 | 3 | 22 |
| Y | Hallstead | 5. 1. 36. | | | | |
| Z | Mill Pasture | 0. 3. 28. | | 61 | 2 | 39 |
| | | 6. 1. 24. | | 68 | 0 | 23 |
| P\* | Bank | | | 3 | 2 | 25 |
| Q | Round Meadow | | | 3 | 3 | 29 |
| R | Calf Croft | | M | 1 | 2 | 2 |
| S | How Meadow | | M | 3 | 2 | 27 |
| T | Eller Croft | | | 3 | 3 | 24 |
| U | Clod | | | 0 | 1 | 14 |
| V | Upper Flatt | | | 6 | 1 | 25 |
| W | Lower Flatt | | | 4 | 3 | 36 |
| X | Marled pit Earth | | | 5 | 2 | 0 |
| | | | | 33 | 3 | 22 |
| | | Total | | 102 | 0 | 5 |

\*     [Fields P - X are labelled '40 Jno. Buckley for his part of Shaw Hall']

---

**146**     John Winterbottom     Shawhouses and Deanshaw bankes (L.M.)

2 Dwelling Houses and Bays for Outhousing all new built

| | | | | A. | R. | P. |
|---|---|---|---|---|---|---|
| A | Lower Ley | | | 1 | 1 | 16 |
| B | Upper Ley | | | 1 | 2 | 23 |
| C | Golbron | | | 3 | 1 | 11 |
| D | Upper Clough | | M | 1 | 0 | 13 |
| E | Lower Clough | | M | 1 | 0 | 0 |
| F | Foot | | | 1 | 0 | 30 |
| G | Long New Meadow | | M | 2 | 0 | 14 |
| H | Clew Meadow | | M | 0 | 3 | 16 |
| I }<br>K } | Deanshaw bankes | [1. 0. 12.]<br>[1. 0. 17.] | | 2 | 0 | 29 |
| L | Hare holes | | | 0 | 1 | 9 |
| | | | | 15 | 0 | 1 |

---

In 1789   James

**147**     Executors Timothy Whitehead      SHAWHOUSES (L.M.)

2 Houses to wit, 1 old one & 1 new built with several Bays of
Outhousing. Also a new House (but a very indifferent one) built in
Golbron Clough in which 2 Families dwell.

| | | | | A. | R. | P. |
|---|---|---|---|---|---|---|
| B | Kilnhill | | | 0 | 1 | 34 |
| C | Broadleighen | | | 0 | 0 | 30 |
| D | Neither Field | | | 2 | 2 | 23 |
| E | Broad Dole | | M | 2 | 2 | 18 |
| F | Long Meadow | | M | 2 | 0 | 10 |
| G | Marled Earth | | M | 0 | 3 | 2 |
| H | Slids | | M | 0 | 1 | 24 |
| I | Croft | | | 2 | 0 | 30 |
| K | Whicken butt | | | 1 | 1 | 0 |
| L | Eyebridge | | | 3 | 0 | 0 |
| M }<br>N } | Great Golbron | [2. 0. 18.]<br>[2. 2. 8.] | | 4 | 2 | 26 |
| O | Little Golbron | | | 0 | 3 | 37 |
| P | Knowl | | M | 0 | 2 | 25 |
| Q | Lower Meadow | | M | 0 | 2 | 25 |
| R | Calf hey | | | 1 | 1 | 30 |
| S | Near Croft | | | 1 | 1 | 2 |
| | | | | 25 | 0 | 36 |

---

**148**     James Whitehead      UPPER MILL (L.M.)

2 Dwelling Houses with one of them new built with several Bays of
Outhousing

| | | | | A. | R. | P. |
|---|---|---|---|---|---|---|
| A | Housing Fold &c | | | 0 | 1 | 10 |
| B | Lee | | M | 3 | 2 | 7 |
| C | Flegm | | | 3 | 2 | 19 |
| D | Flegm Meadow | | M | 1 | 2 | 26 |
| E | Shore      4. 1. 20.<br>Shrogg    0. 2. 24. | | | 5 | 0 | 4 |
| F | Pick hill | | | 0 | 3 | 39 |
| G | Three nook | | | 2 | 0 | 2 |
| H | Great Field | | | 4 | 2 | 3 |
| I | Little Field | | | 0 | 2 | 33 |
| K | Wood | | | 0 | 3 | 31 |
| L | Intake | | | 2 | 0 | 10 |
| M | Damside | | | 0 | 0 | 27 |
| | | | | 25 | 2 | 11 |

---

**149**     Henry Whitehead      WOODS (L.M.)

A large Quantity of Building in which 12 or 13 Families dwell

| | | | | A. | R. | P. |
|---|---|---|---|---|---|---|
| A | Croft at Dobcross | | | 0 | 1 | 22 |
| B | | | | 1 | 0 | 35 |
| C | | | | 0 | 3 | 9 |
| D | | | | 1 | 1 | 0 |
| E | | | | 1 | 1 | 0 |
| F | | At Platthill | | 0 | 3 | 35 |
| G | | | | 1 | 3 | 8 |
| H | | | | 1 | 1 | 29 |
| I | | | | 1 | 2 | 10 |
| K | | | | 2 | 0 | 9 |
| L | | | | 1 | 2 | 30 |
| M | | | | 1 | 0 | 20 |
| N | | | | 0 | 3 | 31 |
| O | Upper Intake | | | 1 | 1 | 33 |
| P | Meadow | At Nabend | M | 1 | 1 | 4 |
| Q }<br>R } | Tenter Intakes | | | 2 | 0 | 20 |
| | | | | 21 | 1 | 15 |

---

**150**     Henry Whitehead      MOOR GREEN (L.M.)

No Housing

| | | | | A. | R. | P. |
|---|---|---|---|---|---|---|
| A }<br>B } | Moorgreen | | M | 2 | 2 | 20 |

---

**151**     John Whitehead      BROWNKNOTTHILL (L.M.)

One Dwelling House and several Bays of Outhousing

| | | | | A. | R. | P. |
|---|---|---|---|---|---|---|
| | Housing Fold and Garden | | | 0 | 0 | 21 |
| A | Great Meadow | | M | 2 | 2 | 8 |
| B | Lower Field | | | 2 | 2 | 0 |
| C | Upper Field | | | 1 | 2 | 32 |
| D | Marled Earth | | | 2 | 3 | 29 |
| E | Little Meadow | | M | 1 | 2 | 5 |
| | | | | 11 | 1 | 15 |

## 152 Mr. Ra: Whitehead Executors     LIDYATE (Q.M.)

One good Dwelling House Woll Shop and Outhousing

| | | | A. | R. | P. |
|---|---|---|---|---|---|
| A | House Garden &c | | 0 | 1 | 10 |
| B | Garden Field | | 3 | 3 | 15 |
| C | Middlemost Field | | 3 | 1 | 15 |
| D | Highmost Field | | 4 | 1 | 21 |
| E | Kenworthy Meadow | M | 2 | 3 | 11 |
| F | Bent Meadow | M | 0 | 3 | 30 |
| G} H} | Lower Meadows | M | 3 | 1 | 10 |
| | | | 18 | 3 | 32 |

## 153 Edmund Whitehead     UPPER LIDYATE (Q.M.)

One Dwelling House with about   Bays of Outhousing

| | | | A. | R. | P. |
|---|---|---|---|---|---|
| A | Housing and Croft | | 0 | 1 | 9 |
| B | Great Meadow | M | 3 | 1 | 14 |
| C | Little Meadow | M | 0 | 3 | 24 |
| D | Watered Meadow | M | 1 | 3 | 17 |
| E | White Field | | 3 | 1 | 1 |
| F | Long Meadow | M | 1 | 0 | 15 |
| G | Thorp | | 1 | 3 | 15 |
| H | Cote Field | | 3 | 2 | 0 |
| | | | 16 | 0 | 15 |

## 154 James Winterbottom     KNARR (S.M.)

One tolerable good Dwelling House one very old & one new built with several Bays of Outhousing

| | | | A. | R. | P. |
|---|---|---|---|---|---|
| A | Housing Waste &c | | 0 | 1 | 27 |
| B | Long Croft | | 0 | 3 | 39 |
| C | Brier Hey | | 0 | 3 | 28 |
| D | New Ridd | | 0 | 0 | 36 |
| E | New Meadow | M | 1 | 3 | 13 |
| F} G} | Maghey | | 3 | 0 | 33 |
| H | Clough Meadow | M | 2 | 0 | 15 |
| I | Middlemost Field | | 3 | 1 | 22 |
| K | Kiln Field with the Croft | | 1 | 3 | 28 |
| L | Stony Acre | M | 2 | 1 | 34 |
| M | Rough Knarr | | 5 | 0 | 12 |
| N | New Field | | 2 | 3 | 1 |
| O | Acre | | 1 | 3 | 0 |
| | Lett to James Winterbottom | | 27 | 0 | 8 |
| P | Bent M with the Housing therein | | 2 | 0 | 17 |
| Q | Upper Thurstone | | 2 | 2 | 4 |
| R | Spout Field | | 2 | 0 | 24 |
| S | Upperhouse Meadow | M | 1 | 2 | 31 |
| T} U} | Thurstone {2. 2. 31. / 2. 1. 20.} | | 5 | 0 | 11 |
| V | Shutt | | 0 | 2 | 31 |
| W | Calf Pickle | M | 2 | 0 | 6 |
| X | Rough Calf Pickle | | 1 | 3 | 30 |
| | Lett to Jonathan Lees | | 18 | 0 | 34 |
| | | | 45 | 1 | 2 |

In 1789 Executors of

## 155 John Winterbottom     NOONSUNHILL (S.M.)

2 Bays of Building, to wit, one for a Dwelling House and one for Outhousing old Cow House

| | | | A. | R. | P. |
|---|---|---|---|---|---|
| A | House and Garden | | 0 | 0 | 10 |
| B | Croft | | 0 | 2 | 18 |
| C | Intake | | 1 | 0 | 34 |
| D | Meadow | M | 1 | 2 | 10 |
| E | Lower Croft | | 0 | 3 | 34 |
| | | | 4 | 1 | 26 |

## 156 Thomas Winterbottom     (Q.M.)

Two Houses the Upper end of ye Barn with liberty for Thrashing in the Thrashing Bay

| | | | A. | R. | P. |
|---|---|---|---|---|---|
| | Housing Fold &c 1. 12½. of which is | | 0 | 0 | 26 |
| A | Barn Yard | M } | | | |
| B | Lower Bent | M } | 2 | 2 | 15 |
| C | Higher Bent | M | 1 | 2 | 28 |
| D | Acker | | 2 | 1 | 10 |
| E | Higher Hey | | 3 | 3 | 4 |

| | | | A. | R. | P. |
|---|---|---|---|---|---|
| F | Further Shutt | | 4 | 1 | 11 |
| G | Farr Wall Field enlarged out of the Near Wall Field } | | 2 | 1 | 34 |
| H | Rough Meadow | | 1 | 1 | 37 |
| | | | 18 | 3 | 5 |

## 87 James Hollingworth

One very old House ready to drop down ye lower end of ye Barn, with liberty for Thrashing in ye Thrashing Bay

| | | | A. | R. | P. |
|---|---|---|---|---|---|
| | One half of the Fold &c | | 0 | 0 | 26 |
| I | The Near Wall Field when the same shall have 1. 33. laid out of it to the Farr Wall Field | | 1 | 1 | 30 |
| K | Wheat Wood | | 1 | 0 | 37 |
| L | Lower Hey | | 3 | 2 | 9 |
| M | Old Wood | | 1 | 1 | 37 |
| N | Rie Road | | 2 | 2 | 20 |
| O | Lower Croft | | 2 | 0 | 6 |
| P | Lower Meadow | M | 1 | 2 | 14 |
| Q | Kiln Croft | M | 1 | 2 | 24 |
| R | Higher Croft | | 1 | 3 | 33 |
| | | | 17 | 2 | 36 |
| S | Spring Wood | | 1 | 2 | 24 |
| | | | 19 | 1 | 20 |

## 157 Daniel Winterbottom     SHELDERSLOW (Q.M.)

| | | A. | R. | P. |
|---|---|---|---|---|
| A | Croft with a Cottage Built therein | 0 | 1 | 24 |

## 158 Daniel Winterbottom     Pastures and Stonebreaks (Q.M.)

No Housing

| | | | | A. | R. | P. |
|---|---|---|---|---|---|---|
| A | Upperends {2. 2. 36 / 1. 2. 10} | Pastures | | 4 | 1 | 6 |
| B | | | | | | |
| C | Black Pasture | | | 4 | 0 | 6 |
| D | Intake | Stonebreak | M | 1 | 0 | 15 |
| E | Rushy Field | | | 2 | 0 | 14 |
| F | Higher Field | | | 0 | 3 | 16 |
| | | | | 12 | 1 | 17 |

In 1789 Timothy

## 159 Robert Winterbottom     BURNTEDGE (S.M.)

No Housing

| | | | A. | R. | P. |
|---|---|---|---|---|---|
| A | Bank | | 1 | 0 | 32 |
| B | End of Moor | | 0 | 3 | 34 |
| C | Butt | | 0 | 3 | 20 |
| D | Great Meadow | M | 1 | 0 | 38 |
| E | Little Meadow | M | 0 | 3 | 18 |
| F} G} | Lower Intake {1. 2. 18. / 2. 1. 21.} | | 3 | 3 | 39 |
| H | New Intake | | 2 | 3 | 9 |
| I | North Close | | 1 | 0 | 30 |
| | | | 13 | 0 | 20 |

## 160 Jonathan Lees     FOUR ACRES (S.M.)

No Housing

| | A. | R. | P. |
|---|---|---|---|
| A rough, or unimproved Field called 4 Acres | 8 | 1 | 0 |

## 161 John Winterbottom     STRINES (Q.M.)

| | | | A. | R. | P. |
|---|---|---|---|---|---|
| A | Highmost Field | | 1 | 2 | 21 |
| B | Croft | M | 0 | 2 | 5 |
| C | Middle Field | | 1 | 2 | 26 |
| D | Great Field | | 3 | 0 | 24 |
| E | Lowmost Field | | 1 | 3 | 37 |
| F | Meadow | M | 2 | 1 | 28 |
| G | Butt | | 2 | 0 | 4 |
| H | Lane | | 0 | 3 | 6 |
| | | | 14 | 0 | 31 |

N.B. It being pretended that the last mentioned Field called the Lane was a Road for particular Persons; I believe it is not put in John Winterbottom's last Lease.

In 1789   Joseph Whitehead

162   Executors John Wood                     WHARMTONSIDE (L.M.)
      2 Dwelling Houses with 1 Bay of Outhousing erected by John Wood
      the Lessee

|   |                                   |   | A. | R. | P. |
|---|-----------------------------------|---|----|----|----|
| A | Meadow M with the Housing therein |   | 1  | 1  | 20 |
| B | Intake                            |   | 2  | 2  | 34 |
|   |                                   |   | 4  | 0  | 14 |


In 1789   Robert Winterbottom

163   Timothy Wood                            COTTAGES (L.M.)
      A new Building in ye Meadow with several Families dwelling therein,
      also 3 or 4 Families in ye Cottages in Upper Mill Fold

|   |                          |              | A. | R. | P. |
|---|--------------------------|--------------|----|----|----|
| A | Meadow                   | M            | 0  | 2  | 32 |
| B |                          | M { 0. 1. 33. } |    |    |    |
| C | Upper Meadow             | M { 0. 1. 34. } | 0 | 3  | 27 |
| D |                          | { 0. 1. 34. } |    |    |    |
| E | Upper Intakes            | { 0. 2.  4. } | 0 | 3  | 38 |
| F | New Intake               |              | 1  | 1  | 27 |
| G | Cottages in the Upper Mill Fold |       | 0  | 0  | 11 |
|   |                          |              | 4  | 0  | 15 |


In 1789   John Sager

164   David Wood                              RUNNINGHILL (L.M.)
      2 Bays for a Dwelling House wherein 2 Families dwell with 2 Bays of
      Outhousing
      One Dwelling House being 2 Bays lately built adjoyning to an old Barn

|   |                     |   | A. | R. | P. |
|---|---------------------|---|----|----|----|
|   | Housing &c          |   | 0  | 0  | 8  |
| A | Lamb knowl          |   | 0  | 3  | 26 |
| B | Field at Door       |   | 1  | 0  | 33 |
| C | Brow                |   | 0  | 3  | 3  |
| D | Meadow              | M | 2  | 1  | 34 |
| E | Long Lands          |   | 1  | 1  | 17 |
| F | Wardgreen Field     |   | 1  | 1  | 4  |
| G | Lower Wardgreen Field |  | 1  | 3  | 16 |
| H | Lower Meadow        | M | 1  | 2  | 1  |
| I | Firbrow             |   | 1  | 1  | 13 |
| K | Well Field          |   | 1  | 0  | 11 |
|   |                     |   | 13 | 3  | 6  |


165   James Wood                              GREEN (L.M.)

|   |                    |              | A. | R. | P. |
|---|--------------------|--------------|----|----|----|
| A | Meadow             | M            | 1  | 3  | 25 |
| B |                    | { 3. 0. 31. } |    |    |    |
| C | Well Field         | { 1. 1. 35. } | 4 | 2  | 26 |
| D | Lee Shore          |              | 1  | 2  | 10 |
| E | One half of Lee    | M            | 1  | 3  | 29 |
| F | Upper Bank         |              | 3  | 0  | 14 |
| G | ½ Backstone Intake |              | 2  | 1  | 25 |
|   |                    |              | 15 | 2  | 9  |


In 1789   Joshua Radcliffe

166   Joseph Wood                             LONGHOUSE (L.M.)
      2 Dwelling Houses and Outhousing
      A good Dwelling House Barn and Shippen

|   |                   |   | A. | R. | P. |
|---|-------------------|---|----|----|----|
| A | Meadow            | M | 1  | 3  | 25 |
| B | Field next Meadow |   | 0  | 2  | 4  |
| C | Little Intake     |   | 0  | 2  | 30 |
| D | Long Intake       |   | 0  | 3  | 26 |
| E | Lowerend          |   | 0  | 3  | 15 |
| F | Old Field         |   | 1  | 1  | 12 |
| G | Slack Intakes     |   | 2  | 3  | 37 |
| H |                   |   |    |    |    |
|   |                   |   | 9  | 0  | 29 |


In 1789   John

167   Joshua Wood           Tenterhouse and Crompton Cottage (L.M.)
      One Dwelling House lately built being 2 Bays and 3 or 4 Bays of very
      old Building

|   |              |   | A. | R. | P. |
|---|--------------|---|----|----|----|
| A | Waste        |   | 1  | 0  | 37 |
| B | Bank         |   | 0  | 2  | 15 |
| C | Tenter Croft |   | 0  | 1  | 34 |
| D |              |   | 0  | 3  | 17 |
| E | Meadow       | M | 1  | 3  | 6  |
| F | Daubut Field |   | 0  | 2  | 6  |
|   |              |   | 5  | 1  | 35 |


In 1789   Benjamin Lawton

168   Executors John Wood                     (L.M.)

|   |           |   | A. | R. | P. |
|---|-----------|---|----|----|----|
| A | Little New |  | 1  | 0  | 28 |
| B | Rough     |   | 2  | 2  | 9  |
| C | Rough     |   | 2  | 0  | 8  |
| D |           |   |    |    |    |
|   |           |   | 5  | 3  | 5  |


In 1789   Benjamin Lawton

169   Executors John Wood                     COUSINS (L.M.)
      Several Bays of very old Housing
      A very old Thatched House & very bad Outhousing

|   |             |   | A. | R. | P. |
|---|-------------|---|----|----|----|
| A | Meadow      | M | 1  | 2  | 4  |
| B | Bank        |   | 1  | 2  | 35 |
| C | Upper Field |   | 1  | 0  | 37 |
| D | New Field   |   | 1  | 0  | 37 |
|   |             |   | 5  | 3  | 1  |


In 1789   John

170   Abraham Wood                            YEWTREE (L.M.)
      2 Houses and several Bays of Outhousing.  The Roof of ye Barn in bad
      repair.

|   |                   |              | A. | R. | P. |
|---|-------------------|--------------|----|----|----|
|   | Housing Fold &c   |              | 0  | 0  | 22 |
| A | Croft             |              | 0  | 0  | 21 |
| B | Spout Meadow      | M            | 1  | 0  | 9  |
| C | Cranberry Meadow  | M            | 1  | 3  | 35 |
| D | Great Meadow      | M            | 3  | 1  | 6  |
| E | Steelbutts        | M            | 1  | 0  | 31 |
| F | Lower Flatt       |              | 1  | 3  | 16 |
| G | Upper Flatt       |              | 1  | 3  | 3  |
| H | Bank stile        |              | 4  | 0  | 38 |
| I | Clay Field        |              | 2  | 1  | 24 |
| K | Faugh             |              | 1  | 3  | 33 |
| L | Hey Wood          |              | 0  | 2  | 30 |
| M | Lower old Intake  |              | 2  | 0  | 29 |
| N | Upper old Intake  |              | 1  | 2  | 28 |
| O | Hirst Field       | { 4. 1. 29. } | 6 | 0  | 4  |
| P |                   | { 1. 2. 15. } |    |    |    |
|   |                   |              | 30 | 2  | 9  |


                      Joseph and Joshua
171   Joseph Wrigley                          SADDLEWORTHFOLD (L.M.)
      2 Dwelling Houses with 2 Bays of Outhousing all built by Joshua
      Wrigley

|   |                 |   | A. | R. | P. |
|---|-----------------|---|----|----|----|
| A | Little Field    |   | 0  | 0  | 23 |
| B | Near Long Field |   | 1  | 2  | 8  |
| C | Farr Long Field |   | 2  | 1  | 13 |
| D | High Field      |   | 3  | 0  | 12 |
| E |                 |   |    |    |    |
| F | Pingot          | M | 2  | 0  | 33 |
| G | Hey             |   | 4  | 1  | 32 |
| H | Great Bent      | M | 2  | 3  | 3  |
| I | Crossy Lane     | M | 0  | 3  | 0  |
| K | 2 Little Crofts |   | 0  | 0  | 24 |
| L |                 |   |    |    |    |
|   |                 |   | 17 | 1  | 28 |

## 172 — George Wrigley — SADDLEWORTHFOLD (L.M.)

An old Dwelling House being 2 Bays with 3 Bays of old Thatched outhousing and very bad

|   |                 |   | A. | R. | P. |
|---|-----------------|---|----|----|----|
| A | Upper Field     |   | 2  | 0  | 15 |
| B | Near Lower Field|   | 2  | 0  | 0  |
| C | Farr Lower Field|   | 1  | 3  | 25 |
| D | Hanging Acker   |   | 4  | 1  | 30 |
| E | Intake          |   | 1  | 0  | 6  |
| F | Upper Meadow    | M | 2  | 2  | 16 |
| G | Upper Crossy Lane| M | 1 | 0  | 23 |
| H | Little Meadow   | M | 0  | 2  | 2  |
| I | Cromberry Knowl |   | 0  | 1  | 31 |
|   |                 |   | 16 | 0  | 28 |

In 1789 John Smith

## 173 — George Platt — DIGGLEE (LM.)

3 very indifferent Dwelling Houses wtih very old Thatched Outhousing being 7 Bays in all

|   |                      |   | A. | R. | P. |
|---|----------------------|---|----|----|----|
| A | ½ Meadow             | M | 0  | 3  | 11 |
| B | Crofts               | M | 0  | 0  | 16 |
| C | Marshbottom          |   | 2  | 1  | 1  |
| D | Hey Marsh            | M | 3  | 3  | 3  |
| E | Clough               |   | 0  | 2  | 33 |
| F | Clough head          |   | 1  | 0  | 25 |
| G | ½ Rough Broad Meadow |   | 2  | 1  | 13 |
| H | Whore Stones         |   | 4  | 0  | 37 |
| I | Shaw Marsh           |   | 4  | 0  | 0  |
| K | Shaw Lee             | M | 3  | 3  | 6  |
| L | Nun Ing              |   | 2  | 3  | 29 |
| M | ¼ Broad Meadow       |   | 0  | 3  | 30 |
|   | In the Mean Fields   |   | 10 | 1  | 14 |
|   |                      |   | 37 | 1  | 18 |

## 174 — John Wrigley — MIDGREAVE (L.M.)

A good Dwelling House and Outhousing

|   |                   |   | A. | R. | P. |
|---|-------------------|---|----|----|----|
|   | Housing Fold &c   |   | 0  | 0  | 28 |
| A | Field             | M | 2  | 3  | 8  |
| B | Middlemost Meadow | M | 1  | 0  | 23 |
| C | Furthermost Meadow| M | 1  | 3  | 5  |
| D | Clod              |   | 0  | 0  | 31 |
| E | Further Field     |   | 3  | 1  | 10 |
| F | Longlands         |   | 2  | 0  | 21 |
| G H | Stony Fields {1. 1. 4.} {1. 2. 31.} |   | 2 | 3 | 35 |
| I | Marled earth      |   | 1  | 3  | 11 |
| K | Hey               |   | 8  | 1  | 2  |
| L | Limed             |   | 2  | 0  | 8  |
| M | Milking Knowl     | M | 0  | 3  | 9  |
| N | Waste             |   | 0  | 0  | 36 |
| O | Faugh             |   | 0  | 3  | 7  |
| P | Back'oth House    |   | 0  | 2  | 27 |
|   |                   |   | 29 | 0  | 31 |

## 174 — John Smith — WHARMTON DOLE

In 1789 Timothy

## 175 — Robert Winterbottom — (S.M.)

No Housing

|   |            | A. | R. | P. |
|---|------------|----|----|----|
| A | New Intake | 1  | 3  | 35 |

## 176 — Elias Broadbent — (L.M.)

A. One good Dwelling House adjoining to his Brother's Barn erected on a Square piece of Land 18 yards each way being 324 Square Yards part of his Brothers Tenement equal to 10 perches & 7 $\frac{1}{10}$ of a perch

The above Built in a Field called Roughend in his Brother James's Tenement

## 177 — James Wrigley — Wharmtonbrow Cottage (S.M.)

One Bay of Building lately rebuilt by the said James Wrigley

|   |                 | A. | R. | P. |
|---|-----------------|----|----|----|
| A | Cottage and Croft | 0 | 2 | 0 |

## 178 — James Wood — Green for a Housestead (L.M.)

2 Bays of new Building for a Dwelling House

In 1789 Mr. John Bower

## 179 — Henry Lees — for ye Intakes that belong'd Hollins (L.M.)

No Housing

|   |              | A. | R. | P. |
|---|--------------|----|----|----|
| A | Little Meadow| 0  | 1  | 25 |
| B | New Intake   | 2  | 2  | 7  |
| C | Bent         | 2  | 0  | 18 |
| D | Highmost     | 0  | 3  | 28 |
| E | Old Intake   | 1  | 1  | 6  |
|   |              | 7  | 1  | 4  |

## 180 — Jonathan Bradbury — STONE DELF

|   | A. | R. | P. |
|---|----|----|----|
| A | 26 | 1  | 0  |

## 181 — James Rhodes — for a Cottage on Harrop edge (L.M.)

|                   | A. | R. | P. |
|-------------------|----|----|----|
| Cottage and Croft | 0  | 0  | 16 |

## 182 — Mr. James Buckley — a Housestead (L.M.)

In 1789 Executors

## 183 — Mr. John Whitehead — for Delf Bridge Green (L.M.)

## 184 — Benjamin Brierley — Dobcross for a Housestead (L.M.)

## 185 — John Harrop — Dobcross for Kiln Ditch & Nook (L.M.)

|   |            | A. | R. | P. |
|---|------------|----|----|----|
| A | Nook       | 0  | 0  | 12 |
| B | Kiln Ditch | 0  | 1  | 16 |
|   |            | 0  | 1  | 28 |

In 1789 Mr. Samuel Heginbottom

## 186 — Francis Platt — Dobcross Mill Intake (L.M.)

## 187 — James Lees — Building on WHARMTON

## 187 — Mr. Joseph Buckley — 3 Acres HIGH MOOR (Q.M.)

## 188 — Benjamin Lawtons New Inclosure

## 189 — A Teazing Mill

## 190 — Jas. Lees — a Cottage near Upper Mill

## 191 — Benjamin Lawton — part of his Dwellinghouse at Dobcross

## 192 — Mr. John Harrop Junior & Joseph Lawton — Delf Sand Mine on Harropedge

# THE TOTAL SUMS OF THE SEVERAL TENEMENTS

| | | | A. | R. | P. |
|---|---|---|---|---|---|
| 1 | Alexander Scholefield | Wellihole | 26 | 2 | 0 |
| 2 | | Ash hey | | | |
| 3 | Executors Thomas Bradbury | Cott: & Com: | 3 | 0 | 34 |
| 4 | Jno. Bentley | Boarshurst & Saddleworth fold | 22 | 2 | 34 |
| 5 | John Bentley | Lowerhouse | 14 | 1 | 36 |
| 6 | John Bentley | Bentleys | 7 | 2 | 38 |
| 7 | James Bentley | Upperhouse | 5 | 1 | 9 |
| 8 | Michl. Bottomley | Gravemakers and Dial field | 3 | 2 | 38 |
| 9 | John Bradbury | Minsey Cott: & Croft | 0 | 3 | 27 |
| 10 | John Bradbury | Runninghill | 7 | 1 | 15 |
| 11 | Executors Thomas Bradbury | Greenfield | 37 | 2 | 12 |
| 12 | Assignes James Ridgeway | Greenfield | 37 | 3 | 20 |
| 13 | Executors Robt. B. & J.B. | Top of Green | 1 | 2 | 34 |
| 14 | Thomas Bradbury | Fairbanks | 18 | 1 | 11 |
| 15 | Assignes John Bradbury | Abels | 3 | 2 | 4 |
| 16 | Jno. Bradbury | Peters & Slades | 109 | 3 | 19 |
| 17 | Jas. Bradbury | Digglee | 8 | 0 | 29 |
| 18 | Jno. Bradbury | Digglee | 7 | 2 | 24 |
| 19 | Thomas Bradbury | Digglee | 24 | 3 | 30 |
| 20 | James Broadbent | Digglee | 20 | 3 | 26 |
| 21 | Jno. Smith | | 0 | 0 | 9 |
| 22 | Executors Hen: Broadbent | Road & Knottylane Cott: | 2 | 2 | 39 |
| 23 | James Broadbent | Clerk | 28 | 0 | 2 |
| 24 | Robt. Broadbent | Green | 8 | 0 | 0 |
| 25 | Executors James Broadbent | Green | 14 | 1 | 14 |
| 26 | Geo: Broadbent's Executors | Harrup | 37 | 2 | 39 |
| 27 | John Broadbent | Marslands | 10 | 1 | 32 |
| 28 | James Broadbent | Carrhead | 34 | 2 | 12 |
| 29 | James Broadbent | Lee and Warth | 9 | 0 | 3 |
| 30 | George Buckley | Lanehead | 34 | 0 | 34 |
| 31 | William Buckley | Stones | 43 | 2 | 29 |
| 32 | | Burntedgebent | 34 | 3 | 34 |
| 33 | Assignes Jas. Buckley | Greenfield & Dovestone | 152 | 2 | 11 |
| 34 | John Buckley | Barn | 8 | 3 | 38 |
| 35 | John Buckley | Pinfold | 9 | 1 | 37 |
| 36 | Jas. Buckley | Brownhill | 33 | 1 | 22 |
| 37 | James Buckley | Gatehead | 47 | 3 | 33 |
| 38 | Edmd. Buckley | Lidyate | 13 | 0 | 25 |
| 39 | Mr. Jas. Lawton | Frenches Mill | 1 | 2 | 6 |
| 40 | Edmd. Buckley | Newhouses | 15 | 3 | 17 |
| 41 | Tenants of Back o th lee (what is inclos'd) | | 221 | 0 | 0 |
| 42 | Mr. Jos: Buckley | Stonebreaks | 12 | 3 | 15 |
| 43 | Nathl. Broadbent | Runninghill | 7 | 2 | 29 |
| 44 | Isaac Clegg | Lukefields | 10 | 1 | 27 |
| 45 | | Corn Mills | | | |
| 46 | Peter Bradbury | Brownhill | 1 | 2 | 36 |
| 47 | George Dronsfield | Poundstone | 8 | 2 | 5 |
| 48 | | Diggle Delph | | | |
| 49 | | Coalmine | | | |
| 50 | Peter Greave | Knowltop | 13 | 3 | 32 |
| 51 | Gartside's Executors | Heathfields | 8 | 3 | 26 |
| 52 | William Radcliffe | Housestead in Peter Greave's Farm | | | |
| 53 | Mr. Jas. Harropp | Ladcastle | 1 | 1 | 36 |
| 54 | Executors Jas. Harropp | Tamewater | 43 | 3 | 39 |
| 55 | Jno. Buckley | Hollins | 9 | 2 | 26 |
| 56 | Jas. Harropp | Shaws | 12 | 0 | 21 |
| 57 | William Hawkyard | Cloughbottom | 19 | 2 | 35 |
| 58 | John Hazelgreave | Wallhill | 19 | 2 | 21 |
| 59 | Widow Bradbury | new Barn at Runninghill | 8 | 0 | 16 |
| 60 | Executors Jas. Mallalieu | Dungebooth &c | 8 | 0 | 16 |
| 61 | | | | | |
| 62 | Executors Jas. Mallalieu | Ladcastle | 3 | 0 | 39 |
| 63 | Robt: Holden | Cloughbottom | 20 | 1 | 19 |
| 64 | Paul Jas. Holden | David's Smithy | 9 | 1 | 24 |
| 65 | Nathl. Holden | David's Smithy | 9 | 3 | 22 |
| 66 | | | | | |
| 67 | Assignes Thomas Kenworthy | Roundhill | 9 | 0 | 37 |
| 68 | Assignes John Kenworthy | Hobhole | 3 | 3 | 16 |
| 69 | William Kenworthy | Fulling Mill | 1 | 2 | 16 |
| 70 | William Kenworthy | near Quick | 22 | 1 | 12 |
| 71 | William Kenworthy | Quick or Loadhills | 16 | 2 | 1 |
| 72 | Jonathan Lawton | | 0 | 0 | 27 |
| 73 | Mr. Jos. Lawton | Halls | 43 | 2 | 9 |
| 74 | Jos: Lawton | Woodlane Cott: | 0 | 1 | 11 |
| 75 | Jos: & Ben: Lawton | Dobcross | 2 | 3 | 32 |
| 76 | Henry Buckley | Frenches | 15 | 0 | 18 |
| 77 | John Lees | Banktop | 4 | 3 | 14 |
| 78 | John Lees | High Moor | 22 | 0 | 35 |
| 79 | John Lees | High Moor | 2 | 1 | 30 |
| 80 | John Lees | Shelderslow | 6 | 3 | 30 |
| 81 | Jas. Lees | Thurstoneclough | 34 | 1 | 39 |
| 82 | Jonathan Lees | part of Knarr | 18 | 0 | 34 |
| 83 | | | | | |
| 84 | Executors Jas. Mallalieu | Wharmtonbank | 8 | 2 | 6 |
| 85 | George Mallalieu | Whickins | 29 | 0 | 10 |
| 86 | | | | | |
| 87 | John Nield & Mr. Cors: Kenworthy | Quick | 54 | 3 | 30 |
| 88 | John Platt Executors | Shaws Lanehead | 19 | 2 | 38 |
| 89 | Jas. Platt | Hollins | 7 | 2 | 23 |
| 90 | John Platt's Executors | Butterworths | 13 | 1 | 6 |
| 91 | Executors George Platt | Primrosehill | 11 | 0 | 15 |
| 92 | Thomas Platt & William Kenworthy | Woolroad | 17 | 2 | 10 |
| 93 | Thomas Platt | Woolroad | 7 | 3 | 17 |
| 94 | Edmd. Platt | Plattlane | 6 | 3 | 32 |
| 95 | Edmd. Platt | Hollingreave | 11 | 1 | 18 |
| 96 | George Shaw | Pinfold Hey | 31 | 2 | 32 |
| 97 | James Ratcliff | Cott: | | | |
| 98 | Alex: Radcliffe | Wooleys | 12 | 0 | 38 |

| No. | Name | Place | A. | R. | P. |
|---|---|---|---|---|---|
| 99 | Alex: Ratcliffe | Balgreave | 27 | 2 | 36 |
| 100 | William Radcliffe | Cross | 6 | 2 | 10 |
| 101 | William & Joshua Radcliffe | Lanehouse | 1 | 1 | 32 |
| 102 | Joshua Radcliffe | Birches | 9 | 1 | 35 |
| 103 | John Radcliffe | Saddleworthfold | 20 | 0 | 6 |
| 104 | John & William Radcliffe | Cross | 24 | 3 | 33 |
| 105 | Jere: Rhodes & M.B. | Lee Cross | 8 | 0 | 38 |
| 106 | John Rhodes | Green | 28 | 2 | 10 |
| 107 | John Rhodes Executors | Acker | 9 | 1 | 35 |
| 108 | Abraham Rhodes | Deanhead | 35 | 1 | 25 |
| 109 | Abraham Rhodes | part of Knights Pastures | 15 | 2 | 20 |
| 110 | James Rhodes | Intake | 14 | 2 | 8 |
| 111 | James Rhodes | Knowl | 16 | 3 | 18 |
| 112 | Thomas Rhodes Executors | Sunfield | 29 | 0 | 14 |
| 113 | Executors Thomas Rhodes | Shaws or Olivers | 12 | 0 | 20 |
| 114 | Thomas Rhodes Executors | Common | 14 | 0 | 25 |
| 115 | James Rhodes | Thornses | 27 | 1 | 21 |
| 116 | John Lees | Pastures | 8 | 3 | 33 |
| 117 | Jacob Savil | Thorps | 20 | 1 | 29 |
| 118 | Isaac Savil | Cabbin | 17 | 1 | 38 |
| 119 | James Savil | Robuckloe | 26 | 3 | 36 |
| 120 | John Savil | Robuckloe | 9 | 2 | 31 |
| 121 | Abraham Savil | Dicksons & Garlicks | 0 | 0 | 0 |
| 122 | James Scholefield | Hollingreave | 12 | 0 | 31 |
| 123 | John Scholefield | Hollingreave | 12 | 0 | 16 |
| 124 | Joshua Platt | Lanehead | 19 | 0 | 23 |
| 125 | Alex: Scholefield | Gibbs | 22 | 0 | 5 |
| 126 | Robert Scholefield | Brow or Mow Walls | 12 | 2 | 6 |
| 127 | Scholefield Buckley & Bottomley | Tunsd. Clough | 7 | 1 | 30 |
| 128 | Joseph Scholefield | Arthurs | 14 | 3 | 3 |
| 129 | Michael Shaw | Rie top | 17 | 1 | 25 |
| 130 | Robert Andrew | Knowltop | 6 | 1 | 27 |
| 131 | John Sikes | Ambroses | 3 | 1 | 27 |
| 132 | Shaws Executors | Barn | 24 | 2 | 24 |
| 133 | Executors Jas. Buckley | Tamewater | 33 | 1 | 3 |
| 134 | Jas. Shaw | Hollins | 11 | 0 | 10 |
| 135 | George Shaw | Hawkyard | 29 | 0 | 9 |
| 136 | William Shaw | Lowerhouse | 8 | 0 | 17 |
| 137 | Elizabeth Shaw | Boarshurst | 10 | 0 | 17 |
| 138 | Samuel Hegingbottom | Dobcross Mill | 8 | 2 | 36 |
| 139 | Michael Bottomley | Sikes Cottage | 0 | 2 | 1 |
| 140 | Executors Robert Scholefield | Lane head | 17 | 3 | 21 |
| 141 | Mrs. Whitehead | Cottage | 0 | 0 | 0 |
| 142 | Mr. Harrop & Buckleys | | 22 | 2 | 5 |
| 143 | Executors Robert Walker & Scholefield | Whitelee | 8 | 3 | 28 |
| 144 | Martha Whewal | Hollingreave | 34 | 2 | 27 |
| 145 | Mrs. Whitehead & Ratcliffe Whitehead | Shawhall  61. 2. 39 } 40. 1. 6 } | 102 | 0 | 5 |
| 146 | John Winterbottom | Shawhouses and Deanshaw banks | 15 | 0 | 1 |
| 147 | Executors Timo. Whitehead | Shawhouses | 25 | 0 | 36 |
| 148 | James Whitehed | Upper Mill | 25 | 2 | 11 |
| 149 | Henry Whitehead | Woods | 21 | 1 | 15 |
| 150 | Henry Whitehead | Moor Green | 2 | 2 | 20 |

| No. | Name | Place | A. | R. | P. |
|---|---|---|---|---|---|
| 151 | John Whitehead | Brownknotthill | 11 | 1 | 15 |
| 152 | Mr. Ralph Whitehead Executors | Lidyate | 18 | 3 | 32 |
| 153 | Edmd. Whitehead Executors | Upper Lidyate | 16 | 0 | 15 |
| 154 | Jas. Winterbottom | Knarr | 45 | 1 | 2 |
| 155 | John Winterbottom | Noonsun | 4 | 1 | 26 |
| 156 | Thos. Winterbottom & Wm. Newton | Quick | 38 | 0 | 25 |
| 157 | Danl. Winterbottom | Shelderslow | 0 | 1 | 24 |
| 158 | Daniel Winterbottom | Pastures & Stonebreaks | 12 | 1 | 17 |
| 159 | Robt. Winterbottom | Burntedge | 13 | 0 | 20 |
| 160 | Jonathan Lees | 4 Acres | 8 | 1 | 0 |
| 161 | John Winterbottom | Strines | 14 | 0 | 31 |
| 162 | Executors John Wood | Wharmtonside | 4 | 0 | 14 |
| 163 | Executors Timo. Wood | Cottages | 4 | 0 | 15 |
| 164 | David Wood | Runninghill | 13 | 3 | 6 |
| 165 | James Wood | Green | 15 | 2 | 9 |
| 166 | Joseph Wood | Longhouse | 9 | 0 | 29 |
| 167 | Joshua Wood | Tenterhouse & Crompton Cott: | 5 | 1 | 35 |
| 168 | Executors John Wood | | 5 | 3 | 5 |
| 169 | Executors John Wood | Cousins | 5 | 3 | 1 |
| 170 | Abraham Wood | Yewtree | 30 | 2 | 1 |
| 171 | George Wrigley | Saddleworthfold | 17 | 1 | 28 |
| 172 | Joseph Wrigley | Saddleworthfold | 16 | 0 | 28 |
| 173 | George Platt | Digglee | 37 | 1 | 18 |
| 174 | John Wrigley | Midgreave | 29 | 0 | 31 |
| 175 | Robert Winterbottom | | 1 | 3 | 35 |
| 176 | Elias Broadbent | | 0 | 0 | 0 |
| 177 | James Wrigley | Wharmtonbrow Cott: | 0 | 2 | 0 |
| 178 | Jas. Wood | Green a Housestead | 0 | 0 | 0 |
| 179 | Henry Lees | Hollins Intak's | 7 | 1 | 4 |
| 180 | Jonathan Bradbury | Stone Delf | 0 | 0 | 0 |
| 181 | James Rhodes | a Cottage on Harropedge | 0 | 0 | 16 |
| 182 | Mr. James Buckley | a Housestead | | | |
| 183 | Mr. Jno. Whitehead | Delf Bridge Green | | | |
| 184 | Benjamin Brierley | Dobcross a Housestead | | | |
| 185 | John Harrop | Nook (Kiln Ditch is Measured to Dobcross Mill) | 0 | 12 | 0 |
| 186 | Francis Platt | Dobcross Mill Intake was also Measured with the Mill | | | |
| 187 | Mr. Joseph Buckley | 3 Acres on High Moor | 3 | 0 | 0 |
| 188 | James Lees | Building upon Wharmton | | | |
| | | The enclosure upon Wharmton | | | |
| | | New Inclosures on Wharmton | 14 | 0 | 0 |
| | | Total | 3108 | 3 | 2 |

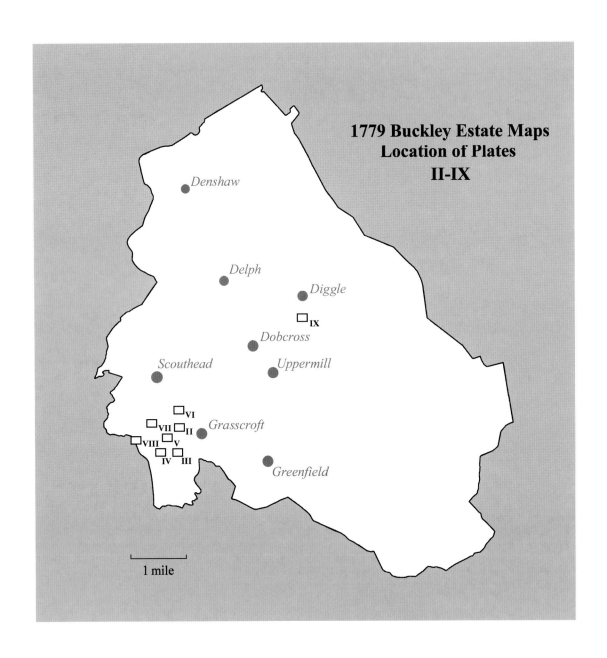

1779 Buckley Estate Maps
Location of Plates
II-IX

Denshaw

Delph

Diggle

IX

Dobcross

Scouthead

Uppermill

VI

VII II

Grasscroft

VIII V

IV III

Greenfield

1 mile

# ESTATES IN THE SEVERAL COUNTIES OF YORK AND LANCASTER AND CHESTER BELONGING TO JOHN BUCKLEY ESQ., 1779

| | |
|---|---|
| *Location:* | Greater Manchester County Record Office (with Manchester Archives), GB127.BR 912.427 W5[1] |
| *Date of Compilation of Maps:* | 1779 |
| *Surveyor:* | Ralph Wood |
| *Material:* | Leather bound volume written on parchment. |
| *Size of Book:* | 5" x 5¾" |
| *Scale of Original:* | 1" : 6 Chains (13⅓" : 1 mile) |
| *Scale of Reproduction:* | Varies with each map |

These thirteen maps and their respective keys are all drawn on vellum and bound up as an attractive leather covered volume (see Figure 3). It is significant that the title is contained in a rococo cartouche and every map is presented in a decorative manner with its own title elaborated with fine penmanship. This little volume of maps seems to fit easily into that category of maps that celebrate possession and were often to be found on the library shelves of gentlemen, or aspiring gentlemen. However the decorative emphasis should not blind us to the fact that these maps are the product of accurate survey and all are drawn at the same scale, although north is not always at the top of the map. John Buckley's bookplate on the front inside cover is in the form of an elaborately executed Coat of Arms and bears witness to his perceived status and pedigree. It is noteworthy that in the key to each map the acreage is described in both Cheshire and Lancashire acres as well as Statute Measure.[2]

John Buckley, although an absentee landlord, was a descendant of perhaps the most important Saddleworth family of the seventeenth century. Originally tenants of the Booths of Dunham Massey, they rose rapidly in wealth and importance during the early seventeenth century, acquiring their freeholder status by buying a large tract of newly enclosed commons on Quick Moor in 1629.[3] Richard Buckley, who had made this addition to the family properties at Grotton and Grottonhead, was thus fully justified in describing himself as 'yeoman of Grottonhead'. Six years later, in 1635, his son, John Buckley was one of the prime movers in the purchase by the tenants of Sir George Booth's leasehold farms in Saddleworth; John Buckley himself acquiring the freehold of Grotton and Grottonhead farms in this way.[4] John Buckley also appears to have been responsible for building Grotton Hall in the 1650s. However, his father Richard, still alive in 1635, was described as occupying 'all that capital messuage at Grottonhead' indicating that the family already had an important house there before the 1650s.

---

[1] Deposited by Messrs Slater Heelis and Co., 28th November 1905.

[2] A Cheshire Acre equals 10,240 square yards. Apparently this unit of measure continued in use well into the nineteenth century. R. Holland, *Glossary of Words Used in the County of Cheshire,* London, English Dialect Society, 1886, pp. 3 and 291. A Lancashire Acre equals 7,840 square yards. See E.H. Smith, 'Lancashire Long Measure' *Transactions of the Historic Society of Lancashire and Cheshire,* Vol. CX for 1958, Liverpool, Historic Society of Lancashire and Cheshire, 1959, pp. 1-14.

[3] Deed of Gift from Richard Buckley to his son, Edmund, 12th February 1632, Newhouses Deeds, M/NH 1, SMA.

[4] Copy of deed, Julian Hunt Collection. H/JH/CAB/1/29, SHS.

Figure 3.  John Buckley's Book of Estate Maps

John Buckley, the son, reputedly a Roundhead during the Civil War, added to the family possessions by purchasing a half of the farm at Hollingreave.[5] This he conveyed to his son, another John, in 1662, who purchased the other half in 1707.[6] He further added to the family estates by acquiring Crawshawbent and Thornlee in 1713.[7]

A third John Buckley succeeded to the estate on the death of this father in 1723 and, by the time of his death in 1738, had further augmented the family possessions, both within and beyond Saddleworth. His properties are listed in his will and include all the Saddleworth farms in the 1779 survey as well as those in Denton, Derker and Pitbank. By the time of his death he was styled gentleman and, befitting his gentry status, was responsible for erecting a gallery in the old Saddleworth church in 1728 for his own use and that of his family. In his will he left a bequest of 40 shillings a year, for ever, to the poor of Saddleworth 'to be laid out in oatmeal on Christmas Day at Grottonhead'.[8] He and his widow Katherine were the last of their line to live at Grottonhead and by the time of the death of Katherine, in 1750, his son Richard Buckley had moved to Stockport. Richard died there in 1764 and was followed by his son, the John Buckley, Esquire, responsible for the survey. He was then a minor.

John came of age and entered into his inheritance in 1780, and perhaps the survey was linked to this event. He was baptised at Nottingham, the home of his mother's family

[5] Raines MSS., Vol. 2, p. 62, Chetham's Library, Manchester and Deed copied by the Enclosure Commissioner, c.1810, H/EA 16. p. 55, SHS.

[6] *Deeds copied by the Enclosure Commissioner,* c.1810, H/EA 16, p. 55, SHS.

[7] *loc. cit.* p. 54. Also, O 447 682, West Riding Registry of Deeds, WYAS (Wakefield).

[8] Will of John Buckley of Grottonhead, gentleman, 1740, WCW Supra, Lancashire County Record Office, Preston.

in 1759, entered Manchester Grammar School in 1772 and had settled at Chester by 1783 when he mortgaged his estate for £2200.[9] In 1788, when part of his farm at Crawshawbent was purchased to build Lydgate church, he was a Lieutenant in 'His Majestie's Royal Regiment of Horse Guards.'[10] He married Frances Fosbrooke, daughter and heiress of Leonard Fosbrooke, Esq., of Shardlow, Derbyshire, in 1793 at Chester and died in 1805.[11]

He was succeeded by his son Richard Fosbrooke Buckley of whom Canon Raines wrote in 1835, 'Richard Buckley Esq., of Chester is the owner of the estate, and the representative of the family and yearly visits the seat of his ancestors during the shooting season.'[12] The family's long connections with Saddleworth ended in 1844 when Richard Buckley disposed of the remaining family estates to Edmund Buckley of Manchester, the wealthy manufacturer and canal carrier and son of the Lydgate publican responsible for building the White Hart Inn.[13]

Figure 4. John Buckley's Bookplate

[9] The Julian Hunt Collection, H/JH/40, SHS.

[10] C.E. Higson, *The Buckleys of Grottonhead in Saddleworth*, Oldham, 1930, p. 11.

[11] *ibid.* p. 12.

[12] Raines MSS., Vol. 2, p. 62, Chetham's Library, Manchester.

[13] 'Old Saddleworth, Grottonhead', *Saddleworth Historical Society Bulletin*, Vol. 15, No. 1, Spring 1985, p. 15, quoting H/JH/35, SHS.

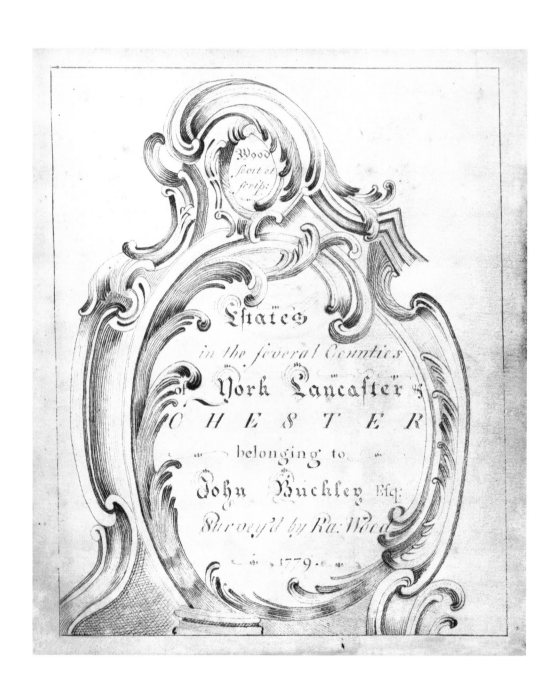

Wood
feat et
scrip:

Estates
in the several Counties
of York Lancaster &
CHESTER
belonging to
John Buckley Esq:
Survey'd by Ra: Wood
1779

Plate I

# I N D E X

| No of Map | Names of Tenements | Parish where situated | Statute | | | Lancashire | | | Cheshire | | |
|---|---|---|---|---|---|---|---|---|---|---|---|
| 1 | Grottenhead | Saddleworth | 74 | 3 | 09 | 46 | 0 | 30 | 35 | 1 | 18 |
| 2 | Crofhawbent | D° | 29 | 3 | 16 | 18 | 1 | 26 | 14 | 0 | 18 |
| 3 | Coverhill | D° | 7 | 0 | 04 | 4 | 1 | 13 | 3 | 1 | 11 |
| 4 | Grotten | D° | 24 | 2 | 05 | 15 | 0 | 22 | 11 | 2 | 14 |
| 5 | Loadhill Platting | D° | 15 | 3 | 02 | 9 | 2 | 35 | 7 | 1 | 32 |
| 6 | Claytons | D° | 30 | 2 | 17 | 18 | 3 | 17 | 14 | 1 | 32 |
| 7 | Thornlee | D° | 11 | 2 | 23 | 7 | 0 | 27 | 5 | 2 | 01 |
| 8 | Hollingrave | D° | 27 | 0 | 16 | 16 | 2 | 36 | 12 | 3 | 11 |
| 9 | Dirker | Oldham | 43 | 3 | 28 | 27 | 0 | 15 | 20 | 3 | 02 |
| 10 | Pitbank | D° | 21 | 1 | 32 | 13 | 0 | 37 | 10 | 0 | 24 |
| 11 | Croftend | Ashton | 34 | 3 | 28 | 21 | 2 | 05 | 16 | 2 | 01 |
| 12 | Robert Fidler | Denton Township | 32 | 2 | 19 | 20 | 0 | 15 | 15 | 1 | 28 |
| 13 | John Cocker | Mottram | 104 | 2 | 30 | 64 | 2 | 27 | 49 | 1 | 36 |

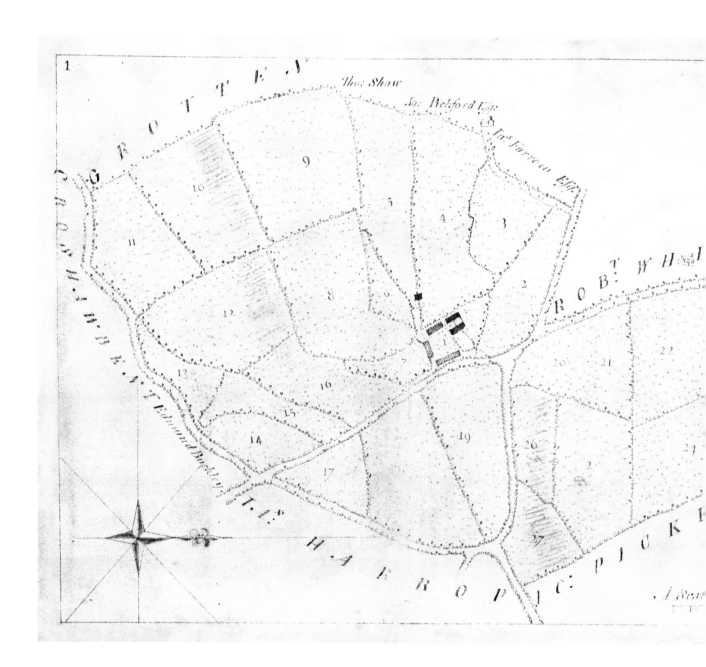

1

GROTT<sup>E</sup> N

Tho: Shaw

Jo: Pickford Esq.

Jas Jarre.. Esq.

9

10

5

4

3

11

R O B.T W H..

8

6

2

12

7

1

22

13

15

16

20 21

14

17

19

26

2

24

27

C: PICK..

H A R O P

A Sc..

Plate II

# S. A D D L E W O R T H

## Grottenhead

| | | Statute |||| Lanc of |||| Chesh |||| Observations |
|---|---|---|---|---|---|---|---|---|---|---|---|---|---|
| | | a | r | p | | a | r | p | | a | r | p | |
| 1 | House Yards Gardens Orchards | 1 | 1 | 08 | | 0 | 3 | 08 | | 0 | 2 | 19 | 1 . 2 . 29 |
| 2 | Old Intake Back | 1 | 3 | 36 | | 1 | 0 | 35 | | 0 | 3 | 29 | 1 . 0 . 19 |
| 3 | Kilnhill | 1 | 3 | 27 | | 1 | 0 | 29 | | 0 | 3 | 25 | 3 . 0 . 04 |
| 4 | Meadow below the house | 3 | 3 | 05 | | 2 | 1 | 13 | | 1 | 3 | 10 | 3 . 2 . 15 |
| 5 | Bent | 3 | 0 | 08 | | 1 | 3 | 21 | | 1 | 1 | 31 | 3 . 3 . 19 |
| 6 | Bent Meadow | 0 | 2 | 19 | | 0 | 1 | 21 | | 0 | 1 | 06 | 4 . 3 . 17 |
| 7 | Stack yard | 0 | 2 | 28 | | 0 | 1 | 28 | | 0 | 1 | 11 | 3 . 0 . 30 |
| 8 | High field | 3 | 3 | 19 | | 2 | 1 | 22 | | 1 | 3 | 12 | 6 . 0 . 02 |
| 9 | Rye Reed | 4 | 3 | 17 | | 3 | 0 | 00 | | 2 | 1 | 07 | 1 . 1 . 08 |
| 10 | Higher Cowhey bank | 3 | 1 | 33 | | 2 | 0 | 21 | | 1 | 2 | 21 | |
| 11 | Lower Dº | 3 | 0 | 05 | | 1 | 3 | 19 | | 1 | 1 | 29 | |
| 12 | Far meadow field | 3 | 2 | 15 | | 2 | 0 | 35 | | 1 | 2 | 24 | |
| 13 | Widow field Bottam | 0 | 3 | 34 | | 0 | 2 | 15 | | 0 | 1 | 33 | |
| 14 | Lower wams field | 1 | 1 | 06 | | 0 | 3 | 07 | | 0 | 2 | 17 | 3 . 1 . 08 |
| 15 | Little wams meadow | 1 | 1 | 33 | | 0 | 3 | 23 | | 0 | 2 | 30 | 4 . 2 . 05 |
| 16 | Near widow field | 2 | 1 | 13 | | 1 | 1 | 30 | | 1 | 0 | 16 | 4 . 0 . 04 |
| 17 | Higher wams field | 1 | 0 | 30 | | 0 | 2 | 37 | | 0 | 2 | 10 | 0 . 1 . 19 |
| 18 | Great wams meadow | 3 | 3 | 00 | | 2 | 1 | 10 | | 1 | 3 | 08 | 1 . 3 . 33 |
| 19 | Long Intake | 3 | 0 | 04 | | 1 | 3 | 18 | | 1 | 1 | 29 | 0 . 2 . 12 |
| 20 | Near Gate intake | 1 | 2 | 29 | | 1 | 0 | 00 | | 0 | 3 | 06 | |
| 21 | Fur Dº | 1 | 1 | 19 | | 0 | 3 | 15 | | 0 | 2 | 23 | 3 . 0 . 24 |
| 22 | Rovings | 3 | 0 | 04 | | 1 | 3 | 18 | | 1 | 1 | 29 | 1 . 3 . 12 |
| 23 | The rough | 4 | 2 | 16 | | 2 | 3 | 16 | | 2 | 0 | 29 | 1 . 1 . 26 |
| 24 | Dicky intake | 3 | 2 | 15 | | 2 | 0 | 36 | | 1 | 2 | 33 | 1 . 2 . 05 |
| 25 | Even intake | 3 | 1 | 09 | | 2 | 0 | 07 | | 1 | 2 | 11 | 0 . 2 . 19 |
| 26 | Near Brow intake | 1 | 1 | 30 | | 0 | 3 | 26 | | 0 | 2 | 32 | 1 . 1 . 38 |
| 27 | Fur Dº | 1 | 2 | 05 | | 0 | 3 | 31 | | 0 | 2 | 36 | |
| a28 | Pole meadow | 2 | 0 | 12 | | 1 | 1 | 06 | | 0 | 3 | 38 | See Map Nº 2 |
| a29 | Great meadow | 4 | 0 | 24 | | 2 | 2 | 12 | | 1 | 3 | 32 | See Map Nº 4 |
| a30 | Dagger | 0 | 2 | 12 | | 0 | 1 | 18 | | 0 | 1 | 04 | Dº |
| a31 | Clough meadow | 1 | 1 | 08 | | 0 | 3 | 07 | | 0 | 2 | 18 | Dº |
| | Total | 74 | 3 | 09 | | 46 | 0 | 30 | | 35 | 1 | 18 | |

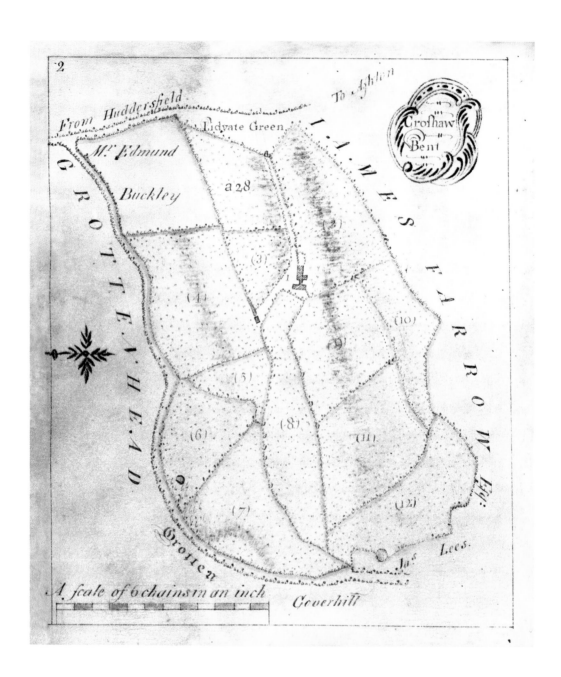

2

From Huddersfield

To Ashton

Lidyate Green

Mr Edmund

Buckley

Croshaw Bent

a 28

(3)

(4)

(9)

(10)

(5)

(8)

(6)

(11)

(7)

(12)

Jas Lees

A scale of 6 chains in an inch

Groreu

Goverhill

G R O T T E H E A D

I. d. WES FARROW Esq.

Plate III

# S A D D L E W O R T H

| Nº | Croshawbent — John Woolley | Statute | | | Lancash. | | | Chesh. | | | Observations |
|----|----------------------------|---|---|---|---|---|---|---|---|---|---|
| | | a | r | p | a | r | p | a | r | p | |
| 1 | House Barn Fold Lane &c | 0 | 2 | 12 | 0 | 1 | 17 | 0 | 1 | 03 | |
| 2 | Highfield | 3 | 2 | 11 | 2 | 0 | 32 | 1 | 2 | 30 | |
| 3 | Little meadow | 1 | 0 | 13 | 0 | 2 | 27 | 0 | 2 | 02 | |
| 4 | Slackfield | 4 | 0 | 13 | 2 | 2 | 03 | 1 | 3 | 29 | .. |
| 5 | Half acre | 0 | 3 | 20 | 0 | 2 | 10 | 0 | 1 | 29 | |
| 6 | Clod meadow | 2 | 0 | 24 | 1 | 1 | 12 | 1 | 0 | 03 | |
| 7 | Clodfield | 3 | 1 | 08 | 2 | 0 | 06 | 1 | 2 | 09 | |
| 8 | Longmeadow | 2 | 3 | 38 | 1 | 3 | 15 | 1 | 1 | 26 | |
| 9 | Croft | 2 | 2 | 36 | 1 | 2 | 29 | 1 | 1 | 06 | |
| 10 | Backmeadow | 1 | 3 | 00 | 1 | 0 | 12 | 0 | 3 | 12 | |
| 11 | Old limed | 3 | 1 | 27 | 2 | 0 | 17 | 1 | 2 | 19 | |
| 12 | Bent | 3 | 1 | 08 | 2 | 0 | 06 | 1 | 2 | 10 | |
| | Total | 29 | 3 | 16 | 18 | 1 | 26 | 14 | 0 | 18 | |

3

Coverhill
in
Saddleworth

GROTTEN.

Whit Lees

THO: SHAW.

A scale of 6 Chains in an inch

Plate IV

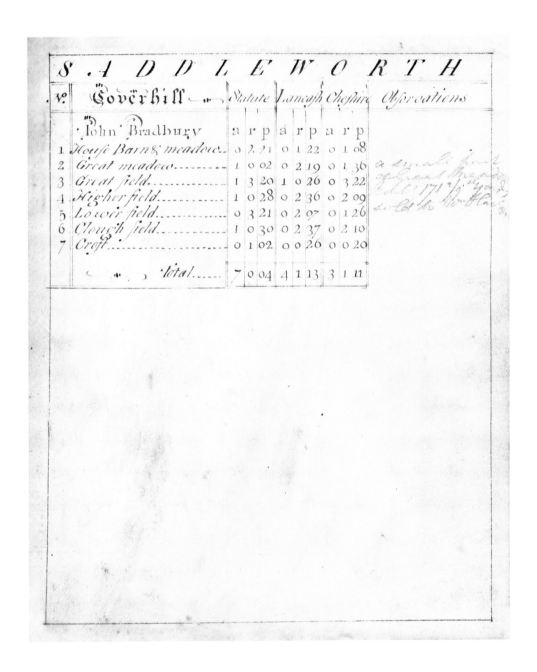

| **SADDLEWORTH** | | | | | | | | | | |
|---|---|---|---|---|---|---|---|---|---|---|
| Nº | Coverhill | Statute | | | Lancash | | | Cheshire | | | Observations |
| | John Bradbury | a | r | p | a | r | p | a | r | p | |
| 1 | House Barn & meadow | 0 | 2 | 21 | 0 | 1 | 22 | 0 | 1 | 08 | a small part |
| 2 | Great meadow | 1 | 0 | 02 | 0 | 2 | 19 | 0 | 1 | 36 | of Great meadow |
| 3 | Great field | 1 | 3 | 20 | 1 | 0 | 26 | 0 | 3 | 22 | Cont 171 ½ yards |
| 4 | Higher field | 1 | 0 | 28 | 0 | 2 | 36 | 0 | 2 | 09 | in Col in Mr Black's |
| 5 | Lower field | 0 | 3 | 21 | 0 | 2 | 07 | 0 | 1 | 26 | |
| 6 | Clough field | 1 | 0 | 30 | 0 | 2 | 37 | 0 | 2 | 10 | |
| 7 | Croft | 0 | 1 | 02 | 0 | 0 | 26 | 0 | 0 | 20 | |
| | total | 7 | 0 | 04 | 4 | 1 | 13 | 3 | 1 | 11 | |

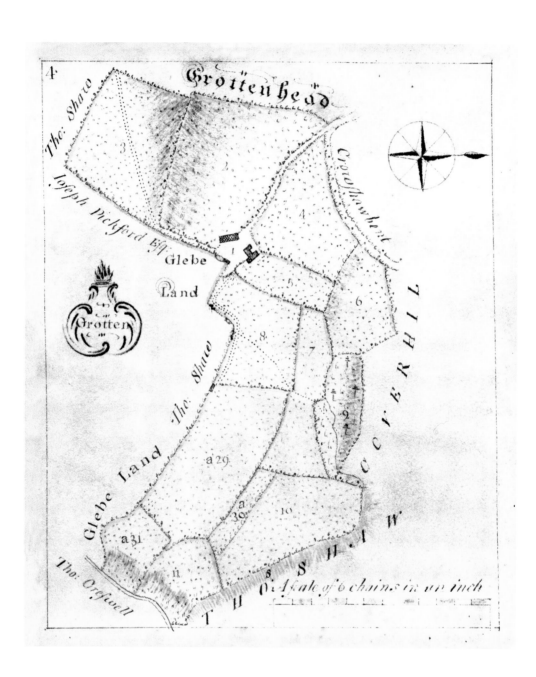

4

Grottenhead

Tho: Shaw

Joseph Pickford Efq

Glebe

Land

Grotten

3

2

Crossharehst

1

4

5

6

Glebe Land

Tho: Shaw

8

7

9

a 29

a 30

a 31

10

11

Tho: Orgswell

T H O S S H . A W

0 A Scale of 6 chains in an inch

C O V E R H I L L

Plate V

# S. A D D L E W O R T H

| Nº Grotten | Statute | | | Lancash | | | Cheshire | | | Observations |
|---|---|---|---|---|---|---|---|---|---|---|
| John Ratcliffe | a | r | p | a | r | p | a | r | p | |
| 1 House, Barn Gard.ⁿ folder | 0 | 1 | 20 | 0 | 0 | 37 | 0 | 0 | 29 | |
| 2 Bank | 4 | 3 | 02 | 2 | 3 | 30 | 2 | 1 | 00 | |
| 3 Acre | 3 | 1 | 32 | 2 | 0 | 21 | 1 | 2 | 21 | |
| 4 Broad meadow | 2 | 3 | 02 | 1 | 2 | 33 | 1 | 1 | 09 | |
| 5 Little Dº | 1 | 0 | 25 | 0 | 2 | 34 | 0 | 2 | 07 | |
| 6 Round field | 1 | 2 | 28 | 1 | 0 | 05 | 0 | 3 | 06 | |
| 7 Little knotbirch | 1 | 3 | 19 | 1 | 0 | 25 | 0 | 3 | 21 | |
| 8 Fold meadow | 2 | 1 | 33 | 1 | 2 | 02 | 1 | 0 | 26 | |
| 9 Clough | 1 | 0 | 28 | 0 | 2 | 30 | 0 | 2 | 09 | |
| 10 Great knotbirch | 3 | 1 | 18 | 2 | 0 | 12 | 1 | 2 | 14 | |
| 11 Clough field | 1 | 1 | 38 | 0 | 3 | 27 | 0 | 2 | 32 | |
| Total | 24 | 2 | 05 | 15 | 0 | 22 | 11 | 2 | 14 | |

109

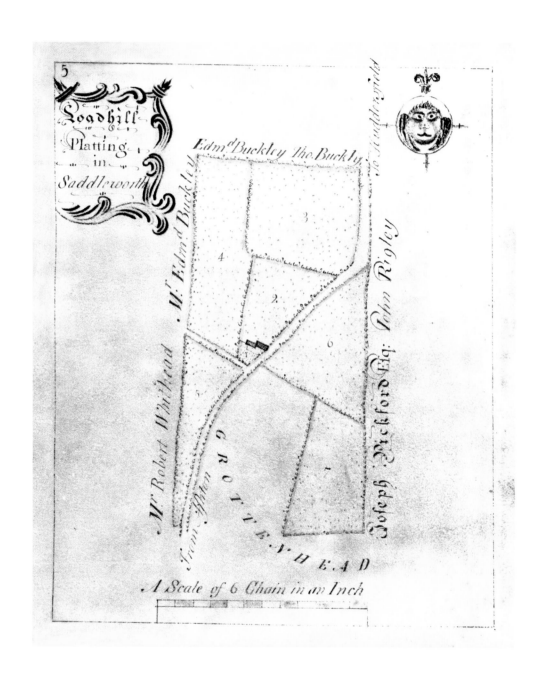

5

Loadhill
or
Platting
in
Saddleworth

Edm<sup>d</sup> Buckley  Tho. Buckly

To Huddersfield

M<sup>r</sup> Edm<sup>d</sup> Buckley

3

4

2

6

7

John Rigley

Joseph Pickford Esq<sup>r</sup>

M<sup>r</sup> Robert Whithead

Grotehead

GROTE HEAD

A Scale of 6 Chain in an Inch

Plate VI

# S. A D D L E W O R T H

| r. Loadhill Plaiting | Statute | | | Lancash. | | | Cheshire | | | Observations |
|---|---|---|---|---|---|---|---|---|---|---|
| Jno Whittaker | a | r | p | a | r | p | a | r | p | |
| 1 House fold &c | 0 | 0 | 33 | 0 | 0 | 20 | 0 | 0 | 16 | |
| 2 Plaiting field | 1 | 2 | 20 | 1 | 0 | 00 | 0 | 3 | 03 | |
| 3 Newhouse field | 3 | 1 | 30 | 2 | 0 | 20 | 1 | 2 | 20 | |
| 4 Meadow | 3 | 1 | 00 | 2 | 0 | 01 | 1 | 2 | 06 | |
| 5 Intake | 1 | 2 | 14 | 0 | 3 | 36 | 0 | 3 | 00 | |
| 6 Threenookfield | 2 | 3 | 33 | 1 | 3 | 12 | 1 | 1 | 23 | |
| 7 Rough field | 2 | 2 | 32 | 1 | 2 | 26 | 1 | 1 | 04 | |
| Total | 15 | 3 | 02 | 9 | 2 | 35 | 7 | 1 | 32 | |

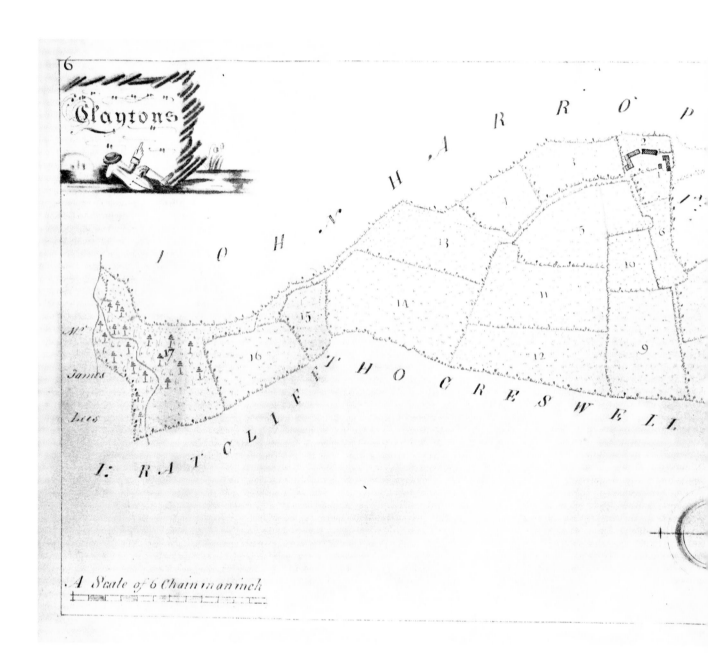

Plate VII

# S A D D L E W O R T H

| Nᵒ Claytons | Statute | | | Lancash. | | | Cheshire | | | Observations |
|---|---|---|---|---|---|---|---|---|---|---|
| John Lawton | a | r | p | a | r | p | a | r | p | |
| 1 Houses Barn Orchd foldw | 0 | 1 | 21 | 0 | 0 | 37 | 0 | 0 | 29 | |
| 2 Pingothead | 0 | 0 | 37 | 0 | 0 | 22 | 0 | 0 | 17 | |
| 3 Pingot | 1 | 1 | 12 | 0 | 3 | 10 | 0 | 2 | 20 | |
| 4 Copy | 1 | 0 | 09 | 0 | 2 | 24 | 0 | 2 | 00 | |
| 5 Stones | 2 | 1 | 06 | 1 | 1 | 26 | 1 | 0 | 13 | |
| 6 Dᵒ above Orchard | 0 | 3 | 12 | 0 | 2 | 01 | 0 | 1 | 22 | |
| 7 New meadow | 1 | 2 | 01 | 0 | 3 | 28 | 0 | 2 | 33 | |
| 8 Highmost field | 1 | 3 | 15 | 1 | 0 | 22 | 0 | 3 | 20 | |
| 9 Middle high field | 2 | 2 | 12 | 1 | 2 | 15 | 1 | 0 | 34 | |
| 10 Stones meadow | 0 | 3 | 14 | 0 | 2 | 02 | 0 | 1 | 23 | |
| 11 Near long field | 2 | 3 | 09 | 1 | 2 | 37 | 1 | 1 | 12 | |
| 12 Fur Dᵒ | 2 | 1 | 34 | 1 | 2 | 03 | 1 | 0 | 26 | |
| 13 Near long shut | 2 | 0 | 35 | 1 | 1 | 19 | 1 | 0 | 08 | 2 0 35 |
| 14 Fur Dᵒ | 3 | 2 | 08 | 2 | 0 | 31 | 1 | 2 | 29 | |
| 15 Little hurst head | 0 | 3 | 30 | 0 | 2 | 12 | 0 | 1 | 30 | |
| 16 Clough meadow | 1 | 3 | 14 | 1 | 0 | 21 | 0 | 3 | 19 | |
| 17 Clough | 3 | 3 | 28 | 2 | 1 | 27 | 1 | 3 | 17 | |
| Total | 30 | 2 | 17 | 18 | 3 | 17 | 14 | 1 | 32 | |

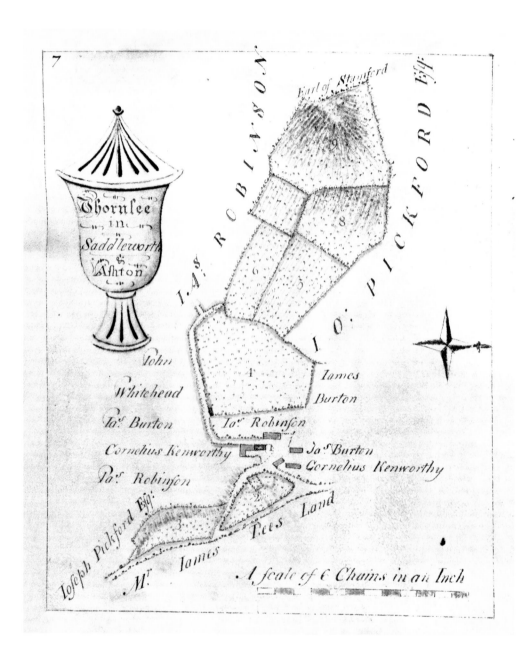

7

Thornlee
in
Saddleworth
&
Ashton

Iohn
Whitehead
Ias Burton
Cornelius Kenworthy
Ias Robinfon

I. As ROBINSON

Earl of Stamford

9

8

7

6

5

4

3

2

1

Ias Robinfon

James
Burton

Ias Burton
Cornelius Kenworthy

Iofeph Pickford Efqr

Mr James

Tees Land

A scale of 6 Chains in an Inch

I O: PICKFORD Efqr

Plate VIII

# S. A D D L E W O R T H

N° **Thornlee** ... Statute Lancash Cheshire Observations

| Widow Shaw | | a | r | p | a | r | p | a | r | p | |
|---|---|---|---|---|---|---|---|---|---|---|---|
| 1 | House | | " | | | " | | | " | | |
| 2 | Green | 0 | 2 | 20 | 0 | 1 | 21 | 0 | 1 | 08 | |
| 3 | Park | 0 | 3 | 29 | 0 | 2 | 12 | 0 | 1 | 30 | |
| 4 | Meadow | 2 | 3 | 08 | 1 | 2 | 36 | 1 | 1 | 12 | |
| 5 | Roundfield | 1 | 2 | 00 | 0 | 3 | 28 | 0 | 2 | 33 | |
| 6 | Long field | 1 | 0 | 25 | 0 | 2 | 34 | 0 | 2 | 08 | These 5 pieces |
| 7 | Little field | 0 | 2 | 29 | 0 | 1 | 27 | 0 | 1 | 11 | are in Ashton parish |
| 8 | Colehill | 1 | 0 | 29 | 0 | 2 | 36 | 0 | 2 | 10 | |
| 9 | Shakerhill | 2 | 3 | 03 | 1 | 2 | 33 | 1 | 1 | 09 | |
| | Total | 11 | 2 | 23 | 7 | 0 | 27 | 5 | 2 | 01 | |

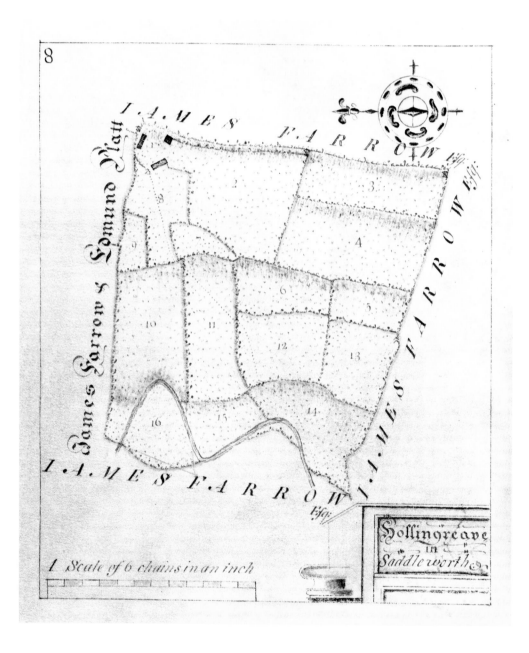

8

I.A.M.E.S    F.A.R.R.O.W Esqr.

Edmund Platt

James Farrow &

James Farrow

1
2
3
4
5
6
7
8
9
10
11
12
13
14
15
16

I.A.M.E.S F.A.R.R.O.W I.A.M.E.S F.A.R.R.O.W Esqr.

Esqr.

Hollingreave in Saddleworth

1 Scale of 6 chains in an inch

Plate IX

# S A D D L E W O R T H

| № | Hollingreave | Statute | | | Lancash | | | Chesh | | | Observations |
|---|---|---|---|---|---|---|---|---|---|---|---|
| | Isaac Bottamley | a | r | p | a | r | p | a | r | p | |
| 1 | Houses Barn field &c...... | 0 | 1 | 24 | 0 | 1 | 00 | 0 | 0 | 30 | |
| 2 | Nearfield | 3 | 2 | 05 | 2 | 0 | 29 | 1 | 2 | 27 | |
| 3 | Higherfarfield | 1 | 3 | 10 | 1 | 0 | 19 | 0 | 3 | 07 | |
| 4 | Lower D° | 3 | 1 | 37 | 2 | 0 | 24 | 1 | 2 | 23 | |
| 5 | Little field | 0 | 3 | 33 | 0 | 2 | 14 | 0 | 1 | 32 | |
| 6 | Cowhey | 1 | 1 | 34 | 0 | 3 | 24 | 0 | 2 | 30 | |
| 7 | Croft | 0 | 1 | 31 | 0 | 1 | 05 | 0 | 0 | 34 | |
| 8 | Barn croft | 1 | 2 | 07 | 0 | 3 | 33 | 0 | 3 | 10 | |
| 9 | Round croft | 0 | 1 | 28 | 0 | 1 | 03 | 0 | 0 | 32 | |
| 10 | Lower meadow | 3 | 1 | 00 | 2 | 0 | 01 | 1 | 2 | 06 | |
| 11 | Foley D° | 2 | 1 | 14 | 1 | 1 | 30 | 1 | 0 | 17 | |
| 12 | Rushy field | 1 | 3 | 15 | 1 | 0 | 22 | 0 | 3 | 19 | |
| 13 | Marldearth | 1 | 2 | 00 | 0 | 3 | 28 | 0 | 2 | 33 | |
| 14 | Bottams | 1 | 3 | 37 | 1 | 0 | 35 | 0 | 3 | 30 | |
| 15 | Holme | 1 | 0 | 03 | 0 | 2 | 19 | 0 | 1 | 37 | |
| 16 | Clod | 1 | 0 | 18 | 0 | 2 | 30 | 0 | 2 | 04 | |
| | Total | 27 | 0 | 16 | 16 | 2 | 36 | 12 | 3 | 11 | |

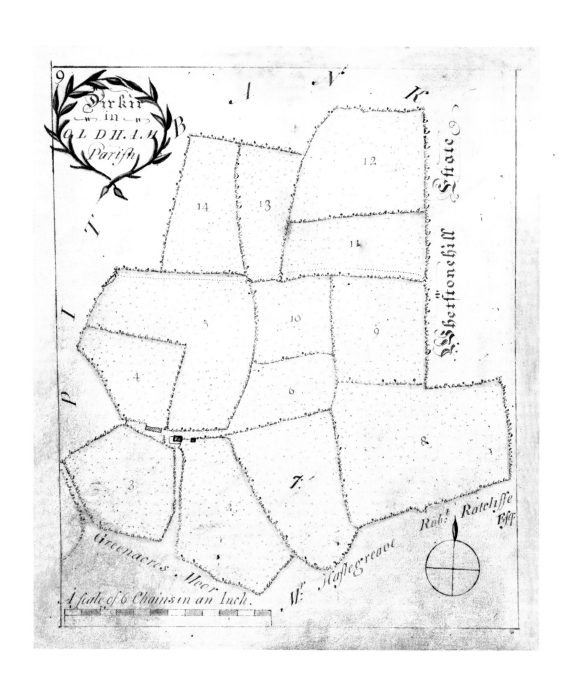

Dirkir in OLDHAM Parish

A scale of 6 Chains in an Inch.

Plate X

## O L D H A M Parish

| № | Order | Statute | | | Lancash | | | Cheshire | | | Observations |
|---|---|---|---|---|---|---|---|---|---|---|---|
| | Joseph Dunkerly | a | r | p | a | r | p | a | r | p | |
| 1 | House Barn Garden fold &c | 0 | 1 | 28 | 0 | 1 | 02 | 0 | 0 | 32 | |
| 2 | Kiln meadow | 4 | 0 | 00 | 2 | 1 | 35 | 1 | 3 | 23 | |
| 3 | Wams | 2 | 3 | 04 | 1 | 2 | 34 | 1 | 1 | 10 | |
| 4 | Barn meadow | 2 | 0 | 30 | 1 | 1 | 16 | 1 | 0 | 06 | |
| 5 | Croft | 5 | 0 | 28 | 3 | 0 | 31 | 2 | 1 | 31 | |
| 6 | Little field | 1 | 3 | 17 | 1 | 0 | 24 | 0 | 3 | 20 | |
| 8 | Higher Broad Meadow | 6 | 2 | 30 | 4 | 0 | 20 | 3 | 0 | 25 | |
| 7 | Marled Earth | 3 | 0 | 15 | 1 | 3 | 25 | 1 | 1 | 34 | |
| 9 | Lower Broad Meadow | 1 | 3 | 07 | 1 | 0 | 17 | 0 | 3 | 15 | |
| 10 | Long field | 3 | 3 | 11 | 2 | 1 | 17 | 1 | 3 | 09 | |
| 11 | Back of stone wall | 3 | 0 | 08 | 1 | 3 | 20 | 1 | 1 | 31 | |
| 12 | Meadow hill | 3 | 3 | 26 | 2 | 1 | 26 | 1 | 3 | 16 | |
| 13 | Cote meadow | 2 | 1 | 20 | 1 | 1 | 34 | 1 | 0 | 20 | |
| 14 | Hard field | 2 | 3 | 04 | 1 | 2 | 34 | 1 | 1 | 10 | |
| | Total | 43 | 3 | 28 | 27 | 0 | 15 | 20 | 3 | 02 | |

= Part of the Croft laid into the Barn meadow
Little field laid to the Lower Broad meadow —
for Pasture
= Back of the stone wall and Meadow hill
laid together — pasture ———
= Cote Meadow and Hardfield laid
together — pasture

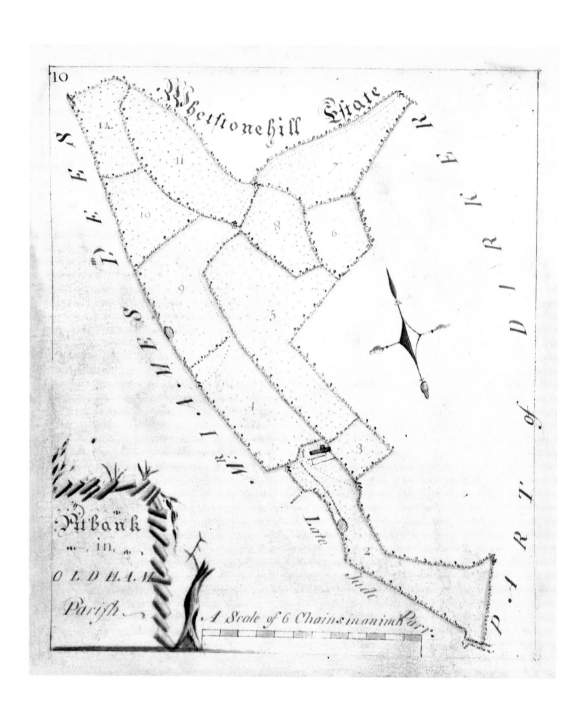

Whetstonehill Estate

Nubank
in,
OLDHAM
Parish

A Scale of 6 Chains in an inch Part.

Plate XI

# OLDHAM Parish

| No | Pitbank | Statute | | | Lancash | | | Cheshire | | | Observations |
|----|---------|---|---|---|---|---|---|---|---|---|---|
| | John Hilton | a | r | p | a | r | p | a | r | p | |
| 1 | House field Garden | 0 | 1 | 31 | 0 | 1 | 03 | 0 | 0 | 34 | |
| 2 | Cockpit | 2 | 2 | 03 | 1 | 2 | 08 | 1 | 0 | 30 | |
| 3 | New meadow | 0 | 2 | 20 | 0 | 1 | 21 | 0 | 1 | 08 | |
| 4 | Field at back of house | 2 | 1 | 06 | 1 | 1 | 26 | 1 | 0 | 13 | |
| 5 | Stonepit field | 3 | 2 | 08 | 2 | 0 | 31 | 1 | 2 | 29 | |
| 6 | Little Bent | 1 | 0 | 36 | 0 | 3 | 02 | 0 | 2 | 13 | |
| 7 | Crooked acre | 2 | 0 | 06 | 1 | 1 | 03 | 0 | 3 | 34 | |
| 8 | Threenook | 1 | 1 | 02 | 0 | 3 | 04 | 0 | 2 | 15 | |
| 9 | Marlpit field | 2 | 2 | 00 | 1 | 2 | 10 | 1 | 0 | 32 | |
| 10 | Little field | 1 | 1 | 18 | 0 | 3 | 14 | 0 | 2 | 23 | |
| 11 | Barley field | 2 | 1 | 34 | 1 | 2 | 03 | 1 | 0 | 27 | |
| 12 | Little meadow | 1 | 0 | 22 | 0 | 2 | 33 | 0 | 2 | 06 | |
| | Total | 21 | 1 | 32 | 13 | 0 | 37 | 10 | 0 | 24 | |

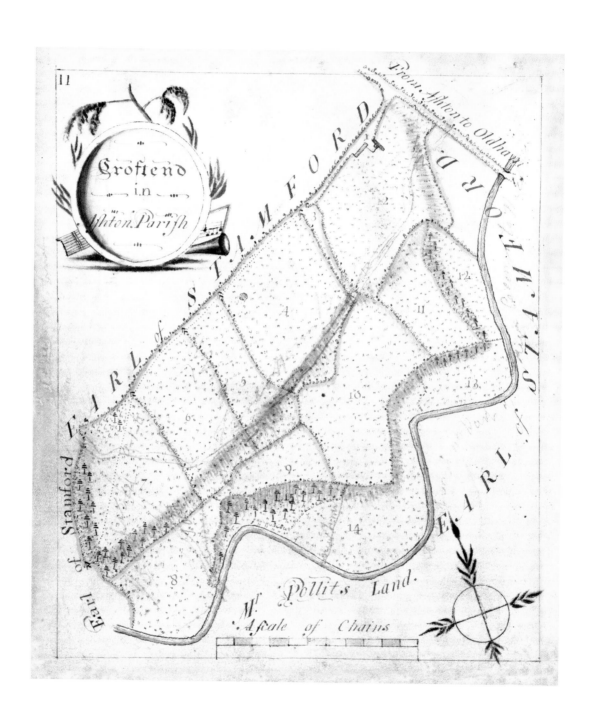

11

Croftend in Ashton Parish

EARL of STAMFORD

From Ashton to Oldham

EARL of ST. VE

Earl of Stamford

2

13

4

5

6

7

8

10

9

12

11

13

14

EARL of ST. VE

Mr Pollits Land.

A Scale of Chains

Plate XII

# ASHTON Parish

| № Croftend | Statute | | | Lancash: | | | Cheshire | | | Observations |
|---|---|---|---|---|---|---|---|---|---|---|
| Sam.l Stanffield | a | r | p | a | r | p | a | r | p | |
| 1 House Barnfeld Lane &c | 0 | 0 | 36 | 0 | 0 | 22 | 0 | 0 | 17 | |
| 2 Croftend | 4 | 0 | 04 | 2 | 1 | 37 | 1 | 3 | 24 | |
| 3 A driving way | 0 | 0 | 38 | 0 | 0 | 23 | 0 | 0 | 18 | |
| 4 Crooked acre | 4 | 1 | 08 | 2 | 2 | 25 | 2 | 0 | 03 | |
| 5 Fir meadow | 2 | 1 | 04 | 1 | 1 | 25 | 1 | 0 | 12 | |
| 6 Nearhey | 3 | 0 | 11 | 1 | 3 | 23 | 1 | 1 | 32 | |
| 7 Fir D.o | 4 | 0 | 34 | 2 | 2 | 16 | 1 | 3 | 39 | |
| 8 Long eye | 2 | 2 | 11 | 1 | 2 | 13 | 1 | 0 | 34 | |
| 9 Little field | 1 | 1 | 00 | 0 | 3 | 03 | 0 | 2 | 14 | |
| 10 Two acre | 3 | 3 | 07 | 2 | 1 | 14 | 1 | 3 | 10 | |
| 11 Wheat field | 1 | 2 | 17 | 0 | 3 | 38 | 0 | 3 | 01 | |
| 12 Calfbank meadow | 1 | 1 | 00 | 0 | 3 | 03 | 0 | 2 | 14 | |
| 13 Barley croft | 1 | 1 | 27 | 0 | 3 | 20 | 0 | 2 | 27 | |
| 14 Warth & round eye | 3 | 1 | 31 | 2 | 0 | 20 | 1 | 2 | 20 | |
| 15 Garr | 1 | 1 | 00 | 0 | 3 | 03 | 0 | 2 | 14 | |
| Total | 31 | 3 | 28 | 21 | 2 | 05 | 16 | 2 | 01 | |

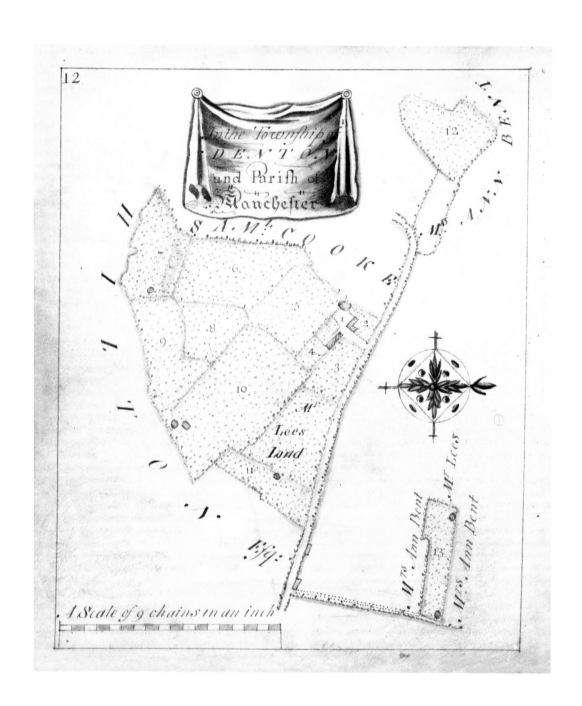

12

In the Township of
DENTON
and Parish of
Manchester

S.A.M.ᵣ COOKE
M.ᵣ ANN BENT

12

6

5

1 2

8 4

9

3

10

M.ᵣ
Lees
Land

11

M.ʳˢ Ann Bent
M.ʳ Lees

M.ʳ Lees

13

M.ʳˢ Ann Bent

A Scale of 9 chains in an inch

Plate XIII

# DENTON Township

| Nᵒ | | Statute | | | Lancashire | | | Cheshire | | Observations |
|----|----------------------|---|---|----|---|---|----|---|---|----|---|
| | Robt Fidler | a | r | p | a | r | p | a | r | p | |
| 1 | House fold Garden &c | 0 | 2 | 30 | 0 | 1 | 28 | 0 | 1 | 12 | |
| 2 | Barn Croft | 0 | 1 | 29 | 0 | 0 | 38 | 0 | 0 | 33 | |
| 3 | Bean acre | 1 | 1 | 23 | 0 | 3 | 17 | 0 | 2 | 25 | |
| 4 | Croft | 0 | 1 | 31 | 0 | 1 | 03 | 0 | 0 | 34 | |
| 5 | Blackcroft | 3 | 0 | 00 | 1 | 3 | 20 | 1 | 1 | 29 | |
| 6 | Wheat field | 4 | 0 | 30 | 2 | 2 | 13 | 1 | 3 | 30 | |
| 7 | Cockshut | 2 | 3 | 04 | 1 | 2 | 34 | 1 | 1 | 10 | |
| 8 | Round meadow | 2 | 0 | 00 | 1 | 0 | 37 | 0 | 3 | 31 | |
| 9 | Longshut | 3 | 2 | 25 | 2 | 1 | 01 | 1 | 3 | 00 | |
| 10 | Cowhey | 6 | 3 | 31 | 4 | 1 | 08 | 3 | 1 | 05 | |
| 11 | Whiteleach | 1 | 3 | 20 | 1 | 0 | 25 | 0 | 3 | 22 | |
| 12 | Tomcroft | 3 | 1 | 21 | 2 | 0 | 13 | 1 | 2 | 15 | |
| 13 | Acre | 1 | 3 | 09 | 1 | 0 | 18 | 0 | 3 | 10 | |
| | Total | 32 | 2 | 19 | 20 | 0 | 15 | 15 | 1 | 28 | |

126

Plate XIV

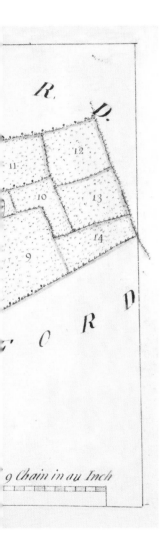

9 Chain in an Inch

| MOTTRAM Parish | | | | | | | | | | |
|---|---|---|---|---|---|---|---|---|---|---|
| | | Statute | | | Lancaſh: | | | Cheſhire | | Observations |
| John Cocker | a | r | p | a | r | p | a | r | p | |
| 1 Houſe Barnfield Lane | 0 | 3 | 21 | 0 | 2 | 07 | 0 | 1 | 26 | |
| 2 Barn meadow | 5 | 1 | 02 | 3 | 1 | 00 | 2 | 1 | 38 | |
| 3 Far meadow | 4 | 2 | 37 | 2 | 3 | 37 | 2 | 0 | 37 | |
| 4 Bread meadow | 6 | 0 | 06 | 3 | 2 | 36 | 2 | 3 | 16 | |
| 5 Dº Dº top | 2 | 3 | 27 | 1 | 3 | 08 | 1 | 1 | 21 | |
| 6 Dirty meadow | 3 | 1 | 26 | 2 | 0 | 17 | 1 | 2 | 18 | |
| 7 Calf croft | 1 | 1 | 00 | 0 | 3 | 03 | 0 | 2 | 14 | |
| 8 Dead lane | 1 | 3 | 15 | 1 | 0 | 22 | 0 | 3 | 19 | |
| 9 Black earth | 6 | 0 | 36 | 3 | 3 | 15 | 2 | 3 | 31 | |
| 10 Lower cote edge | 2 | 0 | 14 | 1 | 1 | 05 | 0 | 3 | 38 | |
| 11 Wheat edge | 2 | 3 | 31 | 1 | 3 | 10 | 1 | 1 | 23 | |
| 12 Sour dock | 3 | 0 | 00 | 1 | 3 | 16 | 1 | 1 | 27 | |
| 13 Higher cote edge | 3 | 0 | 28 | 1 | 3 | 33 | 1 | 2 | 0 | |
| 14 Round edge | 2 | 1 | 07 | 1 | 1 | 26 | 1 | 0 | 13 | |
| 15 Greenings | 7 | 1 | 23 | 4 | 2 | 10 | 3 | 2 | 00 | |
| 16 Wood in Dº | 3 | 0 | 14 | 1 | 3 | 25 | 1 | 1 | 33 | |
| 17 Higher marlfield | 4 | 2 | 30 | 2 | 3 | 23 | 2 | 0 | 34 | |
| 18 Lower Dº | 5 | 3 | 25 | 3 | 2 | 24 | 2 | 3 | 11 | |
| 19 Little marehey meadow | 2 | 2 | 20 | 1 | 2 | 23 | 1 | 1 | 01 | |
| 20 Long Dº Dº | 3 | 3 | 35 | 2 | 1 | 32 | 1 | 3 | 20 | |
| 21 Snape | 5 | 1 | 22 | 3 | 1 | 13 | 2 | 2 | 07 | |
| 22 Broad marehey | 8 | 3 | 00 | 5 | 1 | 24 | 4 | 0 | 22 | |
| 23 Long Dº | 5 | 0 | 14 | 3 | 0 | 23 | 2 | 1 | 24 | |
| 24 Barley croft | 3 | 0 | 35 | 1 | 3 | 38 | 1 | 2 | 03 | |
| 25 Wood in Dº | 1 | 3 | 19 | 1 | 0 | 25 | 0 | 3 | 21 | |
| 26 A Wood | 6 | 3 | 17 | 4 | 0 | 12 | 3 | 0 | 19 | |
| Total | 104 | 2 | 30 | 64 | 2 | 27 | 49 | 1 | 36 | |

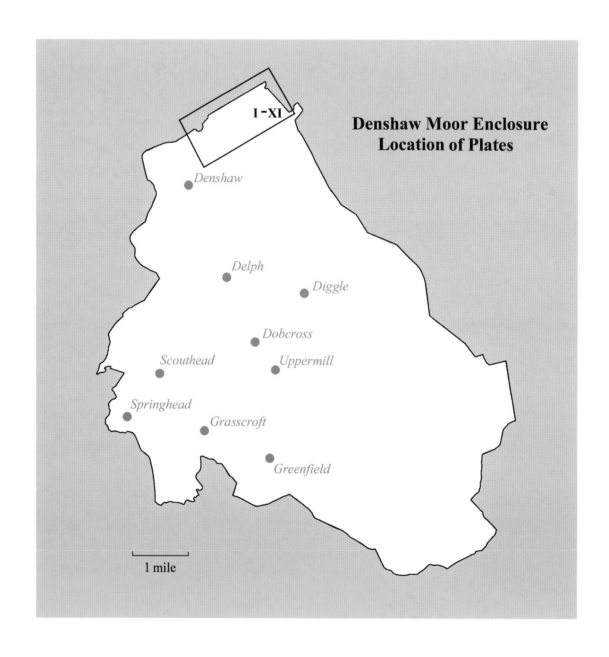

I -XI

**Denshaw Moor Enclosure
Location of Plates**

Denshaw

Delph

Diggle

Dobcross

Scouthead

Uppermill

Springhead

Grasscroft

Greenfield

1 mile

# THE ENCLOSURE MAPS OF
# DENSHAW MOOR, 1808-12

Parliamentary enclosure swept through northern England in the late eighteenth and early nineteenth centuries. Inevitably Saddleworth was caught up in this movement and two enclosure acts implemented the process in the township: the Denshaw Moor Act of 13th March 1809 and the Saddleworth Act of 2nd June 1810. Of these two acts the one for Denshaw proved by far the more straightforward to implement and it provides a textbook study of how a parliamentary enclosure act should operate in an upland area.

The Denshaw Moor common rights belonged exclusively to the owners of properties within Denshaw. At the time of the sale of Friarmere by Henry VIII in 1544 Denshaw consisted of three or four tenements and, in the century that followed, these grew by subdivision into eight or more[1]. Early deeds indicate that each of these tenements was allocated a proportion of the common rights on the Moor, eighths being the usual share[2]. It is not clear what pressures led to the expensive process of parliamentary enclosure; clearly it must not have been possible to achieve agreement between the various interested parties. Nor is it known who the prime movers were in pressing for enclosure. What is clear is that some benefitted more than others.

This situation contrasts strongly with the enclosure of Oxhey, an area of approximately 140 acres, some twenty years earlier. Here all the parties were in agreement as to their shares. All that was needed was an independent party to be paid to make an impartial allotment of the ground. There was no loss of land and no opportunity for the Crown to take its share[3].

---

[1] The extent of the monastery's holding in Denshaw is given in the Minister's Accounts of 1538-9. Ralph Chetham, and Christipher Chetham hold, inter alia, a moiety of Denshaw late in the tenure of Robert Wrigley; Henry Gartside, William Gartside son of Henry Gartside, deceased, Richard and John Gartside hold the other moiety (apparently in two portions). Ministers Accounts 29 & 30 Hen VIII. No 132, TNA. In 1649 Richard Holt & Jane, his wife, sold the freehold of 16 tenements in 'Tame, Ould Tame, New Tame, Denshawe, Swinescroft, Hilbrighthope and Sadleworth' to the tenants, among these were nine Gartsides. Feet of Fines CP 25(2) 612, TNA.

[2] The purchase of his farm from Holt by John Gartside of Denshaw, yeoman (son of Raphe Gartside of the same, yeoman), in 1649 includes 'Also the eighth part of one moor or moss in Denshawe and Hilbrighthope called Denshawe Moore'. Biddle, Thorns, Welsford & Barnes Documents, No 81, WYAS (Leeds). A similar clause was in Robert Gartside's purchase at the same time; 'the eight parte of one moore or mose lying and being in Denshaw and Hilbrighthope or one of them called Denshaw Moore'. Morgan Brierley MSS now lost but from A.J. Howcroft's notes on the MSS in The Howcroft Collection, H/HOW/53, SHS.

[3] Award of the Division of Oxhey, 29 May 1790, DF 46 55, West Riding Registry of Deeds, WYAS (Wakefield).

# ROUGH PLAN OF DENSHAW MOOR
## (PLATES I - IV)

| | |
|---|---|
| *Location:* | Bolton Archives and Local Studies, ZAL 537 |
| *Date of Compilation of Map:* | No date given (c.1808) |
| *Surveyor:* | John Albinson of Bolton |
| *Material:* | Paper |
| *Size of Original:* | 43¼" x 26¼" |
| *Scale of Original:* | 1" : 4 chains (20" : 1 mile) |
| *Scale of Reproduction:* | 12⅔" : 1 mile |

John Albinson of Bolton (1774-1854), the surveyor for the Denshaw Moor Act, produced this map along with the four others reproduced below. The appointment of a Bolton man as surveyor should come as no surprise since one of the two Commissioners appointed to implement the act was Ralph Fletcher of Bolton (1757-1832).[1] Fletcher was a prominent Bolton citizen and Treasurer to the Great Bolton Improvement Trustees, effectively the town council of Bolton. Interestingly John Albinson was appointed clerk to the trustees in 1800, a post which he retained until 1841 and he must have worked closely with Fletcher in Bolton for many years.[2]

Although undated, this rough map presumably dates from the beginning of Albinson's involvement with the Denshaw Moor enclosure project because it shows the area in an unenclosed and unimproved state. The purpose of this map was clearly to establish the extent of the land to be enclosed and to fix the boundaries of the moor. It shows that initially there was uncertainty as to the boundaries of Denshaw Moor with Butterworth, Ripponden and Marsden. This rough draft shows a much larger area than appears on the maps of 1812.

The map captures a landscape in the process of evolution. The line of the newly opened Newhey to Huddersfield turnpike is clearly marked. At the same time, in the vicinity of Readycondean Head, a stretch of the proposed turnpike, which would have bypassed Denshaw and taken a route over Ogden Edge appears . Boundaries are shown for Grange Hey and Castleshaw Moor Backside, specific details that do not appear on later maps. The original route of Rapes Highway, the 'Prime and Pack Route from Marsden' is shown. Moreover at the boundary where the road enters Saddleworth, Rapes Gate is recorded as well as a boundary stone. The watershed is indicated in various places, implying that at this stage Albinson considered that this was the line of the boundary.

The map throws useful light on the working practices of surveyors at this period, drafting their maps on spare pieces of paper. Examination of the map shows that it has been drawn on the reverse side of at least six printed statements of the accounts of the Great Bolton Improvement Trustees for 31st December 1801 to 31st December 1807. No doubt Albinson had plenty of surplus copies of this document, which records his not unprofitable involvement with the enterprise, for he received £344 06s 09d for 'Salary of Clerk, and Commissioner's Business' in this six year period.

---

[1] *Oxford Dictionary of National Biography*, Oxford, Oxford University Press, 2004, article under Ralph Fletcher.

[2] Introduction to the Handlist of the Albinson Collection (ZAL), Bolton Archives and Local Studies.

# PLAN OF DENSHAW MOOR
## (PLATES V - VIII)

| | |
|---|---|
| *Location:* | Bolton Archives and Local Studies, ZAL 1186 |
| *Date of Compilation of Map:* | 1808 |
| *Surveyor:* | John Albinson of Bolton |
| *Material:* | Paper |
| *Size of Original:* | 51" x 26¼" |
| *Scale of Original:* | No scale given but 1" : 4 chains (20" : 1 mile) |
| *Scale of Reproduction:* | 10¾" : 1 mile |

This map is dated 1808, which shows that detailed preparations were made before application for an enclosure act was made to Parliament. The Act received royal assent on the 13th March 1809. This map appears to have been constructed originally to show the features of Denshaw Moor before enclosure and is a fair copy of the 'Rough Plan of Denshaw Moor' (Plates I - IV). Like the 'Rough Plan' it records many significant features, many of which are unique to this map. It is the earliest map to record the village of Denshaw and the position of buildings recently created around the newly formed cross roads. The map also sheds light on the shape and size of the hamlet of Denshaw. Details such as the position of the newly erected guide post, a milestone and the toll bars are shown at Junction. Another milestone on the Oldham to Ripponden Turnpike road is marked as it crosses Coldgreave Pasture recording the distance to various towns. The position of a Cock Pit on Denshaw Moor, which is not marked on any other map is also indicated. In addition to these more transient features of the landscape, this map is the first to record the present boundary with Butterworth township which is also the Lancashire and Yorkshire boundary. A number of physical features along the boundary are recorded. A particularly significant one appears to be the willow at Readycondean Head. This is mentioned in the 1499 description of the boundary of Marsden. Although the willow is unlikely to have survived to 1808, its position may have been embedded in legal and local memory.[6]

The Black Ditch next to the sheep wash on Ragstone Brook is an important boundary feature and records the division of Grange Hey and Crawshaw Hey. It is not marked on later maps and is probably an ancient man-made feature. An intriguing feature only found on this map is Peg O'Noants well. The name almost certainly explains the building called Peggy Well House which appears on later maps.

The map contains large numbers of pencil lines some of which may well indicate the lines of survey which were measured on the ground, the orientation being determined by compass bearings. These measurements would facilitate the triangulation of the Moor and allow the construction of the present map

Towards the end of the process of enclosure, when the Enclosure Award Map (Plate XI) was being planned out, Albinson clearly used this map to work out the lines of division of the final lots. In the top right corner of the map is his list of the claimants and the areas they received dated March 1812.

---

[6] A Boundarie of the Manor of Marsden in the fourteenth year of the Reigne of King Henrie the seventhe, Radcliffe of Rudding Park Collection, WYAS (Leeds).

# PLAN OF PART OF DENSHAW MOOR TO BE SOLD BY AUCTION, 1810
## (PLATE IX)

| | |
|---|---|
| *Location:* | Bolton Archives and Local Studies, ZAL 1267 |
| *Date of Compilation of Map:* | 1810 |
| *Surveyor:* | John Albinson of Bolton |
| *Material:* | Paper |
| *Size of Original:* | 21½" x 16⅜" |
| *Scale of Original:* | No scale given but 1" : 8 chains (10" : 1 mile) |
| *Scale of Reproduction:* | 6¾" : 1 mile |

Enclosure was a costly process and one of the most popular methods of financing it was to sell, by auction, a portion of the land to be enclosed. This course was adopted in the case of the Denshaw Moor Act and the map reproduced here was drawn up to show the lots to be auctioned. It must have been a bitter blow to the commoners to realise that the area to be auctioned comprised just over a third of the whole area covered by the Denshaw Moor. This seems to be a generous allocation, especially in view of the fact that the area auctioned off to finance the Saddleworth Act comprised just two per cent of the total area to be enclosed. Perhaps this disparity can be explained by the fact that the enclosure process involved certain fixed costs irrespective of the area to be enclosed. Denshaw Moor was a small area of relatively poor land so, inevitably, the proportion of it required to finance the implementation of the act was relatively large.

The purchasers of the lots at the auction are recorded on the map. The list is reproduced below:

## LOTS SOLD

| Lot Number | Purchaser | Acres | Roods | Perches |
|---|---|---|---|---|
| 1 | John Taylor | 9 | 1 | 22 |
| 2 | John Taylor | 14 | 1 | 24 |
| 3 | John Taylor | 15 | 1 | 11 |
| 4 | Joshua Radcliffe | 24 | 0 | 37 |
| 5 | John Taylor | 8 | 1 | 16 |
| 6 | John Taylor | 11 | 1 | 22 |
| 7 | John Taylor | 11 | 3 | 30 |
| 8 | John Taylor | 19 | 1 | 20 |
| 9 | James Whitehead | 1 | 1 | 28 |
| **Total** | | **115** | **3** | **10** |

It is perhaps noteworthy that John Taylor, who purchased nearly all the lots, was an absentee landlord who had recently acquired farms with common rights at Brimmycroft, in the hamlet of Denshaw and at Calf Hey Barn. He had also recently purchased the Junction Inn and Junction estate.

As with the other maps there are many interesting details that go beyond the immediate purpose of indicating the lots to be sold. Like the 1808 'Plan of Denshaw Moor' (Plates V - VIII) it shows the hamlet of Denshaw and the newly formed road junction centred on the Junction Inn. The original route taken by the Rapes Highway to Rochdale beyond the turnpike road was apparently still in use and is shown on the map.

# PLAN OF DENSHAW MOOR WITH THE NEW ROADS LAID OUT, 1810
## (PLATE X)

| | |
|---|---|
| *Location:* | Bolton Archives and Local Studies, ZAL 1235 |
| *Date of Compilation of Map:* | 1810 |
| *Surveyor:* | John Albinson of Bolton |
| *Material:* | Paper |
| *Size of Original:* | 26⅜" x 17¾" |
| *Scale of Original:* | No scale given but 1" : 4 chains (20" : 1 mile) |
| *Scale of Reproduction:* | 11¼" : 1 mile |

A crucial stage in transforming open moorland into enclosed, and therefore improvable, land was to plan a network of roads which would provide access to the new allotments the Commissioner was to make. This map shows the new pattern of roads that were required for the Denshaw Moor enclosure. These roads included existing routes, suitably modified by a certain amount of straightening out and detailed re-routing; an example of this is the Rapes Highway. By contrast the two other roads, Fair Springs Occupation Road and Dowry Occupation Road on the final map (Plate XI), are, at least in part, new roads as can be verified by Albinson's earlier maps (Plates I to VIII). Interestingly, the little branch road running north east from the Rapes Highway to 'Redikin Dean Brook' appears never to have been built. Certainly it does not appear on either the 1822 Vestry Map or first edition six inches to one mile Ordnance Survey sheet surveyed between 1849 and 1851; neither does the sheep wash on the same stream.

Figure 5. Denshaw Moor from the air. Few traces remain of the enclosure process
but the linear ditch marking its northern boundary is clearly visible.

# PLAN OF DENSHAW MOOR TO ACCOMPANY
## THE ENCLOSURE AWARD, 1812
## (PLATE XI)

| | |
|---|---|
| *Location:* | Bolton Archives and Local Studies, ZAL 1208 |
| *Date of Compilation of Map:* | 1812 |
| *Surveyor:* | John Albinson of Bolton |
| *Material:* | Paper |
| *Size of Original:* | 35¼" x 20¾" |
| *Scale of Original:* | 1" : 4 chains (20" : 1 mile) |
| *Scale of Reproduction:* | 8½" : 1 mile |

This map was drawn up at the end of the process of Parliamentary enclosure in Denshaw. It is a good example of a relatively simple enclosure map. Two Commissioners, John Shaw and Ralph Fletcher, had been appointed by the act to represent the two major interests in Denshaw Moor: the Crown and the freeholders. Their job was relatively easy in that the area concerned was small, some 427 acres, and land was eventually allotted to only twenty-two claimants. As a result barely three years were required to implement the act. The Enclosure Award was published on 7th May 1813 and this map accompanied it.

On the top right-hand corner of the map is a faint note, probably in the hand of John Albinson, dated July 6th 1813 addressed to Jonathan Teal, a surveyor who had been active in Saddleworth during the 1790s. The note is difficult to decipher but it may indicate that Teale was working on behalf of the Crown and had requested a sketch of the land allotted to the King. The King's claim arose because Friarmere was land which had belonged to Roche Abbey and had been seized by the Crown at the Dissolution. In the end the Crown was awarded a modest 21a 0r 16p.

At the time when the farmsteads of Denshaw were subdivided, the title deeds were quite clear as to how the common rights were to be allocated. However, by the time of Enclosure, this clarity had disappeared and some landowners with dubious rights were successful in the pursuit of spurious claims[7].

The map sets out the new landscape as planned by the Commissioners. As was so often the case in upland areas, there is a considerable disparity between the planned landscape and that which actually emerged. A comparison between the Award map and the first edition six inches to one mile Ordnance Survey map surveyed between 1849 and 1851 shows that walls have been built around less than half the new allotments of land. This failure to fence off the new allotments was in direct contravention of the terms of the Act. Several factors may explain this. The land was of poor quality a.id may well not have been worth walling, which was after all, quite an expensive undertaking. Equally, much land changed hands as soon as it had been awarded so that walls were not required around every allotment as adjacent lots were held by the same owner.

John Taylor of Manchester acquired other allotments on the moor in the years following 1813, perhaps with the aim of creating a grouse shooting estate. This was ultimately achieved by the 1860s when John Gartside of Ashton-under-Lyne, the

---

[7] For example, David Kelsall and Jesse Ainsworth's award of 44a 3r 0p was totally disproportionate to their eighth share as evidenced in the title of two purchase deeds dated 1773. BQ 569 747 and BQ 570 748. West Riding Registry of Deeds. WYAS (Wakefield).

founder of Gartside's Breweries purchased John Taylor's estate and supplemented this by purchases from other parties. He built a large mansion at Dowry as a weekend retreat and shooting lodge, though he died before his project was completed. The mansion was short-lived. It was demolished less than thirty years later following the acquisition of the moor by Oldham Corporation for the construction of the Dowry, Crooked Gate and Readycon Dean reservoirs. Today, apart from the good quality land sold in 1809, there is little evidence of parliamentary enclosure to be seen. The remains of the ambitious Gartside estate are equally elusive.

## Allotments from the Enclosure Award
### (also Showing the Estates Claiming Common Rights)[8]

| | | A. | R. | P. |
|---|---|---|---|---|
| A | The King [Chief Lord] | 21 | 0 | 16 |
| B | Rev. James Buckley Curate of The Chapel of Dobcross [Boothsteads] | 28 | 2 | 0 |
| C | Abraham Milnes of Boostage Edge, Saddleworth School master [Boothsteads Edge] | 2 | 1 | 0 |
| D | Abraham Gartside of Syke in Butterworth, Co. Lancs., Farmer [Farm in Denshaw Fold] | 4 | 2 | 2 |
| E | William Armitage of Rastrick, Co. York, Merchant [Ralph's Farm] | 8 | 0 | 26 |
| F | John Clegg of Manchester, Co. Lancs., Gentleman [Calf Hey] | 3 | 3 | 19 |
| G | Joshua Radcliffe of Saddleworth, Gentleman [Bowkhouse] | 25 | 1 | 0 |
| H | Thomas Milnes of Saddleworth, Clothier [Dowry Greens] | 9 | 2 | 28 |
| I | Martha Harrop of Bardsley, Co. Lancs., Spinster [Dowry Greens] | 3 | 0 | 8 |
| J | Jonah Harrop of Copster Hill, Oldham, Co. Lancs., Gentleman [Dowry Greens] | 10 | 3 | 10 |
| K | Benjamin Buckley of Linfitts, Saddleworth, Gentleman [Farm in Denshaw Fold &c] | 37 | 2 | 33 |
| L | John Taylor of Manchester Co. Lancs., Esquire [Brimmycroft] | 29 | 2 | 25 |
| M | James Milnes of Hey-house, Saddleworth, Inn Keeper [Rough Hey Side] | 7 | 2 | 30 |
| N | Benjamin Gartside of Cherry-Clough, Saddleworth, Farmer [Cherry Clough] | 7 | 0 | 36 |
| O | William Greenwood of Delph, Saddleworth, Grocer [Cherry Clough] | 4 | 1 | 28 |
| P | Rev. James Hargreaves of Ogden in Butterworth, Co. Lancs. [Cherry Clough] | 3 | 1 | 28 |
| Q | Samuel Gartside of Syke in Butterworth, Co. Lancs., Yeoman [Farm in Denshaw Fold] | 4 | 1 | 0 |
| R | John Taylor of Manchester Co. Lancs., Esquire [Calf Hey Barn Estate] | 5 | 0 | 24 |
| S | David Kelsall of Mottram, Co. Chester, Farmer [Farm in Denshaw Fold &c] / Jesse Ainsworth of Wickenhole in Butterworth. Co. Lancs., Gentleman [Denshaw Mill & Land] | 44 | 3 | 0 |
| T | William Horton Lloyd of London, Co. Middlesex, Esquire [Slack Gate] | 24 | 3 | 0 |
| U | John Schofield of Old Tame, Saddleworth, Yeoman [Brewery or Martin Estate] / James Schofield of Old Tame, Saddleworth, Yeoman [Brewery or Martin Estate] / Joseph Schofield of Liverpool, Co Lancs., Brewer [Brewery or Martin Estate] | 9 | 2 | 10 |
| V | Thomas Gartside of Friar Lodge, Saddleworth, Esquire [Woodbrow] | 6 | 2 | 13 |
| | | 302 | 0 | 38 |

---

[8] The list printed here is that recorded on the map with the addition of places of residence, occupation and status taken from the Enclosure Award, QE2/6, WYAS (Wakefield). The estates owned by the respective parties from which their common rights derived are listed in square brackets. This information has been compiled from numerous deeds collated by Mike Buckley.

Plate I

138

Plate II

Plate III

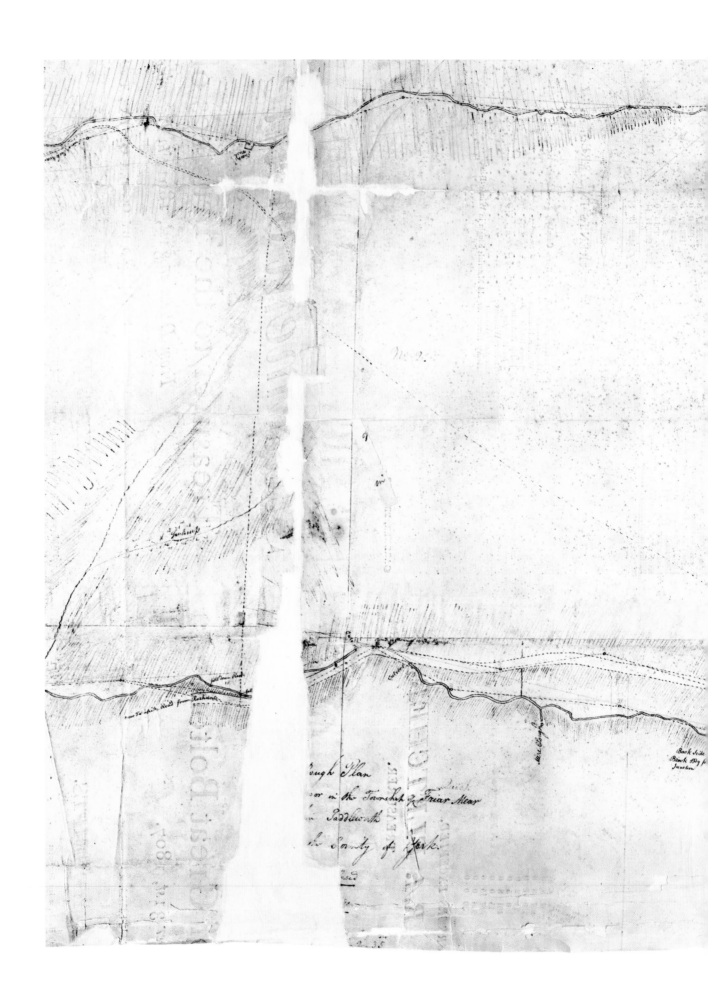

Plate IV

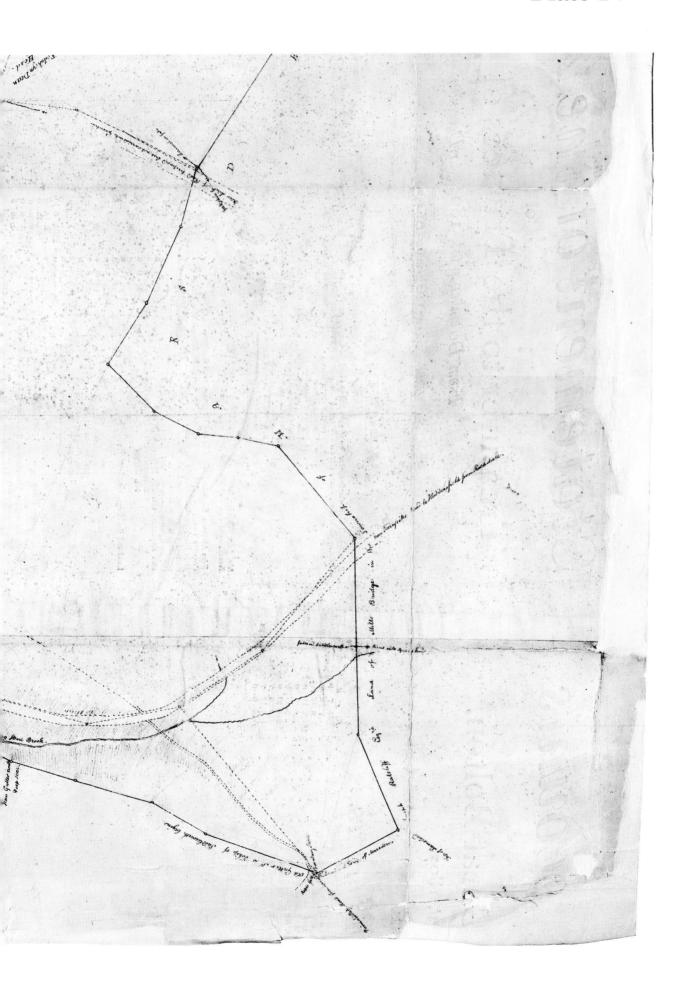

143

Plate V

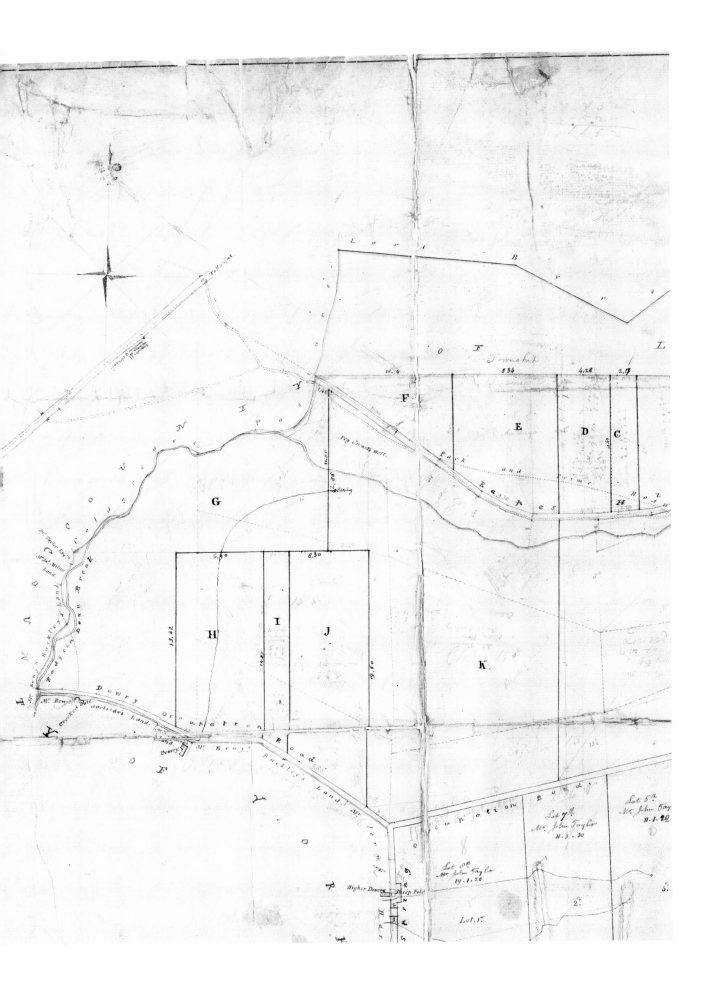

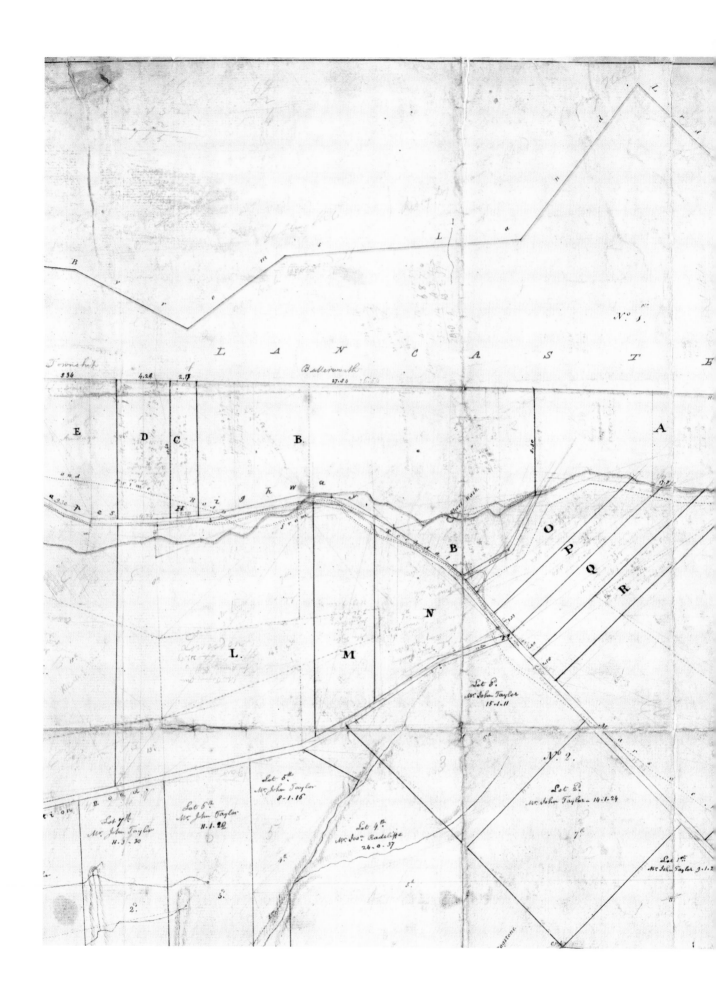

Plate VI

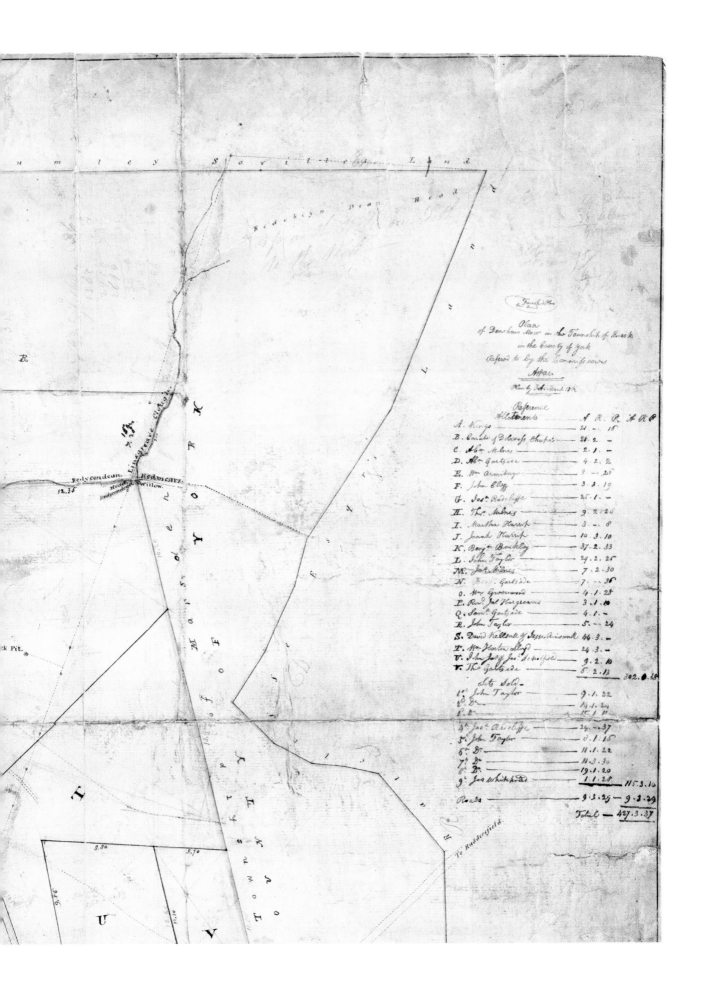

Plate VII

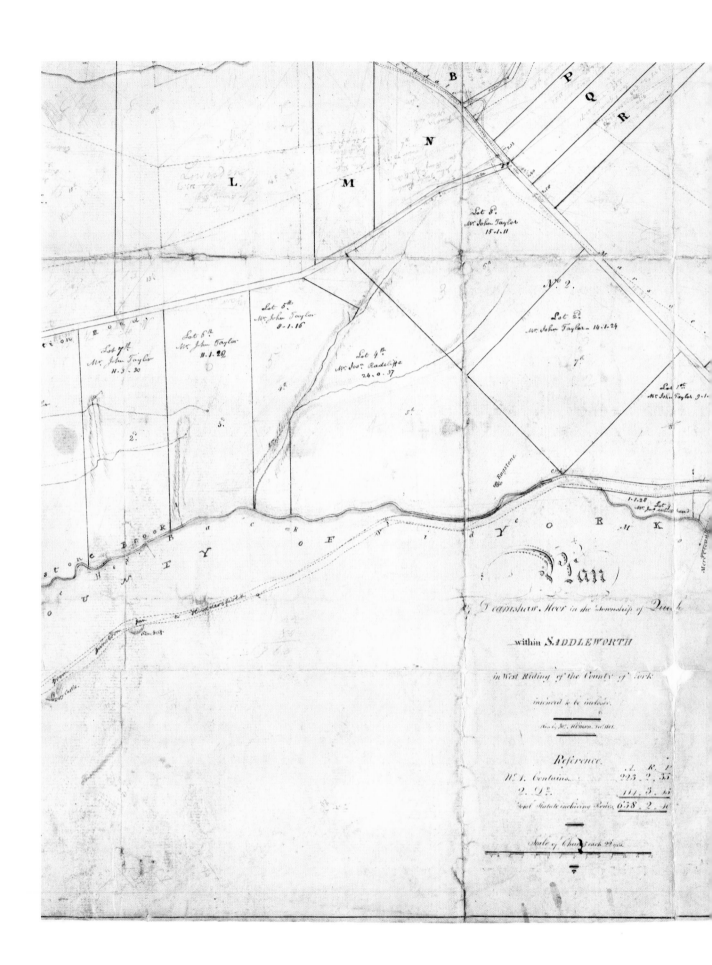

L.

M

N

B

P

Q

R

Lot 8.
Mr John Taylor
15.1.11

No. 2.

Lot 6.
Mr John Taylor
9.1.16

Lot 3.
Mr John Taylor — 14.1.24

7th.

Lot 6th.
Mr John Taylor
11.1.22

Lot 4th.
Mr Jos Radcliffe
24.0.37

Lot 7th.
Mr John Taylor
11.3.30

Lot 1st.
Mr John Taylor 9.1.

1.1.28

Plan

of Ramshaw Moor in the Township of Quick

within SADDLEWORTH

in West Riding of the County of York

intended to be inclosed.

Reference.

| | A. R. |  |
|---|---|---|
| No 1. Contains | 223.2.35 |  |
| 2. Do | 414.3. |  |
| Total Statute including Roads | 638.2. |  |

Scale of Chains each 22 yds.

150

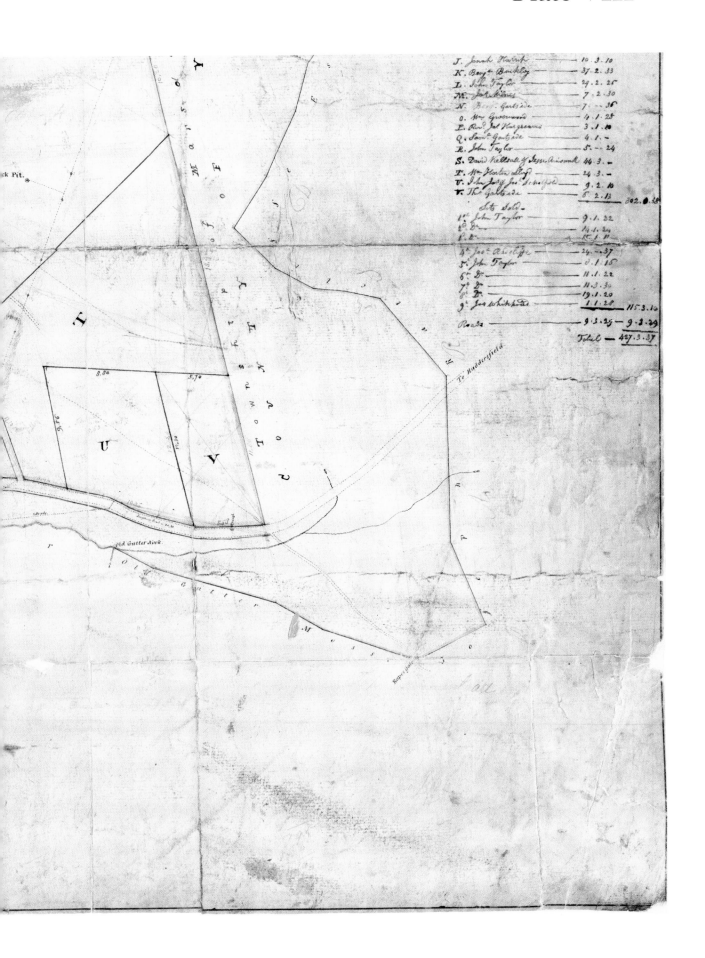

Plate VIII

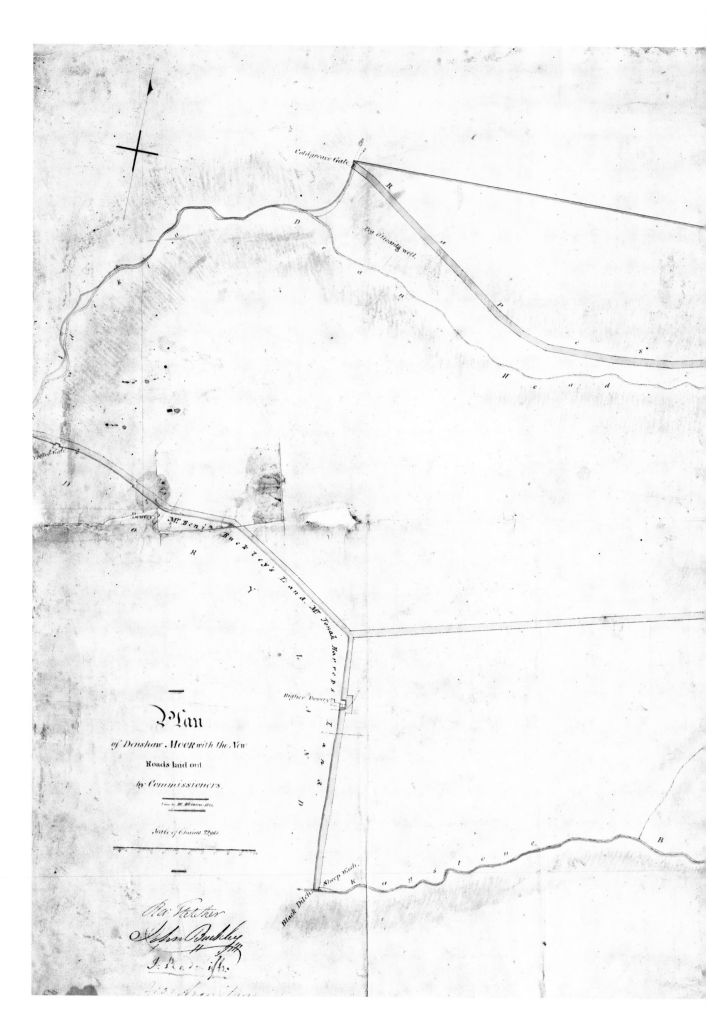

Coldgreave Gate.

Peg O'leary's well.

Crooked Gate

Mr Benjn Buckley's Land

Mr Jonah Harrop's

Higher Dowry

Plan
of Denshaw MOOR with the New
Roads laid out
by Commissioners.

Scale of Chains 22 Yds.

Black Ditch

Sheep Wash

152

Plate IX

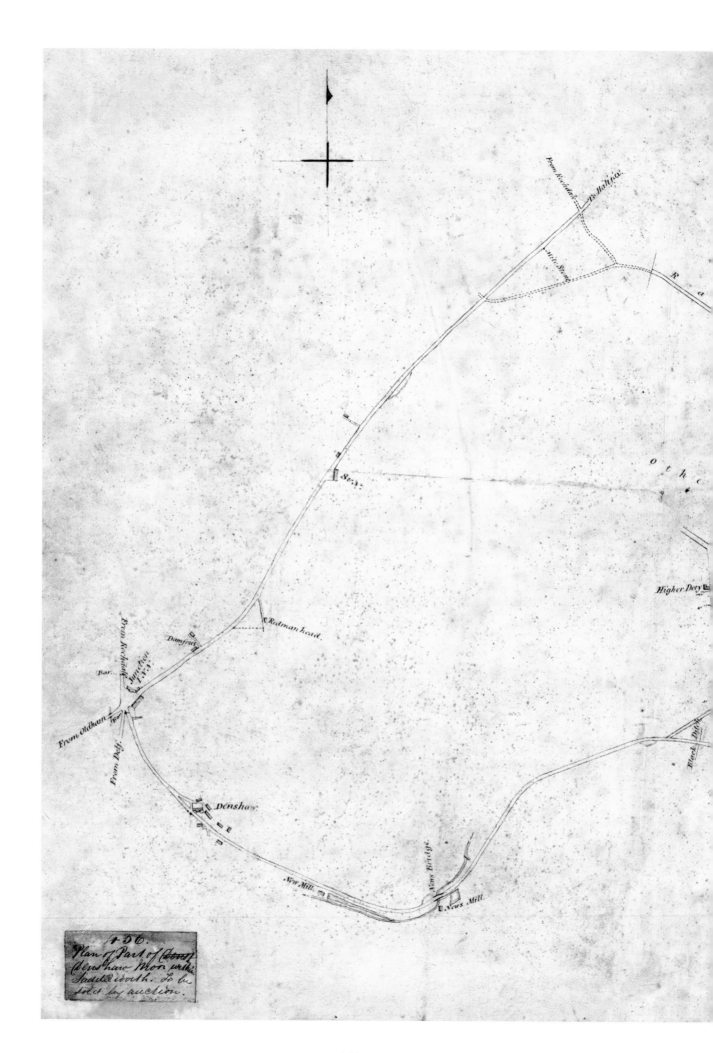

From Rochdale
To Halifax
Mile Stone
R a
From Rochdale
Damfires
Bar
Junction I.V.P.
From Oldham
From Delph
Redman head
Sew.
o t h
Higher Doy
Black Ditch
Denshaw
New Mill
News Bridge
News Mill

+56.
Plan of Part of Coast
Denshaw Moor within
Saddleworth. To be
Sold by auction.

Plate X

Plan

*of part of Denshaw Moor within*

SADDLEWORTH

*To be Sold by*

AUCTION.

*Plan by Wm Robinson 1810*

Reference.

| | A:R:P. |
|---|---|
| Lot 8th Contains | 19. 1. 20 |
| 7th Do | 11. 3. 30 |
| 6th Do | 11. 1. 22 |
| 5th Do | 8. 1. 16 |
| 4th Do | 21. . 37 |
| 3d Do | 15. 1. 11 |
| 2d Do | 14. 1. 24 |
| 1st Do | 9. 1. 22 |
| 9th Do | 1. 1. 28 |
| Total Statute | 115. 3. 10 |

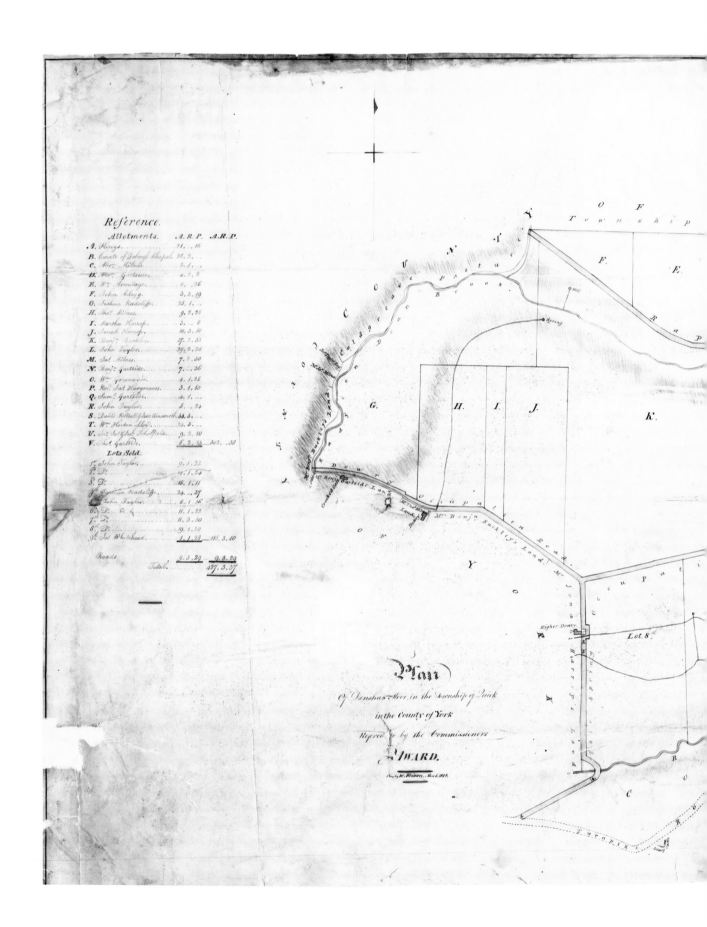

Reference.

| Allotments. | A.R.P. | A.R.P. |
|---|---|---|
| A. Kings | 31. . 16 | |
| B. Curate of Deberg Chapel | 33. 2. | |
| C. Abr. Milnes | 2. 1. | |
| D. Abr. Gartside | 4. 2. 2 | |
| E. Wm Armitage | 8. . 26 | |
| F. John Clegg | 5. 3. 19 | |
| G. Joshua Radcliffe | 25. 1. | |
| H. Thos. Milnes | 9. 2. 23 | |
| I. Martha Harrop | 3. . 8 | |
| J. Jonah Harrop | 10. 3. 10 | |
| K. Benj. Buckley | 17. 2. 33 | |
| L. John Taylor | 29. 2. 26 | |
| M. Jas. Milnes | 7. 2. 30 | |
| N. Benj. Gartside | 7. . 36 | |
| O. Wm. Greenwood | 4. 1. 28 | |
| P. Rev. Jas. Hargreaves | 3. 1. 10 | |
| Q. Sam. Gartside | 4. 1. | |
| R. John Taylor | 5. . 24 | |
| S. David Kelsall & Jno. Ainsworth | 44. 3. | |
| T. Wm. Horton Lloyd | 24. 3. | |
| U. Jas. Jas. Robt. Schofield | 9. 3. 10 | |
| V. Thos. Gartside | 6. 3. 13 | 502. . 38 |

Lots Sold.

| | A.R.P. | |
|---|---|---|
| 1. John Taylor | 9. 1. 22 | |
| 2. Do. | 14. 1. 34 | |
| 3. Do. | 15. 1. 11 | |
| 4. Joshua Radcliffe | 24. . 37 | |
| 5. John Taylor | 6. 1. 16 | |
| 6. Do. Do. | 4. 1. 22 | |
| 7. Do. | 11. 3. 30 | |
| 8. Do. | 19. 1. 20 | |
| 9. Jas. Whitehead | 1. 1. 28 | 115. 3. 40 |
| Roads | 9. 3. 29 | 9. 3. 29 |
| Total. | | 627. 3. 37 |

Plan

Of Denshaw Moor in the Township of Quick

in the County of York

Referred to by the Commissioners

J. WARD.

Made by W. Milnes, March 1819.

Plate XI

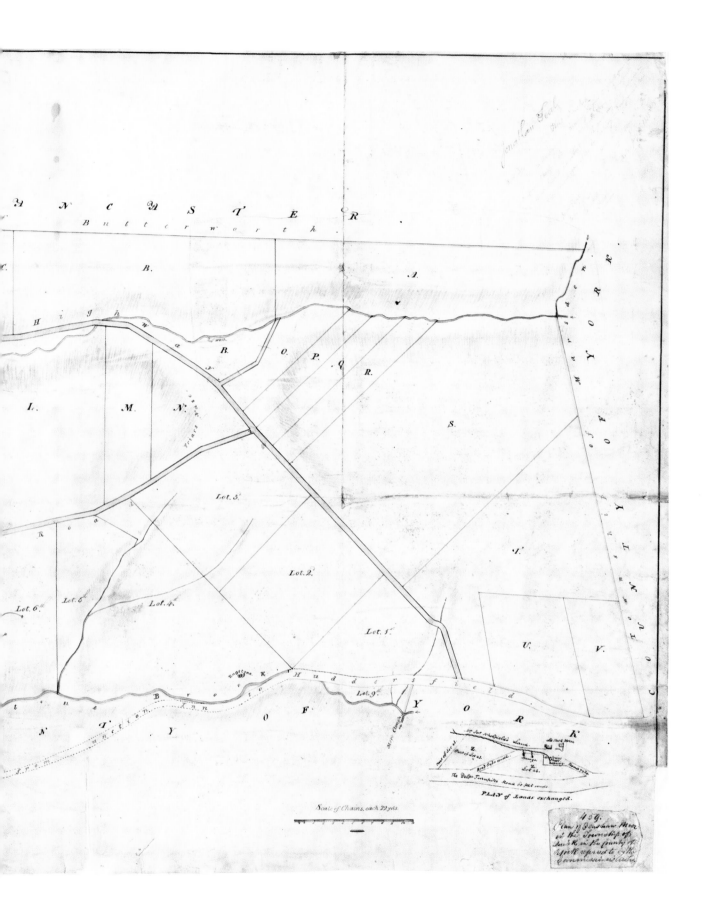

PLAN of Lands exchanged.

Scale of Chains, each 22 yds.

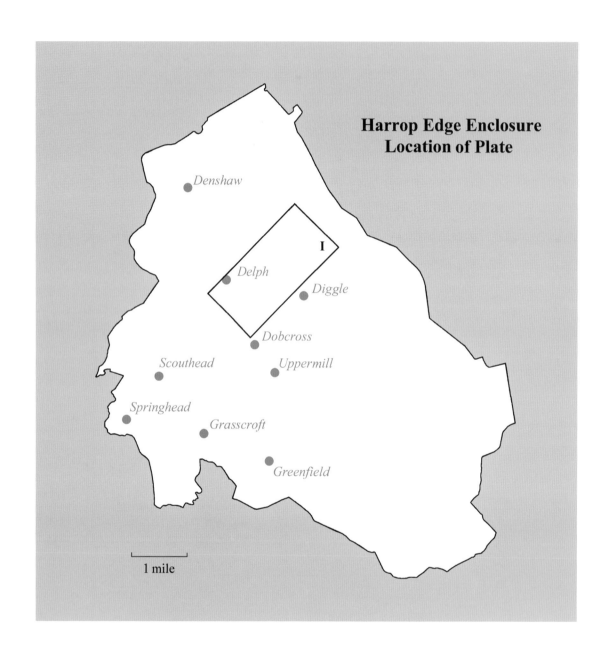

**Harrop Edge Enclosure**
**Location of Plate**

Denshaw

I

Delph

Diggle

Dobcross

Scouthead

Uppermill

Springhead

Grasscroft

Greenfield

1 mile

158

# PLAN OF HARROP EDGE SITUATE WITHIN THE PARISH OF SADDLEWORTH AS SOLD IN LOTS, 1810

| | |
|---|---|
| *Location:* | Reproduced from a copy in the hands of Mike Buckley. Location of original unknown |
| *Date of Compilation of Maps:* | 1810 |
| *Surveyor:* | Joel Hawkyard |
| *Material:* | Unknown |
| *Size of Original:* | Unknown |
| *Scale of Original:* | 1" : 6 Chains (13⅓" : 1 mile) |
| *Scale of Reproduction:* | Approximately 5½" : 1 mile |

The *Act for Inclosing Lands In The Parish of Saddleworth* received the royal assent on 2nd June 1810. The Commissioner, Ralph Fletcher, was also working concurrently on the Denshaw enclosure and there are interesting comparisons between the process of enclosure in the two locations. One similarity is that part of the common land was sold by auction to provide funds to carry out the process of enclosure. Harrop Edge was no doubt chosen as the area to be auctioned because it was one of the most attractive pieces of common available. The area was significantly lower than most of the unenclosed land and access was easy from Dobcross, a prosperous and growing community.

This map shows how the land was set out for auction. It also shows some land that had been sold privately before the auction. This is a reminder that the Commissioner had the power to sell off small amounts of land to individuals. This was most often done where a little piece of common land lay adjacent to an existing holding and it made sense to add it to the field. Examples of this can be found in several road-side locations, notably at the southern end of the 'Middle Highway' which we now know as Harrop Edge Lane.

The auction of Harrop Edge took place on four days beginning on 7th November 1810 and 328 acres 1 rood and 35 perches were sold raising a total of £8,600 5s. 2½d. It was held at the Kings Head Inn (now the Swan) which was the major public venue in Dobcross, then the principal village of the district. Figure 7 shows the poster advertising the auction listing the lots to be sold[1]. It is clear from the text that multiple copies of the enclosure plans had been produced by Hawkyard. These could be:

> *seen at the House of the said John Wrigley; at the Office of Mr. Mellor, Solicitor, Ashton-under-line; or at Mr. Joel Halkyard's, Land Surveyor, No. 9, Pine Street, Manchester.*

The area to be enclosed contained not only the large rectangular plots carved out of the common but also small areas of waste alongside the turnpike road leading over Stanedge. This map is not only about the sale of land but also the construction of a new landscape. For example, the line of the old pack horse route over Harrop Edge was all but obliterated by the newly laid out Middle Highway.

---

[1] The Shaw Papers, H/SHAW/29, SHS.

The boundaries of the lots depicted on this map were, in many cases, translated into stone walls on the ground as can be seen by a comparison with later maps. This process appears to have been quite rapid. There is evidence that most of the walls required had been built by 1812 because in July of that year Ralph Fletcher received a complaint that some walls had not been built: the implication is that most were already in existence. As it happened this was not the only problem that the Commissioner was to have with Harrop Edge; the Rhodes family of Bleak Hey Nook claimed that some of the land sold at the auction belonged to them and it was not until 1819 that this matter was resolved.[2] Not every lot had to be walled individually as some adjacent lots were bought by the same man; for example lots three, four and five were all bought by Jonathan Harrop and lots seventeen, eighteen, nineteen and twenty were purchased by John Harrop.

Nevertheless, Joel Hawkyard's map was to have a significant landscape impact. Unlike Denshaw Moor, where little now is visible of the enclosure process, Harrop Edge, characterised as it is by the regular rectangular fields and the long straight occupation road, remains the most visible example of Parliamentary enclosure in Saddleworth.

Figure 6. Harrop Edge. A striking example of early nineteenth century Parliamentary enclosure.

[2] A.J. Petford, 'The Process of Enclosure in Saddleworth, 1625-1834', *Transactions of the Lancashire and Cheshire Antiquarian Society*, Manchester, printed for the society, Vol. 84, 1987, p. 110.

# SADDLEWORTH.

# TO BE SOLD BY AUCTION,

## BY MR. JOHN PLATT,

## At the House of Mr. John Wrigley, Innkeeper, Dobcross, Saddleworth,

in the County of York, on the 7th. 8th. and 9th. Days of NOVEMBER, 1810, at 3 o'Clock in the Afternoon, of each of the said Days,

**(In Lots, and subject to such Conditions as will be then and there produced.) BY ORDER of *RALPH FLETCHER, Esq.* the Commissioner appointed under an Act of Parliament passed in the *50th.* Year of the Reign of his present Majesty, intituled "An Act for inclosing Lands in the Parish of Saddleworth in the West-Riding of the County of York," in pursuance of the said Act, and also of another Act of Parliament intituled "An Act for consolidating in one Act, certain provisions usually inserted in Acts of Inclosure, and for facilitating the mode of proving the several Facts usually required on the passing of such Acts,**

## *About three Hundred Acres of Land,*

Statute Measure, (being Part of the Lands authorised to be inclosed by Virtue of the Act first above mentioned) and called by the name of PLATT-HILL, or *HARROP-EDGE*, and the Waste up to Wimber-lee-Lane, in Saddleworth aforesaid, through and over which runs the Turnpike-Road, leading from Manchester to Huddersfield.

LOT.

**1.** **A parcel of Common, lying on the Northwesterly side of Platt-hill or Harrop Edge aforesaid, adjoining the higher side of the turnpike road near *Midge Grove*: containing by admeasurement 12a. 3r. 29p. or thereabouts, be *the same more or less*.**

**2.** A PARCEL OF COMMON, lying on the said North-Westerly side of *Platt-Hill*, or *Harrop-Edge* aforesaid, adjoining the northerly side of the *1st.* Lot, & containing by admeasurement 12a. 2r. 10p or thereabouts, be *the same more or less*,

**3.** A PARCEL of COMMON, lying on the said North Westerly side of *Platt Hill or Harrop Edge* aforesaid, adjoining the northerly side of the *second Lot*, and containing by admeasurement 11a. 1r. 25p. or thereabouts, *be the same more or less*,

**4.** A PARCEL of COMMON, lying on the said North-westerly side of *Platt Hill or Harrop Edge* aforesaid, adjoining the northerly side of the *third Lot*, and containing by admeasurement 10a. 3r. 30p or thereabouts, *be the same more or less*

**5.** A PARCEL of COMMON, lying on the said North-westerly side of *Platt Hill, or Harrop Edge* aforesaid, adjoining the northerly side of *the fourth Lot*, and containing by admeasurement 11a. 0r. 33p or thereabouts, *be the same more or less*,

**6.** A PARCEL of COMMON, lying on the said North-westerly side of *Platt Hill or Harrop Edge* aforesaid, adjoining the northerly side of *the fifth Lot*, and containing by admeasurement, 11a. 1r. 15p or thereabouts, *be the same more or less*.

**7,** A PARCEL of COMMON, lying on the said North-westerly side of *Platt-hill, or Harrop-edge* aforesaid, adjoining the northerly side of *the sixth Lot*, and containing by admeasurement *10a. 3r.* 33*p* or thereabouts, *be the same more or less*,

**8,** A PARCEL of COMMON, lying on the said North-westerly side of *Platt-hill, or Harrop edge* aforesaid, adjoining the northerly side of *the seventh Lot*, and containing by admeasurement 10*a* 0*r* 35*p* or thereabouts, *be the same more or less*.

**9.** A PARCEL of COMMON, lying on the said North-westerly side of *Platt-hill, or Harrop-edge* aforesaid, adjoining the northerly side of *the eighth Lot*, and containing by admeasurement 13*a* 2*r* 5*p* or thereabouts, *be the same more or less*.

**10.** A PARCEL of COMMON, lying on the said north-westerly side of *Platt-hill, or Harrop-edge*, aforesaid, adjoining the northerly side of *the ninth Lot*, and containing by admeasurement 6*a* 2*r* 14*p* or thereabouts, *be the same more or less*.

**11.** A PARCEL of COMMON, lying on the said north-westerly side of *Platt hill, or Harrop edge* aforesaid, adjoining the northerly side of *the tenth Lot*, and containing by admeasurement 8*a* 0*r* 22*p* or thereabouts, *be the same more or less*.

**12,** A PARCEL of COMMON, lying on the said north-westerly side of *Platt-hill, or Harrop-edge*, aforesaid, adjoining the northerly side of *the eleventh Lot*, and containing by admeasurement, 8*a* 2*r* 22*p* or thereabouts, *be the same more or less*.

**13.** A PARCEL of *COMMON*, lying on the said north-westerly side of *Platt-hill or Harrop edge* aforesaid, and adjoining the northerly side of a Bridle Road laid out on the north easterly side of *the twelfth Lot*, and containing by admeasurement, 4*a* 0*a* 10*p*. or thereabouts, *be the same more or less*.

**14.** A PARCEL of *COMMON*, lying on the said north-westerly side of *Platt-hill, or Harrop edge* aforesaid, adjoining the northerly side of *the thirteenth Lot*, and running up to the Way-Mark, containing by admeasurement 3*a* 2*r* 34*p*. or thereabouts, *be the some more or less*.

**15.** A PARCEL of *COMMON*, lying on the top or south-easterly side of *Platt.hill, or Harrop edge* aforesaid, adjoining the northerly side of a new laid out road, leading from Long-Lane towards Midge Grove, and containing by admeasurement 9*a* 2*r* 3*p*. or thereabouts, *be the same more or less*.

**16,** A PARCEL of COMMON, lying on the top or south-easterly side of *Platt-hill or Harrop edge* aforesaid, adjoining the northerly side of *the fifteenth Lot*, and containing by admeasurement 8*a* 0*r* 31*p* or thereabouts, *be the same more or less*,

**17,** A PARCEL of COMMON, lying on the top or south-easterly side of Platt-hill, or Harrop-edge aforesaid, adjoining the northerly side of *the sixteenth Lot* and containing by admeasurement 8*a* 12*r* 6*p* or thereabouts *be the same more or less*.

**18.** A PARCEL of COMMON, lying on the top or south-easterly side of Platt-hill, or Harrop-edge aforesaid, adjoining the northerly side of *the 17th* Lot, and containing by admeasurement 8*a* 2*r* 22*p* or thereabouts, *be the same more or less*.

**19,** A PARCEL of COMMON, lying on the top or south easterly side of Platt-hill or Harrop-edge aforesaid, adjoining the northerly side of *the 18th. Lot*, and containing by admeasurement 8*a* 3*r* 26*p* or thereabouts, *be the same more or less*.

**20,** A PARCEL of COMMON, lying on the top or south-easterly side of Platt-hill, or Harrop-edge aforesaid, adjoining the northerly side of *the 19th Lot*, and containing by admeasurement, 9*a* 1*r* 2*p* or thereabouts, *be the same more or less*.

**21,** A PARCEL of COMMON, lying on the top or south-easterly side of Platt-hill, or Harrop-edge aforesaid, adjoining the northerly side of *the 20th Lot*, and containing by admeasurement 9A 2R 24P or thereabouts, *be the same more or less*,

**22.** A PARCEL of COMMON, lying on the top or south-easterly side of Platt hill or Harrop-edge aforesaid, adjoining the northerly side of the *21st, Lot*, and containing by admeasurement 9A 3R 31P or thereabouts, *be the same more or less*.

**23.** A PARCEL of COMMON, lying on the top or south-easterly side of Platt-hill or Harrop-edge aforesaid, adjoining the northerly side of *the 22nd. Lot*, and containing by admeasurement 9*a* 3*r* 14*p* or thereabouts, *be the same more or less*.

**24,** A PARCEL of COMMON, lying on the top or south-easterly side of Platt-hill, or harrop.edge aforesaid, adjoining the northerly side of the *23d Lot*, and containing by admeasurement 9*a* 2*r* 12*p* or thereabouts, *be the same more or less*.

**25.** A PARCEL of COMMON, lying on the top, or south-easterly side of Platt-hill or Harrop-edge aforesaid, adjoining the northerly side of the *24th* Lot, and containing by admeasurement 8*a*, 3*r*, 21*p* or thereabouts, *be the same more or less*,

**26.** A PARCEL of *COMMON*; lying on the top, or south easterly side of Platt-hill, or Harrop-edge, aforesaid, adjoining the south easterly ends of the *16th, 17th, and 18th*, Lots, and containing by admeasurement, 6*a* 3*r* 8*p*. or thereabouts, *be the same more, or less*.

**27.** *A PARCEL* of *COMMON*, lying on the south-easterly side of Platt-hill, or Harrop-edge aforesaid, adjoining the southerly end of the *26th*. Lot, and containing by admeasurement, 3*a* 2*r* 14*p*, or thereabouts, be *the same more or less*.

**28.** *A PARCEL* of *COMMON*, lying on the south-easterly side of Platt-hill, or Harrop-edge aforesaid, adjoining the southerly side of the *27th*, Lot, and containing by admeasurement 5a 1r 1p. or thereabouts, *be the same more or less*,

**29,** *A PARCEL* of COMMON, lying on the south easterly side of Platt-hill or Harrop-edge aforesaid, near Nab-End, and adjoining a new laid out road, running between this and the *28th*, Lot, and containing by admeasurement 3*a* 3*r* 24*p* or thereabouts, *be the same more or less*,

**30,** A PARCEL OF COMMON, lying on the south easterly side of *Platt-Hill*, or *Harrop-Edge* aforesaid, adjoining the south easterly side of the *29th* Lot, & containing by admeasurement 2a. 1r. 0p or thereabouts, be *the same more or less*,

**31.** A PARCEL of COMMON, lying on *Platt Hill or Harrop Edge* aforesaid, adjoining the north-easterly side of the Turnpike road leading from Dobcross to Delph, and also adjoining the south easterly side of a new laid out road to be called the Middle Highway, containing by admeasurement 1a. 3r. 9p. or thereabouts, *be the same more or less*,

**32.** A PARCEL of COMMON, lying on *Platt Hill or Harrop Edge* aforesaid, adjoining the north westerly side of the middle highway, and the south-westerly side of Slack Pit, and containing by admeasurement 0a: 1r. 26p or thereabouts, *be the same more or less*

**33.** A PARCEL of COMMON, lying on *Platt Hill or Harrop Edge* aforesaid, adjoining the south-easterly side of the middle high way, and opposite to Slack Pit aforesaid, and containing by admeasurement 4a. 0r. 31p or thereabouts, *be the same more or less*,

**34.** A TRIANGULAR PARCEL of COMMON, lying on *Platt Hill or Harrop Edge* aforesaid, adjoining the north-easterly side of *the 33d Lot*, and containing by admeasurement, 2a. 1r. 10p or thereabouts, *be the same more or less*.

**35.** A PARCEL of COMMON, lying on *Platt hill, or Harrop edge* aforesaid, adjoining the North-westerly side of the middle highway, and opposite *the 34th Lot*, and containing by admeasurement, *5a*, 1r, 35p or thereabouts, *be the same more or less*,

**36.** A PARCEL of COMMON, lying on the north-westerly side of *Platt hill, or Harrop.edge* aforesaid, adjoining the lower side of the turnpike road, near Midge Grove aforesaid, containing by admeasurement 0*a*. 1*r* 20*p*. or thereabouts, *be the same more or less*.

**37,** A small PARCEL of COMMON, lying on *Platt.hill, or Harrop edge*, aforesaid, adjoining the lowerside of the turnpike road, and also adjoining the northerly end of *the 36th Lot*, and containing by admeasurement 0*a* 3*r* 36*p* or thereabouts, *be the same more or less*.

**38,** A PARCEL of COMMON, lying on *Platt hill, or Harrop edge* aforesaid, adjoining the lower side of the turnpike road, and also adjoining the northerly end of *the 37th, Lot*, and containing by admeasurement 0*a* 3*r* 33*p*, or thereabouts, *be the same more or less*.

**39,** A PARCEL of COMMON, lying on *Platt hill, or Harrop edge* aforesaid, adjoining the lower-side of the turnpike road, and also adjoining the northerly side of a new laid out road leading to Sand-bed running between this and the 38th. Lot, and containing by admeasurement 2*a* 2*r* 19. or thereabouts, *be the same more or less*.

**40,** A PARCEL of COMMON, lying on *Platt hill, or Harrop edge* aforesaid, adjoining the lower-side of the turnpike-road, and also adjoining the northerly side of the *39th* Lot, and containing by admeasurement, 4*a* 1*r* 12*p*, or thereabouts, *be the same more or less*.

**41.** A PARCEL of *COMMON*, lying on Platt-hill, or Harrop-edge aforesaid, adjoining the northerly side of Delph highway, at or near Sandbed, containing by admeasurement, 1*a* 0*r* 21*p*. or thereabouts, *be the same more or less*.

**42.** A PARCEL of *COMMON*, lying on Platt-hill, or Harrop-edge aforesaid, adjoining the northerly side of Delph highway, and also adjoining a new laid out road, leading to Intake Nook, running between this and the north-easterly side of the *41st Lot*, containing by admeasurement 1*a* 3*r* 17*p*. or thereabouts, *be the same more or less*.

**43.** A PARCEL of COMMON, lying on Platt-hill or Harrop-edge aforresaid, adjoining the lowerside of the turnpike road, and also adjoining a new laid out road, leading to Causeway-Set, running between this and *the 42d, Lot*, and containing by admeasurement 4A 1R 17P, or thereabouts, *be the same more or less*.

**44** A small PARCEL of COMMON, lying on Platt-hill or Harrop-edge aforesaid, adjoining the lower side of the turnpike road, and opposite the Old Pack Horse, and containing by admeasurement 0*a* 3*r* 11*p*. or thereabouts, be *the same more or less*.

**45.** A PARCEL of COMMON, lying on Platt-hill or Harrop-edge aforesaid, adjoining the lower side of the turnpike road, and also adjoining a new laid out road, leading to the Old Pack-Horse aforesaid, running between this and the *44th Lot*, containing by admeasurement 1a 3r 11p. or thereabouts, *be the same more or less*.

**46,** A small PARCEL of *COMMON*, lying on *Platt-hill, or Harrop edge* aforesaid, adjoining the Lower-side of the Turnpike-road, and also adjoining the north easterly end of 45th Lot, and containing by admeasurement 0*a* 2*r* 30*p*. or thereabouts, *be the same more or less*.

**47,** *A* PARCEL of COMMON, lying on *Platt-hill or Harrop edge* aforesaid, adjoining the lower-side of the Turnpike-road, and also adjoining a new laid out Road, leading from the said Turnpike-road to Waters-Gate, containing by admeasurement 1*a* 0*r* 22*p* or thereabouts, *be the same more or less*.

**48** A PARCEL of COMMON, lying on Platt-hill, or Harrop-edge aforesaid, adjoining the lower-side of the Turnpike-road, and also adjoining the easterly end of the 47th Lot, and containing by admeasurement 1*a* 0*r* 6*p* or thereabouts, be *the same more or less*.

**49.** A PARCEL of Waste Land lying between Platt-hill, or Harrop.edge aforesaid, and Wimber-lee-lane, adjoining the lower side of the Turnpike-Road, and also adjoining the north-easterly end of the 48th Lot, and containing by admeasurement 1*a*. 0*r*, 32*p*. or thereabouts, *be the seme more or less*,

**50.** A small PARCEL of Waste Land, lying between Platt-hill or Harrop-edge aforesaid, and Wimber-lee Lane, adjoinining the north-westerly side of the Turnpike-Road at Blakehey-Nook, and also adjoining the new laid out Road running between this and the 49th Lot, and containing by admeasurement, *a*0 1*r* 3*p*, or thereabouts, *be the same more or less*.

**51,** *A PARCEL* of Waste Land lying between Platt-hill or Harrop-edge aforesaid, and Wimber-lee-Lane, adjoining the north-westerly side of the old Turnpike-Road there, and called or known by the name of the Knowl-brow, containing by admeasurement 3*a* 0*r* 33*p* or thereabouts, *be the same more or less*

**52.** A small *PARCEL* of Waste-Land, adjoining the south-side of the Turnpike-Road at Blakehey-Nook aforesaid, and also adjoining the Road leading to Dean-head, and containing by admeasurement 0*a* 1*r* 10*p* or thereabouts, *be the same more or less*.

**53.** *A PARCEL* of Waste-Land, lying on the south-easterly side of the Turnpike-road at Blakehey-Nook aforesaid, and containing by admeasurement, 0*a* 2*r*, 6p. or thereabouts, *be the same more, or less*

**54.** A PARCEL of Waste-Land, adjoining the south-easterly side of the Turnpike-road near Blakehey-Nook aforesaid, and also adjoining the south-westerly side of a new laid out Road leading to Warrock-hill-foot, running between this and the south westerly end of the 53d Lot, and containing by admeasurement 1*a*, 0*r*, 6*p*. or thereabouts, *be the same more or less*,

**55,** A PARCEL of COMMON, lying on Platt-hill, or Harrop-edge aforesaid, adjoining the south easterly-side of the said Middle-highway, and also adjoining a new laid out road, leading to Carr-head, running between this and the south westerly-end of the 54 Lot, and containing by admeasurement 3a 3r 5p. or thereabouts, *be the same more or less*.

NOTE.——Any Person or Persons who shall become a Purchaser or Purchasers of any of the said Lots will be required to Pay down a deposit of £10. per Cent upon the Purchase Money, in part thereof, agreeable to the Directions of the last above mentioned Acts.

☞ PLANS of the said Lots may be seen at the House of the said JOHN WRIGLEY; at the Office of MR. MELLOR, Solicitor, Ashton-under-line; or at MR. JOEL HALKYARD'S, Land Surveyor, No. 9, Pine Street, Manchester; and the Lots will be shewn to any Person wishing to view the same, by JOSEPH WRIGLEY, of Saddleworth-Fold.

Nicholson, Printer,

Figure 7. Poster Advertising the Auction of the Lots on Harrop Edge.

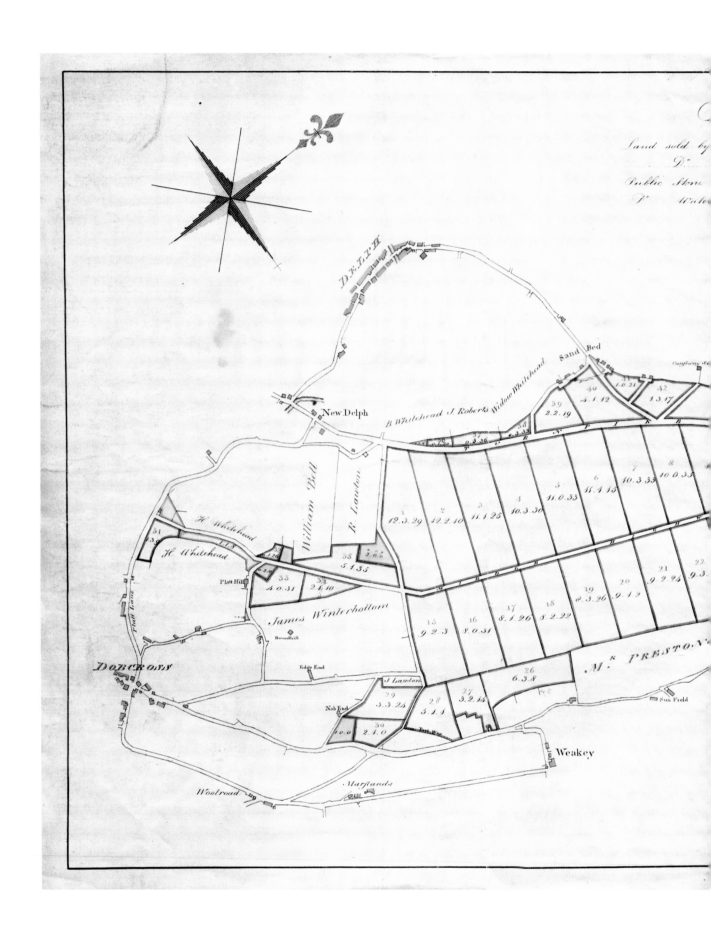

Land sold by

Dº

Public Stone

Dº Water

DELPH

Sand Bed

New Delph

B Whitehead  J. Roberts  Widow Whitehead

39
2.2.19

40
5.1.12

1.0.24

42
4.3.17

Canflurry Sc

38
4.3.33

37
0.3.36

8
10.0.33

7
10.3.33

William Bell

R. Lawton

H. Whitehead

H. Whitehead

Platt Hill

51
1.3.9

1.1.8

32
4.1.26

35
5.1.35

36
2.2.6

6
11.1.15

5
11.0.33

4
10.3.30

3
11.1.25

2
12.2.10

1
12.3.29

33
4.0.31

34
2.1.40

21
9.2.24

22
9.3.

20
9.2.4

19
8.3.26

17
8.1.26

18
8.2.22

James Winterbottom

Roundhill

15
9.2.3

16
8.0.31

Edge End

Mˢ PRESTON

DOBCROSS

J Lawton

Nab End

29
3.3.24

28
5.1.5

27
3.2.44

26
6.3.8

Sun Field

30
10.0

2.1.0

Fart Rᵉᵉ

Weakey

Woolroad

Marslands

162

Plate I

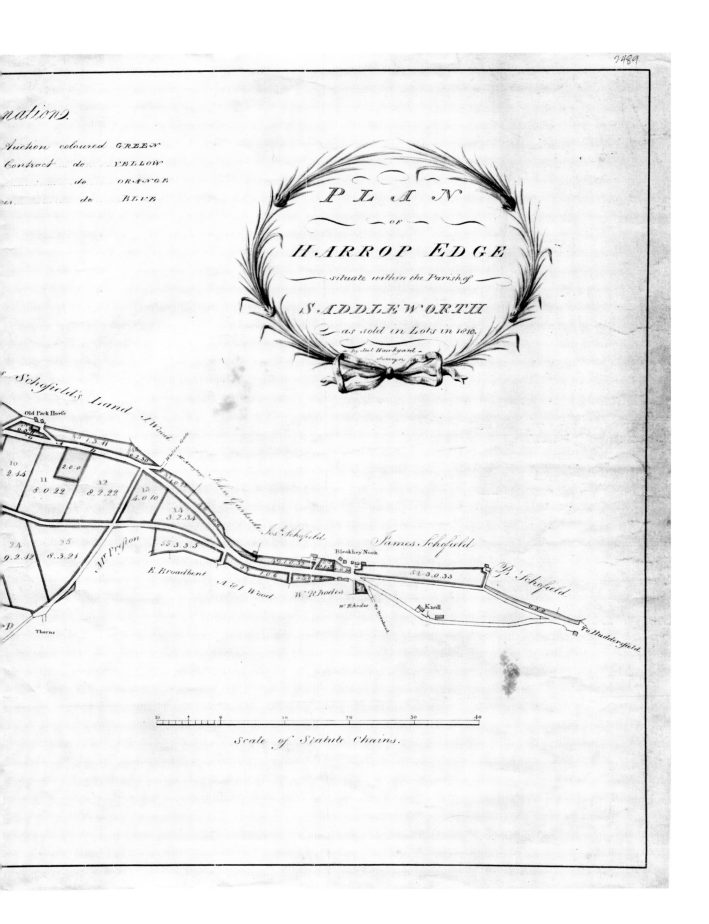

Scale of Statute Chains.

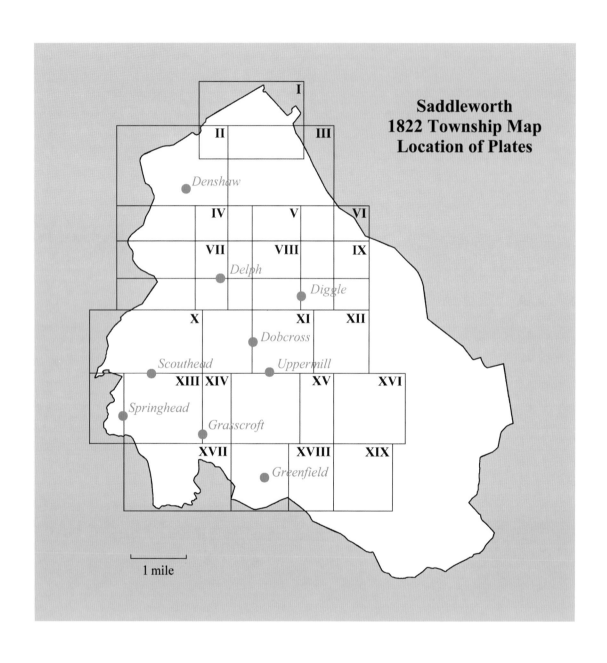

**Saddleworth
1822 Township Map
Location of Plates**

I

II    III

Denshaw

IV    V    VI

VII    VIII    IX

Delph

Diggle

X    XI    XII

Dobcross

Scouthead    Uppermill

XIII XIV    XV    XVI

Springhead

Grasscroft

XVII    XVIII    XIX

Greenfield

1 mile

# PLAN OF THE TOWNSHIP OF QUICK AND PARISH OF SADDLEWORTH IN THE WEST RIDING OF THE COUNTY OF YORK, 1822

| | |
|---|---|
| *Location:* | Saddleworth Historical Society Archives |
| *Date of Compilation of Map:* | 1816-22 |
| *Surveyors:* | Joel Hawkyard, James Monk, Mr. Dunn, Mr. Johnson and Joseph Shaw. |
| *Material:* | Paper mounted on linen |
| *Size of Original:* | 82" x 79" |
| *Scale of Original:* | 1" : 6 Chains (13⅓" : 1 mile) |
| *Scale of Reproduction:* | Approximately 8½" : 1 mile |

The most impressive of the Saddleworth maps in its detail and coverage is this Vestry Map of 1822. It was produced to facilitate a re-rating of the township, and was intended to be complete in its coverage. In the end some of the commons in the east of the township were omitted, but apart from this the original intention was fulfilled. The production of this map was a long and complex procedure: the task of surveying the whole of Saddleworth was daunting enough in itself, but the difficulties were exacerbated by the unwillingness of the vestry to pay more than the bare minimum for the work.

On the 4th July 1816, the Vestry committee for the new valuation of the parish ordered that an advertisement be inserted in one of the Leeds and one of the Manchester papers for a surveyor. On the 1st August Joel Hawkyard, James Monk and a Mr. Johnson presented themselves to the Committee, and Hawkyard was chosen, the other two being paid £1 for their attendance. The Vestry defined Hawkyard's task thus:

> *...the whole of the Township including the Commons be surveyed and planned. The inclosed lands containing about 8,700 acres, and the unenclosed lands about 7,000 acres and a proper map of the whole on a proper scale on paper to be backed in linen with a Field Book and a Book of Reference and that the whole be completed in eighteen months from the time of entering into the engagement.*[1]

For this work Hawkyard was to receive £240. In September 1817 he was granted £80 of this, but failed to finish the map in the required time. Therefore, at a full Vestry meeting in October 1818, it was resolved to sue him, a strong action, but one justified by the circumstances, for no alteration in the Parish assessment could be made until the map and survey were finished. As the Vestry recorded,

> *...the persons appointed to value this township have been prevented from making their valuation as expeditiously as they otherwise would have done.*[2]

In February 1819, however, Hawkyard managed to stay legal proceedings,

> *...having stated to this meeting that the Survey of Saddleworth is in great forwardness, he having four persons at work thereon regularly and that he will complete the same in a hansome style on or before 20th April next.*

---

[1] Saddleworth, Vestry Minute Books, Vol. III, 1816-1835, 4th July 1816, O9/3/1/3-4, Greater Manchester County Record Office (with Manchester Archives).

[2] *ibid.* 28th October, 1818.

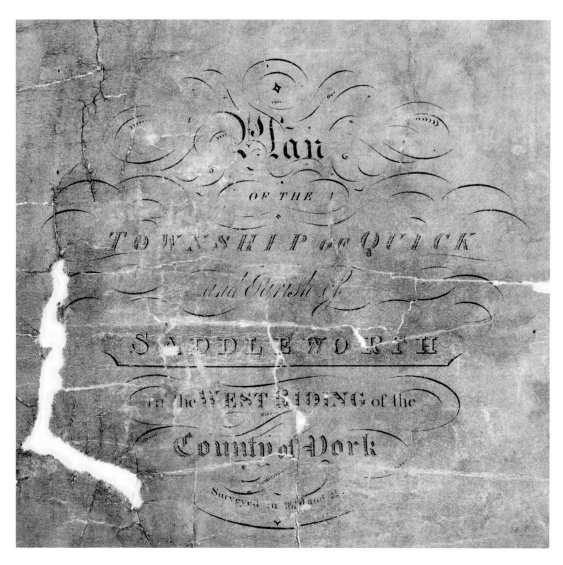

Figure 8. The Cartouche on the 1822 Vestry Map.

The 20th April came and went; the finished product was promised for the end of December, but the Vestry resolved to pay Hawkyard off and engage another surveyor to finish it. In December 1819, James Monk of Atherton in Lancashire, one of the unsuccessful candidates for the original contract, was chosen. He was to have fifteen months to finish the work and was to be paid at the rate of 6d per acre. This time the Vestry was determined to exercise a stricter supervision, and demanded a report every two months from the surveyor and valuers. A few days before the end of the fifteen months, four plans containing 4,000 acres had been produced and approved, but 2,300 acres remained. Monk had in fact been ill, so that

> *...he has not been out in the exercise of his profession for a whole day within the time he placed himself within the service of this Township.*[3]

[3] Saddleworth, Vestry Minute Books, Vol. III, 1816-1835, 4th April, 1821, O9/3/1/3-4, Greater Manchester County Record Office (with Manchester Archives).

It was impossible for him to fulfil his contract (which he bound himself to observe in the penal sum of £100) and therefore Monk was requested to attend a meeting of the Valuation Committee on 18th April. This he did, and promised to have all complete by 15th September. As he said,

> ... he has come into the Township with a view of proceeding and that he shall proceed forthwith and that he intends to remain until the survey is finished.[4]

Understandably, the Committee was not impressed by Monk's profession of intent, and it was resolved to give him only one month's trial and to inspect his work at the end of May. By this date only 700 more acres had been surveyed, but since Monk was now employing a surveyor it was agreed to continue with him and inspect the work again on 21st June. Monk did not appear on that date, and he and his employee were ordered to attend a full Vestry meeting on 29th June.

Mr. Dunn, his surveyor, did attend, but a letter from Mr. Robert Martin, surgeon, explained that Monk was too ill to come.[5] The Vestry decided that Monk should continue to employ Dunn and that the Survey Committee should inspect the work in a fortnight. Therefore on 13th July Monk and his assistant attended, and Monk assured the Committee that he had engaged Mr. Johnson and Joseph Shaw to assist him, and that all would be complete by 15th September.

When the Committee met on 29th August, it was greeted by a letter from Monk explaining that he was kept away by illness. His assistant, Dunn, gave them more disquieting news. He said that Monk had left the parish on the 18th, and that he had not yet returned, and that it was now impossible to complete the survey by 15th September. The Committee thereupon resigned its commission in the following minute:

> Mr. Monk having exhibited to this Committee a conduct of the most negligent character and broken every engagement which from time to time he has made, having made promises in the most solemn and serious manner and in a few days acted in direct opposition to them, this Committee is obliged to surrender its trust to the Vestry with the strongest expression of discontent with Mr. Monk.[6]

By January 1822 Mr. Monk was dead and his widow applied to the Vestry to be released from his commitments. The Vestry agreed, and also stated that her husband's work would be paid for at 3d per acre. In May this was increased to 7d per acre:

> ...on the grounds of justice and humanity and also because your Committee have found it necessary to excite some hope of public liberality or run great hazard of the suspension of the survey.[7]

Perhaps the Vestry regretted that they had not been more liberal with their payments in the first place and got the work done more rapidly. Ultimately the survey was

---

[4] *ibid.* 18th April, 1821.

[5] The identity of Mr. Dunn is obscure, but he may be the Joseph Dunn of Ashton-under-Lyne referred to in S. Bendall (editor), *Dictionary of Land Surveyors and Local Map-Makers of Great Britain and Ireland 1530-1850*, Second Edition, Vol. 1, London, The British Library, 1997, p. 158.

[6] Saddleworth, Vestry Minute Books, Vol. III, 1816-1835, 29th August, 1821, O9/3/1/3-4, Greater Manchester County Record Office (with Manchester Archives).

[7] *ibid.* 19th January, 1822.

completed, presumably by Dunn, Johnson and Shaw, and it was received by the Vestry on 9th May 1822. Perhaps not surprisingly, it bears no mapmaker's name.

Once the survey was finished it took the valuers little time to do their work, and the new valuation was ready by 16th August.

Despite the generally decayed state, parts of the map are in reasonable condition (see Figure 10) and could be reproduced. However, because of the poor state of the rest of the map (see Figure 9), and the difficulties this presented, a hand drawn copy of the map was published in 1983 in *Saddleworth Surveyed*.[8] Surprisingly, shortly after publication, another copy of the map was discovered in the archives of Heywood, Hartley and Whipp, Chartered Surveyors of Oldham[9]. This map, on paper, is dated 1863 and comprises six sheets accompanied by a reference map showing how the six sheets relate to each other. It is not clear who was responsible for this map however it is endorsed in the bottom of the right hand corner of the first sheet 'Cop[d]. April 27[th]1863 Jno Beedham Ex[d]. J.W.W'. Neither the purpose of this copy nor the identity of Jno Beedham or J.W.W. are at present known.

Figure 9. The Quick area, an example of the extremely decayed
state of the lower part of the 1822 Vestry Map.

At twice the scale of the Vestry Map, the 1863 Map contains much important detail omitted from its predecessor. However, an area approximately 25% of the total stretching from Denshaw, via Delph, Dobcross, and Diggle, to Saddleworth Church is missing. Fortunately those areas damaged or decayed on the Vestry Map are in good condition on the 1863 Map, and the missing areas on the 1863 Map are to a large degree readable on the Vestry Map. So, by combining the two, a reasonably complete picture emerges.

---

[8] *Saddleworth Surveyed*, Uppermill, SHS, 1983, pp. 70-101.

[9] Heywood, Hartley and Whipp Collection, Uncatalogued, Oldham Local Studies and Archives.

Valuable information only found on the 1863 Map relates to footpaths and watercourses, particularly those associated with early mills. The map however, although twice the scale, is less accurately drawn than the Vestry version and appears to have been a freehand copy of an earlier, and probably more accurate source. The fact that it was accompanied by a reference map, yet a section is missing, points to the possibility that it was a copy of an incomplete survey by either Hawkyard or Monk, and that the 1863 draughtsman had access to some of the original survey plans. Unfortunately, the fate of the original surveyors' plans from which it was apparently copied remains a mystery.

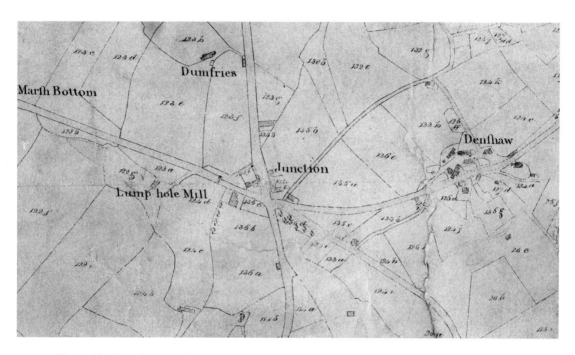

Figure 10. Denshaw on the 1822 Vestry Map, an area of the map still in good condition

With the availability of both the Vestry Map and the 1863 version, and their complementary nature, it has been possible to reconstruct the complete Township map with greater detail and accuracy than in the version printed in *Saddleworth Surveyed* where the Township map was essentially a copy of the Vestry Map of 1822. In the present publication the map presented is a synthesis of the 1822 and 1863 versions. We have therefore referred to it as the Reconstructed Version. In the missing section of the 1863 Map, the Vestry version has been exclusively used whereas in the damaged areas of the Vestry version, the 1863 Map has provided the missing detail. Close scrutiny of the two maps indicates that neither is entirely accurate nor free from error; both contain mistakes and omissions. However, the Vestry version is the more accurately drawn, even though at half the scale of the other, and has been used in the Reconstructed Version as the primary source for Plates I to XII. For the remaining plates the 1863 copy has been used with corrections from the Vestry Map. The detail on both maps has been compared, and the more accurate and complete source adopted in each specific instance. There are major differences in the shape of buildings between the two, and again, neither appears to be entirely accurate. In each case what appears to be the more correct representation has been adopted.

The colouring on the Vestry Map has been reproduced and interpreted as accurately as possible even though heavily faded and indistinct in places. This is particularly the case with the roads where the light brown colour has all but disappeared. Considerable difficulty has been experienced here and some errors may have been made.

One important difference in the Reconstructed Map reproduced here is its orientation. In both the Vestry Map and the 1863 copy the top of the map was drawn 34° to the West of true North. The Reconstructed Version has North at the top. This enables easier comparison with later maps and, to facilitate this further, the same scale and arrangement of plates as the first edition 6 inches to 1 mile Ordnance Survey map, reproduced in *Mapping Saddleworth Volume I,* have been adopted.

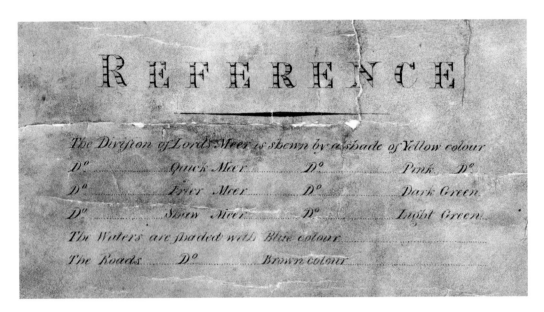

Figure 11. Key to the 1822 Vestry Map indicating Mere boundary, road and river colours.

Another important difference between the Vestry Map and the 1863 copy is the designation of the fields and enclosures. In the Vestry Map each field or enclosure is numbered and a key was created to record the acreage and ownership; apparently this is the Field Book referred to in the original commission. The 1863 Map contains only acreages and gives no indication of ownership; which is another indication that this map was copied from a surveyors working document.

Neither the Field Book nor the Book of Reference has survived. A copy of the Field Book covering Shawmere and Quickmere was made by the Lees historian, C.E. Higson, in the 1920s and is reproduced here.[10] This records the names of the owner and tenant of each plot; however, it is extremely confusing in places with multiple names listed. Some of these may have been later additions and annotations to the original: but, if so, Higson makes no distinction between the two. No information relating to the Lordsmere and Friarmere divisions has survived, but the 1863 Map gives the acreages for each field. This has been used to produce a reconstructed key for Friarmere and Lordsmere. The names of estates have been taken from the map where recorded but where none is provided estate names current at the time have been used.

---

[10] The Higson Collection, H.359, Oldham Local Studies and Archives.

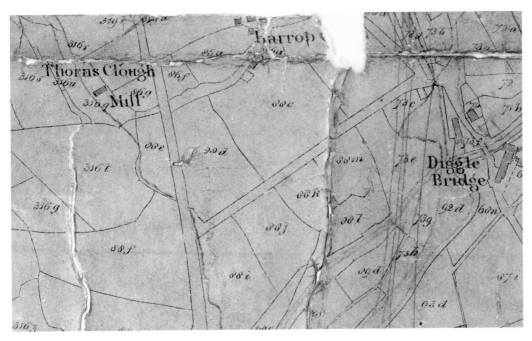

Figure 12. Later additions to the 1822 Vestry Map showing the deviation of the
Huddersfield Narrow Canal brought about by the railway in 1849.

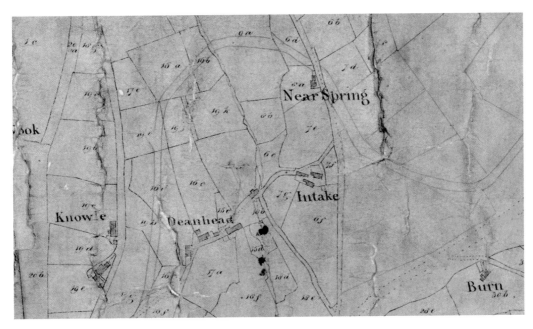

Figure 13. The new route, c.1840, of the Austerlands to Wakefield Turnpike Road
shown on the 1822 Vestry Map together with later enclosures.

Denshaw Moor

| A | R | P |
|---|---|---|
| 255 | 2 | 16 |

141b

141a

130q

142

130p

130o

138e

127i

**Dorey**

129b

**Dorey**

130n

127m

127n

128a

128b **Daisey**

140l

140n

143a

140m

127l

129a

131b

131a

130m

129d

129c

127o

127p

127q

128c

128d

128e

128f

131c

129e

128h

127r

130k

130l

129g

128g

129f

Plate I

124x

143c

ne

From Rochdale

Old Road

**Marsh**

**Cherry Clough**

**Briney Croft**

**Bosset**

**Lump-hole Mill**

**Junctio**

**Edge**

**Calf-hey**

**Whitehead Mill**

**Wood-brow**

**Barracks**

140h

138h

127h

Su

127e

127g

Sun

127f

138g

138f

124g

121d

140f

121b

121a

121e

140e

120a

120b

121c

120c

120d

140g

138g

119d

120e

120g

121g

121f

124f

140d

140c

140b

119c

119e

119f

119b

120f

140a

117f

121h

119g

117e

116h

118c

124e

140a

137a

119a

116g

118b

123c

130

117c

117d

116i

118a

123d

123h

116f

116j

118a

117b

116d

122a

123e

123f

116e

123b

117a

116c

116k

116l

122f

122g

123a

123g

116b

122c

122e

124d

135a

115d

Lump-hole Mill

135f

136c

113f

115c

124b

124c

136b

135

Edge

122d

124a

136a

135d

115b

135e

135c

115a

133a

114c

124h

114b

114a

114d

113a

124i

114e

112c

114f

113b

111n

112b

113c

28a

112a

111a

111d

112c

111e

112d

113d

111b

111f

111i

111m

24m

Wood-brow

111h

111i

111g

Barracks

24i

111c

Plate II

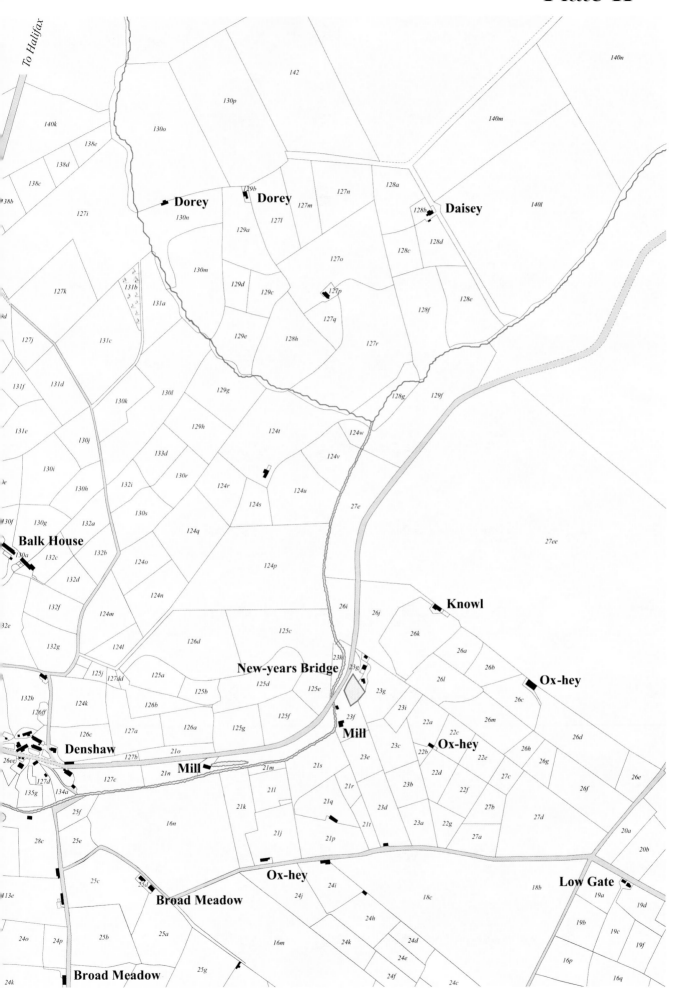

140n

143b

143c

143a

140m

140l

128b **Daisey**

128d

128e

128f

129f

27ee

1a

**Knowl**

26k

26a

1v

26l

26b

**Ox-hey**

26c

1w

22a

26m

22c

1x

**Ox-hey**

22b

26h

22e

26g

1y

22d

27c

1z

1u

22f

27b

1A

23a

22g

27d

27a

1B

20c

1C

20a

**Broadhead**

18b

20b

1D

20d

20f

1J

1B

**Low Gate**

18c

20e

1I

19a

20g

1E

1H

1c

1F

24d

19d

19e

19b

19c

19h

1G

1K

19f

1M

16p

19g

19i

**Low Bank**

1L

48a

1c

16q

1F

**Castle shaw**

1N

24c

176

Plate III

Castle Shaw Moor

| A | R | P |
|---|---|---|
| 619 | 0 | 0 |

3a

3f

3b

3d

3c

2a

2b

2c

Oaken hill Lea

2d

13b

13c

13a

Roughs

13d

12i

11f

11e

12g

12h

11c

11a

14

1e

11b

11d

12e

12a

12f

2f

12c

hill

1d

12d

12b

1o

Stanedge Foot

2d

1b

20gg

10a

2b

1j

1c

1a

9b

Wood-brow

Barracks

Martin

Stile-house

Old Tame

Horiest

Hethey Hill

Mantle Gate

Slack Coat Mill

Hollin-bank

New Barn

Rams Clough

Dodle

Bank Field

Hanson-house

Bank

Grains Bar

Ship

Coatmans

Tame Croft

Coatman Heights

*From Oldham*

178

Plate IV

**Broad Meadow**

**Slack Gate**

**Hey**

**Slack**

**Hey**

**Moorcroft**

**Upper Grange**

**Heights Chapel**

**Heights**

**Grange**

**Milcroft**

**Barn**

**New Barn**

**Delves Greaves**

**Hull Mill**

**Frier Lodge**

**Linfits**

**Stubbing**

**Carr Coat**

**Delph Barn**

**Dale**

**Top of Wood**

**Bank**

Plate V

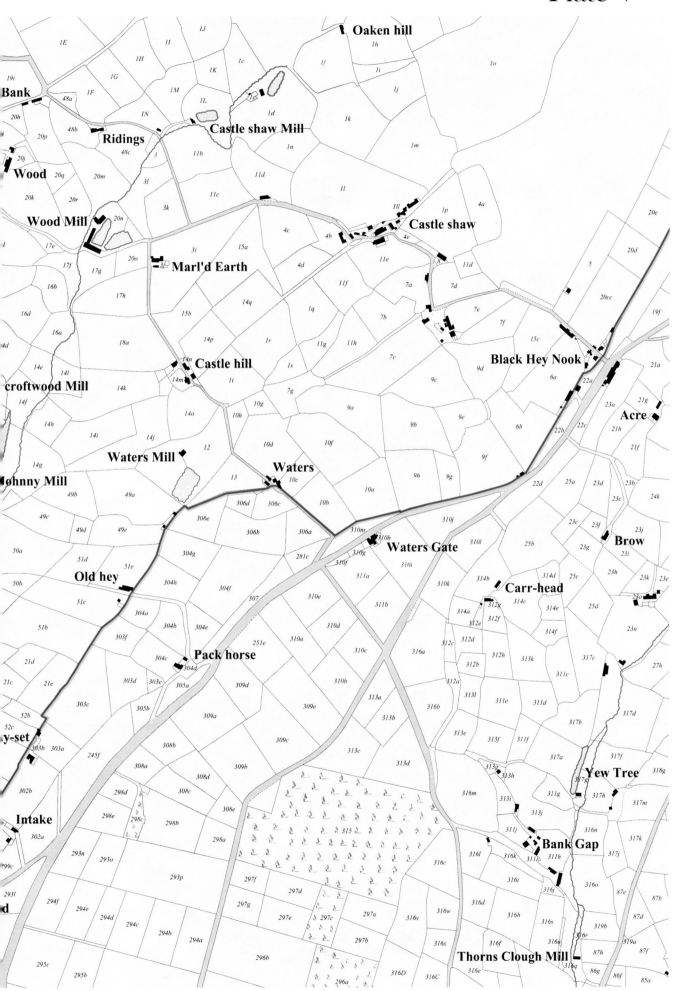

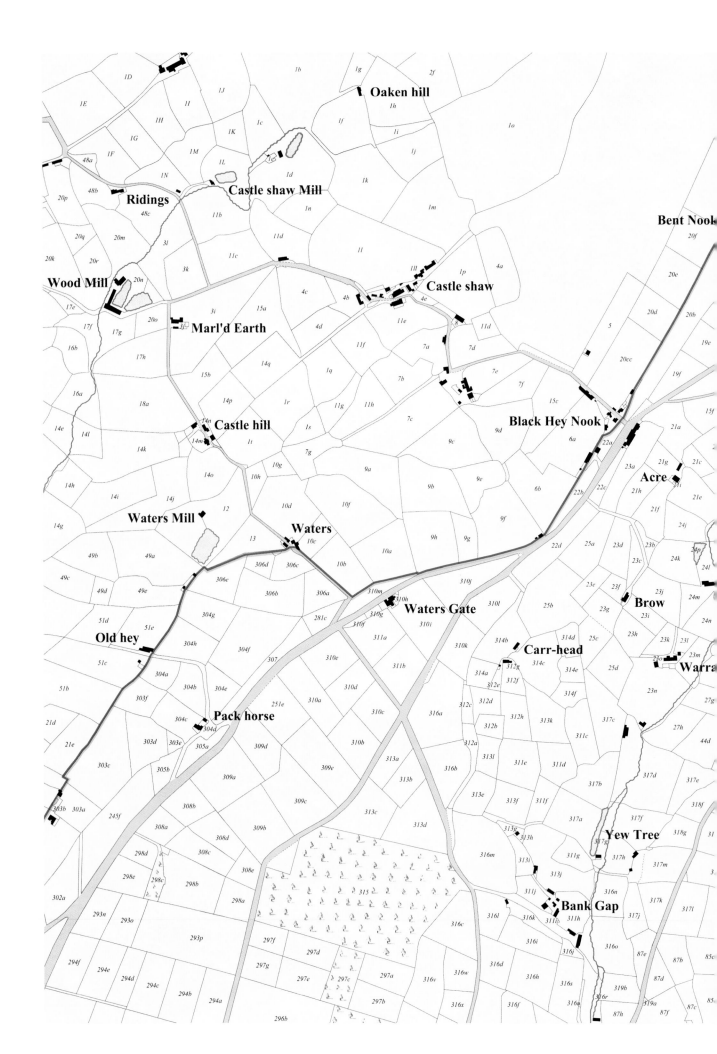

**Oaken hill**

**Ridings**

**Castle shaw Mill**

**Wood Mill**

**Bent Nook**

**Marl'd Earth**

**Castle shaw**

**Castle hill**

**Black Hey Nook**

**Acre**

**Waters Mill**

**Brow**

**Waters**

**Old hey**

**Waters Gate**

**Carr-head**

**Warra**

**Pack horse**

**Yew Tree**

**Bank Gap**

Plate VI

Hollin-bank

100d          100g

100c   100b   100a          100h   100i          104d   104f

100j

104e

97g     97f   97e   97c          **Rams Clough**

97h                              97d     97b

**Dodle**          98d     98b   98a

98c   96e                96c   96b

96d                95a

99e     99a     99b

99d     99c

**Hanson-house**

72r          69U

72s

72q

72o

97a

96a

95f          72p

95e

78B          72i

95d

Bank Fi

95c          78C          78A

95b

78D

**Bank**

95g

78V

78X          78W   78U   78G   78F   78E

78R

**Grains Bar**

78Y   78Z   78T          78K          78Q          78x

**Ship**          78S          78I

*From Oldham*                    78J   78N   **Coatmans**

78O

78K   78M

**Coatman Heights**          78L          78bb

78aa

79a

196h          196a

196b

196c

196d

196e   186c          187a          191h

186a   **High Lee**   187b          191g

186b          187c

183g          182a   187d          191e   191f

183f          182d

183e   183c          182c   182b   187e   **Grean Leach**   187f   **Jerico**

181j          191d   192a   192h

183d          182e   181i

183b          181h   188b          190   193h          **Shilo**

184e   184d                181g          189          193a

173c   173a          184c   **Harbour**   183a          179e   188a   191c

173b

174d   **Luke-lane**   177c          184a          179d          191b          193b

174c          175a          184b          185          191a

174e          177b   174b                179c          181c

175b                177a                181f

172d   175e   176a   174a          178a                193b

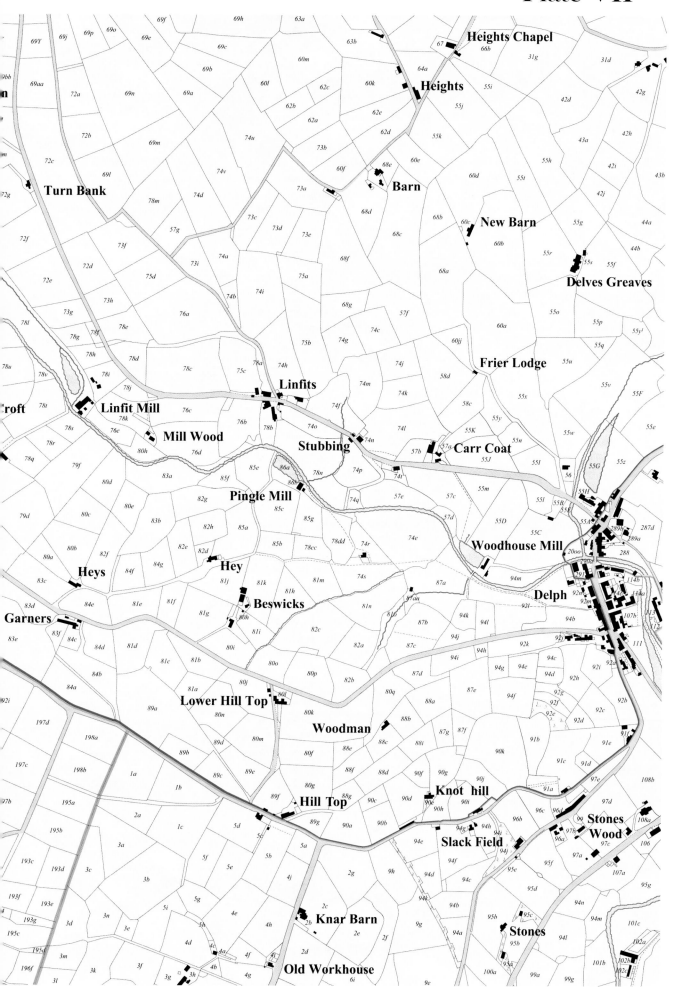

Plate VII

185

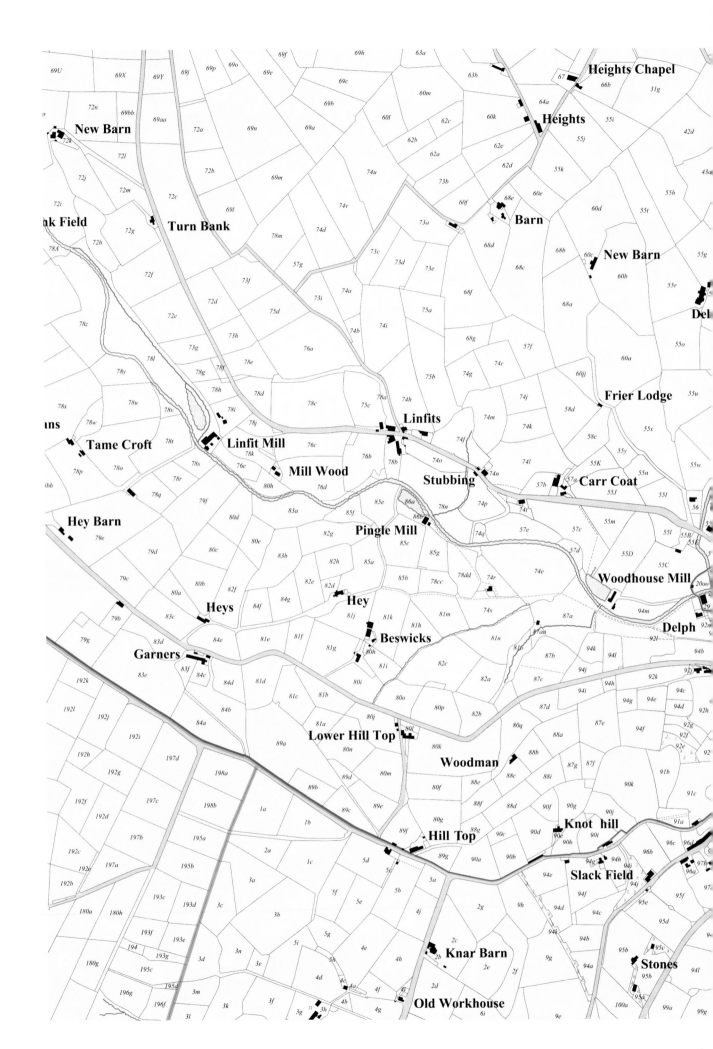

New Barn

69U    69X    69Y    69j    69p    69o    69e    69f    69h    63a    67    Heights Chapel
72n    69bb   69aa                     69c    69b    60m    63b    64a    66b    31g
69    72k              72a             69n    69a    60l    62c    60k    Heights    55i
72l                                                 62b    62a    62e    62d    55j    42d
72j    72m    72c                     69m    74u    73b    60f    68e    60e    55k    43a
72i    72h    72g    Turn Bank        78m    74d    73a    Barn    68d    60c    New Barn    55h    55g
nk Field              72f    73f      73c    73d    73e    68f    68c    68b    60b    55t    55r    Del
78A    78z    72d    75d    73i    74a    75a    68a    57f    60a    60jj    55o
72e    73g    73h    76a    74b    74i    75b    68g    57f    60a    55u
78l    78y    78g    78f    78e    76a    75c    78a    74h    74j    58d    Frier Lodge
78x    78u    78h    78d    78c    75c    Linfits    74m    74k    58c    55x
ns    78w    78v    78i    78j            78a    74f    74l    55y    55w    55K    55n
Tame Croft    78t    Linfit Mill    76c    76b    78b    74o    74n    57b    57a    Carr Coat    55J
78p    78o    78k    76e    Mill Wood    76d    Stubbing    74p    57c    55l    56
bb    78r    79f    80h    83a    85e    86a    78n    74q    57e    57c    55m    55l    55B
Hey Barn    78q    79d    80d    82g    85f    Pingle Mill    85c    74r    74e    57d    55D    55C
79e    80c    80e    83b    82h    85a    85g    78cc    78dd    74e    Woodhouse Mill    20oo
79c    80b    82f    82e    82d    Hey    85b    81m    74s    87a    94m
Heys    83c    84f    84g    81j    81k    81h    81n    87aa    94k    94l    Delph
79b    83d    84e    81e    81f    80h    Beswicks    81i    82c    87b    94j    92k    92j
Garners    83e    84c    84d    81d    81g    80i    82a    87c    94i    94h    94c    94d
192k    83f    84b    81c    81b    80o    80p    82b    87d    87e    94g    94e    92g
192l    192j    84a    89a    81a    80j    80k    80q    88a    88b    87g    87f    94f    92f
192i    197d    80n    80m    Lower Hill Top    Woodman    88c    88i    91b    91c
192h    198a    89d    80f    88e    90k
192g    197c    198b    1a    89b    80g    88f    88d    90f    90g    90j    Knot hill    91a
192f    192d    197b    195a    1b    89c    89e    80g    88g    90c    90d    90e    90h    96c    96d
192c    197a    195b    2a    1c    89f    Hill Top    89g    90a    90b    Slack Field    94g    94h    96b    97
192e    193c    193d    3a    5d    5c    5b    5a    90d    94e    94j    96a    96a
180a    180h    193f    193e    3c    3b    5f    5e    2g    9h    94d    94f    95f
194    193g    3d    3n    5g    5i    4e    2c    2e    2f    94k    94c    95e    95d
180g    195c    196f    3m    3k    3f    3g    3h    4d    4c    4a    4f    4j    2d    Knar Barn    9g    95b    94a    Stones    95c    94l
196g    4b    4g    Old Workhouse    6i    9e    100a    99a    99g

Plate VIII

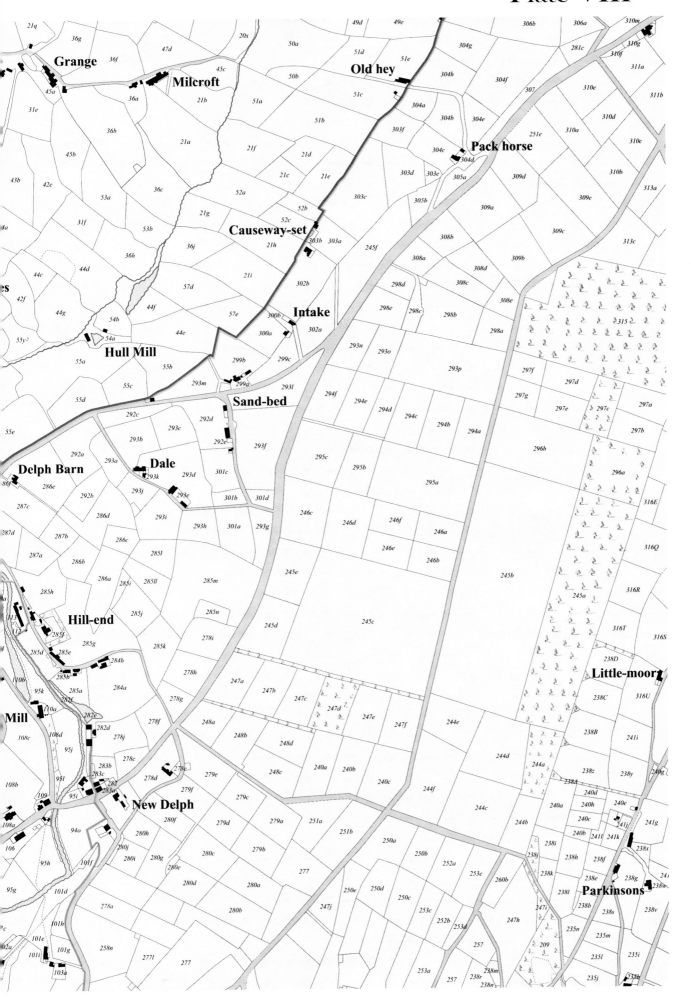

**Waters Gate**

**Brow**

**Carr-head**

**Warrack-hill Foot**

**Thurstons**

**Ridge**

**Yew Tree**

**Court**

**Bank Gap**

**Thorns Clough Mill**

**Harrop Green**

**Dig lee**

**Sun Field**

**Diggle Bridge**

**Little-moor**

**Warth Mill**

**Lee Cross**

**Fairbankes**

**Wrigley Mill**

**Parkinsons**

**Hollingreave**

Plate IX

183f

183e

183

183d

173c · 173a · 184e · 184d

173b

174d · **Luke-lane** · 184c · **Harbour**

174c · 177c · 184

174e · 175a · 184b

175b · 177b · 174b · 177a

175e · 176a · 174a · 178a

172d · 175c · **Roebuck-law** · 174a

**Cabin** · 175d · 178b

172c · 175k · 176b · 176f

172a · 175f · 175j · 176d · 176c · 176e

170i · 170g

170h · 175g · 175i

**Toulon Mill** · 170d · 170e · 175h · 156d · 147

170c · **Green Lane** · 156e

170a · 170b · 156g · **Far Barn** · 147s

169 · 168d · 157a · 156f · 156c

168c · 168e · **Strines**

168b · 155g · 155h 157c 157b · 156a 156b

168a · 157e · 157d · 155d 155c 155b · 155a

157f · 158a

158c · 158b · 155f · 155e · 17

160g 160f 160e · 159j · 159i · 159k

160h · 160d · 159h · 159a

161a · 161c · 160c · 159g · 159b · 159c · 125k

161b · 161h · **Top of Meadow**

161d · 164c · 164d · 161g · 160b · 160a · 159f · 159e 159d

161e · **Low Brook** · 162a · 162b · 154c · 154e

164b · 164e · 161f · 154b · 154d

165c · 120f · **Pastures**

165d · 165b · 163f · 163e · 164a · **Back o'th law** · 162c · 162d · 154b

165e · 165a · 163c · 154a

167a · 165f · **New Road Head** · 163d · 125h · **Greaves**

166 · 134p · 120d · 125l · **Old Nath**

167b · **Rough Law** · 163b · 136c

167c · 163a · 125j · 125g · 128d

125i · 125f

167e · 167d · **Thorns**

120c · 126e · 127b

**Waterhead Mill** · 126d · 127c · 128

125d · **Nook** · 127a

**Austerlands** · 126c · 126b · **Three Crowns**

125 · 125b · 126a · 125e · 120b

190

Plate X

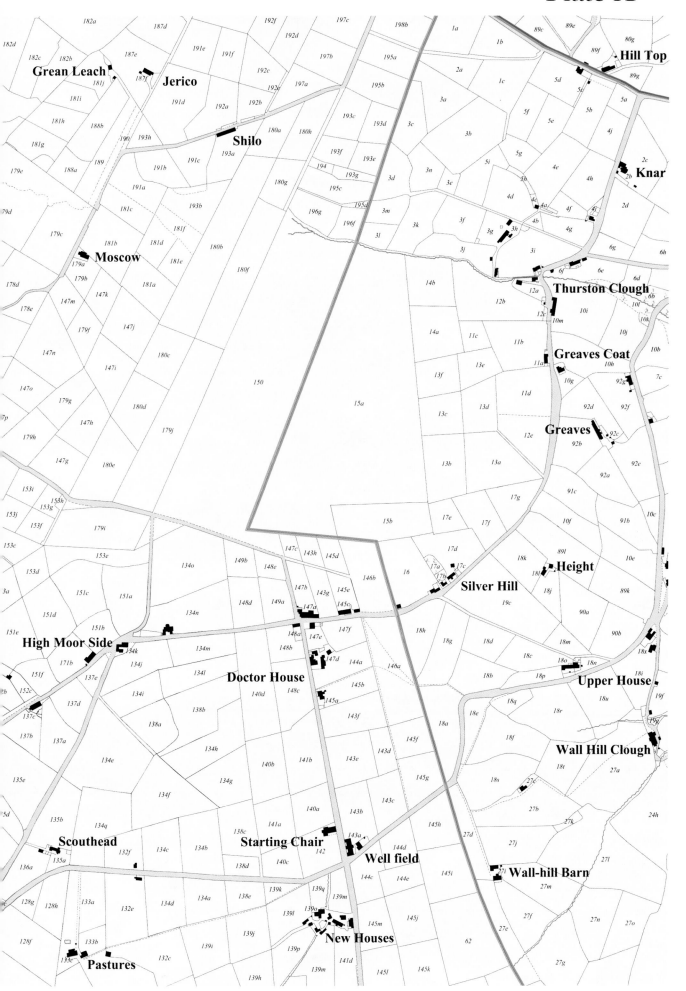

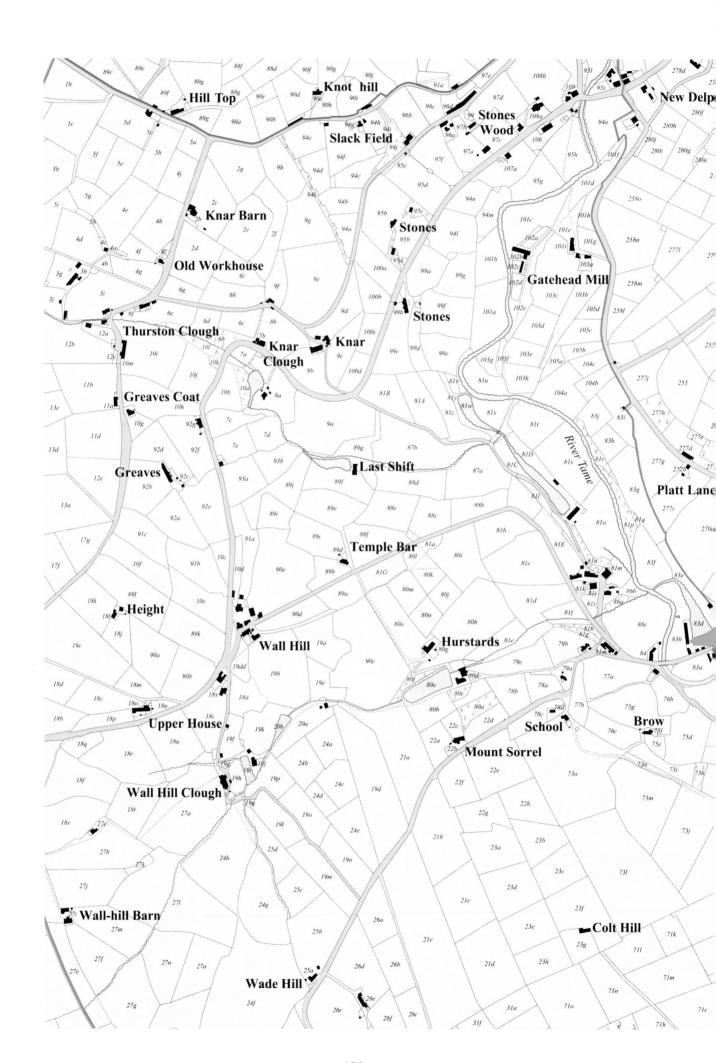

Hill Top
Knot hill
Knar Barn
Slack Field
Stones Wood
New Delp
Stones
Stones
Old Workhouse
Gatehead Mill
Thurston Clough
Knar Clough
Knar
Greaves Coat
Last Shift
River Tame
Greaves
Platt Lane
Temple Bar
Height
Hurstards
Wall Hill
Upper House
Mount Sorrel
School
Brow
Wall Hill Clough
Wall-hill Barn
Colt Hill
Wade Hill

192

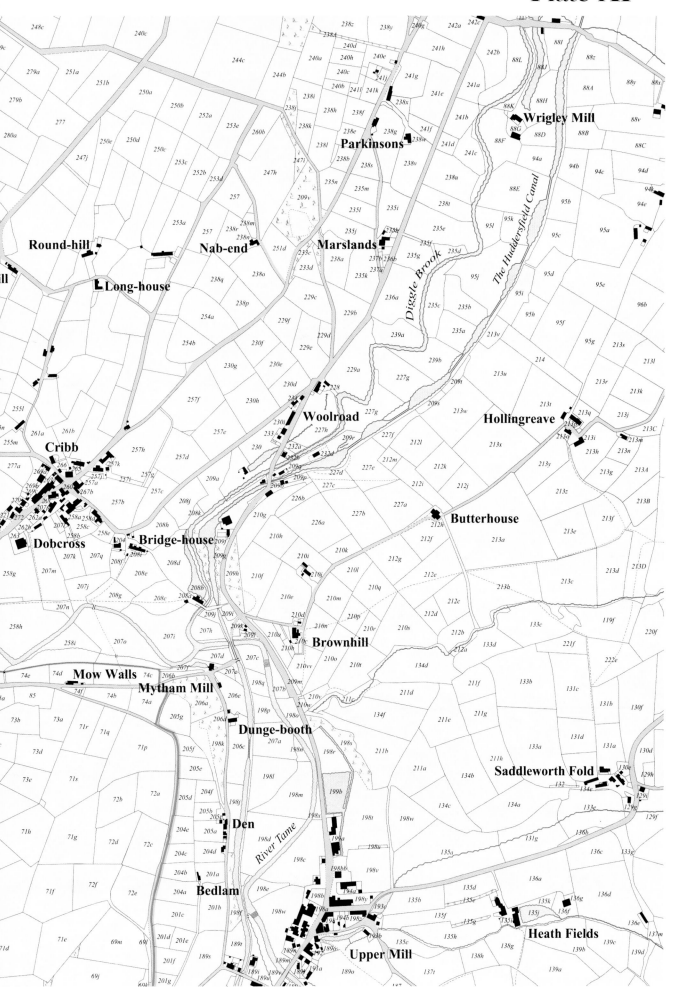

Plate XI

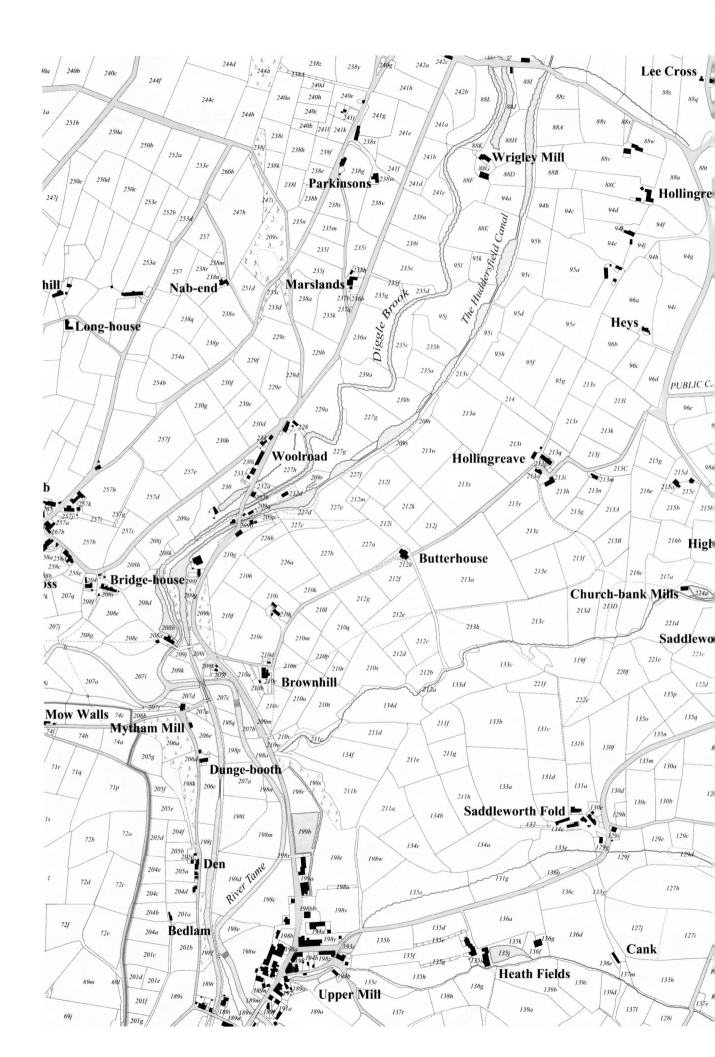

Lee Cross

Wrigley Mill

Hollingre

Parkinsons

Nab-end

Marslands

Heys

Long-house

Woolroad

Hollingreave

Butterhouse

Church-bank Mills

Bridge-house

Saddlewo

High

Mow Walls

Brownhill

Saddleworth Fold

Mytham Mill

Dunge-booth

Den

Saddleworth Fold

Bedlam

Cank

Heath Fields

Upper Mill

The Huddersfield Canal

Diggle Brook

River Tame

PUBLIC C.

194

Plate XII

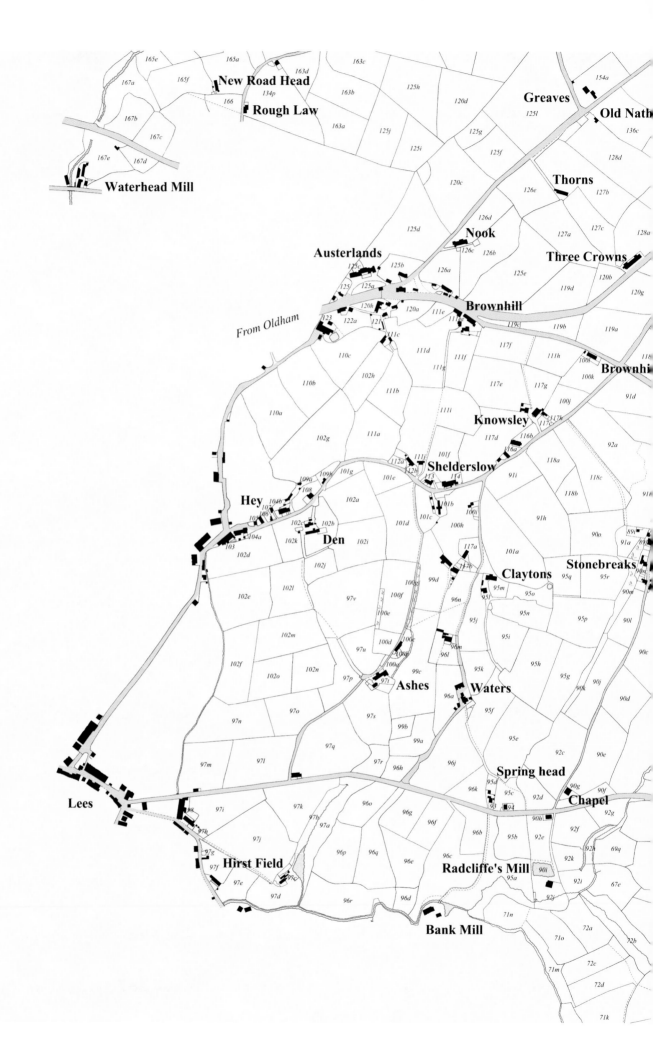

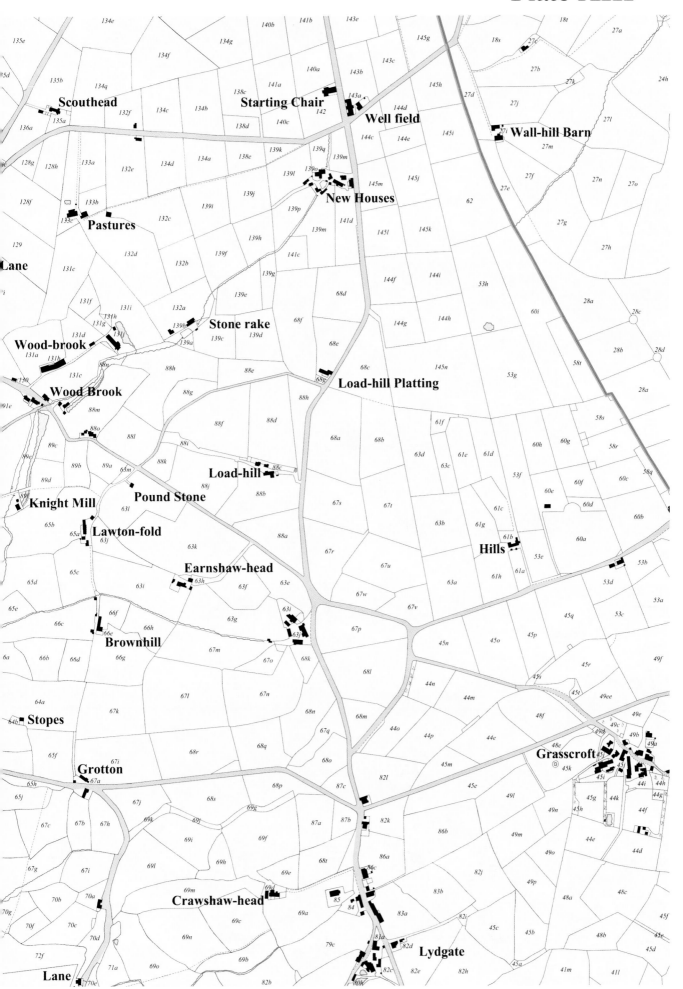

Plate XIII

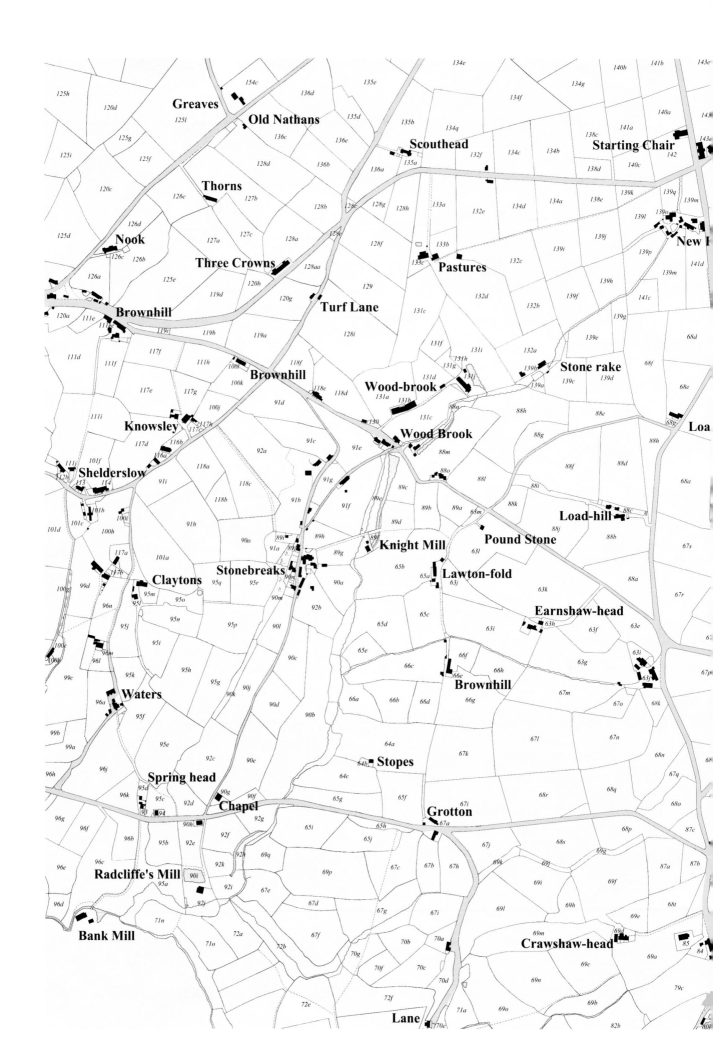

Greaves
Old Nathans
Scouthead
Starting Chair
New
Thorns
Pastures
Nook
Three Crowns
Stone rake
Turf Lane
Brownhill
Brownhill
Wood-brook
Wood Brook
Knowsley
Shelderslow
Load-hill
Knight Mill
Pound Stone
Lawton-fold
Claytons
Stonebreaks
Earnshaw-head
Waters
Brownhill
Stopes
Spring head
Grotton
Chapel
Radcliffe's Mill
Bank Mill
Crawshaw-head
Lane

198

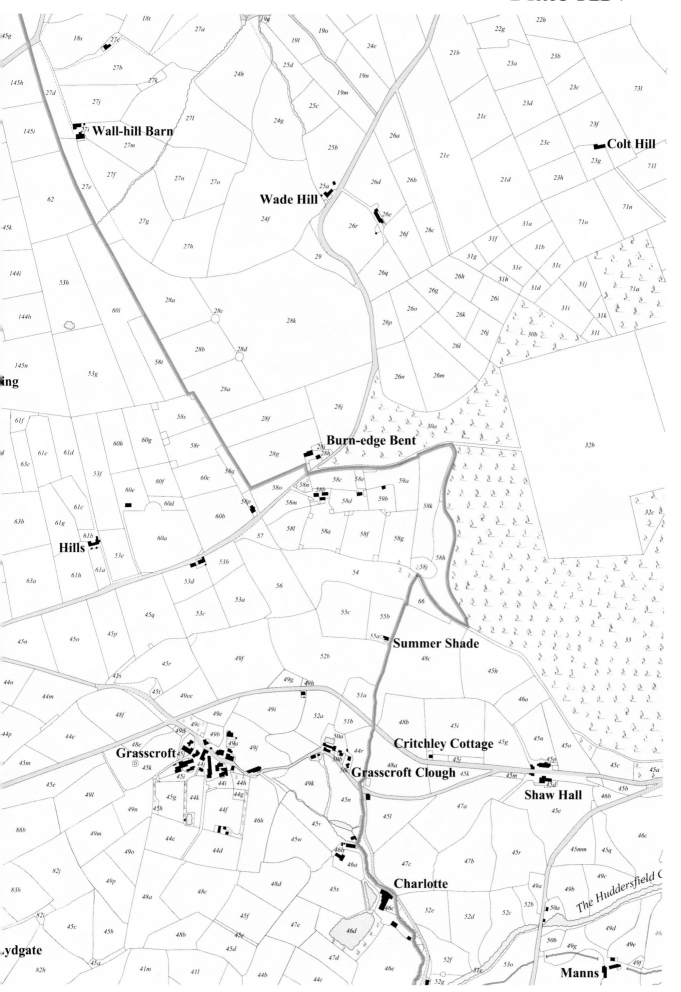

Plate XIV

Wall-hill Barn

Colt Hill

Wade Hill

Burn-edge Bent

Hills

Summer Shade

Critchley Cottage

Grasscroft

Grasscroft Clough

Shaw Hall

Charlotte

Manns

The Huddersfield C

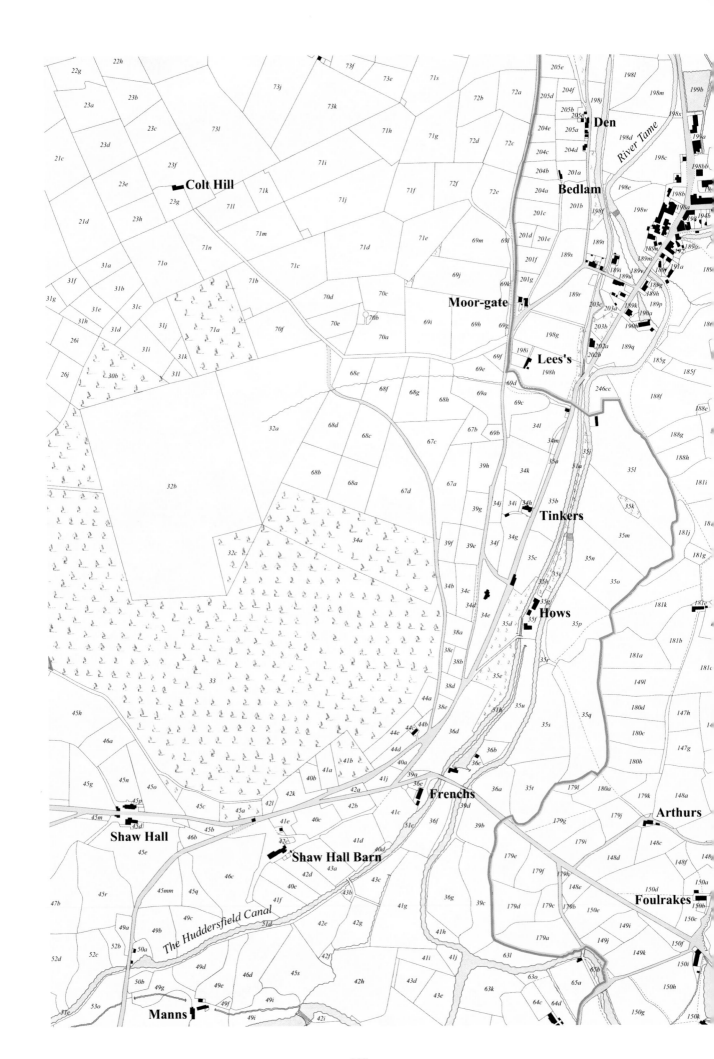

Colt Hill

Den

Bedlam

Moor-gate

Lees's

Tinkers

Hows

Frenchs

Arthurs

Shaw Hall

Shaw Hall Barn

Foulrakes

The Huddersfield Canal

Manns

River Tame

Plate XV

211a
134b
134c
w
135a
135b
135c
135d
135e
135f
135g
135h
138g
138h
137t
137s
138i
182f
184e
184d
182g
185d 185c
184c
186g
184b
188b
188a
184a
189d
189c
189e
88i
182e
182c
182d
182b
182a
144a
144b
145g
145j
147a
147c
145l
nders
145k
7d
150pp
149e
arshurst
150n
150m
150o
150s

**Saddleworth Fold**
130e
130c
130b
132
134e
129h
133e
129i
129g
131g
136b
136c
133g
136a
136d
129f
129d
129e
129c
129b
136g
135k
135i
135f
135j
136f
**Heath Fields**
138g
139b
139c
139d
136e
**Cank**
137m
133h
139a
137l
128i
139e
137k
139f
128j
137q
137k
139g
138f
137i
137d
184d
137p
137o
139h
138k
**Cross**
**Shaws**
186f
186e
137n
138l
128m
182h
182i
186d
186c
138m
128l
128k
141a
141b
141c
140a
**Ballgreave**
185a
186b
186a
144d
137w
137v
140e
140c
140b
144f
140d
**Knowl-top**
**RyeTop**
182c
144c
144e
143a
140j
140k
140f
182d
141d
140i
140h
143b
141e
140l
**Goulburn Clough**
**Knowl-top**
143d
143c
141f
140m
141g
141h
142f
143h
143g
140n
142a
142c
142e
143j
143k
143f
143e
145a
142b
142d
141i
141l
158b
141m
141n
145b
141n
153s
**White Brook Head**
158c
158i
158h
143l
143m
145d
145c
145r
145s
151d
154ll
158d
158g
158e
158f
**Fur-lane**
145f
145p
145q
151c
153r
157b
147b
146b
145o
141o
153q
154n
154l
158a
149b
149a
145m
145n
154b
153m
153n
154k
155a
149c
146c
154a
154d
154e
154f
154c
154m
**Tunstead**
141q
141r
149d
146d
**School**
152b
152c
152e
153l
153o
155c
155b
156g
157a
146e
153k
153j
153i
153p
155d
155g
155h
151a
152a
152d
150C
151b
152f
152g
155e
155f
**Hawkyard**
155i
156f
156a
150D
153b
153a
154h
154g
183a
154j
183b
**Shepherds Green**
156h
156e
156b
155k
150B
150E
153c
153g
154i
183c
156i
156c
159cc
150A

**Intake**
123c
124c
126d
115b
115c
116d
123d
114n
114m
124d
114l
114k
114b
121e
115d
131f
133i
124e
129a
126c
127e
115e
114d
127g
126a
114c
127h
127j
127i
128d
128e
127f
114i
128b
128a
128c
128f
135r
137e
128h
128g
138c
137a
138a
138b
137c
135l
**Rogue-hole**
137b
138e
137f
138d
137g
137h

201

124c
126d
115b
114n
114m
124d
115c
116d
112a
116b
115d
116c
116a
121e
114l
114k
114b
114e
133i
115e
114d
114f
127e
114c
114g
114h
114j
127f
114i
128f
138c
135r

Upper Wood
159ii
159jj
159kk

141n
141m
141l
158b
White Brook Head
155j
158c
158i
158h
154ll
158g
158d
158e
158f
158a
157b
154l
160b
155a
160c
160a
156g
157a
Binn Green
160d
160e
160i
160g
155h
160h
160f
155j
155i
161a
Hawkyard
156f
156a
161c
161b
156b
155k
159v
161e
161d
161e
161f

# Plate XVI

ay Gap

1610

**Thornlee Brook**

**Lane**

**Thornlee**

**Crown Point**

**Butt**

**Quick Edge**

**Li**

**Carr-hill**

**Baguley**

**Baguley Knowle**

**Mosley**

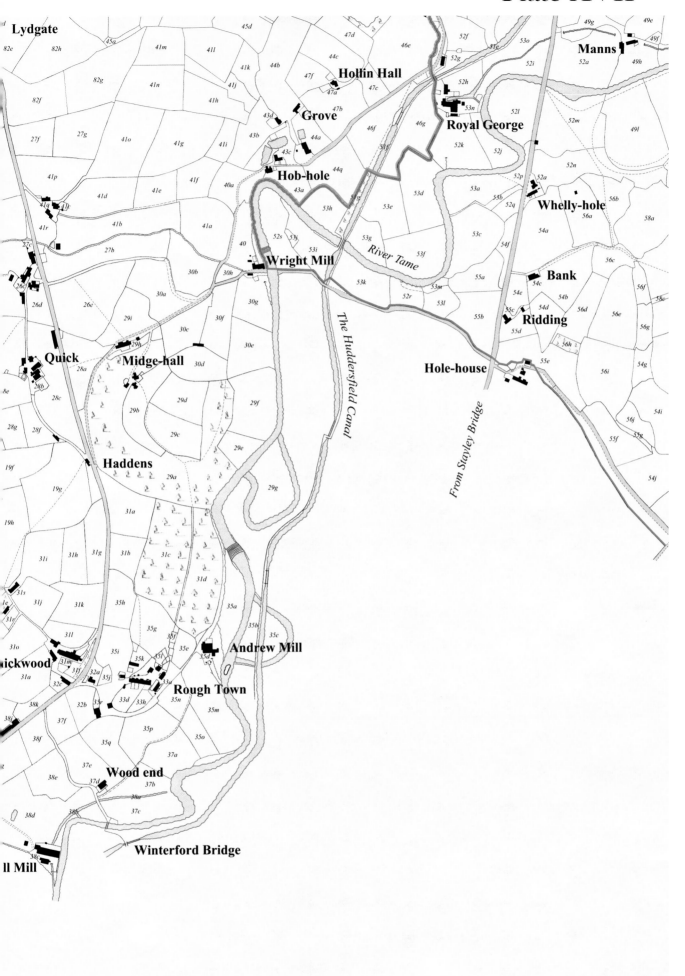

Plate XVII

Lydgate

Hollin Hall

Grove

Hob-hole

Wright Mill

*River Tame*

Royal George

Manns

Whelly-hole

Bank

Ridding

Hole-house

Quick

Midge-hall

Haddens

*The Huddersfield Canal*

*From Stayley Bridge*

Andrew Mill

Rough Town

ickwood

Wood end

Winterford Bridge

ll Mill

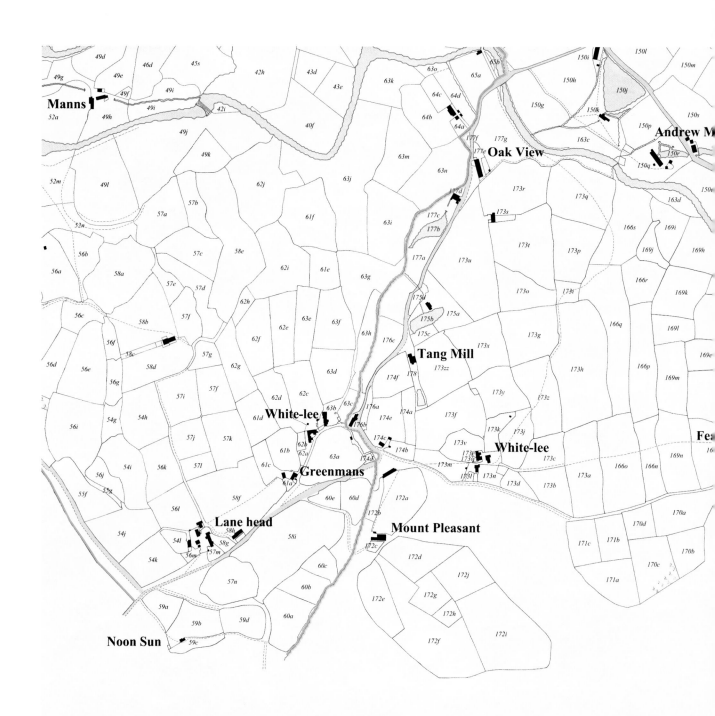

Plate XVIII

Shepherds Green

Hollin Bank

Side Bank

Greenfield Mill

Greenfield

Dove Stone

Greenfield Barn

Slack-head

Kinder Intake

Plate XIV

# 1822 QUICKMERE TOWNSHIP MAP.
## KEY TO FIELD NUMBERS AND ESTATE OWNERSHIP

## Baguley Hill

*John Wild* — Self

| 1a | 0 | 2 | 7 | Mary Wild |
|---|---|---|---|---|

*G.Bramall* — Self

| 2a | 0 | 2 | 27 | John Taylor |
|---|---|---|---|---|
| b | 0 | 0 | 10 | " |
| c | 1 | 0 | 24 | " |
| d | 2 | 0 | 5 | " |
| e | 1 | 0 | 21 | " |
| f | 0 | 1 | 3 | " |
| g | 4 | 1 | 26 | " |

## Baguley Hill

*Rob Whitehead*

| 3 | 0 | 0 | 12 |
|---|---|---|---|
| 4 | 0 | 0 | 17 |

*Edward Greaves Esq* — H. Kenworthy

| 5a | 0 | 0 | 13 | John Andrew |
|---|---|---|---|---|
| b | 1 | 2 | 38 | Ab. Wood |
| c | 0 | 2 | 7 | " |
| d | 0 | 3 | 34 | " |
| e | 0 | 0 | 13 | Robt & John Andrew |
| f | 0 | 1 | 10 | " |
| g | 2 | 3 | 13 | " |

6, 7 8, 9, 10, 11, are all small plots

*Edward Greaves Esq*

| 12a | 3 | 2 | 3 | |
|---|---|---|---|---|
| b | 0 | 0 | 16 | |
| c | 2 | 0 | 28 | G. Rook |
| d | 1 | 2 | 25 | " |
| e | 1 | 3 | 32 | " |
| f | 0 | 0 | 17 | Jos Scholefield |
| g | 1 | 2 | 31 | G. Rook |
| h | 1 | 2 | 27 | " |
| i | 1 | 3 | 21 | " |
| j | 1 | 3 | 18 | " |
| k | 1 | 3 | 36 | " |
| l | 1 | 3 | 31 | " |
| m | 2 | 0 | 22 | |

## Baguley

*E. Leigh Esq*

| 15a | 0 | 0 | 16 | |
|---|---|---|---|---|
| b | 1 | 0 | 20 | Mary Wild, E. Lees |
| c | 2 | 1 | 18 | " |
| d | 3 | 0 | 7 | " |
| e | 2 | 3 | 3 | " |
| f | 1 | 2 | 39 | " |

## Top of Quick Edge

*Leigh Esq* — Jno Buckley

| 15g | 0 | 3 | 29 | Jas Buckley |
|---|---|---|---|---|
| h | 0 | 0 | 15 | " |
| i | 1 | 0 | 35 | " |
| j | 0 | 3 | 10 | " |
| k | 1 | 3 | 3 | " |
| l | 1 | 3 | 7 | Jas Lawton |
| m | 2 | 1 | 23 | " |
| n | 2 | 2 | 12 | " |
| o | 3 | 0 | 33 | " |
| p | 0 | 2 | 31 | " |
| | 0 | 0 | 13 | Lane |

*Whitehead*  Ed Lilley  Messrs L.G.Barlow R. Dunkerley

| 16a | 2 | 3 | 20 | " | " |
|---|---|---|---|---|---|
| b | 2 | 0 | 6 | " | " |
| c | 0 | 2 | 10 | " | " |
| d | 1 | 2 | 39 | " | " |

*Execs late Jas Kershaw* — Jos Kershaw

| 17a | 0 | 0 | 13 | House |
|---|---|---|---|---|
| b | 4 | 0 | 18 | |

*Thos Mellor* — Robert Dunkerley

| 18a | 1 | 0 | 2 | " |
|---|---|---|---|---|
| b | 0 | 0 | 9 | Buildings " |
| c | 0 | 0 | 14 | |

## Little Hague

*Leigh Esq* — Geo Andrew, Jno Taylor

| 19b | 2 | 2 | 19 | " |
|---|---|---|---|---|
| c | 3 | 2 | 39 | " |
| d | 1 | 1 | 35 | " |
| e | 2 | 2 | 1 | " |
| f | 2 | 0 | 27 | " |
| g | 4 | 2 | 3 | " |
| h | 3 | 1 | 11 | " |
| i | 4 | 3 | 4 | " |
| j | 1 | 2 | 7 | " |
| k | 0 | 3 | 36 | " |
| l | 1 | 0 | 2 | 4 Bldgs & Road " |

## Butt

*E. Leigh Esq* — Rob Andrew

| 20a | 7 | 3 | 33 | " |
|---|---|---|---|---|
| c | 1 | 1 | 13 | " |
| d | 1 | 2 | 4 | " |
| e | 0 | 0 | 29 | House &c " |
| f | 0 | 1 | 39 | " |
| g | 0 | 3 | 34 | " |
| | 0 | 3 | 33 | |

## Back of Quick Edge

*Edw. Greaves Esq* — Benj Buckley

| 21a | 0 | 3 | 23 | James Buckley |
|---|---|---|---|---|
| b | 0 | 2 | 11 | " |
| c | 0 | 3 | 9 | " |
| d | 0 | 0 | 14 | " |
| e | 1 | 0 | 8 | " |
| f | 0 | 3 | 35 | " |
| g | 4 | 0 | 25 | Jno Scholefield |
| h | 1 | 1 | 19 | " |
| i | 2 | 2 | 10 | " |
| j | 0 | 0 | 12 | " |
| k | 0 | 2 | 6 | " |
| l | 1 | 1 | 10 | " |
| m | 0 | 0 | 24 | " |
| n | 0 | 0 | 19 | } Brookbank " |
| o | 0 | 2 | 14 | " |
| p | 1 | 0 | 3 | |

*Robert Moss*  Samuel Buckley Jos Clayton or occ

| 22a | 1 | 0 | 27 | |
|---|---|---|---|---|
| b | 0 | 0 | 23 | House &c " |
| c | 0 | 0 | 32 | " |
| d | 3 | 2 | 13 | " |

## Quick Edge

*John Whitehead* — Self

| 23a | 1 | 2 | 36 | " |
|---|---|---|---|---|
| b | 0 | 2 | 30 | " |
| c | 1 | 1 | 0 | " |
| d | 0 | 2 | 35 | " |
| e | 1 | 2 | 27 | " |
| f | 2 | 2 | 21 | " |
| g | 0 | 2 | 36 | " |
| h | 2 | 0 | 16 | " |
| i | 2 | 0 | 24 | " |
| j | 0 | 1 | 13 | " |
| k | 0 | 1 | 17 | " |
| l | 0 | 1 | 26 | " |
| m | 1 | 2 | 19 | " |

*Thos Whitehead* — Self

| 24a | 0 | 2 | 26 | " |
|---|---|---|---|---|
| b | 1 | 3 | 17 | " |
| c | 1 | 0 | 10 | " |
| d | 2 | 0 | 38 | " |
| e | 0 | 1 | 27 | Reservoir " |
| f | 0 | 3 | 34 | " |
| g | 1 | 3 | 3 | Ben Street |
| h | 0 | 0 | 11 | Bldgs  J. Hilton / B Street |
| i | 2 | 3 | 27 | New do " |
| j | 2 | 1 | 8 | " |
| k | 0 | 1 | 11 | Bldgs  Ben Street |
| l | 0 | 3 | 10 | " |
| m | 0 | 0 | 36 | " |
| n | 2 | 1 | 2 | " |
| o | 0 | 3 | 35 | " |
| p | 2 | 0 | 12 | " |
| q | 3 | 2 | 4 | " |

## Crown Point

*Rev Myddleton* — Samuel Buckley

| 25a | 1 | 1 | 37 | " |
|---|---|---|---|---|
| b | 1 | 0 | 15 | " |
| c | 0 | 0 | 20 | Bldgs &c " |
| d | 0 | 2 | 35 | " |
| e | 3 | 0 | 39 | " |
| f | 0 | 3 | 24 | " |

*Robert Kenworthy, Self* — Sophia Kenworthy

| 26a | 5 | 2 | 30 | " |
|---|---|---|---|---|
| b | 2 | 1 | 11 | " |
| c | 0 | 3 | 7 | " |
| d | 0 | 2 | 6 | Bldgs " |
| e | 3 | 2 | 28 | " |

*Rev W. Kenworthy* — Self

| 27a | 0 | 0 | 19 | Hse & Gdns |
|---|---|---|---|---|
| | | | | Mrs.Sidebottom occr |
| b | 2 | 3 | 36 | " |
| c | 0 | 0 | 38 | Hse & Gdns " |
| d | 2 | 2 | 22 | Mrs Sidebottom owner |
| e | 4 | 2 | 11 | " |
| f | 1 | 1 | 37 | Rev Cowell |
| | | | | Execs R. Kenworthy |
| g | 3 | 1 | 38 | " |

*Tabitha Kenworthy* — Jno Hilton

| 28a | | | | J. Kenworthy |
|---|---|---|---|---|
| | | | | Eli Fielding occr & Sam Seal |
| b | 0 | 2 | 39 | House &c   Jno Hilton |
| c | 3 | 1 | 24 | " |
| d | 3 | 2 | 27 | Stone Pit " |
| e | 1 | 2 | 3 | " |
| f | 0 | 3 | 29 | " |
| g | 1 | 0 | 2 | " |
| h | 4 | 2 | 26 | " |
| i | 2 | 0 | 6 | " |
| j | 2 | 1 | 24 | " |
| k | 4 | 2 | 20 | " |
| l | 2 | 3 | 31 | " |

## Midge Hill

*Tabitha Kenworthy* — Jas Nield

| 29a | 12 | 2 | 16 | Wood   Sam Seal |
|---|---|---|---|---|
| b | 2 | 0 | 12 | " |
| c | 2 | 0 | 7 | " |
| d | 1 | 3 | 28 | " |
| e | 1 | 0 | 1 | " |
| f | 2 | 3 | 27 | " |
| g | 2 | 2 | 7 | " |
| h | 0 | 2 | 28 | Garden   John Neild |
| i | 1 | 3 | 37 | " |

*James Nield* — Self

| 30a | 2 | 2 | 22 | School |
|---|---|---|---|---|
| | | | | Execs Jas Nield Jno Nield |
| b | 2 | 0 | 21 | " |
| c | 1 | 2 | 33 | " |
| d | 1 | 2 | 27 | " |
| e | 2 | 0 | 24 | " |
| f | 1 | 3 | 16 | " |
| g | 1 | 3 | 14 | " |
| h | 0 | 1 | 6 | " |

## Quickwood

*Hardman, J. Nield* — W.Winterbottom

| 31a | 2 | 0 | 35 | |
|---|---|---|---|---|
| b | 1 | 1 | 4 | " |

## Roughtown

*Themselves* — W.Winterbottom

| 31c | 4 | 2 | 23 | Plantation " |
|---|---|---|---|---|
| d | 3 | 3 | 10 | " |
| e | 0 | 0 | 38 | "  C. Winterbottom |
| f | 0 | 0 | 25 | " |
| g | 1 | 3 | 19 | Owen Jones |
| h | 1 | 1 | 17 | " |
| i | 2 | 0 | 10 | C. Winterbottom |
| j | 1 | 2 | 17 | " |
| k | 2 | 0 | 20 | Owen Jones |
| l | 1 | 0 | 6 | " |
| m | 0 | 0 | 12 | " |
| n | 2 | 0 | 32 | Garden " |

## (continued)

| Plot | a | r | p | Note |
|---|---|---|---|---|
| o | 2 | 0 | 9 | " |
| p | 0 | 2 | 35 | Buildings " |
| q | 1 | 2 | 20 | " |
| r | 0 | 1 | 5 | " |
| s | 0 | 0 | 20 | W. Winterbottom |

*James Nield* — Self

| Plot | a | r | p |
|---|---|---|---|
| 32a | 0 | 0 | 37 |
| b | 0 | 3 | 31 |
| c | 0 | 0 | 34 |

N.B. Those omitted are very small gardens &c

| Plot | a | r | p | Note |
|---|---|---|---|---|
| 33a | | | | Gardens |
| b | | | | Fold &c |
| c | 0 | 1 | 4 | Gardens |
| d | 0 | 1 | 20 | Thos Morehouse |
| | | | | Ralph Lawton |

*Late Neild Execs   Jno Andrew   Jno Buckley occ*

| Plot | a | r | p | Note |
|---|---|---|---|---|
| 35a | 2 | 1 | 6 | |
| b | 0 | 3 | 3 | " |
| c | 0 | 3 | 8 | " |
| d | 0 | 2 | 1 | House " |
| e | 0 | 2 | 32 | Owen Jones " |
| f | 0 | 0 | 29 | Grdn  Jno Neild " |
| g | 1 | 3 | 35 | " |
| h | 1 | 2 | 4 | " |
| i | 1 | 1 | 19 | " |
| j | 0 | 0 | 32 | " |
| k | 0 | 2 | 28 | " |
| l | 0 | 0 | 34 | " |
| m | 3 | 1 | 14 | " |
| n | 0 | 3 | 37 | " |
| o | 0 | 3 | 29 | " |
| p | 1 | 3 | 35 | " |
| q | 1 | 2 | 38 | " |
| r | 0 | 0 | 39 | Waste " |

*Huddersfield Canal Co.*

| Plot | a | r | p | Note |
|---|---|---|---|---|
| 36a | 0 | 1 | 7 | Plantation |
| b | 0 | 2 | 36 | Canal |

## Wood End

*John Platt   Self   Edw Wright   Jno Buckley*

| Plot | a | r | p | Note | Note |
|---|---|---|---|---|---|
| 37a | 1 | 3 | 3 | " | " |
| b | 1 | 1 | 20 | " | " |
| c | 1 | 3 | 20 | " | " |
| d | 0 | 0 | 18 | " | " |
| e | 1 | 3 | 29 | " | " |
| f | 1 | 0 | 5 | " | " |

## Cresswell Mill

*N. Buckley* — N. Buckley

| Plot | a | r | p | Note |
|---|---|---|---|---|
| 38a | 0 | 2 | 25 | " |
| b | 0 | 1 | 9 | " |
| c | 0 | 2 | 14 | " |

## Carr Hill

*N. Buckley* — Self

| Plot | a | r | p | Note |
|---|---|---|---|---|
| 38d | 5 | 2 | 2 | N. Buckley |
| e | 1 | 2 | 28 | " |
| f | 1 | 0 | 11 | " |
| g | 2 | 2 | 4 | " |
| h | 0 | 2 | 13 | " |
| i | 2 | 1 | 22 | " |
| j | 0 | 0 | 26 | " |
| k | 0 | 2 | 31 | Gardens " |

*Daniel Woolley Self Owner & Occupier*

| Plot | a | r | p | Note |
|---|---|---|---|---|
| 39 | 1 | 1 | 10 | Buildings & Gardens |

## Wright Mill

*Samuel Seel   James Seel   Owner & Occ*

| Plot | a | r | p | Note |
|---|---|---|---|---|
| 40 | 1 | 3 | 26 | Wood &c |

## Quick

*Wrigley Buckley*   —   Whitehead ........ &c

| Plot | a | r | p | Note |
|---|---|---|---|---|
| 41a | 2 | 3 | 3 | W. Radcliffe |
| b | 3 | 2 | 13 | Widow Whitehead |
| c | 0 | 0 | 32 | Buildings |
| d | 2 | 1 | 19 | W. Radcliffe |
| e | 1 | 1 | 19 | Mrs Whitehead |
| f | 1 | 1 | 30 | Eli Fielding |
| g | 3 | 1 | 22 | Widow Whitehead |
| h | 1 | 3 | 29 | " |
| i | 0 | 3 | 17 | Eli Fielding |

*Wrigley & Co*

| Plot | a | r | p | Note |
|---|---|---|---|---|
| 41j | 1 | 0 | 10 | Mrs Whitehead |
| k | 0 | 3 | 31 | Eli Fielding |
| l | 2 | 0 | 30 | W. Whitehead |
| m | 1 | 2 | 30 | W.R. |
| n | 2 | 2 | 10 | " |
| o | 3 | 3 | 8 | " |
| p | 2 | 2 | 6 | " |
| q | 0 | 1 | 4 | Buildings |
| r | 0 | 3 | 20 | " |
| s | 2 | 4 | 7 | " |

No 42 omitted - No place on Plan

## Hob Hole

*W. Kenworthy* — Isaac Beesley occr

| Plot | a | r | p |
|---|---|---|---|
| 43a | 1 | 2 | 31 |
| b | 0 | 3 | 34 |
| c | 0 | 2 | 4 |
| d | 0 | 0 | 36 |

*Harrop*

| Plot | a | r | p |
|---|---|---|---|
| 44a | 1 | 0 | 11 |
| b | 3 | 1 | 37 |
| c | 1 | 3 | 7 |

## Grasscroft

*Jno Harrop*

| Plot | a | r | p | Note |
|---|---|---|---|---|
| 44d | 1 | 2 | 21 | |
| e | 1 | 2 | 25 | |
| f | 1 | 1 | 32 | |
| g | 0 | 0 | 18 | |
| h | 0 | 2 | 20 | |
| i | 0 | 1 | 10 | Road |
| j | 0 | 1 | 36 | House & Garden |
| k | 0 | 3 | 17 | |
| l | 2 | 2 | 22 | |
| m | 2 | 1 | 38 | |
| n | 1 | 1 | 25 | |
| o | 1 | 3 | 9 | |
| p | 2 | 1 | 15 | |

## Hob Hole

*Harrop*

| Plot | a | r | p | Note |
|---|---|---|---|---|
| 44q | 2 | 1 | 33 | Messrs Whitehead |
| r | 1 | 0 | 25 | |

## Grasscroft

*James Harrop* — Self

| Plot | a | r | p | Note |
|---|---|---|---|---|
| 45a | 0 | 0 | 32 | |
| b | 1 | 2 | 33 | |
| c | 2 | 0 | 19 | |
| d | 1 | 2 | 25 | |
| e | 0 | 0 | 23 | |
| f | 2 | 0 | 22 | |
| g | 0 | 3 | 35 | |
| h | 0 | 0 | 25 | |
| i | 0 | 2 | 24 | Road |
| j | 0 | 1 | 33 | Garden |
| k | 2 | 2 | 12 | |
| l | 2 | 2 | 13 | |
| m | 1 | 1 | 5 | |
| n | 2 | 0 | 4 | |
| o | 3 | 1 | 4 | |
| p | 2 | 0 | 17 | |
| q | 3 | 1 | 20 | |
| r | 2 | 2 | 7 | |
| s | 0 | 0 | 21 | Wood |
| t | 0 | 0 | 21 | |
| u | 1 | 3 | 17 | |
| v | 1 | 2 | 11 | |
| w | 2 | 1 | 38 | |
| x | 2 | 1 | 17 | |

## Grove

*James Wright* — Self

| Plot | a | r | p | Note |
|---|---|---|---|---|
| 46a | 0 | 2 | 26 | Garden |
| b | 0 | 1 | 14 | Yard |
| c | 1 | 0 | 14 | |
| d | 2 | 2 | 11 | |
| e | 4 | 0 | 21 | |
| f | 2 | 0 | 35 | |
| g | 1 | 3 | 39 | |
| h | 2 | 1 | 24 | |

## Holling Hall

*Miss Taylor* — Jno Winterbottom

| Plot | a | r | p | Note |
|---|---|---|---|---|
| 47a | 0 | 1 | 6 | House |
| b | 2 | 1 | 9 | |
| c | 0 | 2 | 26 | |
| d | 1 | 1 | 19 | |
| e | 1 | 2 | 38 | |
| f | 1 | 0 | 39 | |

## Grasscroft

*Miss Taylor* — James Lord ?

| Plot | a | r | p |
|---|---|---|---|
| 48a | 3 | 1 | 21 |
| b | 1 | 2 | 10 |
| c | 3 | 0 | 19 |
| d | 2 | 1 | 20 |
| e | 0 | 1 | 31 |
| f | 2 | 3 | 8 |

*W. Shaw* — Self

| Plot | a | r | p |
|---|---|---|---|
| 49a | 0 | 0 | 17 |
| b | 0 | 1 | 31 |
| c | 0 | 1 | 16 |
| d | 0 | 0 | 6 |
| e | 0 | 2 | 31 |
| ee | 1 | 2 | 21 |
| f | 5 | 0 | 22 |
| g | 0 | 1 | 18 |
| h | 0 | 0 | 13 |
| i | 2 | 0 | 16 |
| j | 2 | 0 | 25 |
| k | 2 | 0 | 18 |
| l | 2 | 2 | 10 |
| m | 1 | 3 | 38 |
| n | 1 | 1 | 14 |
| o | 1 | 2 | 2 |
| p | 1 | 3 | 6 |

## Grasscroft Clough

*Exec. J. Kenworthy*

| Plot | a | r | p |
|---|---|---|---|
| 50a | 0 | 1 | 23 |
| b | 0 | 1 | 10 |

*Miss Taylor* — Jas Wright

| Plot | a | r | p |
|---|---|---|---|
| 51a | 0 | 3 | 22 |
| b | 0 | 2 | 26 |

*Thos Whitehead*

| Plot | a | r | p |
|---|---|---|---|
| 52a | 2 | 1 | 5 |
| b | 5 | 3 | 8 |

## Burnedge

*Jas Harrop* — Thos Winterbottom

| Plot | a | r | p |
|---|---|---|---|
| 53a | 1 | 3 | 22 |
| b | 1 | 0 | 6 |
| c | 1 | 2 | 7 |
| d | 1 | 1 | 31 |
| e | 1 | 1 | 29 |
| f | 3 | 0 | 20 |
| g | 5 | 0 | 3 |
| h | 4 | 0 | 33 |

*James Lord* — Jno Grindrod

| Plot | a | r | p |
|---|---|---|---|
| 54 | 3 | 2 | 8 |

## Summer Shade

*John Taylor*

| Plot | a | r | p |
|---|---|---|---|
| 55a | 0 | 0 | 12 |

*Thos Ammon Platt*

| Plot | a | r | p |
|---|---|---|---|
| 55b | 1 | 1 | 11 |
| c | 2 | 2 | 10 |

## Burnedge

*Jas Kenworthy*

| Plot | a | r | p |
|---|---|---|---|
| 56 | 2 | 3 | 3 |

## Kerchief Nook

| Plot | a | r | p | Note |
|---|---|---|---|---|
| 57 | 0 | 2 | 11 | Waste |

## Burnedge

*Jas Lees Esq*

| Plot | a | r | p | Note |
|---|---|---|---|---|
| 58a | 1 | 3 | 1 | |
| b | 0 | 1 | 12 | Buildings |
| c | 0 | 3 | 20 | |
| d | 0 | 3 | 5 | |
| e | 0 | 0 | 32 | Buildings |

| | | | | |
|---|---|---|---|---|
| f | 1 | 3 | 32 | |
| g | 1 | 2 | 31 | |
| h | 2 | 0 | 33 | |
| j | 0 | 1 | 29 | Plantation |
| k | 2 | 2 | 9 | |
| l | 1 | 0 | 30 | |
| m | 0 | 2 | 38 | |
| n | 0 | 0 | 32 | |
| o | 1 | 0 | 2 | |
| p | 0 | 0 | 32 | Waste |
| q | 0 | 1 | 38 | |
| r | 1 | 2 | 31 | |
| s | 1 | 2 | 27 | |
| t | 1 | 3 | 28 | |

## Burnedge

| | | | |
|---|---|---|---|
| 59a | 1 | 3 | 14 |
| b | 0 | 2 | 28 |

## Hills

*Jas Wright* — Self

| | | | |
|---|---|---|---|
| 60a | 3 | 3 | 32 |
| b | 2 | 2 | 26 |
| c | 1 | 2 | 35 |
| d | 0 | 1 | 26 |
| e | 1 | 0 | 29 |
| f | 1 | 0 | 11 |
| g | 1 | 3 | 26 |
| h | 1 | 2 | 38 |
| i | 6 | 0 | 18 |

## Hills

*Thomas Shaw* — Wm Platt

| | | | | |
|---|---|---|---|---|
| 61a | 0 | 2 | 4 | " |
| b | 0 | 1 | 13 | " |
| c | 1 | 1 | 19 | " |
| d | 1 | 2 | 22 | " |
| e | 1 | 2 | 24 | " |
| f | 0 | 1 | 22 | " |
| g | 1 | 3 | 0 | " |
| h | 1 | 3 | 24 | " |

*Thomas Shaw*

| | | | | |
|---|---|---|---|---|
| 62 | 4 | 2 | 29 | Rob. Buckley |

*Thos Mayall (Miles Mayall)* — Isaac Clayton

| | | | | | |
|---|---|---|---|---|---|
| 63a | 3 | 0 | 34 | | " |
| b | 3 | 2 | 4 | | " |
| c | 1 | 0 | 4 | | " |
| d | 2 | 3 | 26 | | " |
| e | 2 | 0 | 4 | | R.Whitehead |
| f | 1 | 3 | 20 | | " |
| g | 3 | 2 | 15 | | " |
| h | 0 | 1 | 31 | Waste | M.M. |
| i | 3 | 2 | 18 | | " |
| j | 1 | 0 | 10 | | " |
| k | 5 | 3 | 5 | | " |
| l | 3 | 0 | 11 | | " |
| m | 0 | 0 | 35 | | " |

## Stopes

*Jno Mayall*

| | | | | |
|---|---|---|---|---|
| 64a | 4 | 3 | 6 | |
| b | 0 | 0 | 15 | Garden |
| c | 2 | 0 | 29 | |

## Lawton Fold

*Hey Chapel* — Jas Cooper

| | | | | | |
|---|---|---|---|---|---|
| 65a | 0 | 1 | 4 | House | " |
| b | 4 | 2 | 5 | | " |
| c | 2 | 0 | 13 | | " |
| d | 3 | 1 | 18 | | " |
| e | 0 | 3 | 22 | | " |
| f | 2 | 0 | 22 | | " |
| g | 1 | 2 | 22 | | " |
| h | 0 | 1 | 30 | | " |
| i | 2 | 1 | 32 | | " |
| j | 1 | 3 | 2 | | J.Smith |
| k | | | | | Houses &c |

## Brown Hill

*Thos Shaw* — Jas Smith

| | | | | | |
|---|---|---|---|---|---|
| 66a | 1 | 3 | 2 | | " |
| b | 1 | 2 | 15 | | " |
| c | 2 | 2 | 32 | | " |
| d | 1 | 0 | 26 | | " |
| e | 0 | 1 | 3 | House | " |
| f | 0 | 3 | 11 | | " |

| | | | | |
|---|---|---|---|---|
| g | 3 | 0 | 2 | " |
| h | 1 | 1 | 7 | " |

## Grotton

*R.F.Buckley*

| | | | | |
|---|---|---|---|---|
| 67a | 0 | 0 | 37 | Jno Lees |
| b | 1 | 0 | 32 | " |
| c | 2 | 1 | 3 | " |
| d | 0 | 2 | 22 | " |
| e | 1 | 1 | 38 | J.Lees |
| f | 2 | 3 | 37 | " |
| g | 4 | 2 | 28 | " |
| h | 1 | 2 | 10 | " |
| i | 3 | 3 | 20 | " |
| j | 1 | 2 | 37 | " |
| k | 3 | 1 | 27 | " |
| l | 4 | 3 | 0 | T.Shaw |
| m | 2 | 3 | 23 | " |
| n | 3 | 2 | 37 | " |
| o | 0 | 2 | 16 | J.Shaw |
| p | 3 | 0 | 2 | " |
| q | 1 | 0 | 33 | " |
| r | 2 | 3 | 26 | T.Shaw |
| s | 2 | 3 | 28 | " |
| t | 3 | 1 | 27 | " |
| u | 3 | 1 | 10 | J.Shaw |
| v | 1 | 1 | 34 | " |
| w | 1 | 1 | 25 | " |

## Load Hill Platting

*R.F.Buckley Esq*

| | | | | | |
|---|---|---|---|---|---|
| 68a | 4 | 0 | 33 | | Abm " |
| b | 2 | 3 | 2 | | " |
| c | 3 | 0 | 12 | | " |
| d | 2 | 2 | 36 | | " |
| e | 1 | 2 | 29 | | " |
| f | 3 | 3 | 36 | | " |
| g | 0 | 0 | 31 | Gardens | " |
| h | 1 | 1 | 28 | | " |

## Grotton Head

*R.F.Buckley*

| | | | | | |
|---|---|---|---|---|---|
| 68i | 0 | 1 | 30 | House | Thos Shaw |
| j | 0 | 1 | 37 | | " |
| k | 0 | 3 | 0 | | " |
| l | 3 | 2 | 20 | | " |
| m | 1 | 0 | 23 | | " |
| n | 2 | 1 | 12 | | " |
| o | 1 | 1 | 37 | | J.S. |
| p | 1 | 2 | 18 | | T.S. |
| q | 2 | 1 | 11 | | " |
| r | 3 | 1 | 33 | | " |
| s | 2 | 1 | 34 | | " |
| t | 1 | 3 | 0 | | " |

## Croft Shaw Bent

*R.F.Buckley Esq* — Self

| | | | |
|---|---|---|---|
| 69a | 3 | 1 | 22 |
| b | 1 | 2 | 24 |
| c | 2 | 3 | 13 |
| d | 0 | 1 | 32 |
| e | 0 | 3 | 26 |
| f | 3 | 3 | 34 |
| g | 0 | 1 | 38 |
| h | 1 | 0 | 8 |
| i | 2 | 0 | 4 |
| j | 0 | 0 | 36 |
| k | 0 | 1 | 8 |
| l | 2 | 3 | 31 |
| m | 2 | 3 | 24 |
| n | 2 | 3 | 35 |
| o | 3 | 0 | 35 |
| p | 4 | 0 | 22 |
| q | 1 | 0 | 33 |

## Cover Hill

*R.F.Buckley* — Sam Wood

| | | | | |
|---|---|---|---|---|
| 70a | 0 | 2 | 7 | " |
| b | 1 | 0 | 28 | " |
| c | 1 | 2 | 34 | " |
| d | 0 | 3 | 14 | |
| e | 0 | 0 | 37 | |
| f | 0 | 3 | 10 | |
| g | 1 | 0 | 10 | |

## Lane

*Rob Lawton, Jos Holden* — W.Hayes occr

| | | | | | |
|---|---|---|---|---|---|
| 71a | 1 | 0 | 14 | | " |
| b | 2 | 1 | 38 | | " |
| c | 1 | 1 | 32 | | " |
| d | 1 | 0 | 14 | | " |
| e | 0 | 3 | 26 | | |
| f | 0 | 0 | 18 | Gardens & Buildings | |
| g | 0 | 0 | 24 | Gardens & Buildings | |
| h | 3 | 0 | 22 | | |
| i | 1 | 3 | 35 | | |
| j | 0 | 3 | 36 | Holden own | Heyes |
| k | 2 | 2 | 4 | " | " |
| l | 0 | 2 | 15 | " | " |
| m | 1 | 0 | 20 | " | " |
| n | 1 | 0 | 35 | " | " |
| o | 1 | 3 | 0 | " | " |

## Lane

*Hrs Shaw, Mrs Shaw ownr* — Wm Hayes occ

| | | | | | |
|---|---|---|---|---|---|
| 72a | 1 | 2 | 14 | | " |
| b | 2 | 2 | 36 | | " |
| c | 1 | 1 | 27 | | " |
| d | 1 | 2 | 36 | | " |
| e | 2 | 2 | 34 | | " |
| f | 3 | 0 | 1 | | " |
| g | 0 | 0 | 22 | Yard | " |

## Thornlee

*R.F.Buckley* — Jos Shaw occr

| | | | | | |
|---|---|---|---|---|---|
| 73a | 0 | 3 | 31 | | " |
| b | 0 | 1 | 33 | | " |
| c | 0 | 0 | 32 | Garden | " |
| d | 2 | 3 | 0 | | " |

## Thornlee

*David Lilley, Jas Lees own* — Josh Lees occr

| | | | | | |
|---|---|---|---|---|---|
| 75a | 0 | 2 | 5 | | " |
| b | 0 | 2 | 10 | | " |
| c | 0 | 1 | 0 | Buildings | " |
| d | 0 | 3 | 18 | | " |

## Thornlee

*Rob Kenworthy* — Self

| | | | |
|---|---|---|---|
| 76 | 0 | 2 | 31 |

## Wormhole

*Widow Whitehead  R. Whitehead owner*  Self

| | | | | |
|---|---|---|---|---|
| 77 | 0 | 1 | 12 | Grdn |
| | | | | Chas Whitehead occ |
| 78a | 0 | 0 | 30 | Bldgs |

*Tabitha Kenworthy*

| | | | | |
|---|---|---|---|---|
| b | 0 | 3 | 10 | G.Mayall occ |

## Lydgate

*Rich Wilson* — Self

| | | | |
|---|---|---|---|
| 79a | 2 | 0 | 7 |
| b | 3 | 1 | 13 |
| c | 3 | 1 | 8 |

## Lydgate

*Mary Wrigley & Sons* — Selves

| | | | | |
|---|---|---|---|---|
| 80a | 3 | 2 | 28 | |
| b | 2 | 3 | 37 | |
| c | 2 | 0 | 11 | |
| d | 2 | 1 | 13 | |
| e | 3 | 0 | 39 | |
| f | 1 | 0 | 35 | |
| g | 3 | 0 | 17 | |
| h | 0 | 1 | 38 | Gardens |

## Lydgate

*Exec Jno Mayall* — Jas Clayton

| | | | | |
|---|---|---|---|---|
| 81a | 0 | 0 | 19 | Buildings |
| b | 3 | 0 | 17 | |
| c | 1 | 1 | 21 | |

## Lydgate

*Eliz Bostock* — Self

| | | | |
|---|---|---|---|
| 82a | 3 | 3 | 11 |
| b | 2 | 3 | 24 |

| | A | R | P | |
|---|---|---|---|---|
| c | 0 | 1 | 30 | |
| d | 0 | 1 | 2 | |
| e | 2 | 2 | 21 | |
| f | 2 | 3 | 4 | |
| g | 3 | 1 | 30 | |
| h | 3 | 2 | 19 | |
| i | 0 | 0 | 33 | |
| j | 3 | 0 | 30 | |

## Lydgate

*John Bostock Jno Robinson    Abr Lees own*

| | A | R | P |
|---|---|---|---|
| 82k | 1 | 0 | 28 |
| l | 2 | 1 | 36 |

## Lydgate

*John Boden Kitty Whitehead Ex J. Boden own*

| | A | R | P |
|---|---|---|---|
| 83a | 2 | 0 | 28 |
| b | 2 | 2 | 5 |

*M. Newton*

| | A | R | P | |
|---|---|---|---|---|
| 84 | 0 | 1 | 17 | Buildings & Fold |

*Rev J.C.Attye, Ab Wood Stalybridge Chapel own*

| | A | R | P |
|---|---|---|---|
| 86a | 1 | 3 | 38 |
| b | 3 | 3 | 19 |

*John Harrison, Pub House, Ab Wood,*
*Ed Buckley own*

| | A | R | P |
|---|---|---|---|
| 86c | 0 | 0 | 31 |
| 87a | 1 | 3 | 10 |
| b | 0 | 2 | 31 |
| c | 0 | 2 | 29 |

## Load Hill

*Rob Whitehead        Self*

| | A | R | P | |
|---|---|---|---|---|
| 88a | 2 | 1 | 31 | |
| b | 3 | 0 | 20 | |
| c | 0 | 2 | 16 | Buildings |
| d | 3 | 3 | 0 | |
| e | 1 | 1 | 37 | |
| f | 3 | 3 | 20 | |
| g | 1 | 0 | 3 | |
| h | 4 | 0 | 38 | |
| i | 0 | 2 | 0 | Road |
| j | 3 | 0 | 19 | |
| k | 0 | 2 | 19 | |
| l | 2 | 1 | 0 | |
| m | 3 | 1 | 17 | |
| n | 0 | 2 | 22 | |
| o | 0 | 0 | 27 | Buildings |

## Stonebreaks

*Knights*

| | A | R | P | |
|---|---|---|---|---|
| 89a | 0 | 3 | 38 | Jos Lockwood |
| | | | | W.Taylor |
| b | 1 | 0 | 21 | " |
| c | 1 | 0 | 5 | " |
| d | 1 | 1 | 23 | " |
| e | 1 | 0 | 15 | " |
| f | 0 | 0 | 29 | House " |
| g | 1 | 0 | 36 | M.Buckley |
| | | | | W.Taylor |
| h | 0 | 3 | 13 | " |
| i | 0 | 0 | 39 | Waste & Garden |
| j | 0 | 1 | 6 | |

## Stonebreaks

*Jno Radcliffe Esq  Mrs Radcliffe*

| | A | R | P | | |
|---|---|---|---|---|---|
| 90a | 1 | 3 | 34 | R.Lees | |
| b | 6 | 1 | 1 | Mrs Radcliff | Self |
| c | 1 | 2 | 35 | " | " |
| d | 1 | 2 | 38 | " | " |
| e | 2 | 3 | 9 | R.Lees | |
| f | 0 | 2 | 16 | " | |
| g | 0 | 0 | 20 | Chapel Yard | |
| h | 0 | 0 | 22 | House | Josh H. |
| i | 0 | 0 | 18 | Reservoir | |
| j | 2 | 0 | 17 | Mrs Radcliffe ow & occ | |
| k | 0 | 1 | 39 | " | " |
| l | 1 | 0 | 29 | " | " |
| m | 0 | 2 | 32 | " | " |
| n | 0 | 1 | 30 | Bldgs " | " |
| o | 2 | 0 | 27 | Maria Radffe | |
| | | | | Hy Buckley | |

## Crowthorn

*Jno Radcliffe Esq*

| | A | R | P | | |
|---|---|---|---|---|---|
| 91a | 0 | 1 | 28 | Waste | |
| b | 2 | 1 | 25 | | M.Buckley |
| c | 1 | 1 | 8 | | Mrs Radcliffe |
| | | | | | Mary Buckley |
| d | 2 | 1 | 8 | " | " |
| e | 1 | 3 | 36 | " | " |
| f | 2 | 2 | 37 | " | " |
| g | 0 | 2 | 29 | " | " |

*Jos & Stewart Buckley*

| | A | R | P | |
|---|---|---|---|---|
| 91aa | 0 | 2 | 29 | House & Garden |

*John Radcliffe Josh Haughton*

| | A | R | P | | |
|---|---|---|---|---|---|
| 91b | 3 | 2 | 3 | | |
| c | 1 | 2 | 0 | | |
| 92a | 3 | 0 | 21 | Mary Radliffe | |
| | | | | Mary Buckley | |
| b | 1 | 3 | 16 | " | R.Lees |
| c | 2 | 3 | 36 | " | " |
| d | 1 | 0 | 3 | " | " |
| e | 0 | 2 | 0 | W.Taylor owner & occ | |
| f | 1 | 2 | 24 | " | " |
| g | 0 | 3 | 35 | " | " |
| h | 0 | 0 | 25 | " | " |
| i | 1 | 0 | 27 | " | " |
| j | 1 | 0 | 17 | " | " |
| k | 0 | 3 | 3 | " | " |

## Springhead

*Jos Taylor*

| | A | R | P | |
|---|---|---|---|---|
| 93 | 0 | 0 | 20 | Buildings |

*Esther Buckley*

| | A | R | P | |
|---|---|---|---|---|
| 94 | 0 | 0 | 17 | Buildings |

## Claytons

*R.F.Buckley Esq      Wm Taylor owr & occ*

| | A | R | P |
|---|---|---|---|
| 95a | 3 | 2 | 11 |
| b | 1 | 1 | 29 |
| c | 0 | 3 | 0 |
| d | 0 | 1 | 0 |
| e | 3 | 1 | 15 |
| f | 2 | 0 | 2 |
| g | 2 | 1 | 8 |
| h | 2 | 3 | 10 |
| i | 1 | 2 | 15 |
| j | 1 | 1 | 21 |
| k | 1 | 0 | 8 |
| l | 0 | 1 | 7 |
| m | 0 | 1 | 12 |
| n | 1 | 1 | 23 |
| o | 0 | 3 | 9 |
| p | 2 | 2 | 14 |
| q | 1 | 1 | 11 |
| r | 1 | 3 | 19 |

## Walkers

*John    Jos Jones owner   Josh Jones*

| | A | R | P | | |
|---|---|---|---|---|---|
| 96a | 1 | 1 | 28 | Mayall | Jas Mayall |
| b | 1 | 0 | 24 | Buckley | W. Buckley |
| c | 3 | 2 | 8 | " | " |
| d | 0 | 2 | 7 | " | " |
| e | 1 | 2 | 24 | " | " |
| f | 1 | 1 | 10 | " | " |
| g | 1 | 1 | 33 | " | " |
| h | 0 | 2 | 26 | J.Mayall | J.Mayall |
| i | 0 | 1 | 21 | " | " |
| j | 3 | 0 | 18 | W.B. | W.Buckley |
| k | 0 | 3 | 37 | " | " |

*Jos Taylor occ & owner*

| | A | R | P | | |
|---|---|---|---|---|---|
| l | 0 | 2 | 27 | | |
| m | 0 | 1 | 0 | Orchard | " |
| n | 1 | 1 | 34 | " | |
| o | 1 | 1 | 36 | Jas Mayall occr | |
| p | 2 | 0 | 28 | " | |
| q | 2 | 1 | 13 | " | |
| r | 2 | 2 | 24 | " | |

## Ashes

*Jno Booth            Self*

| | A | R | P | |
|---|---|---|---|---|
| 97a | 1 | 2 | 22 | |
| b | 0 | 3 | 30 | |
| c | 0 | 2 | 10 | |
| d | 1 | 1 | 26 | |
| e | 0 | 3 | 37 | |
| f | 0 | 3 | 7 | Gardens |

| | A | R | P | |
|---|---|---|---|---|
| g | 0 | 0 | 10 | " |
| h | 0 | 0 | 20 | " |
| i | 1 | 3 | 39 | Buildings |
| j | 4 | 0 | 19 | " |
| k | 2 | 1 | 1 | " |
| l | 3 | 0 | 4 | " |
| m | 2 | 1 | 18 | " |
| n | 2 | 3 | 23 | " |
| o | 1 | 3 | 28 | " |
| p | 1 | 1 | 24 | " |
| q | 3 | 2 | 36 | " |
| r | 0 | 2 | 33 | " |
| s | 2 | 0 | 35 | " |
| t | 0 | 2 | 3 | " |
| u | 1 | 1 | 8 | " |
| v | 4 | 0 | 30 | " |

## Latham

*Jno Buckley Execs*

| | A | R | P | |
|---|---|---|---|---|
| 99a | 1 | 0 | 34 | |
| b | 0 | 1 | 31 | " |
| c | 3 | 2 | 11 | " |
| d | 1 | 3 | 30 | |

## Woodmans

*Jos Taylor's Execs*

| | A | R | P | |
|---|---|---|---|---|
| 100a | 0 | 1 | 0 | Hugh Andrew |
| b | 0 | 0 | 19 | Buildings " |
| c | 0 | 1 | 0 | " |
| d | 0 | 2 | 13 | " |
| e | 0 | 0 | 28 | " |
| f | 2 | 0 | 11 | " |
| g | 0 | 0 | 28 | " |
| h | 2 | 0 | 30 | Luke Clayton |
| i | 0 | 0 | 21 | Building |
| j | 0 | 0 | 32 | R.Tetlow |
| | | | | Mrs Taylor own |
| k | 1 | 1 | 1 | " " |
| l | 0 | 0 | 24 | Gardens |

## Shelderslow

*Jos Taylor*

| | A | R | P | |
|---|---|---|---|---|
| 101a | 3 | 2 | 30 | Stephen Bridge |
| b | 0 | 1 | 12 | Buildings " |
| c | 0 | 2 | 27 | Exec J.Taylor |
| d | 2 | 2 | 4 | " |
| e | 0 | 3 | 23 | " |
| f | 1 | 2 | 9 | " |
| g | 0 | 1 | 31 | " |

## Hey

*Walker Esq*

| | A | R | P | |
|---|---|---|---|---|
| 102a | 2 | 0 | 18 | Hargreaves |
| b | 1 | 0 | 26 | " |
| c | 0 | 1 | 22 | House & Waste |
| d | 3 | 2 | 4 | Hargreaves |
| e | 3 | 0 | 25 | " |
| f | 2 | 1 | 25 | " |
| g | 4 | 1 | 23 | " |
| h | 1 | 2 | 9 | " |

## Den

*Walker Esq           Orlando Buckley occ*

| | A | R | P | |
|---|---|---|---|---|
| 102i | 2 | 1 | 15 | O.B. |
| j | 0 | 3 | 14 | " |
| k | 1 | 0 | 26 | " |
| l | 2 | 0 | 1 | " |
| m | 2 | 2 | 21 | " |
| n | 1 | 2 | 35 | " |
| o | 1 | 2 | 25 | " |
| f | 1 | 2 | 9 | " |
| 103 | 0 | 0 | 22* | |
| 104a | 0 | 0 | 22* | |
| b | 0 | 1 | 6* | |
| 105* | | | | |
| 106 | 0 | 0 | 10* | |
| 107 | 0 | 0 | 10* | |

*Hart Bracewell*

| | A | R | P | |
|---|---|---|---|---|
| 108 | 0 | 1 | 0 [36]* | |
| 109a* | | | | |
| b* | | | | |

*[N.B. Numbers 103 to 107 and 109 omitted on Higson copy, details from Vestry and 1863 maps.]

## Austerlands

*Jos Seville* — Self — R.Kenworthy

| | a | r | p | |
|---|---|---|---|---|
| 110a | 3 | 1 | 10 | " |
| b | 2 | 2 | 19 | " |
| c | 2 | 1 | 3 | " |

## Austerlands

*Walker Esq* — W.Dale occ

| | a | r | p | |
|---|---|---|---|---|
| 111a | 2 | 1 | 3 | " |
| b | 1 | 3 | 37 | " |
| c | 0 | 0 | 29 | " |
| d | 3 | 0 | 36 | W.Wrigley |
| e | 0 | 1 | 20 | B.Buckley |
| f | 1 | 1 | 19 | " |
| g | 0 | 0 | 20 | " |
| h | 1 | 2 | 3 | " |
| i | 3 | 3 | 19 | " |
| j | 0 | 0 | 19 | Buildings |

## Shelderslow*

*[N.B. Numbers 112 to 115 omitted on Higson copy, details from Vestry and 1863 maps.]

| | a | r | p | | |
|---|---|---|---|---|---|
| 112a* | | | | | |
| b* | | | | | |
| 113 | 0 | 0 | 39* | | |
| 114* | | | | | |
| 116a | 0 | 0 | 16 | Croft | Messrs Cooper |
| b | 0 | 1 | 15 | | Mrs Driver |
| 117a | 0 | 1 | 30 | | " |
| b | 0 | 0 | 22 | | Buckley |
| c | 0 | 1 | 22 | Knowsley | Mrs Driver |
| d | 2 | 3 | 39 | | " |
| e | 2 | 3 | 0 | J.Jackson | Driver |
| f | 1 | 2 | 23 | " | " |
| g | 1 | 0 | 10 | " | " |

## Three Lane Ends

*Cath Byrom* — Mrs Robinson occ

| | a | r | p | | |
|---|---|---|---|---|---|
| 118a | 1 | 2 | 20 | | Nancy Robinson |
| b | 0 | 3 | 35 | | " |
| c | 2 | 3 | 34 | | " |
| d | 2 | 0 | 9 | | " |
| e | 0 | 0 | 9 | Buildings | " |
| f | 1 | 3 | 38 | | " |

## Austerlands

*Rob Lees* — Jas Heywood occ

| | a | r | p |
|---|---|---|---|
| 119a | 2 | 2 | 25 |
| b | 1 | 0 | 2 |
| c | 0 | 1 | 0 |
| d | 2 | 2 | 5 |

## Austerlands

*James Lees* — Jos Lees

| | a | r | p | | |
|---|---|---|---|---|---|
| 120a | 0 | 1 | 36 | | Jas Heywood |
| b | 0 | 3 | 4 | | " |
| c | 3 | 3 | 24 | | " |
| d | 2 | 3 | 20 | | " |
| e | 0 | 0 | 32 | | " |
| f | 3 | 0 | 5 | | " |
| g | 1 | 3 | 29 | | " |
| h | 0 | 1 | 16 | Gardens | " |
| 121 | 0 | 0 | 39 | Buildings | |
| 122a | 0 | 3 | 15 | Reservoir | |
| b | 0 | 0 | 20 | " | |
| 123 | 1 | 0 | 23* | | |

*[N.B. Numbers 123 and 124 omitted on Higson copy, details of 123 from Vestry and 1863 maps.]

## Austerlands

*Edm Lees*

| | a | r | p | | |
|---|---|---|---|---|---|
| 125a | 0 | 1 | 3 | Jon Lees | Self |
| b | 0 | 3 | 19 | | Saml Lees |
| c | 0 | 2 | 10 | | |
| d | 4 | 0 | 9 | | |
| e | 4 | 1 | 39 | | |
| f | 1 | 3 | 14 | | |
| g | 0 | 3 | 17 | | |
| h | 3 | 0 | 0 | | |
| i | 1 | 2 | 39 | | |
| j | 2 | 1 | 21 | | |

| | a | r | p | | |
|---|---|---|---|---|---|
| k | 9 | 0 | 39 | | |
| l | 6 | 1 | 0 | | Esther Mayall |
| | | | | | Jon Lees occ |

## Nook

*Rich Brown* — Messrs Mallalieu — Mary Tithes occ

| | a | r | p |
|---|---|---|---|
| 126a | 1 | 1 | 26 |
| b | 2 | 2 | 35 |
| c | 0 | 0 | 33 |
| d | 1 | 1 | 34 |
| e | 2 | 0 | 6 |

## Thorpes

*Benj H. Allen Esq* — Jos Lawton occ

| | a | r | p | |
|---|---|---|---|---|
| 127a | 2 | 2 | 14 | " |
| b | 3 | 3 | 21 | " |
| c | 1 | 3 | 30 | " |

## Turf Lane

*Walker*

| | a | r | p | |
|---|---|---|---|---|
| 128 | 2 | 1 | 8 | Charles Buckley |
| aa | 1 | 0 | 21 | " |
| i | 5 | 1 | 34 | Wm Wrigley |

## Scouthead

*Jon Lees*

| | a | r | p | | |
|---|---|---|---|---|---|
| 128b | 2 | 0 | 5 | | Jon Lees |
| c | 0 | 0 | 12 | | " |
| d | 4 | 1 | 4 | | " |
| e | 0 | 0 | 9 | | " |
| f | 3 | 0 | 34 | | " |
| g | 0 | 2 | 1 | R.Lees | W.Jackson |
| h | 1 | 3 | 5 | | M.Wrigley |

## Turf Lane

*Jas Taylor*

| | a | r | p | | |
|---|---|---|---|---|---|
| 129 | 3 | 1 | 14 | J.Taylor | B.Buckley |

## Wood Brook

*Jno Robinson* — Self (Jno & Thos)

| | a | r | p |
|---|---|---|---|
| 131a | 2 | 1 | 36 |
| b | 0 | 0 | 26 |
| c | 2 | 0 | 0 |
| d | 1 | 1 | 7 |
| e | 3 | 0 | 21 |
| f | 0 | 2 | 31 |
| g | 0 | 1 | 17 |
| h | 0 | 0 | 11 |
| i | 3 | 0 | 26 |
| j | 0 | 2 | 30 |

## Stonerake

*Execs D.Bentley* — W.Taylor

| | a | r | p | |
|---|---|---|---|---|
| 132a | 2 | 1 | 30 | " |
| b | 1 | 2 | 24 | " |
| c | 2 | 3 | 1 | " |
| d | 3 | 2 | 31 | " |
| e | 2 | 3 | 7 | " |
| f | 1 | 1 | 14 | " |

## Pastures

*Jno Waring* — Booth & Hall

| | a | r | p | |
|---|---|---|---|---|
| 133a | 1 | 1 | 32 | " |
| b | 0 | 2 | 28 | " |
| c | 0 | 3 | 0 | " |

## High Moor Side

*Matthew Driver* — Jno Whitehead

| | a | r | p | | |
|---|---|---|---|---|---|
| 134a | 1 | 2 | 10 | B | Jas Radcliffe |
| b | 2 | 1 | 4 | MD | G.Bardsley |
| c | 1 | 3 | 17 | Bn | Garlic |
| d | 2 | 0 | 26 | Bn | Jno Radcliffe |
| e | 3 | 3 | 5 } | Bn | Garlic |
| | 1 | 0 | 0 } | | |
| f | 3 | 1 | 5 | R.Bur | Garlic |
| g | 2 | 1 | 20 | MD | E.Bardsley |
| h | 2 | 1 | 37 | MD | Ed. Bardsley occ |
| i | 1 | 2 | 18 | Burton | Garlic |
| j | 2 | 1 | 2 | " | " |
| k | 0 | 0 | 22 | " | " |
| l | 1 | 2 | 14 | " | " |
| m | 1 | 1 | 15 | " | " |
| n | 2 | 3 | 5 | M.D. | J.Whitehead |
| o | 4 | 1 | 19 | " | " |

| | a | r | p | | |
|---|---|---|---|---|---|
| p | 3 | 2 | 28 | " | Jon Jackson |
| q | 3 | 1 | 12 | S.Wrigley own & occ | |

## Scouthead

*Jos Mellor* — W.Jackson

| | a | r | p | | |
|---|---|---|---|---|---|
| 135a | 0 | 2 | 7 | Bldgs & Grdn | Lees |
| b | 2 | 1 | 35 | | |
| c | 4 | 1 | 6 | | Miles Wrigley |
| d | 1 | 0 | 21 | | " |

## Scouthead

*Execs of late Jas Jackson* — W.Jackson occ

| | a | r | p |
|---|---|---|---|
| 136a | 1 | 1 | 38 |
| b | 1 | 3 | 34 |
| c | 2 | 0 | 33 |
| d | 2 | 3 | 14 |
| e | 1 | 3 | 25 |

## Herdslow

*Peter Fletcher* — Ed Lees own & occ

| | a | r | p | |
|---|---|---|---|---|
| 137a | 1 | 3 | 5 | " |
| b | 1 | 1 | 8 | " |
| c | 0 | 0 | 22 | " |
| d | 1 | 1 | 33 | " |
| e | 0 | 2 | 29 | " |

## Starting Chair

*Jno & Jos Radcliffe* — P.Seville

| | a | r | p | |
|---|---|---|---|---|
| 138a | 1 | 3 | 17 | " |
| b | 2 | 2 | 4 | " |
| c | 2 | 0 | 3 | " |
| d | 0 | 3 | 2 | " |
| e | 1 | 0 | 17 | " |

## Stonerake

*Jas Broadbent* — Self

| | a | r | p | | |
|---|---|---|---|---|---|
| 139a | 0 | 1 | 12 | | R.Shaw |
| b | 0 | 2 | 0* | | " |
| c | 1 | 2 | 10 | | " |
| d | 2 | 0 | 13 | | " |
| e | 1 | 2 | 34 | | " |
| f | 2 | 0 | 3 | | " |
| g | 0 | 3 | 2 | B.Wrigley | B.W |
| h | 1 | 2 | 10 | " | " |
| i | 1 | 3 | 29 | " | " |
| j | 1 | 1 | 19 | " | " |
| k | 0 | 1 | 37 | " | " |
| l | 1 | 3 | 28 | " | " |
| m | 0 | 3 | 10 | P.S. | P.S. |
| n | 2 | 1 | 14 | B.Wrigley | B.W |
| o | 0 | 0 | 14 | " | " |
| p | 1 | 1 | 25 | P.Seville | P.S. |
| q | 0 | 2 | 14 | B.Wrigley | B.W |

*[N.B. Number 129b omitted on Higson copy, details from Vestry and 1863 maps.]

| | a | r | p | |
|---|---|---|---|---|
| 140a | 1 | 3 | 1 | P.S. |
| b | 2 | 1 | 32 | " |
| c | 1 | 0 | 32 | B.W. |
| d | 3 | 2 | 30 | " |

## Wellfield

*Peter Saville*

| | a | r | p | |
|---|---|---|---|---|
| 141a | 1 | 3 | 22 | P.S. |
| b | 2 | 2 | 22 | " |
| c | 0 | 3 | 35 | " |
| d | 1 | 2 | 24 | " |

| | a | r | p | |
|---|---|---|---|---|
| 142 | 1 | 2 | 37 | P.Seville |

## Doctor House

*Mary Buckley John Howard* — occ Jno Lees

| | a | r | p | | |
|---|---|---|---|---|---|
| 143a | 0 | 0 | 34 | House | Jas Buckley |
| b | 2 | 0 | 17 | | " |
| c | 1 | 3 | 2 | | " |
| d | 0 | 3 | 35 | | " |
| e | 2 | 0 | 39 | | " |
| f | 2 | 1 | 37 | | " |
| g | 1 | 0 | 30 | | " |
| h | 0 | 2 | 33 | | " |

## Doctor House

*Geo Collins*

| | | | | |
|---|---|---|---|---|
| 144a | 1 | 2 | 21 | |
| b | 0 | 1 | 29 | |
| c | 1 | 1 | 38 | |
| d | 1 | 1 | 14 | Buildings &c |
| e | 1 | 0 | 10 | |
| f | 2 | 0 | 22 | |
| g | 1 | 2 | 39 | |
| h | 1 | 3 | 35 | |
| i | 2 | 0 | 25 | |

## Doctor Lane

*Jon Wrigley    Jno, Ben & Thos Wrigley*

| | | | | |
|---|---|---|---|---|
| 145a | 0 | 0 | 28 | House & Garden |
| b | 1 | 1 | 13 | Wrigley Jno Lees occ |
| c | 0 | 3 | 12 | |
| d | 0 | 3 | 2 | |
| e | | | | |
| f | 1 | 2 | 0 | |
| g | 2 | 0 | 10 | |
| h | 2 | 1 | 0 | |
| i | 2 | 2 | 23 | |
| j | 2 | 1 | 2 | |
| k | 2 | 0 | 25 | |
| l | 1 | 3 | 18 | |
| m | 1 | 2 | 12 | |
| n | 6 | 2 | 38 | |

## Dole

*Jno Harrop & Co*

| | | | | |
|---|---|---|---|---|
| 146a | 4 | 0 | 4 | Ass. Jos Harrop Collins |
| b | 2 | 1 | 25 | Stonepit W.Buckley |

## Doctor Lane Head

*John Buckley*

| | | | | |
|---|---|---|---|---|
| 147a | 0 | 0 | 0 | House |
| b | 1 | 0 | 12 | Mr Waring Ann Smethurst |
| c | 0 | 1 | 36 | W.Shaw Scanlan occ |
| d | 0 | 0 | 13 | "  " |
| e | 0 | 1 | 21 | "  " |
| f | 1 | 1 | 12 | R.Buckley own & occ. |
| g | 1 | 3 | 15 | "  " |
| h | 1 | 3 | 26 | "  " |
| i | 2 | 2 | 0 | "  " |
| j | 2 | 1 | 32 | "  " |
| k | 1 | 0 | 18 | |
| m | 1 | 0 | 7 | Scanlan  S.Shaw |
| n | 3 | 2 | 12 | Smethurst & Scanlan |
| o | 1 | 2 | 34 | Ann Smethurst |
| p | 1 | 1 | 29 | Scanlan  S.Shaw |
| q | 2 | 0 | 13 | Smethurst |
| r | 1 | 2 | 20 | Scanlan  W.Shaw |
| s | 3 | 0 | 10 | R.Buckley |

## Doctor Lane Head

| | | | | |
|---|---|---|---|---|
| 148a | 0 | 0 | 19 | Thos Buckley Jno Harrison occ. |
| b | 1 | 0 | 17 | "  " |
| c | 2 | 1 | 6 | "  " |
| d | 1 | 2 | 24 | "  " |
| e | 1 | 0 | 4 | "  " |

## High Moor

*Edm Wrigley*

| | | | | |
|---|---|---|---|---|
| 149a | 1 | 2 | 32 | P.Seville |
| b | 1 | 0 | 12 | " |

## High Moor

*Leigh & Taylor*

| | | | | |
|---|---|---|---|---|
| 150 | 29 | 1 | 7 | |
| 150a | 24 | 1 | 7 | W.Dunkerley occ |
| b | 4 | 0 | 0 | " own & occ |
| c | 1 | 0 | 0 | improved " " |

## High Moor

*M.Fletcher*

| | | | | |
|---|---|---|---|---|
| 151a | 2 | 2 | 34 | Edm Lees own & occ |
| b | 1 | 1 | 2 | |
| c | 2 | 1 | 30 | |
| d | 2 | 2 | 4 | |
| e | 2 | 3 | 15 | |
| f | 1 | 0 | 12 | |

## High Moor

*Jas Gartside*

| | | | | |
|---|---|---|---|---|
| 152a | 1 | 2 | 20 | Sam Lees (Soho) J.Dunkerley |
| b | 0 | 3 | 7 | " " |
| c | 0 | 1 | 32 | " " |

## High Moor

*Execs late James Kershaw*

| | | | | |
|---|---|---|---|---|
| 153a | 1 | 0 | 29 | Edm Fielding |
| b | 1 | 0 | 18 | |
| c | 1 | 1 | 18 | |
| d | 1 | 0 | 24 | |
| e | 1 | 3 | 26 | |
| f | 0 | 3 | 15 | |
| g | 0 | 2 | 9 | |
| h | 0 | 0 | 28 | |
| i | 0 | 3 | 20 | |
| j | 0 | 3 | 12 | |

## Thorpes

*Jno Greaves   James Greaves  own*

| | | | | |
|---|---|---|---|---|
| 154a | 1 | 3 | 32 | Miles Beaumont occ |
| b | 1 | 3 | 29 | " |
| c | 3 | 2 | 19 | W.Graham |
| d | 2 | 2 | 2 | Miles Beumont |
| e | 1 | 0 | 33 | W.Graham |
| f | 1 | 0 | 7 | " |

## Strines

*Edw Ainsworth, Lord Stamford*

| | | | | | |
|---|---|---|---|---|---|
| 155a | 8 | 0 | 13 | | Ed Fielding |
| b | 1 | 1 | 5 | S.Lees | Eli Chadwick |
| c | 1 | 1 | 38 | " | " |
| d | 1 | 0 | 15 | " | " |
| e | 1 | 1 | 19 | " | " |
| f | 1 | 3 | 15 | " | " |
| g | 1 | 2 | 13 | S.Lees | Thos Smith |
| h | 0 | 0 | 23 | " | |

## Higher Barn

*Seville*    S.Lees Jno Mills

| | | | | |
|---|---|---|---|---|
| 156a | 1 | 1 | 0 | " |
| b | 0 | 0 | 32 | " |
| c | 1 | 2 | 28 | " |
| d | 2 | 0 | 18 | " |
| e | 0 | 1 | 36 | " |
| f | 1 | 0 | 34 | " |
| g | 2 | 3 | 6 | " |

## Strines

*Seville*    S.Lees Thos Smith

| | | | | |
|---|---|---|---|---|
| 157a | 4 | 1 | 18 | " |
| b | 1 | 1 | 29 | " |
| c | 0 | 1 | 14 | " |
| d | 1 | 2 | 32 | " |
| e | 1 | 3 | 1 | " |
| f | 10 | 1 | 30 | Jas Cocker |
| g | 3 | 0 | 0 | |

## Red House

*Jno Scholes*    Sam Lees Geo Seville occ

| | | | | |
|---|---|---|---|---|
| 158a | 1 | 1 | 5 | " |
| b | 2 | 0 | 31 | " |
| c | 1 | 3 | 20 | " |

## Top of Meadows

*Abm Clegg J.Taylor*    J.Shaw occ

| | | | | |
|---|---|---|---|---|
| 159a | 1 | 3 | 35 | " |
| b | 3 | 1 | 4 | " |
| c | 0 | 3 | 10 | " |
| d | 0 | 2 | 20 | " |
| e | 0 | 2 | 33 | " |
| f | 0 | 1 | 17 | " |
| g | 2 | 2 | 33 | J.Shaw |
| h | 2 | 0 | 4 | " |
| i | 0 | 2 | 24 | " |
| j | 2 | 0 | 37 | " |
| k | 1 | 3 | 18 | " |

## Top of Meadows

*Jno, Geo & Hugh Shaw owners*

| | | | | |
|---|---|---|---|---|
| 160a | 1 | 3 | 38 | Jas Shaw occ |
| b | 1 | 3 | 33 | " |
| c | 1 | 3 | 14 | " |
| d | 1 | 3 | 2 | " |
| e | 1 | 1 | 23 | " |
| f | 0 | 3 | 10 | " |
| g | 1 | 3 | 39 | " |
| h | 2 | 2 | 20 | " |

## Low Brook

*Execs late Abr Seville E.Moss, J. Greenwood*

| | | | | |
|---|---|---|---|---|
| 161a | 1 | 2 | 4 | |
| b | 0 | 3 | 23 | |
| c | 1 | 1 | 21 | |
| d | 5 | 3 | 30 | |
| e | 3 | 3 | 15 | |
| f | 1 | 0 | 31 | |
| g | 0 | 0 | 33 | |

Revised

*E.Moss late Greenwood*

| | | | | |
|---|---|---|---|---|
| 161a | 1 | 2 | 24 | |
| b | 0 | 3 | 23 | |
| c | 1 | 1 | 21 | |
| d | 0 | 3 | 0 | |
| d | 0 | 2 | 30 | |
| d | 4 | 2 | 0 | Waterworks J.Ingham Moss |
| e | 3 | 3 | 15 | |
| f | 1 | 0 | 31 | |
| g | 0 | 0 | 33 | |

## Pastures

*W.Lees  Sam Lees*    Peter Platt occ

| | | | | |
|---|---|---|---|---|
| 162a | 1 | 1 | 12 | " |
| b | 1 | 1 | 28 | " |
| c | 3 | 1 | 13 | " |
| d | 6 | 3 | 8 | " |

## Back o'th Low

*Ann Dale  Abel Dale own & occ*

| | | | | |
|---|---|---|---|---|
| 163a | 1 | 2 | 13 | |
| b | 2 | 1 | 19 | |
| c | 1 | 3 | 21 | |
| d | 1 | 0 | 36 | |
| e | 1 | 2 | 10 | |
| f | 0 | 3 | 12 | |

## Back o'th Low

    Betty Buckley occr

| | | | | |
|---|---|---|---|---|
| 164a | 0 | 0 | 36 | " |
| b | 3 | 0 | 25 | " |
| c | 0 | 3 | 34 | " |
| d | 1 | 1 | 21 | " |
| e | 2 | 0 | 4 | " |

## New Road Head

*Jas Harrop*

| | | | | |
|---|---|---|---|---|
| 165a | 3 | 0 | 20 | |
| b | 1 | 0 | 14 | |
| c | 2 | 2 | 39 | |
| d | 0 | 2 | 1 | |
| e | 0 | 3 | 15 | |
| f | 2 | 0 | 20 | |

## Waterhead Mill

*W.Booth*

| | | | |
|---|---|---|---|
| 166 | 0 | 2 | 10 |

## Waterhead Mill

*Jos Lees*

| | | | | |
|---|---|---|---|---|
| 167a | 2 | 1 | 13 | |
| b | 1 | 0 | 28 | |
| c | 1 | 0 | 32 | Bowling Green |
| d | 0 | 1 | 16 | |
| e | 2 | 1 | 24 | |

## Strines

*E.Ainsworth*    Jno Dunkerley

| | | | | | |
|---|---|---|---|---|---|
| 168a | 0 | 0 | 39 | S.Lees | Cocker |
| b | 5 | 3 | 19 | " | Jos Cocker |
| c | 1 | 3 | 2 | " | " |
| d | 1 | 2 | 14 | " | " |
| e | 3 | 2 | 35 | " | Thos Smith |

## Four Acre

*Sidebottom Esq*

| | | | |
|---|---|---|---|
| 169 | 5 | 3 | 25 |

## Green Lane

*Jno Winterbottom*

| | | | | |
|---|---|---|---|---|
| 170a | 2 | 0 | 5 | |
| b | 1 | 1 | 29 | |
| c | 2 | 1 | 10 | |
| d | 2 | 1 | 16 | |
| e | 1 | 2 | 20 | |
| f | 0 | 1 | 37 | |
| g | 1 | 1 | 36 | |
| h | 2 | 3 | 22 | |
| i | 3 | 1 | 20 | |
| j | 11 | 2 | 13 | |

## High Moor

*Geo Schofield*

| | | | | |
|---|---|---|---|---|
| 171 | 2 | 0 | 0 | S.Lees own & occ |
| b | 1 | 1 | 27 | |

## Cabin

*Peter Seville*

| | | | |
|---|---|---|---|
| 172a | 0 | 3 | 28 |
| b | 3 | 2 | 7 |
| c | 3 | 1 | 2 |
| d | 2 | 0 | 8 |

## Roebuck Low

*W.Nicholson & others* — Buckley occr

| | | | |
|---|---|---|---|
| 173a | 2 | 1 | 25 |
| b | 0 | 2 | 0 |
| c | 0 | 1 | 24 |

## Roebuck Low

*Mrs Wilde*

| | | | | |
|---|---|---|---|---|
| 174a | 0 | 1 | 7 | Ex Jno Gartside J.Schofield |
| b | 1 | 3 | 15 | |
| c | 1 | 1 | 32 | |
| d | 1 | 1 | 14 | |
| e | 3 | 1 | 33 | |

## Roebuck Low

*Abm Whitehead*

| | | | | |
|---|---|---|---|---|
| 175a | 1 | 1 | 32 | Jas Whitehead Jno Rhodes |
| b | 1 | 1 | 2 | " |
| c | 2 | 1 | 5 | " |
| d | 1 | 3 | 34 | " |
| e | 3 | 3 | 38 | " |
| f | 2 | 3 | 26 | W.Whitehead Nancy Mills |
| g | 2 | 3 | 28 | " |
| h | 0 | 0 | 29 | " |
| i | 1 | 3 | 33 | " |
| j | 1 | 3 | 13 | " |
| k | 1 | 0 | 0 | " |

## Roebuck Low

*Gorton Chapel & Robt Winterbottom*

| | | | | | |
|---|---|---|---|---|---|
| 176a | 1 | 2 | 9 | J.K. | Edm Lees |
| b | 0 | 1 | 27 | J.Radcliffe | |
| c | 2 | 1 | 13 | " | |
| d | 3 | 0 | 11 | E.Lees | |
| e | 3 | 2 | 31 | " | |
| f | 1 | 2 | 2 | " | |

## Roebuck Low

*Marsden Chapel*

| | | | | |
|---|---|---|---|---|
| 177a | 2 | 0 | 8 | Robt Lees Jas Buckley |
| b | 0 | 2 | 26 | Schofield |
| c | 4 | 0 | 36 | J.Buckley |

## Two Acre Lane

*J.& P. Seville*

| | | | | |
|---|---|---|---|---|
| 178a | 2 | 3 | 30 | R.W. |
| b | 2 | 0 | 3 | " |
| c | 2 | 3 | 2 | " |
| d | 2 | 2 | 5 | " |
| e | 0 | 3 | 23 | " |
| f | 2 | 0 | 29 | J.Greenwood |
| g | 1 | 1 | 13 | " |

## Moscow

*Jas Lawton, R.Lawton* — Betty Brierley

| | | | | |
|---|---|---|---|---|
| 179a | 0 | 0 | 29 | B.B |
| b | 0 | 3 | 18 | " |
| c | 3 | 0 | 4 | " |
| d | 4 | 0 | 13 | " |
| e | 2 | 2 | 38 | " |
| f | 1 | 1 | 16 | " |
| g | 1 | 2 | 20 | " |
| h | 1 | 3 | 34 | " |
| i | 3 | 2 | 33 | " |
| j | 6 | 3 | 35 | " |

## Badger Edge

*Jos Lees*

| | | | | |
|---|---|---|---|---|
| 180a | 1 | 2 | 22 | Jos Lees own & occ |
| b | 7 | 1 | 8 | " |
| c | 2 | 1 | 8 | Scanlan occ |
| d | 2 | 2 | 35 | " |
| e | 3 | 0 | 35 | " |
| f | 5 | 0 | 11 | Jas Lees |
| g | 1 | 1 | 30 | " |
| h | 2 | 0 | 9 | " |

## Green Leech

*W.Whitehead, Jno Greenwood*

| | | | |
|---|---|---|---|
| 181a | 2 | 0 | 4 |
| b | 2 | 3 | 15 |
| c | 1 | 1 | 22 |
| d | 1 | 0 | 0 |
| e | 0 | 2 | 29 |
| f | 1 | 0 | 16 |
| g | 1 | 2 | 21 |
| h | 1 | 1 | 23 |
| i | 0 | 3 | 34 |
| j | 1 | 1 | 16 |

## New

*Mark Seville* — Abr Smith

| | | | | |
|---|---|---|---|---|
| 182a | 4 | 2 | 16 | " |
| b | 1 | 2 | 11 | " |
| c | 2 | 0 | 8 | " |
| d | 2 | 3 | 4 | " |
| e | 3 | 1 | 5 | " |

## New

*Jas Rhodes*

| | | | | |
|---|---|---|---|---|
| 183a | 0 | 1 | 38 | |
| b | 3 | 1 | 28 | |
| c | 0 | 3 | 23 | |
| d | 1 | 2 | 37 | Jas Rhodes |
| e | 1 | 1 | 26 | " |
| f | 1 | 3 | 25 | Sally Tweedale Jno Winterbottom |
| g | 4 | 1 | 12 | |

## Harbour

*Betty & W.Buckley* — Jno Scholes

| | | | | |
|---|---|---|---|---|
| 184a | 1 | 2 | 27 | |
| b | 1 | 3 | 28 | |
| c | 0 | 1 | 5 | |
| d | 5 | 3 | 16 | |
| e | 1 | 0 | 34 | |
| 185 | 0 | 2 | 34 | Waste |

## High Lee

*A.Winterbottom own & occ*

| | | | | |
|---|---|---|---|---|
| 186a | 0 | 1 | 9 | A.W |
| b | 2 | 1 | 0 | " |
| c | 2 | 3 | 0 | " |

## Jericho

*Jesse Ainsworth*

| | | | | |
|---|---|---|---|---|
| 187a | 2 | 0 | 36 | John Buckley Frank Brierley |
| b | 2 | 0 | 32 | " |
| c | 2 | 0 | 13 | " |
| d | 1 | 2 | 29 | " |
| e | 2 | 2 | 22 | " |
| f | 0 | 0 | 3 | Buildings " |

## Near Jericho

*W.Whitehead* — J.Greenwood

| | | | | |
|---|---|---|---|---|
| 188a | 1 | 0 | 21 | " |
| b | 2 | 0 | 35 | " |

## Near Jericho

*W.Whitehead.* — J.G.

| | | | | |
|---|---|---|---|---|
| 189 | 1 | 0 | 36 | |

## Near Jericho

| | | | | |
|---|---|---|---|---|
| 190 | 0 | 2 | 38 | J.G. |

## Shilo

*Jno Whitehead* — Self

| | | | | |
|---|---|---|---|---|
| 191a | 1 | 2 | 8 | Jno Wood Snr |
| b | 1 | 1 | 16 | |
| c | 1 | 1 | 23 | |
| d | 3 | 2 | 21 | |
| e | 1 | 3 | 4 | |
| f | 1 | 1 | 35 | |
| g | 2 | 1 | 29 | |
| h | 2 | 1 | 17 | |

## Shilo

*Abr Whitehead* — Self

| | | | | |
|---|---|---|---|---|
| 192a | 2 | 0 | 28 | Taylor Benskins |
| b | 1 | 1 | 0 | |
| c | 1 | 2 | 0 | |
| d | 1 | 3 | 32 | |
| e | 0 | 0 | 30 | Buildings |
| f | 2 | 0 | 14 | |
| g | 1 | 2 | 4 | |
| h | 0 | 2 | 30 | |
| i | 2 | 1 | 4 | |
| j | 1 | 3 | 25 | |
| k | 0 | 3 | 28 | |
| l | 1 | 3 | 35 | |

## Shilo

*Jos Whitehead*

| | | | | |
|---|---|---|---|---|
| 193a | 1 | 3 | 10 | Jno Wood Jnr |
| b | 1 | 3 | 19 | |
| c | 1 | 3 | 12 | |
| d | 1 | 2 | 8 | |
| e | 0 | 3 | 36 | |
| f | 1 | 0 | 2 | |
| g | 0 | 1 | 27 | |
| h | 0 | 3 | 16 | |

## Shilo

| | | | |
|---|---|---|---|
| 194 | 0 | 1 | 0 |

## Thurston Clough

*James Taylor, Mrs Taylor*

| | | | | |
|---|---|---|---|---|
| 195a | 1 | 2 | 36 | " |
| b | 1 | 3 | 17 | " |
| c | 1 | 2 | 25 | " |
| d | 0 | 1 | 3 | Lane " |

## Rough

*John Lees* — Self

| | | | | |
|---|---|---|---|---|
| 196a | 3 | 2 | 5 | John Lees |
| b | 3 | 0 | 13 | " |
| c | 2 | 3 | 6 | " |
| d | 10 | 0 | 31 | " |
| e | 3 | 2 | 23 | Sam Clark occ |
| f | 0 | 3 | 19 | " |
| g | 1 | 1 | 28 | " |
| h | 9 | 0 | 18 | " |

## Badger Edge

*James Lawton*

| | | | |
|---|---|---|---|
| 197a | 1 | 2 | 0 |
| b | 2 | 1 | 19 |
| c | 2 | 0 | 22 |
| d | 2 | 1 | 21 |

## Badger Edge *(To Friar Mere)*

| | | | | |
|---|---|---|---|---|
| 198a | 2 | 0 | 25 | Wid. Lawton own & occ |
| b | 2 | 0 | 19 | |

## Hill Top

*Jon Lees, Jno Buckley, own & occ*

| 1a | 2 | 2 | 2 |
|----|---|---|---|
| b | 2 | 0 | 7 |
| c | 2 | 1 | 22 |

## Knarr Barn

*Thos Bridock*      Rhodes Bradbury

| 2a | 1 | 0 | 39 |
|----|---|---|----|
| b | 0 | 0 | 21 |
| c | 2 | 0 | 26 |
| d | 2 | 1 | 33 |
| e | 2 | 0 | 25 |
| f | 1 | 3 | 14 |
| g | 2 | 2 | 13 |
| House & Barn | | | |

## Knarr Lane

*Gaml Buckley*

House
"
"
"
"

## Thurston Clough

*Jas Taylor own & occ*

| 3a | 2 | 1 | 11 |
|----|---|---|----|
| b | 4 | 0 | 35 |
| c | 1 | 3 | 29 |
| d | 1 | 2 | 29 |
| e | 0 | 1 | 29 |
| f | 1 | 2 | 33 |
| g | 0 | 2 | 39 |
| h | 0 | 1 | 14 |
| i | 2 | 2 | 20 |
| House, Barn &c | | | |
| James Hilton - house | | | |
| Jno Bottomley - House | | | |

## Thurston Clough

*Jno Taylor*

| j | 2 | 0 | 7 |
|---|---|---|---|
| k | 2 | 0 | 28 |
| l | 0 | 3 | 22 |
| m | 1 | 0 | 25 |
| n | 1 | 1 | 7 |
| J.Lees Cott | | | |
| R. Lawton House | | | |
| " | " | | |

## Valenciennes

*Execs J.Schofield*

| 4a | 0 | 0 | 17 | Jas Lawton |
|----|---|---|----|------------|
| b | 0 | 0 | 25 | |
| c | 0 | 0 | 13 | |
| d | 1 | 3 | 30 | |
| e | 3 | 1 | 9 | |
| f | 0 | 2 | 31 | |
| g | 1 | 0 | 31 | |
| h | 2 | 0 | 1 | |
| i | 0 | 0 | 34 | |
| j | 1 | 1 | 38 | |
| House, Barn &c | | | | |

## Hill Top

*J.Shaw*      Jas Hilton occ

| 5a | 0 | 2 | 37 |
|----|---|---|----|
| b | 2 | 3 | 7 |
| c | 0 | 0 | 33 |
| d | 1 | 3 | 22 |
| e | 1 | 1 | 30 |
| f | 1 | 1 | 33 |
| g | 0 | 3 | 6 |
| h | 0 | 0 | 37 |
| i | 1 | 3 | 4 |
| House & Barn | | | |

## Knarr Clough

*Exec Jno Lees*

| 6a | 0 | 1 | 20 |
|----|---|---|----|

## Thurston Clough

*Exec Jno Lees*      Jno Buckley

| 6b | 0 | 3 | 36 |
|----|---|---|----|
| c | 0 | 3 | 15 |
| d | 0 | 2 | 17 |
| e | 1 | 0 | 39 |
| f | 0 | 0 | 15 |
| g | 0 | 2 | 39 |
| h | 1 | 1 | 27 |
| House & Barn | | | |
| Sol Cook - Cottage | | | |

*James Seville*

| 6i | 1 | 1 | 21 | Thos Greaves |
|----|---|---|----|--------------|

## Knarr

*Jno & Rob Winterbottom*      Thos Greaves

| 7a | 0 | 1 | 34 | |
|----|---|---|----|---|
| b | 0 | 0 | 37 | |
| c | 1 | 0 | 16 | |
| d | 0 | 3 | 39 | |
| e | 1 | 0 | 34 | |
| Law. Haigh - Barn Cottage | | | | |
| 8a | 1 | 2 | 36 | Jno Kenworthy |
| b | 1 | 2 | 26 | Tho Dyson occ |
| 9a | 3 | 0 | 0 | " |
| aa | 1 | 0 | 32 | J.Kenworthy |
| b | 1 | 2 | 23 | " |
| c | 1 | 1 | 19 | " |
| d | 1 | 1 | 39 | " |
| e | 4 | 1 | 39 | Jno Winterbottom / Jno Kenworthy |
| f | 0 | 3 | 23 | " |
| g | 2 | 3 | 20 | " |
| h | 1 | 3 | 33 | " |
| Robt Winterbottom - Stone Quarry | | | | |
| Jos Lees | | | | |

## Wall Hill

*Jno Greaves*

| 10a | 0 | 1 | 29 | |
|-----|---|---|----|---|
| b | 1 | 0 | 24 | J.Rhodes |
| c | 0 | 2 | 9 | " |
| d | 0 | 1 | 30 | " |
| e | 2 | 0 | 9 | " |
| f | 1 | 3 | 2 | Jon Bradbury |
| House & Barn | | | | |

## Greave Cote

*Jno Greaves*

| g | 0 | 2 | 4 | | J.Bradbury |
|---|---|---|---|---|------------|
| h | 2 | 1 | 13 | | " |
| i | 3 | 2 | 4 | | " |
| j | 1 | 3 | 5 | | " |
| k | 0 | 0 | 17 | Waste | " |
| l | 0 | 2 | 10 | | " |
| m | 0 | 0 | 14 | Building | |
| House & Barn | | | | | |

## Thurston Clough

*Jno Greaves*

| 11a | 0 | 0 | 12 | Joel Schofield |
|-----|---|---|----|----------------|
| b | 3 | 2 | 26 | " |
| c | 1 | 0 | 14 | |
| d | 2 | 2 | 27 | |
| House & Barn | | | | |

*Betty Greaves*

| 12a | 0 | 1 | 23 | | Joel Schofield |
|-----|---|---|----|---|----------------|
| b | 3 | 2 | 27 | | " |
| c | 0 | 0 | 17 | Yard | " |
| d | 2 | 2 | 18 | | " |

## Thurston Clough

*Thos Greaves*

| 13a | 3 | 0 | 35 |
|-----|---|---|----|
| b | 2 | 2 | 19 |
| c | 1 | 2 | 31 |
| d | 1 | 2 | 26 |
| e | 1 | 1 | 26 |
| f | 1 | 2 | 26 |
| House & Barn | | | |

*Driver & Schofield*      J.Greaves occ

| 14a | 2 | 2 | 32 |
|-----|---|---|----|
| b | 2 | 2 | 0 |

## Great Dole

*Lord Stamford*

| 15a | 28 | 2 | 2 | |
|-----|----|---|---|---|
| b | 3 | 1 | 36 | incl stonepit |

## Silver Hill

*M.Buckley*      Geo Collins

| 16 | 2 | 3 | 9 | incl stonepit |
|----|---|---|---|---------------|
| Gamaliel Buckley | | | | H |
| " | | | | |
| Ex H. Buckley | | | | " |

## New Inn

*Thos Worsley*    Plantation

| 17a | 0 | 0 | 35 | Croft | J.Seville |
|-----|---|---|----|-------|-----------|
| b | 0 | 0 | 15 | Garden | " |
| c | 0 | 0 | 30 | Croft | " |
| d | 2 | 0 | 23 | | " |
| e | 0 | 3 | 38 | | " |
| f | 1 | 3 | 21 | | " |
| g | 1 | 2 | 18 | | " |
| House, Barn & Cottage | | | | | |

## Upper Houses

*Mary Buckley,*      R.Buckley occ

| 18a | 2 | 2 | 27 | " |
|-----|---|---|----|---|
| b | 1 | 2 | 38 | " |
| c | 1 | 2 | 25 | " |
| d | 1 | 2 | 14 | " |
| e | 1 | 0 | 1 | " |
| f | 1 | 3 | 4 | " |

## Upper House

*Jno Schofield*

| 18j | 0 | 3 | 27 | Hulley occ |
|-----|---|---|----|------------|
| k | 1 | 3 | 37 | " |
| l | 0 | 0 | 17 | " |
| House & Barn | | | | |

## Upper Houses

*M. Buckley occr*

| 18m | 0 | 3 | 39 | R.B. |
|-----|---|---|----|------|
| n | 0 | 1 | 2 | " |
| o | 0 | 1 | 10 | " |
| p | 0 | 2 | 37 | " |
| q | 0 | 2 | 15 | " |
| r | 3 | 0 | 27 | " |
| s | 3 | 2 | 17 | " |
| t | 2 | 0 | 0 | " |
| u | 2 | 2 | 31 | " |
| 19dd | 0 | 2 | 6 | J.Worth |
| House & Barn | | | | |

## Wall Hill

*Execs Hy Buckley*      Jos Rhodes

| 18g | 2 | 0 | 33 | | Js Cooper |
|-----|---|---|----|---|-----------|
| h | 2 | 0 | 13 | | " |
| i | 1 | 3 | 9 | | " |
| ii | 1 | 0 | 20 | | " |
| x | 0 | 0 | 39 | House | " |

## Wall Hill

*Richard Cooper*

| | | | | |
|---|---|---|---|---|
| 19a | 1 | 2 | 34 | J.Worth |
| b | 3 | 3 | 9 | " |
| c | 4 | 2 | 28 | " |
| d | 5 | 0 | 6 | " |
| House | | | | |

## Wall Hill Clough

*Execs Hy Buckley*    S&J Wrigley occrs

| | | | | |
|---|---|---|---|---|
| 19e | 0 | 3 | 35 | |
| f | 0 | 3 | 12 | J.Buckley occ |
| g | 0 | 0 | 12 | Gardens " |
| h | 0 | 2 | 0 | R.Buckley occ |
| i | 0 | 1 | 1 | " |
| j | 0 | 0 | 35 | " |
| k | 1 | 2 | 14 | " |
| House & ½ Barn | | | | |
| l | 1 | 1 | 29 | J.Cocker occ |
| m | 2 | 0 | 35 | |
| n | 1 | 2 | 36 | |
| o | 1 | 2 | 1 | |
| p | 1 | 0 | 39 | |
| q | 0 | 0 | 12 | |

## Shelter Mill

*J. & S. Wrigley*    selves

| | | | | |
|---|---|---|---|---|
| 20a | 1 | 2 | 25 | " |
| b | 0 | 1 | 0 | " |
| John Wood | Mill & Cottages | | | |

## Wharmton

*M.Eastwood*    occ J.Wild

| | | | |
|---|---|---|---|
| 21a | 4 | 2 | 31 |
| b | 3 | 2 | 13 |
| c | 3 | 0 | 6 |
| d | 3 | 2 | 31 |
| e | 8 | 3 | 39 |

## Mount Sorrel

*J.Wright*    occ J.Broadbent

| | | | | |
|---|---|---|---|---|
| 22a | 0 | 3 | 30 | Abr Dyson |
| b | 0 | 0 | 34 | " |
| c | 0 | 1 | 27 | " |
| d | 0 | 2 | 38 | " |
| e | 3 | 0 | 4 | " |
| f | 1 | 2 | 0 | " |
| g | 1 | 1 | 15 | " |
| h | 1 | 2 | 29 | " |
| House & Barn | | | | |

## Wharmton

*Execs Jas Andrew*    occ Ab Pogson

| | | | |
|---|---|---|---|
| 23a | 2 | 0 | 18 |
| b | 1 | 2 | 23 |
| c | 1 | 0 | 12 |
| d | 2 | 1 | 17 |
| e | 2 | 0 | 13 |
| f | 2 | 3 | 25 |
| g | 0 | 3 | 12 |
| h | 1 | 2 | 38 |
| House & Barn | | | |
| House | | | |

## Wade Hill

*Jos Harrop*

| | | | | |
|---|---|---|---|---|
| 24a | 1 | 1 | 1 | |
| b | 1 | 1 | 32 | |
| c | 1 | 1 | 6 | |
| d | 0 | 2 | 19 | |
| e | 1 | 3 | 3 | |
| f | 9 | 1 | 17 | Clough |
| g | 3 | 0 | 36 | |
| h | 4 | 2 | 25 | |

## Wade Hill

*Jno Harrop*

| | | | |
|---|---|---|---|
| 25a | 0 | 0 | 20 |
| b | 3 | 1 | 6 |
| c | 1 | 0 | 32 |
| c | 1 | 2 | 12 |
| House & Barn | | | |

## Dobcross Chapel

               Edm Schofield

| | | | | |
|---|---|---|---|---|
| 26a | 1 | 2 | 27 | |
| b | 1 | 2 | 4 | |
| c | 1 | 1 | 22 | |
| d | 2 | 3 | 8 | Wm Buckley |
| e | 0 | 1 | 8 | Lane &c |
| f | 1 | 1 | 10 | |
| g | 0 | 3 | 34 | |
| h | 1 | 1 | 22 | |
| i | 1 | 1 | 16 | |
| j | 1 | 0 | 22 | |
| k | 1 | 0 | 3 | |
| House & Barn | | | | |
| l | 2 | 0 | 26 | Hugh Whitaker |
| m | 3 | 1 | 4 | Geo Rhodes |
| n | 1 | 2 | 37 | |
| o | 1 | 2 | 24 | |
| p | 1 | 1 | 7 | |
| q | 1 | 2 | 37 | |
| r | 3 | 1 | 0 | |
| House & ½ Barn | | | | |

## Wallhill Barn

*Jno Kenworthy Cooke*

| | | | | |
|---|---|---|---|---|
| 27a | 5 | 1 | 32 | |
| b | 3 | 1 | 2 | |
| c | 0 | 0 | 28 | Yard &c |
| d | 1 | 2 | 38 | |
| House & Barn | | | | |
| e | 2 | 0 | 0 | J.Buckley |
| f | 2 | 1 | 4 | |
| g | 3 | 1 | 30 | |
| h | 3 | 0 | 27 | |
| House & Barn | | | | |
| i | 0 | 0 | 28 | |
| House & Barn Self | | | | |
| j | 2 | 2 | 29 | |
| k | 0 | 0 | 39 | |
| l | 6 | 3 | 35 | |
| m | 2 | 2 | 8 | |
| n | 2 | 2 | 19 | |
| o | 2 | 0 | 30 | |
| House & Barn | | | | |

## Burnedge Bent

*Jos Lees*           Sam Schofield

| | | | |
|---|---|---|---|
| 28a | 4 | 3 | 7 |
| b | 2 | 3 | 10 |
| c | 0 | 0 | 11 |
| d | 0 | 0 | 11 |
| e | 2 | 1 | 35 |
| f | 3 | 0 | 35 |
| g | 3 | 1 | 30 |
| h | 0 | 1 | 9 |
| i | 0 | 0 | 12 |
| j | 3 | 1 | 27 |
| k | 14 | 3 | 15 |
| House & Barn | | | |

## Wharmton

*Jos Lees Esq*

| | | | |
|---|---|---|---|
| 29 | 1 | 0 | 35 |

## Wharmton

*Execs of J.Taylor*

| | | | | |
|---|---|---|---|---|
| 30a | 9 | 2 | 28 | Plantation |
| b | 3 | 2 | 36 | Moor |

## Wharmton

*Robt Wood own & occ*

| | | | |
|---|---|---|---|
| 31a | 1 | 0 | 30 |
| b | 1 | 1 | 29 |
| c | 0 | 3 | 12 |
| d | 0 | 2 | 2 |
| e | 0 | 3 | 32 |
| f | 0 | 3 | 7 |
| g | 0 | 2 | 2 |
| h | 0 | 1 | 38 |
| i | 1 | 0 | 17 |
| j | 1 | 1 | 6 |
| k | 0 | 2 | 38 |
| l | 0 | 2 | 36 |
| House & Barn Tamewater | | | |

## Wharmton

*Mallalieu*           Roberts& Co

| | | | |
|---|---|---|---|
| 32a | 11 | 3 | 22 |
| b | 26 | 0 | 22 |
| c | 1 | 3 | 35 |

## Wharmton

*Lees & Co*

| | | | |
|---|---|---|---|
| 33 | 74 | 1 | 11 |

## Tinkers

*Jas Whitaker*

| | | | |
|---|---|---|---|
| 34a | 9 | 3 | 24 |
| b | 0 | 3 | 6 |
| c | 0 | 3 | 31 |
| d | 0 | 0 | 20 |
| e | 2 | 0 | 32 |
| f | 0 | 2 | 28 |
| g | 1 | 0 | 25 |
| h | 0 | 0 | 24 |
| i | 0 | 1 | 12 |
| j | 0 | 2 | 26 |
| k | 2 | 0 | 34 |
| l | 1 | 3 | 0 |
| m | 0 | 0 | 16 |
| House, Barn & Cottages | | | |

## Halls

*Edw Brown*

| | | | |
|---|---|---|---|
| 35a | 0 | 1 | 4 |
| b | 2 | 1 | 14 |
| c | 1 | 1 | 10 |
| d | 1 | 1 | 30 |
| e | 1 | 2 | 3 |
| f | 0 | 2 | 23 |
| g | 0 | 0 | 15 |
| h | 0 | 0 | 23 |
| i | 0 | 1 | 25 |
| j | 0 | 1 | 12 |
| k | 0 | 1 | 2 |
| l | 6 | 2 | 31 |
| m | 4 | 2 | 20 |
| n | 2 | 0 | 7 |
| o | 1 | 3 | 16 |
| p | 3 | 2 | 22 |
| q | 5 | 0 | 36 |
| r | 0 | 1 | 15 |
| s | 3 | 2 | 16 |
| t | 2 | 2 | 13 |
| u | 1 | 2 | 26 |
| House & Barn | | | |

## Frenches

*Jas Buckley & Co*

| | | | |
|---|---|---|---|
| 36a | 1 | 1 | 33 |
| b | 0 | 2 | 4 |
| c | 0 | 2 | 7 |
| d | 2 | 3 | 28 |
| e | 0 | 0 | 37 |
| f | 1 | 2 | 0 |
| g | 2 | 3 | 28 |

## French Mill

*Platt & Co*

| | | | | |
|---|---|---|---|---|
| | 0 | 2 | 19 | Mill &c |

## Warmton Brow

*J.Mallalieu*

| | | | |
|---|---|---|---|
| 38a | 0 | 3 | 7 |
| b | 0 | 1 | 15 |
| c | 0 | 1 | 23 |
| d | 0 | 1 | 36 |
| e | 0 | 1 | 18 |

## Frenches

*J.Buckley*

| | | | |
|---|---|---|---|
| 39a | 0 | 0 | 26 |
| b | 1 | 3 | 12 |
| c | 2 | 3 | 16 |
| d | 0 | 1 | 18 |
| e | 0 | 3 | 19 |
| f | 0 | 2 | 28 |
| g | 0 | 3 | 16 |
| h | 1 | 1 | 26 |
| House &c | | | |

## Shaw Hall Bank

*J.Buckley*

| 40a | 0 | 1 | 8 |
|---|---|---|---|
| b | 0 | 2 | 10 |
| c | 1 | 0 | 26 |
| d | 0 | 0 | 30 |
| e | 1 | 0 | 7 |
| f | 2 | 3 | 38 |

House & Barn

*John & William Buckley*

| 41a | 0 | 2 | 33 |
|---|---|---|---|
| b | 1 | 1 | 25 |
| c | 1 | 2 | 19 |
| d | 2 | 0 | 30 |
| e | 0 | 1 | 17 |
| f | 1 | 0 | 29 |
| g | 3 | 2 | 33 |
| h | 0 | 2 | 6 |
| i | 0 | 3 | 14 |
| j | 0 | 1 | 32 |

House & Barn

*Henry Buckley*

| 42a | 0 | 0 | 37 | |
|---|---|---|---|---|
| b | 0 | 2 | 38 | |
| c | 0 | 0 | 13 | Buildings |
| d | 1 | 0 | 17 | |
| e | 1 | 3 | 23 | |
| f | 0 | 0 | 31 | |
| g | 1 | 2 | 17 | |
| h | 4 | 2 | 19 | |
| i | 0 | 0 | 31 | |
| j | 0 | 1 | 32 | |
| k | 1 | 0 | 0 | |
| l | 0 | 0 | 37 | |

House
House & ⅔ Barn

*Jno & Wm Buckley*

| 43a | 1 | 1 | 28 |
|---|---|---|---|
| b | 0 | 1 | 5 |
| c | 1 | 1 | 6 |
| d | 1 | 0 | 33 |
| e | 1 | 1 | 24 |

House & ⅓ Barn

## French Top

*Messrs Lees & Co*

| 44a | 0 | 2 | 19 | |
|---|---|---|---|---|
| b | 0 | 0 | 39 | Croft |
| c | 0 | 0 | 10 | Buildings |
| d | 0 | 2 | 14 | |
| e | 1 | 0 | 14 | |

House & Barn

*T & A. Platt*

| 45a | 0 | 3 | 1 |
|---|---|---|---|

## Shaw Hall

*Fr & Ammon Platt*

| 45b | 0 | 1 | 18 | |
|---|---|---|---|---|
| c | 1 | 0 | 31 | |
| d | 0 | 1 | 18 | Garden & Buildings |
| e | 3 | 3 | 34 | |
| f | 0 | 1 | 10 | |
| g | 2 | 0 | 13 | |
| h | 3 | 2 | 10 | |
| i | 3 | 1 | 35 | |
| j | 0 | 1 | 19 | |
| k | 0 | 3 | 37 | |
| l | 1 | 4 | 16 | |
| m | 0 | 0 | 30 | |
| mm | 1 | 0 | 39 | |

House & Barn

| n | 1 | 2 | 19 |
|---|---|---|---|
| o | 1 | 2 | 33 |
| p | 0 | 0 | 10 |
| q | 1 | 1 | 0 |
| r | 3 | 3 | 11 |

House & Part of Barn
Cottage

| s | 2 | 3 | 37 |
|---|---|---|---|

## Critchley Cottage

*Marsden Chapel*

| 46a | 1 | 1 | 28 |
|---|---|---|---|
| b | 0 | 1 | 25 |
| c | 5 | 0 | 0 |
| d | 2 | 2 | 22 |

House &c

*Samuel Buckley*

| 47a | 3 | 3 | 20 |
|---|---|---|---|
| b | 3 | 2 | 28 |
| c | 3 | 0 | 38 |

House & Barn

*Execs J.Kenworthy*

| 48a | 3 | 0 | 24 |
|---|---|---|---|
| b | 2 | 0 | 6 |
| c | 6 | 3 | 17 |

## Mans

*N.W.Hewitt Esq*

| 49a | 0 | 1 | 16 |
|---|---|---|---|
| b | 1 | 3 | 16 |
| c | 2 | 0 | 3 |
| d | 1 | 1 | 38 |
| e | 1 | 2 | 33 |
| f | 0 | 0 | 22 |
| g | 1 | 2 | 17 |
| h | 1 | 1 | 4 |
| i | 1 | 2 | 31 |
| j | 6 | 1 | 38 |
| k | 1 | 1 | 32 |
| l | 4 | 1 | 30 |

House, Barn & Warehouse

## Mans Wharf

*Canal Co*

| 50a | 0 | 1 | 5 |
|---|---|---|---|
| b | 0 | 1 | 26 |

House

*Canal Co*

| 51a | 1 | 2 | 20 | |
|---|---|---|---|---|
| b | 1 | 0 | 38 | |
| c | 1 | 0 | 6 | |
| d | 1 | 3 | 8 | |
| e | 1 | 0 | 10 | |
| f | 1 | 2 | 22 | |
| g | 0 | 1 | 22 | Plantation |

## Gibbs

*Jos Harrop*

| 52a | 3 | 1 | 22 |
|---|---|---|---|
| b | 0 | 2 | 35 |
| c | 1 | 3 | 29 |
| d | 2 | 1 | 33 |
| e | 1 | 2 | 39 |

House &c

## Royal George

| 52f | 1 | 1 | 36 |
|---|---|---|---|
| g | 0 | 1 | 35 |
| h | 0 | 3 | 27 |
| i | 1 | 1 | 32 |
| j | 1 | 1 | 2 |
| k | 2 | 2 | 14 |

House & ½ Barn

## Wellihole

*Jos Harrop*

| 52l | 2 | 3 | 0 | |
|---|---|---|---|---|
| m | 3 | 3 | 2 | |
| n | 3 | 1 | 12 | |
| o | 0 | 1 | 11 | Fold |
| p | 0 | 1 | 22 | |
| q | 0 | 2 | 6 | |
| r | 0 | 3 | 15 | |
| s | 2 | 0 | 10 | |

House & Barn

## Wellihole

*Jno Schofield*

| 53a | 1 | 3 | 36 |
|---|---|---|---|
| b | 0 | 1 | 10 |
| c | 2 | 3 | 11 |
| d | 2 | 3 | 3 |
| e | 1 | 3 | 33 |
| f | 2 | 2 | 17 |

House & Barn

## Wright Mill

*Jos Harrop*

| 53g | 1 | 0 | 36 |
|---|---|---|---|
| h | 1 | 1 | 18 |
| i | 1 | 2 | 13 |
| j | 0 | 0 | 19 |
| k | 2 | 0 | 6 |
| l | 0 | 3 | 17 |
| m | 0 | 0 | 31 |

## Royal George

*Jos Harrop*

| 53n | 0 | 3 | 33 |
|---|---|---|---|
| o | 1 | 2 | 30 |

## Bank

*Ed & R.Radcliffe*

| 54a | 3 | 2 | 6 |
|---|---|---|---|
| b | 2 | 2 | 28 |
| c | 0 | 0 | 21 |
| d | 1 | 0 | 33 |
| e | 0 | 3 | 3 |
| f | 0 | 2 | 0 |

House & Barn

## Lanehead

| 54g | 0 | 2 | 29 |
|---|---|---|---|
| h | 2 | 1 | 18 |
| i | 2 | 1 | 2 |
| j | 2 | 1 | 22 |
| k | 2 | 0 | 10 |
| l | 0 | 2 | 26 |

House & Barn

## Ridding

*Eli Andrew own & occ*

| 55a | 1 | 1 | 33 | |
|---|---|---|---|---|
| b | 2 | 0 | 38 | |
| c | 0 | 0 | 32 | |
| d | 0 | 3 | 12 | |
| e | 2 | 3 | 6 | |
| f | 1 | 3 | 7 | |
| g | 0 | 0 | 27 | Lane |

House & Barn

## Lanehead

*Sally Schofield own & occ*

| 56a | 2 | 1 | 10 | |
|---|---|---|---|---|
| b | 1 | 2 | 17 | |
| c | 1 | 0 | 6 | |
| d | 1 | 2 | 11 | |
| e | 2 | 3 | 25 | |
| f | 0 | 2 | 19 | |
| g | 0 | 2 | 31 | |
| h | 0 | 1 | 29 | |
| i | 3 | 1 | 34 | |
| j | 0 | 3 | 6 | |
| k | 1 | 2 | 35 | |
| l | 1 | 2 | 21 | |
| m | 0 | 0 | 25 | Croft |

House

*Edw Hollingworth, Thos Schofield own*
*Rev Kay occ*

| 57a | 2 | 1 | 22 |
|---|---|---|---|
| b | 1 | 0 | 34 |
| c | 1 | 2 | 7 |
| d | 1 | 3 | 11 |
| e | 0 | 2 | 24 |
| f | 1 | 0 | 32 |
| g | 0 | 2 | 28 |
| h | 1 | 2 | 5 |
| i | 1 | 3 | 27 |
| j | 1 | 1 | 12 |
| k | 2 | 0 | 20 |
| l | 0 | 2 | 34 |
| m | 0 | 0 | 30 |
| n | 2 | 0 | 15 |

House &c

*Rev B.Dacre*

| 58a | 3 | 2 | 1 |
|---|---|---|---|
| b | 3 | 1 | 4 |
| c | 0 | 1 | 11 |
| d | 2 | 1 | 24 |
| e | 5 | 2 | 7 |
| f | 4 | 3 | 17 |
| g | 0 | 1 | 2 |
| h | 0 | 0 | 16 |
| i | 5 | 2 | 29 |

## Noon Sun

*Mrs Worthington*                G.Winterbottom

| | | | |
|---|---|---|---|
| 59a | 0 | 3 | 27 |
| b | 1 | 2 | 5 |
| c | 0 | 2 | 6 |
| d | 1 | 1 | 5 |
| House &c | | | |

*J.Mellor*                Josh Roberts  Jno Schofield

| | | | |
|---|---|---|---|
| 60a | 2 | 0 | 9 |
| b | 1 | 0 | 13 |
| c | 0 | 3 | 7 |
| d | 1 | 0 | 17 |
| e | 0 | 2 | 18 |

## Greenmans

*Ed Travis*                Jno Bottomley

| | | | |
|---|---|---|---|
| 61a | 0 | 0 | 39 |
| b | 1 | 0 | 23 |
| c | 0 | 2 | 33 |
| d | 1 | 1 | 31 |
| e | 1 | 0 | 37 |
| f | 3 | 0 | 33 |
| House &c | | | |

## Whitelee

*M.Davies*                Rev Kaye, J.Bradbury

| | | | |
|---|---|---|---|
| 62a | 0 | 1 | 6 |
| b | 0 | 0 | 24 |
| c | 1 | 3 | 24 |
| d | 1 | 1 | 39 |
| e | 1 | 3 | 3 |
| f | 2 | 0 | 35 |
| g | 1 | 2 | 28 |
| h | 0 | 1 | 29 |
| i | 3 | 0 | 16 |
| j | 4 | 1 | 33 |
| House &c | | | |

*Jno Roberts Esq*                Jos Roberts, Rob Hadfield

| | | | |
|---|---|---|---|
| 63a | 2 | 1 | 31 |
| b | 0 | 2 | 26 |
| c | 0 | 2 | 26 |
| d | 1 | 3 | 26 |
| e | 1 | 2 | 4 |
| f | 2 | 0 | 14 |
| g | 2 | 1 | 0 |
| h | 1 | 0 | 22 |
| i | 3 | 1 | 1 |
| j | 7 | 1 | 4 |
| k | 1 | 3 | 15 |
| l | 1 | 0 | 25 |
| m | 2 | 2 | 19 |
| n | 3 | 0 | 7 |
| o | 0 | 7 | 8 |

## Haybottom

*J.& F.Hardman, R.Winterbottom own & occ*

| | | | |
|---|---|---|---|
| 64a | 0 | 0 | 37 |
| b | 1 | 3 | 35 |
| c | 0 | 2 | 9 |
| d | 0 | 3 | 29 |

*J.Walker Esq*                John Smith

| | | | | |
|---|---|---|---|---|
| 65a | 1 | 2 | 20 | Garden |
| b | 0 | 0 | 21 | Croft |

## Summer Shade

*J.Lord*

| | | | |
|---|---|---|---|
| 66 | 0 | 2 | 33 |

## Wharmton

*Rob Shaw*

| | | | |
|---|---|---|---|
| 67a | 2 | 1 | 26 |
| b | 1 | 3 | 15 |
| c | 2 | 0 | 1 |
| d | 4 | 1 | 17 |

*Josh Hesslegreave*

| | | | |
|---|---|---|---|
| 68a | 1 | 3 | 27 |
| b | 2 | 0 | 17 |
| c | 1 | 3 | 35 |
| d | 2 | 1 | 2 |
| e | 1 | 1 | 0 |
| f | 1 | 3 | 13 |
| g | 1 | 3 | 9 |
| h | 1 | 0 | 27 |

## Wharmton

*Wm Buckley Execs*

| | | | |
|---|---|---|---|
| 69a | 1 | 1 | 25 |
| b | 0 | 1 | 8 |
| c | 1 | 0 | 4 |
| d | 0 | 2 | 20 |
| e | 0 | 3 | 0 |
| f | 0 | 1 | 15 |
| g | 0 | 0 | 13 |
| h | 2 | 2 | 36 |
| i | 3 | 0 | 0 |
| j | 3 | 0 | 9 |
| k | 0 | 1 | 8 |
| l | 0 | 0 | 30 |
| m | 2 | 3 | 2 |

## Wharmton

*Giles Shaw*

| | | | |
|---|---|---|---|
| 70a | 1 | 3 | 18 |
| b | 0 | 0 | 38 |
| c | 1 | 2 | 22 |
| d | 1 | 3 | 2 |
| e | 1 | 0 | 34 |
| f | 2 | 2 | 7 |

*Jno Harrop*                Chas Harrop

| | | | |
|---|---|---|---|
| 71a | 5 | 0 | 28 |
| b | 1 | 2 | 13 |
| c | 2 | 1 | 18 |
| d | 4 | 2 | 36 |
| e | 2 | 3 | 24 |
| f | 2 | 1 | 36 |
| g | 2 | 3 | 9 |
| h | 2 | 0 | 25 |
| i | 3 | 3 | 37 |
| j | 4 | 2 | 17 |
| k | 1 | 0 | 0 |
| l | 1 | 2 | 28 |
| m | 2 | 0 | 36 |
| n | 2 | 1 | 10 |
| o | 3 | 3 | 27 |
| p | 3 | 2 | 6 |
| q | 1 | 0 | 34 |
| r | 1 | 1 | 16 |
| s | 2 | 3 | 14 |

*Dobcross Chapel*                Ed Hall occ.
*St Peter's, Oldham*

| | | | |
|---|---|---|---|
| 72a | 1 | 3 | 12 |
| b | 1 | 2 | 14 |
| c | 1 | 3 | 7 |
| d | 1 | 2 | 21 |
| e | 1 | 3 | 12 |
| f | 1 | 2 | 29 |

*Ann & Betty Dransfield*                Abm Pogson
*Mary Broadbent*

| | | | |
|---|---|---|---|
| 73a | 1 | 1 | 35 |
| b | 1 | 1 | 28 |
| c | 1 | 0 | 13 |
| d | 1 | 1 | 20 |
| e | 1 | 1 | 11 |
| f | 0 | 3 | 9 |
| g | 1 | 1 | 18 |
| h | 0 | 1 | 2 |
| i | 0 | 3 | 23 |
| j | 0 | 0 | 8 |
| k | 6 | 1 | 12 |
| l | 6 | 1 | 32 |
| m | 3 | 3 | 25 |
| n | 0 | 1 | 27 |
| o | 6 | 2 | 7 |
| House&c | | | |

## Mow Walls

*Saml Harrop, Anne Rhodes own*

| | | | |
|---|---|---|---|
| 74a | 0 | 3 | 18 |
| b | 0 | 3 | 14 |
| c | 1 | 1 | 11 |
| d | 1 | 1 | 8 |
| e | 0 | 2 | 4 |
| f | 0 | 0 | 25 |
| House | | | |

## Brow

*Geo Schofield*                Messrs Wrigley

| | | | |
|---|---|---|---|
| 75a | 0 | 2 | 34 |
| b | 1 | 0 | 0 |
| c | 1 | 0 | 9 |
| d | 2 | 0 | 17 |
| e | 0 | 1 | 18 |

| | | | |
|---|---|---|---|
| f | 0 | 0 | 23 |
| g | 2 | 0 | 6 |

*G.Schofield*                Isaac Hall

| | | | |
|---|---|---|---|
| 76a | 2 | 0 | 10 |
| b | 0 | 3 | 34 |
| c | 0 | 3 | 3 |

## Tamewater

*Harry Whitehead*                Jos Smith

| | | | |
|---|---|---|---|
| 77a | 1 | 3 | 24 |
| b | 0 | 3 | 19 |
| Mill &c | | | |

*Lawrence Fox*

| | | | | |
|---|---|---|---|---|
| 78a | 0 | 3 | 5 | |
| b | 1 | 0 | 25 | |
| c | 0 | 3 | 6 | |
| d | 0 | 0 | 29 | School |

## Wharmton

*Dobcross Chapel*

| | | | | |
|---|---|---|---|---|
| 79a | 0 | 1 | 35 | House & Garden |
| b | 1 | 1 | 18 | |
| c | 1 | 2 | 14 | |

## Husteads

*J. & T.Hardman*

| | | | |
|---|---|---|---|
| 80a | 0 | 2 | 34 |
| b | 1 | 2 | 12 |
| c | 0 | 0 | 34 |
| d | 0 | 2 | 8 |
| e | 0 | 3 | 22 |
| f | 0 | 2 | 7 |
| g | 0 | 1 | 10 |
| h | 4 | 1 | 2 |
| i | 2 | 1 | 36 |
| j | 0 | 3 | 0 |
| k | 0 | 3 | 2 |
| l | 0 | 1 | 14 |
| m | 1 | 0 | 3 |
| n | 0 | 2 | 38 |
| o | 2 | 0 | 30 |

## Tamewater

*Late Josh Harrop*

| | | | | |
|---|---|---|---|---|
| 81a | 0 | 0 | 33 | |
| b | 1 | 2 | 19 | |
| c | 2 | 3 | 15 | |
| d | 2 | 1 | 33 | |
| e | 1 | 2 | 10 | |
| f | 0 | 3 | 23 | |
| g | 0 | 0 | 32 | |
| h | 0 | 1 | 0 | |
| i | 0 | 1 | 5 | |
| j | 0 | 0 | 29 | |
| k | 0 | 0 | 21 | |
| l | 0 | 1 | 13 | |
| m | 0 | 0 | 28 | |
| n | 0 | 1 | 17 | |
| o | 2 | 1 | 8 | |
| p | 0 | 2 | 22 | |
| q | 0 | 0 | 17 | |
| r | 0 | 2 | 4 | |
| s | 2 | 3 | 35 | |
| t | 1 | 3 | 4 | |
| u | 1 | 0 | 12 | |
| v | 0 | 0 | 28 | |
| w | 0 | 2 | 27 | Water |
| x | 1 | 0 | 9 | |
| y | 0 | 1 | 38 | |
| z | 1 | 1 | 31 | |
| A | 1 | 2 | 20 | |
| B | 1 | 2 | 15 | |
| C | 0 | 1 | 36 | |
| D | 0 | 3 | 27 | |
| E | 1 | 1 | 27 | |
| F | 0 | 0 | 35 | |
| G | 1 | 0 | 15 | |

*Messrs Harrop*

| | | | | |
|---|---|---|---|---|
| 82a | 0 | 1 | 10 | Mill & Resr |
| b | 0 | 3 | 24 | * * |

## Walk Mill

*Messrs Harrop*

| | | | |
|---|---|---|---|
| 83a | 1 | 0 | 3 |
| b | 1 | 1 | 17 |
| c | 0 | 2 | 16 |

| | | | |
|---|---|---|---|
| d | 0 | 3 | 12 |
| e | 1 | 1 | 29 |
| f | 1 | 2 | 37 |
| g | 2 | 0 | 0 |
| h | 0 | 2 | 33 |
| i | 1 | 2 | 20 |
| j | 0 | 3 | 25 |

## Tamewater

*J.Ingham*

| | | | |
|---|---|---|---|
| 84 | 0 | 1 | 14 |

## Mineycroft

*Edm Schofield*

| | | | |
|---|---|---|---|
| 85 | 0 | 3 | 18 |

## Tamewater

*Jno Wrigley*

| | | | |
|---|---|---|---|
| 86a | 0 | 1 | 12 |
| b | 0 | 1 | 1 |
| c | 3 | 0 | 21 |

*Peter Stelfox*

| | | | |
|---|---|---|---|
| 87a | 2 | 2 | 22 |
| b | 3 | 3 | 20 |

*Jno Wrigley*

| | | | |
|---|---|---|---|
| 88a | 0 | 3 | 9 |
| b | 1 | 1 | 0 |
| c | 1 | 1 | 3 |
| d | 1 | 3 | 32 |
| e | 2 | 3 | 34 |
| f | 2 | 0 | 4 |

## Wallhill

*Jno Gartside*

| | | | |
|---|---|---|---|
| 89a | 1 | 0 | 5 |
| b | 1 | 0 | 7 |
| c | 2 | 1 | 19 |
| d | 0 | 0 | 34 |
| e | 1 | 3 | 12 |
| f | 1 | 3 | 9 |
| k | 2 | 1 | 4 |
| l | 2 | 3 | 28 |

## Last Shift

*Jno Gartside*

| | | | |
|---|---|---|---|
| g | 1 | 1 | 22 |
| h | 0 | 2 | 9 |

## Mag Hey

*Jno Gartside*

| | | | |
|---|---|---|---|
| i | 1 | 0 | 35 |
| j | 2 | 0 | 32 |

## Wallhill

*James Gartside*

| | | | |
|---|---|---|---|
| 90a | 2 | 1 | 0 |
| b | 1 | 3 | 32 |
| c | 5 | 3 | 4 |
| d | 1 | 0 | 20 |
| e | 4 | 0 | 8 |

*Josh Greaves*

| | | | |
|---|---|---|---|
| 91a | 1 | 0 | 36 |
| b | 1 | 3 | 30 |
| c | 1 | 2 | 26 |

## Greaves

*G.Wright*

| | | | |
|---|---|---|---|
| 92a | 1 | 3 | 18 |
| b | 2 | 0 | 23 |
| c | 0 | 0 | 39 |
| d | 2 | 0 | 7 |
| e | 2 | 2 | 4 |
| f | 2 | 0 | 9 |
| g | 0 | 0 | 14 |

## Mag Hey

*James Wood*

| | | | |
|---|---|---|---|
| 93a | 1 | 1 | 35 |
| b | 1 | 0 | 22 |

## Slackfield

*Mary Lees*

| | | | |
|---|---|---|---|
| 94a | 0 | 2 | 14 |
| b | 1 | 0 | 28 |
| c | 0 | 3 | 20 |
| d | 0 | 3 | 38 |
| e | 1 | 0 | 25 |
| f | 1 | 3 | 4 |
| g | 0 | 0 | 33 |
| h | 0 | 2 | 33 |

## New Delph

*Jas Lees Esq*

| | | | |
|---|---|---|---|
| 94i | 0 | 0 | 20 |
| j | 0 | 2 | 23 |
| k | 0 | 1 | 23 |
| l | 1 | 3 | 30 |
| m | 1 | 0 | 20 |
| n | 1 | 1 | 4 |
| o | 1 | 3 | 25 |

## Stones

*Edwd Lees*

| | | | | |
|---|---|---|---|---|
| 95a | 0 | 1 | 17 | |
| b | 3 | 2 | 33 | |
| c | 0 | 1 | 15 | |
| d | 2 | 0 | 30 | |
| e | 0 | 0 | 15 | |
| f | 1 | 2 | 36 | |
| g | 1 | 2 | 20 | |
| h | 2 | 0 | 13 | |
| i | 0 | 0 | 30 | Bldgs |
| j | 1 | 3 | 1 | |
| k | 1 | 1 | 14 | |
| l | 0 | 0 | 20 | Bldgs |

## Stoneswood

*Jonas Ainley*

| | | | | |
|---|---|---|---|---|
| 96a | 0 | 1 | 6 | |
| b | 1 | 1 | 25 | |
| c | 0 | 2 | 38 | |
| d | 0 | 0 | 35 | Bldgs |

## New Delph

*J.Mallalieu*

| | | | | |
|---|---|---|---|---|
| 97a | 1 | 0 | 20 | |
| b | 0 | 0 | 30 | Bldgs |
| c | 1 | 0 | 20 | |
| d | 1 | 2 | 36 | |
| e | 0 | 2 | 5 | |

*Jno Greaves*

| | | | |
|---|---|---|---|
| 98 | 0 | 0 | 36 |

## Stones

*Jos Lees*

| | | | |
|---|---|---|---|
| 99a | 1 | 1 | 24 |
| b | 0 | 1 | 32 |
| c | 1 | 3 | 22 |
| d | 0 | 3 | 15 |
| e | 1 | 1 | 38 |
| f | 2 | 0 | 25 |
| g | 1 | 1 | 29 |

## Stoneswood

*J.Millns*

| | | | |
|---|---|---|---|
| 100a | 1 | 2 | 4 |
| b | 0 | 3 | 36 |
| c | 0 | 3 | 6 |
| d | 0 | 3 | 19 |

## Gatehead

*Thos Shying*

| | | | |
|---|---|---|---|
| 101a | 2 | 0 | 20 |
| b | 1 | 1 | 23 |
| c | 2 | 0 | 21 |
| d | 1 | 1 | 31 |
| e | 0 | 2 | 3 |
| f | 0 | 0 | 23 |
| g | 0 | 2 | 12 |
| h | 0 | 2 | 4 |
| i | 0 | 0 | 31 |

## Gatehead Mills

*J. Harrop Execs*

| | | | |
|---|---|---|---|
| 102a | 0 | 1 | 18 |
| b | 0 | 0 | 36 |
| c | 0 | 0 | 30 |
| d | 0 | 1 | 3 |
| e | 1 | 0 | 34 |

## Gatehead

*Jos Roberts*

| | | | |
|---|---|---|---|
| 103a | 0 | 0 | 32 |
| b | 1 | 2 | 20 |
| c | 3 | 0 | 7 |
| d | 1 | 1 | 31 |
| e | 1 | 0 | 0 |
| f | 0 | 0 | 32 |
| g | 0 | 2 | 0 |
| h | 1 | 0 | 12 |

## Rood

*Jno Wrigley*

| | | | |
|---|---|---|---|
| 104a | 1 | 3 | 25 |
| b | 1 | 0 | 13 |
| c | 0 | 2 | 31 |

*Jno Bradbury*

| | | | |
|---|---|---|---|
| 105a | 0 | 1 | 35 |
| b | 0 | 2 | 12 |
| c | 0 | 3 | 15 |
| d | 0 | 2 | 19 |

*Edw Kenworthy*

| | | | |
|---|---|---|---|
| 106 | 0 | 3 | 0 |

## New Delph

*Jos Lawton*

| | | | |
|---|---|---|---|
| 107a | 1 | 2 | 8 |
| b | 0 | 1 | 15 |

## New Delph

*G. & S.Ogden*

| | | | |
|---|---|---|---|
| 108a | 0 | 2 | 4 |
| b | 2 | 3 | 9 |
| c | 2 | 3 | 27 |
| d | 0 | 1 | 12 |

*Jos Lawton*

| | |
|---|---|
| 109 | |
| House | |

## Rasping Mill &c

*Lees & Schofield*

| | | | |
|---|---|---|---|
| 110a | 0 | 1 | 1 |
| b | 0 | 2 | 33 |

## Old Delph

*Jos Lawton*

| | | | |
|---|---|---|---|
| 111 | 0 | 2 | 32 |

## Salterabbles

*Robt. Kenworthy*

| | | | |
|---|---|---|---|
| 112 | 0 | 0 | 25 |

*Jno Roberts*

| | | | |
|---|---|---|---|
| 113 | 0 | 0 | 30 |

## Delph

*Jos Shaw*

| | | | |
|---|---|---|---|
| 114a | 0 | 1 | 5 |
| b | 0 | 1 | 14 |

**Stanedge Foot**

| | | | |
|---|---|---|---|
| 1a | 1 | 0 | 7 |
| b | 0 | 0 | 22 |
| c | 6 | 0 | 36 |
| d | 4 | 0 | 20 |
| e | 2 | 0 | 16 |
| 2a | 0 | 0 | 18 |
| b | 1 | 1 | 36 |
| 3 | | | |

**Near Leach**

| | | | |
|---|---|---|---|
| 4 | 4 | 0 | 14 |
| 5 | 6 | 1 | 14 |

**Intake**

| | | | |
|---|---|---|---|
| 6a | 1 | 1 | 3 |
| b | 1 | 1 | 0 |
| c | 1 | 0 | 28 |
| d | 0 | 3 | 21 |
| e | 0 | 2 | 5 |
| f | 2 | 1 | 32 |
| 7a | 1 | 1 | 6 |
| b | 0 | 1 | 25 |
| c | 0 | 3 | 14 |
| d | 1 | 0 | 2 |
| e | 1 | 2 | 25 |
| f | 0 | 1 | 1 |
| g | 0 | 2 | 20 |

**Near Spring**

| | |
|---|---|
| 8a | |
| b | |

**Stanedge Foot**

| | | | |
|---|---|---|---|
| 9a | 4 | 3 | 31 |
| b | 3 | 0 | 17 |
| 10a | 0 | 1 | 4 |
| b | 0 | 0 | 22 |

**Bentleys**

| | | | |
|---|---|---|---|
| 11a | 0 | 0 | 22 |
| b | 1 | 1 | 14 |
| c | 0 | 1 | 19 |
| d | 0 | 0 | 34 |
| e | 1 | 3 | 7 |
| f | 0 | 3 | 20 |
| g | 1 | 1 | 0 |
| 12a | | | |
| b | 0 | 2 | 24 |
| c | 0 | 2 | 2 |
| d | | | |
| e | 1 | 2 | 31 |
| f | 2 | 3 | 3 |
| g | 2 | 0 | 7 |
| h | 1 | 0 | 13 |
| i | 0 | 1 | 15 |

**Roughs**

| | | | |
|---|---|---|---|
| 13a | 1 | 1 | 17 |
| b | | | |
| c | 1 | 1 | 25 |
| d | 3 | 1 | 4 |
| 14 | 2 | 2 | 12 |

**Deanhead**

| | | | |
|---|---|---|---|
| 15a | 2 | 3 | 14 |
| b | 0 | 2 | 31 |
| c | 0 | 0 | 38 |
| d | 0 | 3 | 39 |
| e | 2 | 0 | 1 |
| f | 1 | 0 | 36 |
| 16a | 1 | 2 | 31 |
| b | 1 | 2 | 36 |
| c | 1 | 1 | 34 |
| d | 0 | 3 | 29 |
| e | 0 | 1 | 7 |
| f | 1 | 0 | 25 |

| | | | |
|---|---|---|---|
| 17a | 1 | 2 | 9 |
| b | 0 | 0 | 21 |
| c | 2 | 0 | 26 |
| d | 0 | 3 | 39 |
| e | 0 | 3 | 11 |
| 18a | 1 | 2 | 30 |
| b | 0 | 0 | 25 |
| c | 0 | 1 | 5 |
| d | 0 | 2 | 12 |
| e | 1 | 2 | 9 |
| f | 2 | 0 | 23 |
| g | 0 | 2 | 25 |

**Knowle**

| | | | |
|---|---|---|---|
| 19a | 1 | 0 | 28 |
| b | 2 | 0 | 34 |
| c | 1 | 3 | 36 |
| d | 1 | 1 | 30 |
| e | 1 | 1 | 4 |
| f | 1 | 0 | 23 |
| g | 2 | 1 | 27 |
| h | 1 | 0 | 31 |
| I | 1 | 0 | 34 |
| j | 0 | 2 | 20 |
| k | 1 | 1 | 21 |

**Bent Nook**

| | | | |
|---|---|---|---|
| 20aa | | | |
| b | 4 | 2 | 21 |
| c | 3 | 0 | 36 |
| d | 1 | 2 | 21 |
| e | 2 | 0 | 0 |
| f | 1 | 3 | 17 |
| gg | 6 | 0 | 33 |

**Acre**

| | | | |
|---|---|---|---|
| 21a | 1 | 2 | 26 |
| b | 1 | 0 | 33 |
| c | 0 | 2 | 19 |
| d | 1 | 0 | 4 |
| e | 1 | 2 | 18 |
| f | 1 | 1 | 12 |
| g | 0 | 2 | 26 |
| h | 1 | 0 | 25 |
| i | | | |

**Bleak Hey Nook**

| | | | |
|---|---|---|---|
| 22a | | | |
| b | 0 | 2 | 5 |
| c | 0 | 2 | 12 |
| d | 1 | 3 | 35 |

**Brow**

| | | | |
|---|---|---|---|
| 23a | 1 | 3 | 27 |
| b | 0 | 1 | 12 |
| c | | | |
| d | 1 | 1 | 23 |
| e | 0 | 2 | 37 |
| f | 0 | 2 | 6 |
| g | 0 | 3 | 2 |
| h | 1 | 0 | 19 |
| i | 0 | 3 | 4 |
| j | 1 | 3 | 1 |
| k | 0 | 2 | 17 |
| l | 0 | 1 | 21 |
| m | | | |
| n | 2 | 3 | 22 |
| o | 0 | 1 | 16 |

**Warrack Hill**

| | | | |
|---|---|---|---|
| 24a | 2 | 3 | 41 |
| b | 0 | 1 | 13 |
| c | 0 | 1 | 35 |
| d | 0 | 0 | 34 |
| e | 0 | 2 | 19 |
| f | 0 | 2 | 38 |
| g | 2 | 0 | 14 |
| h | 0 | 1 | 21 |
| i | | | |
| j | 1 | 1 | 9 |
| k | 1 | 2 | 9 |
| l | 0 | 2 | 34 |
| m | 0 | 3 | 37 |
| n | 1 | 0 | 29 |
| o | | | |
| p | 0 | 0 | 24 |

| | | | |
|---|---|---|---|
| 25a | 1 | 3 | 15 |
| b | 3 | 1 | 27 |
| c | | | |
| d | 1 | 2 | 13 |
| 26a | 1 | 0 | 0 |

**Thurstons**

| | | | |
|---|---|---|---|
| 27a | 1 | 0 | 22 |
| b | 1 | 2 | 12 |
| c | 0 | 3 | 31 |
| d | 0 | 0 | 21 |
| e | 1 | 3 | 4 |
| f | 1 | 1 | 25 |
| g | 1 | 0 | 10 |
| h | 1 | 1 | 31 |

**Burn Barn**

| | | | |
|---|---|---|---|
| 28a | 0 | 0 | 27 |
| b | 1 | 1 | 3 |
| c | 1 | 1 | 4 |
| d | 0 | 1 | 36 |
| e | 1 | 0 | 31 |
| f | 1 | 3 | 33 |
| g | 2 | 1 | 21 |
| h | 2 | 1 | 21 |

**Burn Clough**

| | | | |
|---|---|---|---|
| 29a | 3 | 2 | 10 |
| b | 1 | 0 | 34 |

**Burn**

| | | | |
|---|---|---|---|
| 30a | 0 | 1 | 34 |
| b | 2 | 2 | 31 |
| c | 0 | 0 | 22 |
| d | 1 | 3 | 32 |
| e | 1 | 1 | 39 |
| f | 0 | 0 | 39 |

**Burn Clough**

| | | | |
|---|---|---|---|
| 31a | | | |
| b } | 1 | 1 | 20 |
| c | | | |
| 32a | 2 | 1 | 27 |
| b | 2 | 1 | 20 |
| c | 0 | 3 | 39 |
| d | 0 | 2 | 8 |
| e | 0 | 1 | 5 |
| f | 0 | 1 | 33 |
| g | 0 | 1 | 21 |
| h | 2 | 2 | 19 |
| i | 1 | 3 | 18 |
| j | 1 | 1 | 33 |

**Backstone Pit**

| | | | |
|---|---|---|---|
| 33a | 1 | 0 | 5 |
| b | 0 | 2 | 17 |
| c | 1 | 1 | 5 |
| d | 2 | 0 | 16 |
| e | 1 | 1 | 14 |
| 34a | 0 | 0 | 22 |
| b | 0 | 0 | 34 |
| c | 0 | 0 | 23 |
| d | 0 | 0 | 22 |
| e | 0 | 0 | 26 |
| f | 0 | 1 | 30 |
| g | 3 | 1 | 4 |
| 35a | 0 | 0 | 16 |
| b | 1 | 0 | 17 |
| c | 0 | 0 | 20 |
| d | 0 | 0 | 12 |
| e | 0 | 0 | 11 |
| f | 0 | 3 | 7 |
| g | 0 | 2 | 25 |
| h | 1 | 1 | 21 |
| i | | | |
| j | 0 | 0 | 22 |
| 36a | 0 | 3 | 2 |
| b | 0 | 1 | 22 |
| c | 0 | 1 | 29 |
| d | 0 | 1 | 18 |

## Harrop Cote (Coat)

| 37a | 0 | 3 | 21 |
|---|---|---|---|
| b | 0 | 0 | 28 |
| c | 0 | 3 | 29 |
| d | 1 | 0 | 36 |
| e | 1 | 0 | 30 |
| f | 0 | 0 | 12 |
| g | 0 | 2 | 8 |
| h | 0 | 3 | 29 |
| i | 0 | 3 | 24 |
| j | 0 | 2 | 31 |
| k | 0 | 2 | 30 |
| l | 0 | 3 | 28 |
| m | 0 | 0 | 14 |
| n | 2 | 1 | 35 |

## Diggle Edge

| 38a | 0 | 2 | 28 |
|---|---|---|---|
| b | 0 | 1 | 19 |
| c | 0 | 1 | 30 |
| d | 0 | 1 | 22 |
| e | 0 | 2 | 26 |
| f | | | |

## Diggle

| 39a | 1 | 0 | 7 |
|---|---|---|---|
| b | 0 | 3 | 39 |
| c | 1 | 0 | 7 |
| d | 1 | 0 | 12 |
| e | 0 | 0 | 38 |
| f | 1 | 2 | 2 |
| g | 0 | 3 | 13 |
| h | 0 | 2 | 37 |
| i | 3 | 0 | 6 |
| j | 0 | 3 | 4 |
| k | 0 | 3 | 30 |

## Limbo Mill

| 40a | 1 | 3 | 10 |
|---|---|---|---|
| b | 1 | 1 | 15 |
| c | 1 | 0 | 20 |
| d | 1 | 0 | 38 |
| e, f | | | |
| g | 0 | 3 | 36 |
| h | 1 | 1 | 15 |
| i } ii } | 0 | 3 | 18 |
| j | 0 | 3 | 39 |
| k | 2 | 0 | 16 |
| l | 0 | 2 | 6 |

## Backstone Pit

| 41a | 1 | 0 | 16 |
|---|---|---|---|
| b | 1 | 0 | 22 |

## Thurstons

| 42a | 1 | 2 | 7 |
|---|---|---|---|
| b | 1 | 0 | 14 |
| c | 0 | 3 | 32 |
| d | 0 | 3 | 12 |
| e | 0 | 3 | 25 |
| f | 1 | 1 | 15 |
| g | 0 | 3 | 18 |

| 43a | | | |
|---|---|---|---|
| b | 1 | 0 | 17 |
| c | 0 | 2 | 19 |
| d | 1 | 0 | 0 |
| e | 0 | 3 | 20 |
| f | 0 | 3 | 25 |
| g | 0 | 3 | 13 |
| h | 2 | 2 | 23 |

| 44a | 1 | 2 | 13 |
|---|---|---|---|
| b | 1 | 1 | 11 |
| c | 1 | 3 | 9 |
| d | 1 | 2 | 36 |

| 45 | | | |
|---|---|---|---|

| 46a | 3 | 2 | 0 |
|---|---|---|---|
| b | 1 | 1 | 20 |
| c | 1 | 0 | 30 |
| d | 1 | 1 | 17 |

| 47 | 2 | 1 | 33 |
|---|---|---|---|

| 48a | 2 | 1 | 5 |
|---|---|---|---|
| b | 0 | 3 | 12 |
| c | 1 | 0 | 22 |
| d | 2 | 0 | 0 |

## Diggle

| 50a | 0 | 2 | 2 |
|---|---|---|---|
| b | 0 | 3 | 18 |
| c | 1 | 0 | 32 |

| 51a | 0 | 1 | 5 |
|---|---|---|---|
| b | 1 | 1 | 14 |
| c | 0 | 3 | 14 |
| d | 1 | 1 | 11 |
| e | 0 | 3 | 24 |

| 52a | 0 | 3 | 8 |
|---|---|---|---|
| b | 1 | 0 | 5 |
| c | 0 | 2 | 20 |
| d | 1 | 0 | 1 |
| e | 1 | 0 | 4 |
| f | 1 | 1 | 3 |
| g | 1 | 2 | 12 |
| h | 0 | 3 | 19 |
| i | 0 | 3 | 19 |

| 53a | 1 | 1 | 20 |
|---|---|---|---|
| b | 1 | 0 | 37 |
| c | 1 | 0 | 0 |
| d | 1 | 3 | 5 |
| e | 1 | 0 | 32 |
| f | 1 | 1 | 12 |

| 54a | 0 | 1 | 7 |
|---|---|---|---|
| b | 0 | 1 | 20 |
| c | 0 | 2 | 20 |
| d | 1 | 1 | 22 |
| e | 2 | 3 | 27 |
| f | 1 | 1 | 37 |

| 55a | 1 | 2 | 0 |
|---|---|---|---|
| b | 1 | 1 | 4 |
| c | 1 | 0 | 25 |
| d | 1 | 1 | 25 |

| 56 | 56 | 0 | 27 |
|---|---|---|---|

| 57a | 3 | 0 | 22 |
|---|---|---|---|
| b | 0 | 1 | 20 |
| c | 0 | 1 | 15 |
| d | 0 | 2 | 24 |

| 58a | 0 | 2 | 9 |
|---|---|---|---|
| b | 2 | 1 | 25 |
| c | 7 | 2 | 0 |
| d | 3 | 3 | 22 |
| e | 3 | 3 | 13 |

| 60a | 60 | 0 | 0 |
|---|---|---|---|

## Fairbanks

61a, b, c, d e, f g, h, i, j, k, l, m, n, o, p, q, r, s, t

## Back of the Lee

62a, b (Near Marsh Head)

62a, b (Near Back of Lee)

63

64

65a, b

66a, b

67a, b

68a, b, c, d e, f, g, h, i, j, k, l, m, n

69a, b

70a, b, c

71a, b, c, d e, f, g, h

72

74

## Diglee

73a, b, c, d e, f g, h

75a, b, c, d, e, f

76a, b, c, d, e, f, g, h

77a, b, c

## Marsh Head

78a, b, c, d, e, ee, f, g, h

## Diglee

79a, b, c, d

80a, b, c, d

81a, b (on map two 81b)

82a, b

## Court

83a, b, c, d, f, g, h

## Harrop Ridge

84a, b, c, d, e, f, g, h

## Harrop Green

85a, b, c, d

86a, b, c, d, e, ee, f, g

87a, b, c, d, e, f, g, h, i, j

## Harrop Green*

| 88a | 0 | 2 | 34 |
|---|---|---|---|
| b | 2 | 2 | 31 |
| c | 3 | 1 | 21 |
| d | 2 | 0 | 25 |
| e | 0 | 3 | 9 |
| f | 2 | 1 | 32 |
| g | 3 | 1 | 11 |
| h | 1 | 1 | 38 |
| i | 2 | 0 | 38 |
| j | 1 | 1 | 33 |
| k | 0 | 3 | 19 |
| l | 0 | 3 | 34 |
| m | 1 | 0 | 21 |

## Lee Cross*

| 88n | 2 | 3 | 30 |
|---|---|---|---|
| o | 0 | 2 | 31 |
| p | 1 | 2 | 28 |
| q | 3 | 0 | 20 |
| r | 0 | 3 | 6 |
| s | 1 | 2 | 17 |

## Hollingreave*

| 88t | 0 | 2 | 28 |
|---|---|---|---|
| u | 2 | 3 | 0 |
| v | 2 | 2 | 38 |
| w | 0 | 3 | 30 |
| x | 0 | 0 | 22 |
| y | 2 | 0 | 2 |
| z | 1 | 0 | 2 |
| A | 1 | 2 | 18 |
| B | 1 | 0 | 1 |
| C | 1 | 0 | 30 |
| D | 0 | 3 | 17 |
| E | 2 | 3 | 15 |
| F | 2 | 0 | 1 |
| G | 0 | 1 | 21 |
| H | 2 | 1 | 21 |
| I | 0 | 3 | 30 |
| J | 0 | 0 | 13 |
| K | 0 | 1 | 14 |
| L | 1 | 1 | 28 |

## Ward Lane*

| 88M | 0 | 2 | 37 |
|---|---|---|---|
| N | 2 | 1 | 1 |

## Warth Mill

89a, b, c, d, e,

90a, c, d

## Lee

91a, b, c, d, e

93a, b, c, d, e, f

## Canal

92a, b, c, d

## Hollingreave

94a, b, c, d, e, f, g, h, i, j, k

95a, b, c, d, e, f, g, h, i, j, k, l

## Heys

96a, b, c, d, e, f

## Running Hill

97a, b

98a, b

99a, b

## Workhouse

100a, b, c, d e, f g, h, i, j, k

## Running Hill

101a, b, c, d, e, f

| | | | |
|---|---|---|---|
| g* | 3 | 0 | 14 |

h, i, j

102a, b, c, d, e

103a, b, c, d, e

104a, b

105a, b, c, d, e

## Wickens

106a, b, c, d, e, f, g, h, i, j, k, l, m, n, o, p, q, r

## Slades

107a, b, c, d, e, f

108a, b, e, f, g, h

| | | | |
|---|---|---|---|
| i | 2 | 0 | 4 |

109a, b, c, d, e, f, g

110a, b

111a, b,

112a, b, c, d, e, f, g

113a, b, c

## Load Clough

| | | | |
|---|---|---|---|
| 114a | 1 | 1 | 15 |
| b | 1 | 1 | 21 |
| c | 0 | 3 | 23 |
| d | 0 | 3 | 34 |
| e | 0 | 2 | 9 |
| f | 0 | 2 | 16 |
| g | 1 | 0 | 19 |
| h | 1 | 2 | 38 |
| i | 1 | 0 | 1 |
| j | 5 | 2 | 14 |
| k | 1 | 1 | 16 |
| l | 0 | 1 | 15 |
| m | 0 | 2 | 1 |
| n | | | |

## Primrose

| | | | |
|---|---|---|---|
| 115a | 1 | 0 | 16 |
| b | | | |
| c | 1 | 2 | 36 |
| d | 1 | 1 | 14 |
| e | 0 | 2 | 8 |
| f | | | |

## Pob Green

116a, b, c, d, e, f

117a, b, c, d

## Clarks

118a, b, d, e, f, g, h, i, j

| | | | |
|---|---|---|---|
| k | 0 | 0 | 30 |
| l | 0 | 0 | 36 |
| m | 0 | 0 | 36 |

n, o, p, q, r, s, t, u, v, w

| | | | |
|---|---|---|---|
| x | 1 | 1 | 2 |
| y | 1 | 1 | 16 |

## Clarks

| | | | |
|---|---|---|---|
| 119a | | | |
| b | 0 | 0 | 23 |
| c | 1 | 2 | 37 |
| e, f | | | |

## Briggs

120

## Cross Keys Inn

| | | | |
|---|---|---|---|
| 121a | 0 | 1 | 6 |
| b | 0 | 2 | 5 |
| c | 0 | 0 | 30 |
| d | | | |
| e | 1 | 3 | 36 |

## Bank Top

| | | | |
|---|---|---|---|
| 122a | 1 | 2 | 5 |
| b | 0 | 5 | 6 |
| c | 1 | 1 | 12 |
| d | 1 | 1 | 7 |
| e | 1 | 3 | 36 |

## Peters

| | | | |
|---|---|---|---|
| 123a | 0 | 2 | 7 |
| b | 0 | 0 | 30 |
| c | 0 | 3 | 12 |
| d | 2 | 0 | 15 |

## Pob Green

| | | | |
|---|---|---|---|
| 124a | 0 | 1 | 34 |
| b | 0 | 0 | 25 |
| c | 0 | 2 | 28 |
| d | 1 | 1 | 12 |
| e | 1 | 2 | 59 |
| 126a | 0 | 1 | 38 |
| b | 0 | 5 | 25 |
| c | 0 | 1 | 25 |
| d | 1 | 1 | 3 |

## Parsonage

| | | | |
|---|---|---|---|
| 127a | 2 | 0 | 1 |
| b | 2 | 0 | 35 |
| c | 1 | 3 | 35 |
| d | 3 | 2 | 13 |
| e | 0 | 5 | 0 |
| f | 15 | 3 | 26 |
| g | | | |
| h | 4 | 0 | 33 |
| i | 2 | 2 | 16 |
| j | 2 | 2 | 18 |

## Intake

| | | | |
|---|---|---|---|
| 128a | 1 | 0 | 35 |
| b | 1 | 1 | 10 |
| c | 1 | 2 | 12 |
| d | 1 | 3 | 15 |
| e | 1 | 2 | 12 |
| f | 2 | 2 | 17 |
| g | 0 | 3 | 25 |
| h | 0 | 3 | 6 |
| i | 1 | 0 | 24 |
| j | 1 | 0 | 23 |
| k | 0 | 3 | 30 |
| l | 1 | 2 | 28 |
| m | 1 | 1 | 0 |

## Saddleworth Fold

| | | | |
|---|---|---|---|
| 129a | 0 | 3 | 29 |
| b | 1 | 2 | 34 |
| c | 0 | 2 | 19 |
| d | 0 | 2 | 2 |
| e | 0 | 2 | 30 |
| f | 1 | 3 | 11 |
| g | | | |
| h | 0 | 0 | 34 |
| i | 0 | 0 | 21 |
| 130a | 0 | 3 | 15 |
| b | 0 | 3 | 20 |
| c | 0 | 3 | 12 |
| d | 0 | 2 | 2 |
| e | | | |
| f | 2 | 2 | 24 |
| 131a | 1 | 0 | 25 |
| b | 0 | 5 | 39 |
| c | 1 | 0 | 28 |
| d | 0 | 5 | 6 |
| e | 0 | 3 | 6 |
| f | 1 | 0 | 23 |
| g | 2 | 2 | 34 |
| 132 | | | |
| 133a | 4 | 0 | 34 |
| b | 3 | 2 | 17 |
| c | 2 | 2 | 10 |
| d | 1 | 3 | 32 |
| e | 2 | 0 | 31 |
| g | 2 | 2 | 34 |

| | | | |
|---|---|---|---|
| 134a | 2 | 3 | 3 |
| b | 2 | 2 | 25 |
| c | 1 | 2 | 32 |
| d | 2 | 2 | 31 |
| f | 2 | 1 | 37 |

## Heathfields

| | | | |
|---|---|---|---|
| 135a | 5 | 0 | 10 |
| b | 1 | 1 | 9 |
| c | 0 | 3 | 32 |
| d | 1 | 0 | 9 |
| e | 0 | 0 | 25 |
| f | 1 | 3 | 25 |
| g | 1 | 0 | 17 |
| h | 2 | 0 | 3 |
| i | | | |
| j | | | |
| k | 0 | 2 | 4 |
| l | 2 | 0 | 17 |
| m | 0 | 2 | 15 |
| n | 0 | 1 | 30 |
| 0 | 1 | 1 | 30 |
| p | 1 | 1 | 1 |
| q | 1 | 0 | 3 |

## Cank (Abels)

| | | | |
|---|---|---|---|
| 136a | 3 | 0 | 24 |
| b | | | |
| c | 1 | 1 | 13 |
| d | 3 | 1 | 39 |
| e | 0 | 0 | 34 |
| f | 0 | 1 | 17 |
| g | 0 | 0 | 28 |

## Birches

| | | | |
|---|---|---|---|
| 137a | 2 | 3 | 11 |
| b | 1 | 1 | 4 |
| c | | | |
| d | 1 | 2 | 14 |
| e | 0 | 0 | 18 |
| f | 2 | 1 | 34 |
| g | 1 | 1 | 28 |
| h | 1 | 1 | 14 |
| i | 1 | 2 | 22 |

## Cross

| | | | |
|---|---|---|---|
| j | | | |
| k | 0 | 2 | 31 |
| l | 1 | 0 | 23 |
| m | 0 | 1 | 30 |
| n | 1 | 0 | 21 |
| o | | | |
| p | 0 | 2 | 20 |
| q | 1 | 2 | 32 |
| r | 0 | 0 | 16 |
| s | 1 | 2 | 26 |
| t | 3 | 0 | 30 |
| v | 1 | 2 | 35 |
| w | 2 | 0 | 7 |
| 138a | 1 | 0 | 14 |
| b | 0 | 2 | 7 |
| c | 1 | 0 | 7 |
| d | 1 | 2 | 1 |
| e | 0 | 1 | 3 |
| f | 0 | 3 | 7 |
| g | | | |
| h | 0 | 3 | 24 |
| I | 2 | 0 | 5 |
| j | 2 | 3 | 38 |
| k | 0 | 0 | 16 |
| l | 1 | 1 | 1 |
| m | 0 | 2 | 35 |
| n | 0 | 5 | 27 |
| 139a | 2 | 3 | 25 |
| b | 2 | 0 | 5 |
| c | 1 | 1 | 25 |
| d | 0 | 2 | 16 |
| e | 11 | 1 | 26 |
| f | 1 | 1 | 20 |
| g | 1 | 2 | 19 |
| h | | | |

## Rye Top

| | | | |
|---|---|---|---|
| 140a | 3 | 1 | 28 |
| b | | | |
| c | 1 | 0 | 15 |
| d | 0 | 0 | 31 |
| e | 2 | 3 | 7 |
| f | 1 | 0 | 24 |
| g | 1 | 0 | 38 |
| h | 2 | 0 | 35 |

| | | | |
|---|---|---|---|
| I | 1 | 3 | 37 |
| J | 1 | 1 | 38 |
| k | 0 | 2 | 21 |
| l | | | |
| m | 1 | 1 | 24 |
| n | 1 | 2 | 15 |

## Pinfold

| | | | |
|---|---|---|---|
| 141a | 1 | 1 | 19 |
| b | 1 | 2 | 38 |
| c | 2 | 3 | 9 |
| d | 1 | 1 | 0 |
| e | 2 | 1 | 25 |
| f | 2 | 2 | 9 |
| g | 1 | 1 | 18 |
| h | 1 | 3 | 36 |
| I | 0 | 1 | 0 |
| j | 1 | 2 | 9 |
| k | 1 | 1 | 13 |
| l | 1 | 1 | 6 |
| m | 3 | 2 | 9 |
| n | 2 | 0 | 36 |
| o | 1 | 0 | 25 |
| p | 2 | 0 | 3 |
| q | 0 | 2 | 3 |
| r | 0 | 2 | 39 |

## Knowl Top

| | | | |
|---|---|---|---|
| 142a | 2 | 0 | 28 |
| b | 1 | 1 | 24 |
| c | 0 | 2 | 11 |
| d | 1 | 3 | 25 |
| e | 2 | 3 | 9 |
| f | 0 | 2 | 31 |

## Furlane

| | | | |
|---|---|---|---|
| 143a | 2 | 0 | 13 |
| b | 1 | 2 | 20 |
| c | 0 | 3 | 20 |
| d | 1 | 2 | 28 |
| e | 2 | 0 | 24 |
| f | 3 | 0 | 13 |
| g | 1 | 3 | 18 |
| h | 1 | 0 | 32 |
| i | 4 | 2 | 5 |
| j | 1 | 0 | 38 |
| k | 2 | 0 | 3 |
| l | 0 | 3 | 26 |
| m | | | |

## Goulburn Clough

| | | | |
|---|---|---|---|
| 144a | 1 | 2 | 38 |
| b | 1 | 1 | 0 |
| c | 1 | 3 | 7 |
| d | 2 | 0 | 10 |
| e | 1 | 0 | 11 |
| f | 1 | 0 | 18 |

## Furlane

| | | | |
|---|---|---|---|
| 145a | 1 | 3 | 11 |
| b | 1 | 2 | 26 |
| c | 1 | 1 | 20 |
| d | 1 | 1 | 0 |
| e | 1 | 1 | 21 |
| f | 2 | 1 | 11 |
| g | 1 | 3 | 9 |
| h | 1 | 0 | 2 |
| i | 1 | 1 | 30 |
| j | 0 | 3 | 7 |
| k | 1 | 2 | 1 |
| l | 1 | 1 | 10 |
| m | 0 | 0 | 33 |
| n | | | |
| o | 2 | 2 | 10 |
| p | 0 | 1 | 28 |
| q | 2 | 1 | 3 |
| r | 0 | 0 | 24 |
| s | 0 | 2 | 32 |

## Boarshurst School

| | | | |
|---|---|---|---|
| 146a | 0 | 0 | 19 |
| b | 0 | 0 | 24 |
| c | 0 | 0 | 29 |
| d | | | |
| e | 0 | 1 | 29 |

## Furlane

| | | | |
|---|---|---|---|
| 147a | 1 | 1 | 21 |
| b | 2 | 0 | 3 |
| c | | | |

| | | | |
|---|---|---|---|
| d | 1 | 3 | 22 |
| e | 3 | 1 | 3 |
| f | 2 | 1 | 11 |
| g | 1 | 1 | 10 |
| h | 1 | 0 | 15 |
| I | 1 | 1 | 10 |

## Kinders

| | | | |
|---|---|---|---|
| 148a | 2 | 2 | 34 |
| b | 1 | 2 | 22 |
| c | 1 | 0 | 26 |
| d | 1 | 1 | 0 |
| e | 0 | 2 | 9 |
| f | 0 | 2 | 20 |
| g | 0 | 3 | 25 |
| h | 1 | 0 | 17 |
| i | 2 | 2 | 1 |
| j | 0 | 1 | 30 |
| k | 0 | 2 | 8 |

## Lower House, Boarshurst

| | | | |
|---|---|---|---|
| 149a | 1 | 3 | 3 |
| b | 0 | 1 | 28 |
| c | 1 | 1 | 5 |
| d | 1 | 1 | 6 |
| e | 1 | 2 | 31 |
| f | 0 | 3 | 39 |
| g | 0 | 3 | 20 |
| h | | | |
| I | 0 | 3 | 24 |
| j | 0 | 2 | 23 |
| k | 2 | 0 | 14 |
| l | 2 | 0 | 2 |

## Foulrakes

| | | | |
|---|---|---|---|
| 150a | 2 | 3 | 36 |
| b | 0 | 1 | 1 |
| c | 0 | 2 | 32 |
| d | 3 | 2 | 17 |
| e | | | |
| f | 0 | 2 | 6 |
| g | 2 | 1 | 0 |
| h | 2 | 2 | 37 |
| i | | | |
| j | 1 | 3 | 17 |
| k | 1 | 2 | 29 |
| l | 4 | 0 | 0 |
| m | 1 | 2 | 31 |
| n | 0 | 3 | 14 |
| o | 1 | 3 | 24 |
| p | 1 | 2 | 9 |
| pp | 2 | 3 | 7 |
| q | 2 | 1 | 33 |
| r | | | |
| s | 2 | 2 | 30 |
| t | 0 | 3 | 5 |
| u | 2 | 0 | 3 |
| v | 2 | 0 | 36 |
| w | | | |
| x | 1 | 3 | 11 |
| y | 1 | 1 | 37 |
| z | 0 | 3 | 39 |
| A | 2 | 0 | 15 |
| B | 1 | 3 | 2 |
| C | 2 | 2 | 6 |
| D | 0 | 2 | 17 |
| E | | | |

## Boarshurst

| | | | |
|---|---|---|---|
| 151a | 0 | 0 | 25 |
| b | 0 | 0 | 38 |
| c | 1 | 3 | 4 |
| d | 1 | 2 | 0 |

## Tunstead

| | | | |
|---|---|---|---|
| 152a | 2 | 3 | 38 |
| b | 1 | 2 | 4 |
| c | 2 | 0 | 12 |
| d | 0 | 1 | 10 |
| e | 1 | 2 | 25 |
| f | 0 | 3 | 2 |
| g | 0 | 0 | 27 |

## Tunstead

| | | | |
|---|---|---|---|
| 153a | 3 | 1 | 17 |
| b | 1 | 2 | 26 |
| c | | | |
| d | 4 | 1 | 28 |
| e | 0 | 2 | 1 |
| f | | | |
| g | 0 | 2 | 10 |

| | | | |
|---|---|---|---|
| h | | | |
| I | 2 | 1 | 15 |
| J | 2 | 3 | 1 |
| k | 0 | 0 | 4 |
| l | 0 | 1 | 2 |
| m | 2 | 1 | 5 |
| n | 2 | 1 | 33 |
| o | 1 | 1 | 1 |
| p | 0 | 2 | 33 |
| q | 1 | 3 | 2 |
| r | 1 | 0 | 10 |
| s | 0 | 2 | 26 |

## Tunstead

| | | | |
|---|---|---|---|
| 154a | 2 | 3 | 17 |
| b | 0 | 3 | 29 |
| c | 1 | 0 | 37 |
| d | 0 | 3 | 30 |
| e | 1 | 2 | 35 |
| f | 0 | 1 | 2 |
| g | 0 | 1 | 29 |
| h | 0 | 3 | 28 |
| I | 0 | 1 | 15 |
| j | 0 | 2 | 6 |
| k | 2 | 1 | 7 |
| l | 4 | 3 | 22 |
| ll | 3 | 2 | 39 |
| m | | | |
| n | 2 | 2 | 22 |

## Hawkyard

| | | | |
|---|---|---|---|
| 155a | 1 | 1 | 25 |
| b | 1 | 2 | 11 |
| c | 2 | 0 | 1 |
| d | 2 | 3 | 1 |
| e | 2 | 0 | 34 |
| f | 2 | 0 | 25 |
| g | 1 | 2 | 30 |
| h | 2 | 3 | 31 |
| i | 0 | 1 | 3 |
| j | 0 | 0 | 36 |
| k | 5 | 1 | 27 |
| l | 3 | 2 | 2 |
| | | | |
| 156a | 2 | 3 | 9 |
| b | 1 | 3 | 17 |
| c | 1 | 1 | 28 |
| d | 0 | 1 | 21 |
| e | 2 | 0 | 25 |
| f | | | |
| g | 1 | 3 | 17 |
| h | 1 | 1 | 5 |

## Brockley Moor

| | | | |
|---|---|---|---|
| 157a | 8 | 2 | 6 |
| b | 3 | 0 | 38 |

## White Brook Head

| | | | |
|---|---|---|---|
| 158a | 10 | 1 | 34 |
| b | 0 | 3 | 3 |
| c | 4 | 1 | 27 |
| d | 1 | 0 | 26d |
| e | 1 | 0 | 29 |
| f | 1 | 0 | 35 |
| g | 0 | 3 | 9 |
| h | 1 | 1 | 8 |
| i | 1 | 1 | 13 |

## Greenfield

| | | | |
|---|---|---|---|
| 159a | | | |
| b | | | |
| c | 0 | 1 | 6 |
| d | 2 | 0 | 31 |
| e | 0 | 2 | 6 |
| f | 1 | 3 | 25 |
| g | 1 | 2 | 3 |
| h | 1 | 1 | 19 |
| i | 1 | 1 | 5 |
| j | 0 | 2 | 21 |
| m | 5 | 2 | 18 |
| n | 4 | 3 | 1 |
| o | 5 | 3 | 5 |
| p | 3 | 1 | 19 |
| q | | | |
| r | 0 | 1 | 30 |
| s | 8 | 1 | 8 |
| t | 52 | 2 | 22 |
| u | 3 | 2 | 28 |
| v | 25 | 1 | 6 |
| w | 11 | 1 | 26 |
| x | 36 | 1 | 15 |
| y | 1 | 1 | 19 |

| | | | |
|---|---|---|---|
| z | 0 | 2 | 18 |
| A | 0 | 2 | 11 |
| B | 1 | 3 | 11 |
| C | 0 | 1 | 22 |
| D | 7 | 2 | 38 |
| E | 9 | 2 | 3 |
| F | 6 | 3 | 5 |
| G | 1 | 1 | 21 |
| H | 2 | 1 | 15 |
| I | 10 | 2 | 25 |
| J | | | |
| K | 2 | 0 | 28 |
| L | 1 | 0 | 14 |
| M | | | |
| N | 20 | 1 | 12 |
| O | 0 | 1 | 1 |
| P | 0 | 3 | 31 |
| Q | 0 | 3 | 13 |
| R | 1 | 2 | 14 |
| S | | | |
| T | 52 | 2 | 22 |
| U | 3 | 2 | 28 |
| V | 7 | 2 | 4 |
| W | 9 | 2 | 16 |
| X | 0 | 2 | 0 |
| Y | 4 | 2 | 18 |
| Z | 18 | 1 | 4 |
| aa | | | |
| bb | 22 | 3 | 23 |
| cc | 1 | 1 | 19 |
| dd | 26 | 0 | 26 |
| ee | 3 | 2 | 33 |
| ff | 2 | 0 | 10 |
| gg | 1 | 3 | 28 |
| hh | 16 | 0 | 34 |
| ii | 2 | 0 | 7 |
| jj | 1 | 2 | 36 |
| kk | 0 | 0 | 31 |
| ll | 24 | 1 | 23 |
| oo | 5 | 3 | 30 |
| pp | 1 | 0 | 23 |
| qq | 0 | 3 | 19 |
| rr | 1 | 1 | 10 |
| ss | 1 | 0 | 20 |
| tt | 2 | 2 | 17 |
| uu | 3 | 3 | 0 |
| vv | 3 | 1 | 20 |
| ww | | | |
| xx | 1 | 0 | 15 |
| yy | 1 | 3 | 3 |
| zz | 2 | 0 | 1 |
| a | 4 | 3 | 36 |
| b | 1 | 1 | 22 |
| c | 2 | 0 | 12 |
| d | 1 | 3 | 11 |
| e | 0 | 3 | 15 |
| f | 1 | 0 | 3 |
| g | 2 | 0 | 33 |
| h | 2 | 1 | 9 |
| i | 1 | 0 | 14 |
| j | 0 | 2 | 1 |
| k | 1 | 3 | 6 |
| l | 1 | 1 | 30 |
| m | 0 | 3 | 38 |
| n | 0 | 3 | 0 |
| o | 0 | 3 | 38 |
| p | 2 | 0 | 30 |
| q | 1 | 2 | 21 |
| r | 2 | 0 | 12 |
| s | 2 | 0 | 5 |
| t | 0 | 2 | 22 |
| u | 0 | 2 | 11 |
| v | 0 | 3 | 32 |
| w | 1 | 0 | 3 |
| x | 0 | 2 | 6 |
| y | 0 | 2 | 24 |
| z | 0 | 2 | 14 |
| aa | 0 | 2 | 28 |
| bb | 0 | 2 | 20 |
| cc | 0 | 2 | 26 |

### Binn Green

| | | | |
|---|---|---|---|
| 160a | 2 | 2 | 6 |
| b | 1 | 3 | 18 |
| c | 0 | 3 | 15 |
| d | 1 | 0 | 37 |
| e | 2 | 1 | 11 |
| f | 1 | 1 | 38 |
| g | 1 | 1 | 2 |
| h | | | |
| i | 0 | 3 | 9 |

### Ashway Gap

| | | | |
|---|---|---|---|
| 161a | 1 | 1 | 10 |
| b | 1 | 1 | 10 |
| c | | | |
| d | 1 | 1 | 15 |
| e | 0 | 2 | 18 |
| f | 0 | 3 | 8 |
| g | 1 | 2 | 24 |
| h | 1 | 3 | 13 |
| i | 1 | 1 | 15 |
| j | 0 | 1 | 6 |
| k | | | |
| l | 0 | 2 | 16 |
| m | 0 | 0 | 39 |
| n | 0 | 3 | 30 |
| o | 0 | 2 | 36 |
| p | | | |
| q | 16 | 3 | 0 |

### Hollins Plantation

| | | | |
|---|---|---|---|
| 162 | 1 | 2 | 35 |
| 163a | 1 | 1 | 17 |
| b | 3 | 1 | 5 |
| c | 1 | 1 | 31 |
| d | 0 | 3 | 5 |
| e | 0 | 1 | 6 |

### Kinder Intake

| | | | |
|---|---|---|---|
| 164a | 3 | 0 | 26 |
| b | 3 | 0 | 23 |
| c | 0 | 3 | 24 |

### Slack Head

| | | | |
|---|---|---|---|
| 165a | 1 | 2 | 33 |
| b | 1 | 1 | 14 |
| c | 1 | 1 | 19 |
| d | 1 | 2 | 39 |
| e | 3 | 3 | 2 |
| f | 1 | 1 | 7 |
| g | 2 | 1 | 4 |
| h | 2 | 1 | 17 |
| i | 0 | 0 | 27 |
| j | 0 | 3 | 6 |
| k | 1 | 0 | 19 |
| l | 1 | 1 | 35 |

### Fearnlee

| | | | |
|---|---|---|---|
| 166a | 0 | 3 | 31 |
| b | 0 | 1 | 18 |
| c | | | |
| d | 0 | 3 | 8 |
| e | | | |
| f | 0 | 3 | 19 |
| g | 0 | 1 | 37 |
| h | 0 | 1 | 38 |
| i | 1 | 1 | 13 |
| j | 1 | 2 | 30 |
| k | 0 | 0 | 16 |
| l | 0 | 1 | 2 |
| m | 3 | 1 | 20 |
| n | 1 | 2 | 28 |
| o | 3 | 2 | 27 |
| p | 2 | 3 | 39 |
| q | 4 | 7 | 14 |
| r | 1 | 2 | 12 |
| s | 3 | 0 | 24 |

### Fearnlee

| | | | |
|---|---|---|---|
| 167a | 0 | 3 | 3 |
| b | 0 | 0 | 36 |
| c | 0 | 1 | 0 |

### Nook Wood

| | | | |
|---|---|---|---|
| 168a | 3 | 3 | 4 |
| b | 1 | 2 | 23 |
| c | 0 | 0 | 25 |
| d | 0 | 2 | 15 |
| e | 0 | 1 | 32 |

### Fearnlee

| | | | |
|---|---|---|---|
| 169a | 0 | 6 | 28 |
| b | 1 | 0 | 10 |
| c | 4 | 0 | 1 |
| d | 1 | 3 | 2 |
| e | 1 | 0 | 19 |
| f | 2 | 0 | 38 |
| g | 1 | 1 | 26 |
| h | 2 | 0 | 3 |
| i | 1 | 2 | 0 |

| | | | |
|---|---|---|---|
| j | 1 | 3 | 12 |
| k | 2 | 0 | 35 |
| l | 1 | 0 | 12 |
| m | 2 | 0 | 30 |
| n | 2 | 3 | 4 |

### Intake

| | | | |
|---|---|---|---|
| 170a | 2 | 0 | 21 |
| b | 1 | 0 | 23 |
| c | 2 | 1 | 11 |
| d | 0 | 3 | 23 |
| 171a | 2 | 0 | 10 |
| b | 1 | 1 | 13 |
| c | 1 | 1 | 10 |

### Mount Pleasant

| | | | |
|---|---|---|---|
| 172a | 2 | 2 | 6 |
| b | 0 | 1 | 12 |
| c | | | |
| d | 2 | 0 | 22 |
| e | 1 | 3 | 18 |
| f } j | 7 | 1 | 2 |
| g | 0 | 2 | 35 |
| h | 0 | 1 | 33 |
| i | 5 | 1 | 15 |

### Whitelee

| | | | |
|---|---|---|---|
| 173a | 2 | 3 | 13 |
| b | 1 | 2 | 7 |
| c | 1 | 1 | 4 |
| d | 0 | 2 | 14 |
| e | | | |
| f | 3 | 0 | 14 |
| g | 2 | 3 | 26 |
| h | 6 | 0 | 12 |
| i | | | |
| j | 1 | 1 | 34 |
| k | 0 | 2 | 26 |
| l | 0 | 0 | 27 |
| m | 0 | 3 | 30 |
| n | 0 | 2 | 14 |
| o | 1 | 3 | 14 |
| p | 2 | 2 | 14 |
| q | 3 | 2 | 20 |
| r | 3 | 0 | 33 |
| s | 0 | 0 | 26 |
| t | 3 | 3 | 38 |
| u | 2 | 1 | 25 |
| w | | | |
| x | 5 | 0 | 26 |
| y | 1 | 3 | 16 |
| z | 2 | 1 | 26 |
| zz | 2 | 2 | 35 |

### Woolleys

| | | | |
|---|---|---|---|
| 174a | 0 | 2 | 30 |
| b | | | |
| c | | | |
| d | | | |
| e | 1 | 2 | 23 |
| f | 1 | 1 | 11 |

### Bolt Meadow

| | | | |
|---|---|---|---|
| 175a | 1 | 2 | 8 |
| b | 0 | 1 | 17 |
| c | 0 | 0 | ? |
| d | 0 | 1 | 2 |

### Warlow Clough

| | | | |
|---|---|---|---|
| 176a | 0 | 7 | 7 |
| b | 1 | 0 | 29 |
| c | 1 | 1 | 31 |

### Oak View

| | | | |
|---|---|---|---|
| 177a | 0 | 3 | 30 |
| b | 0 | 1 | 22 |
| c | 1 | 0 | 3 |
| d | 0 | 0 | 26 |
| e | 0 | 0 | 19 |
| f | | | |
| g | 3 | 1 | 23 |

### Tang Mill

| | | | |
|---|---|---|---|
| 178 | 0 | 1 | 28 |

## Arthurs

| | | | |
|---|---|---|---|
| 179a | 2 | 0 | 25 |
| b | 0 | 0 | 11 |
| c | 0 | 2 | 39 |
| d | 1 | 2 | 37 |
| e | 1 | 2 | 32 |
| f | 1 | 1 | 21 |
| g | 2 | 2 | 1 |
| h | 0 | 0 | 16 |
| i | 1 | 1 | 9 |
| j | 1 | 0 | 23 |
| k | 0 | 3 | 34 |
| l | 0 | 1 | 34 |

## Carr

| | | | |
|---|---|---|---|
| 180a | 1 | 2 | 29 |
| b | 1 | 2 | 1 |
| c | 1 | 2 | 29 |
| d | 1 | 1 | 37 |

## Carr Barn

| | | | |
|---|---|---|---|
| 181a | 2 | 0 | 20 |
| b | 1 | 2 | 16 |
| c | 2 | 1 | 36 |
| d | 1 | 0 | 37 |
| e | | | |
| f | 2 | 0 | 15 |
| g | 0 | 1 | 19 |
| h | 1 | 3 | 12 |
| I | 1 | 3 | 17 |
| J | 1 | 1 | 1 |
| K | 3 | 3 | 38 |

## Gouldburn Clough

| | | | |
|---|---|---|---|
| 182a | 0 | 3 | 32 |
| b | 0 | 2 | 38 |
| c | 1 | 3 | 34 |
| d | 1 | 2 | 37 |

## Shaws

| | | | |
|---|---|---|---|
| 182e | 2 | 0 | 33 |
| f | 0 | 3 | 9 |
| g | | | |
| h | 1 | 1 | 21 |
| I | 1 | 2 | 39 |
| 184a | 1 | 1 | 3 |
| b | 9 | 0 | 18 |
| c | 1 | 0 | 39 |
| d | 0 | 2 | 33 |
| e | 2 | 2 | 39 |
| f | 9 | 3 | 4 |
| 185a | 2 | 3 | 38 |
| c | | | |
| d | 0 | 0 | 3 |
| e | 2 | 0 | 37 |
| f | 0 | 3 | 9 |
| g | 1 | 1 | 19 |
| 186a | 1 | 1 | 36 |
| b | 1 | 2 | 2 |
| c | 1 | 1 | 9 |
| d | 1 | 1 | 18 |
| e | 1 | 1 | 28 |
| f | 0 | 3 | 18 |
| g | 1 | 1 | 26 |
| h | 1 | 1 | 11 |
| I | 3 | 0 | 28 |
| 187 | 1 | 1 | ? |

## Ballgreave

| | | | |
|---|---|---|---|
| 188a | 1 | 1 | 28 |
| b | 1 | 1 | 31 |
| c | 2 | 2 | 10 |
| d | 1 | 1 | 30 |
| e | 0 | 0 | 19 |
| f | 4 | 1 | 18 |
| g | 1 | 0 | 37 |
| h | 1 | 0 | 39 |
| I | 1 | 3 | 26 |
| J | 0 | 3 | 10 |
| 189a | 2 | 2 | 33 |
| b | 1 | 3 | 14 |
| c | 0 | 3 | 1 |
| d, e | | | |

## Uppermill

| | | | |
|---|---|---|---|
| 189f | 2 | 3 | 32 |
| g | 0 | 0 | 20 |
| h | 0 | 0 | 18 |
| i | 0 | 0 | 21 |
| k | 0 | 1 | 3 |
| l | 0 | 0 | 17 |
| m | 0 | 0 | 19 |
| n | 0 | 1 | 23 |
| o | 4 | 3 | 20 |
| o | 0 | 0 | 17 |
| p | 0 | 3 | 4 |
| q | | | |
| r | 1 | 3 | 37 |
| s | 1 | 3 | 28 |
| t | 0 | 3 | 18 |
| u } v } | 1 | 0 | 17 |
| w | 2 | 0 | 16 |

## Giles Mill

| | | | |
|---|---|---|---|
| 190a | 0 | 0 | 26 |
| b | | | |

## Uppermill

| | | | |
|---|---|---|---|
| 191a | | | |
| 192 | 0 | 1 | 14 |
| 193b | 0 | 0 | 17 |
| c | | | |

## Uppermill Methodist Chapel

| | | | |
|---|---|---|---|
| 194a | 0 | 1 | 5 |
| b | 0 | 0 | 14 |

## Uppermill

| | | | |
|---|---|---|---|
| 198a | 0 | 1 | 28 |
| b | 0 | 0 | 38 |
| c | 2 | 1 | 22 |
| d | 2 | 2 | 8 |
| e | 0 | 1 | 35 |
| f | 0 | 1 | 0 |

## Lees's

| | | | |
|---|---|---|---|
| 198g | 2 | 1 | 9 |
| h | 2 | 0 | 39 |
| i | | | |

## Uppermill

| | | | |
|---|---|---|---|
| 198j, k | | | |
| l | 1 | 2 | 8 |
| m | 1 | 3 | 21 |
| n | 0 | 0 | 34 |
| o | 0 | 1 | 26 |
| p | 0 | 2 | 17 |
| q | 0 | 1 | 23 |
| r | 1 | 0 | 9 |
| s | 1 | 0 | 28 |
| t | 2 | 2 | 29 |
| u | | | |
| v | 1 | 3 | 14 |
| w | 1 | 2 | 38 |
| x | | | |
| y | 0 | 2 | 4 |
| z | 0 | 1 | 9 |
| zz | 0 | 1 | 24 |

## Buckley Mill

| | | | |
|---|---|---|---|
| 199a | 0 | 1 | 0 |
| b | 1 | 0 | 32 |

## Bedlam

| | | | |
|---|---|---|---|
| 201a | 0 | 2 | 21 |
| b | 1 | 1 | 6 |
| c | 1 | 0 | 21 |
| d | 0 | 1 | 23 |
| e | 0 | 1 | 38 |
| f | 0 | 3 | 24 |
| g | | | |

## Uppermill

| | | | |
|---|---|---|---|
| 202a | | | |
| b | | | |
| 203a | | | |
| b | | | |
| c | | | |

## Den

| | | | |
|---|---|---|---|
| 204a | 0 | 3 | 36 |
| b | 0 | 2 | 14 |
| c | 0 | 2 | 3 |
| d | 0 | 2 | 25 |
| e | 0 | 2 | 28 |
| f | 0 | 1 | 36 |
| 205a | | | |
| b | | | |
| c | | | |
| d | | | |
| e | | | |
| f | | | |
| g | | | |

## Dunge Booth

| | | | |
|---|---|---|---|
| 206a | | | |
| b | | | |
| c | 1 | 0 | 34 |
| d | | | |
| e | 0 | 3 | 17 |

## Dobcross

| | | | |
|---|---|---|---|
| 207a | 1 | 1 | 20 |
| b | 0 | 1 | 23 |
| c | 0 | 2 | 21 |
| d | | | |
| e | | | |
| f | | | |
| h | | | |
| i | | | |
| j | 1 | 0 | 1 |
| k | 1 | 0 | 36 |
| l | | | |
| m | 2 | 0 | 35 |
| n | 0 | 1 | 17 |
| o | 3 | 0 | 31 |
| p | | | |
| q | 1 | 0 | 7 |

## Bridge House

| | | | |
|---|---|---|---|
| 208a | | | |
| b | | | |
| c | 1 | 1 | 10 |
| d | 1 | 2 | 23 |
| e | 1 | 1 | 38 |
| f | 0 | 1 | 29 |
| g | 1 | 0 | 9 |
| h | 1 | 0 | 9 |
| j | 0 | 3 | 33 |
| k | | | |

## Woolroad

| | | | |
|---|---|---|---|
| 209a | 1 | 0 | 14 |
| b, c, d, e, f, g, h | | | |
| i | 0 | 1 | 4 |
| j | | | |
| k | 0 | 1 | 4 |
| l, m, o, p, q, r, s, t, v | | | |

## Brownhill

| | | | |
|---|---|---|---|
| 210a | 0 | 2 | 15 |
| b | 0 | 3 | 16 |
| c | 0 | 0 | 27 |
| d | | | |
| e | 2 | 0 | 17 |
| f | 1 | 3 | 30 |
| g | 1 | 0 | 39 |
| h | 1 | 0 | 22 |
| i | 0 | 3 | 28 |
| j | 0 | 1 | 11 |
| k | 0 | 2 | 24 |
| l | 0 | 3 | 7 |
| m | 1 | 0 | 18 |
| n | 1 | 0 | 9 |
| o | 1 | 1 | 30 |
| p | | | |
| q | 1 | 1 | 20 |
| r | 0 | 1 | 31 |
| s | 2 | 2 | 31 |
| t | 1 | 2 | 37 |
| u | 0 | 0 | 25 |
| v | 0 | 1 | 8 |
| vv | 0 | 3 | 16 |
| w | 0 | 0 | 9 |

## Saddleworth Fold

| | | | |
|---|---|---|---|
| 211a | 2 | 0 | 16 |
| b | 2 | 1 | 39 |
| c | 0 | 2 | 30 |
| d | 1 | 1 | 30 |
| e | 1 | 3 | 1 |
| f | 1 | 0 | 36 |
| g | 1 | 0 | 26 |
| h | 1 | 3 | 10 |

## Butterhouse

| | | | |
|---|---|---|---|
| 212a | | | |
| b | 0 | 3 | 6 |
| c | 1 | 0 | 20 |
| d | 0 | 2 | 23 |
| e | 2 | 1 | 10 |
| f | 1 | 1 | 25 |
| g | 1 | 2 | 27 |
| h, i | | | |
| j | 1 | 0 | 38 |
| k | 1 | 0 | 6 |
| l | 1 | 2 | 8 |
| m | | | |

## Hollingreave

| | | | |
|---|---|---|---|
| 213a | 6 | 2 | 32 |
| b | 2 | 3 | 39 |
| c | 2 | 2 | 26 |
| d | 1 | 3 | 3 |
| e | 1 | 3 | 23 |
| f | 1 | 2 | 28 |
| g | 1 | 3 | 7 |
| h | | | |
| i | 1 | 2 | 1 |
| j, k, l, m, n, o, p, q, r, s | | | |
| t | 2 | 3 | 29 |
| u | 3 | 0 | 7 |
| v | | | |
| w | 2 | 2 | 0 |
| x | 3 | 3 | 4 |
| y | 1 | 3 | 9 |
| z | 2 | 1 | 1 |
| A | 1 | 0 | 8 |
| B, C | | | |
| D | 1 | 2 | 23 |
| 214 | | | |

## Sherbrook

215a, b, c, d, e, g, h, i

## High Stile

| | | | |
|---|---|---|---|
| 216a, b | | | |
| c | 2 | 2 | 14 |
| d, e | | | |

218a, b, c

219a, b, c, d

## Church Bank Mills

| | | | |
|---|---|---|---|
| 217a | 1 | 2 | 23 |
| b,c, d | | | |

224a, b, c?

## Cloughbottom

| | | | |
|---|---|---|---|
| 220a, b, c, d | | | |
| e | 1 | 2 | 28 |
| f | 1 | 2 | 24 |
| 221a, b | | | |
| c | 2 | 0 | 8 |
| d | 2 | 2 | 39 |
| e | 1 | 0 | 39 |
| f | 0 | 2 | 8 |
| 222a, b, c, d | | | |
| e | 1 | 3 | 1 |
| 223 | | | |

## Saddleworth Church

225

## Butterworth

| | | | |
|---|---|---|---|
| 227a | 2 | 0 | 18 |
| b | 2 | 0 | 28 |
| c | 0 | 2 | 2 |
| d | | | |
| e | 1 | 2 | 27 |
| f | 0 | 2 | 10 |
| g | 1 | 2 | 28 |

## Wool Road

| | | | |
|---|---|---|---|
| 228 | | | |
| 229a | 2 | 1 | 5 |
| b | 1 | 1 | 35 |
| c | | | |
| d | 0 | 1 | 27 |
| e | 1 | 1 | 35 |
| f | 1 | 0 | 33 |
| 230a, b, | | | |
| c | 1 | 0 | 25 |
| d | 1 | 0 | 13 |
| e | 1 | 0 | 2 |
| f | 1 | 0 | 28 |
| g | 1 | 2 | 1 |
| h | 1 | 2 | 36 |
| 233a, c | | | |
| d | 0 | 2 | 29 |

## Marslands

| | | | |
|---|---|---|---|
| 235a, b, c, d, e, f, g, h, i, j | | | |
| k | 1 | 1 | 6 |
| l, m, n | | | |
| 236a | 2 | 1 | 20 |
| b | | | |

237a ,b

## Holden's Smithy

| | | | |
|---|---|---|---|
| 238a | 1 | 1 | 14 |
| b, e, f, g, h, i, j, k, l | | | |

## Nab End

| | | | |
|---|---|---|---|
| 238m | 0 | 1 | 5 |
| n | | | |
| o | 1 | 3 | 35 |
| p | 1 | 1 | 4 |
| q | 1 | 0 | 8 |
| r | 1 | 0 | 37 |

## Parkinsons

| | | | |
|---|---|---|---|
| 238s, t, u, v, w, x, y, z, A, B, C, D | | | |
| 239a | 1 | 0 | 27 |
| b | 1 | 1 | 39 |

## Harrop Edge

240a, b, c, d, e, f, g, h (240a,b,c twice)

## Holden's Smithy

241a, b, c, d, e, g, h, i, j, k, l

## Weakey

242a, b, c

243

## Harrop Edge

244a, b, c, d, e, f

245a, b, c, d, e, f

246a, b, c, d, e, f

| | | | |
|---|---|---|---|
| 247a, b, c, d, e, f, h, | | | |
| j | 1 | 0 | 6 |

248a, b, c, d

249a, b, c

## Round Hill

| | | | |
|---|---|---|---|
| 250a | | | |
| b | 1 | 0 | 36 |
| c | 1 | 1 | 5 |
| d | 1 | 0 | 3 |
| e | 1 | 0 | 55 |
| 251, a, b | | | |
| 252a, b | | | |
| 253a | 1 | 2 | 20 |
| c | 0 | 5 | 34 |
| d, e | | | |

## Platt-Hill

| | | | |
|---|---|---|---|
| 255j | 0 | 3 | 16 |
| k | 0 | 3 | 38 |
| l | 0 | 2 | 4 |
| m | 0 | 2 | 18 |
| n | 0 | 2 | 26 |
| r | 1 | 1 | 10 |
| s | 1 | 0 | 30 |
| t | 1 | 3 | 17 |
| u | 1 | 3 | 34 |
| w | 0 | 2 | 26 |

## Dobcross

| | | | |
|---|---|---|---|
| 257a | | | 7 |
| b | 2 | 0 | 22 |
| c | 1 | 0 | 2 |
| d | 1 | 2 | 33 |
| e | 1 | 2 | 37 |
| f | 2 | 1 | 7 |
| g | 0 | 0 | 18 |
| h | 2 | 1 | 18 |
| i | 0 | 0 | 30 |
| j | 0 | 0 | 36 |
| k | | | |

## Woods

| | | | |
|---|---|---|---|
| 258a, b | | | |
| c | 0 | 2 | 22 |
| d | 0 | 0 | 24 |
| e | 0 | 1 | 9 |
| g | 3 | 2 | 15 |
| h | 4 | 0 | 4 |
| i | 2 | 0 | 9 |
| j, k | | | |
| l | 0 | 2 | 30 |
| m | 1 | 0 | 26 |
| n | 3 | 1 | 19 |
| o | 1 | 1 | 23 |

## Dobcross

260

## Cribb

| | | | |
|---|---|---|---|
| 261a | 1 | 0 | 7 |
| b | 1 | 0 | 16 |

## Manor House

| | | | |
|---|---|---|---|
| 262a | 0 | 0 | 29 |
| b | 0 | 0 | 6 |

## Dobcross Chapel

263

## Dobcross

265

266

267a, b

## Chancery Lane

| | | | |
|---|---|---|---|
| 269a | | | |
| b | 0 | 1 | 32 |
| c | | | |

## Platt Lane

| | | | |
|---|---|---|---|
| 270a | 5 | 0 | 8 |
| b | 1 | 3 | 36 |
| c | 3 | 1 | 30 |
| d | 0 | 0 | 15 |
| e | | | |

## Woods Lane

| | | | |
|---|---|---|---|
| 271 | 0 | 0 | 28 |

272

273

274a b, c

275

276

## Platt Lane

| | | | |
|---|---|---|---|
| 277a | 1 | 0 | 19 |
| b | | | |
| c | 1 | 3 | 4 |
| d | 1 | 1 | 5 |
| e | 0 | 0 | 37 |
| f | 1 | 0 | 19 |
| g | 2 | 0 | 22 |
| h | 0 | 2 | 28 |
| i | | | |
| j | 1 | 0 | 19 |
| l | | | |
| p | 1 | 1 | 1 |

## Midgreave

| | | | |
|---|---|---|---|
| 278c | 0 | 2 | 28 |
| d | 1 | 0 | 10 |
| e, f, g, h, i, | | | |
| j | 1 | 2 | 26 |

## New Delph

| | | | |
|---|---|---|---|
| 279a | 1 | 2 | 15 |
| b | 1 | 1 | 39 |
| c | 1 | 1 | 34 |
| d | 1 | 1 | 25 |
| e | 2 | 0 | 4 |
| f | 1 | 2 | 6 |
| 280a | 1 | 2 | 27 |
| b | 1 | 3 | 37 |
| c | 2 | 0 | 9 |
| d | 1 | 2 | 39 |
| e | 0 | 0 | 22 |
| f | 1 | 2 | 28 |
| g | 1 | 1 | 4 |
| h | 1 | 0 | 6 |
| i | 0 | 3 | 16 |
| j | | | |
| 281c | 0 | 0 | 13 |

282d, e, f

## Bell Inn

| | | | |
|---|---|---|---|
| 283a | 0 | 0 | 28 |
| b | 0 | 2 | 16 |
| c | | | |

## Hill End

| | | | |
|---|---|---|---|
| 284a | 3 | 1 | 27 |
| b | | | |

285a, b, c, d, e, f, g, h, i, j, k, l, ll, m, n

## Delph Barn

286a, b, c, d, e, f

287a, b, c. d

## Delph

288

## Delph Independent Chapel

289a, b

## Delph

290a, b, c

## Delph Methodist Chapel

291

## Sandbed

292a, b, c, d, e

## Dale

293a, b, c, d, e, f, g, h, i, j, k, l, m, n, o, p

## Harrop Edge

294a, b, c, d, e, f

295a, b, c

296a, b

297a, b, c, d, e, f, g

298a, b, c, d, e

## Sandbed

299a, b, c

301a, b. c d

## Intake

300a, b, c

302a, b

## Causeway Sett

303a, b, c, d, e, f

302a, b

## Packhorse

304a, b, c, d, e, f, g, h

305a,b

307

## Waters

306a, b, c, d, e

## Harrop Edge

308a, b, c, d, e

309a, b, c, d, e

315

## Waters Gate

310a, b, c, d, e, f, g, h, i, j, k, l, m

## Bank Gap

311a, b, c, d, e, f, g, h, i, j

## Carr Head

312a, b, c, d, e, f, g

314a, b, c, d, e, f

## Carr

313a, b, c, d, e, f, g, h, i. j. k. l

## Thorns

316a, b, c, d, e, f, g, h, i. j. k. l, m , n o, p, q, r, s, t, u, v, w, x

## Sunfield

316y, z, A, B, C, D, E, F, G, H, I, J, K, L, M, N, O,      P, Q

## Little Moor

316R, S, T, U, V, W

## Yew Tree

317a, b, c, d,e, f, g, h, j, k, l, m, n

## Ridge

318a, b, c, d,e, f, g

## Thorns

319a, b

## Oakenhill

| | | | |
|---|---|---|---|
| 1a | 80 | 2 | 35 |
| b | 12 | 0 | 16 |
| c | 1 | 3 | 26 |
| d | 4 | 1 | 23 |
| e | | | |
| f | 3 | 0 | 11 |
| g | 0 | 3 | 2 |
| h | 3 | 2 | ? |
| i | 0 | 2 | 30 |
| j | 2 | 2 | 10 |
| k | 4 | 1 | 11 |

## Castleshaw

| | | | |
|---|---|---|---|
| ll | 8 | 1 | 26 |
| ll | | | |
| m | 4 | 1 | 30 |
| n | 1 | 3 | 36 |
| o | 20 | 2 | 1 |
| p | 4 | 0 | 10 |
| q | 2 | 1 | 15 |
| r | 3 | 2 | 2 |
| s | 0 | 3 | 11 |
| t | | | |

## Broadhead

| | | | |
|---|---|---|---|
| u | 22 | 3 | 5 |
| v | 17 | 2 | 21 |
| w | 2 | 1 | ? |
| x | 2 | 2 | 22 |
| y | 2 | 0 | 35 |
| z | 2 | 2 | 27 |
| A | 4 | 0 | 21 |
| B | 4 | 0 | 21 |
| C | | | |
| D | 2 | 0 | 39 |
| E | 3 | 2 | 32 |
| F | 2 | 0 | 23 |
| G | 1 | 3 | 19 |
| H | 2 | 0 | 10 |
| I | 1 | 3 | 36 |
| J | 3 | 3 | 2 |
| K | 1 | 1 | 27 |
| L | 2 | 1 | 2 |
| M | 2 | 1 | 12 |
| N | 1 | 1 | 13 |

## Oaken Hill Lee

| | | | |
|---|---|---|---|
| 2a | 6 | 3 | 21 |
| b | 1 | 1 | 21 |
| c | 7 | 1 | 37 |
| d | 21 | 0 | 35 |
| e | 1 | 2 | 24 |
| f | 3 | ? | 37 |
| 3a | 1 | 2 | 36 |
| b | 1 | 2 | 2 |
| c | 1 | 1 | 27 |
| d | 7 | 3 | 39 |
| e | 1 | 1 | 10 |
| f | 13 | 3 | 14 |

## Marled Earth

| | | | |
|---|---|---|---|
| 3h? | 0 | 1 | 24 |
| i | 4 | 3 | 33 |
| j | | | |
| k | 1 | 2 | 26 |
| l | 1 | 3 | 25 |

## Husteads

| | | | |
|---|---|---|---|
| 4a | 2 | 1 | 11 |
| b | 0 | 3 | 27 |
| c | 2 | 3 | 19 |
| d | 1 | 1 | 25 |
| e | 0 | 0 | 31 |

## Bleak Hey Nook

| | | | |
|---|---|---|---|
| 5 | 2 | 1 | 13 |
| 6a | 3 | 2 | 17 |
| b | 3 | 0 | 25 |

## Higher Castleshaw

| | | | |
|---|---|---|---|
| 7a | 1 | 3 | 5 |
| b | 1 | 3 | 34 |
| c | 3 | 2 | 36 |
| d | 1 | 3 | 0 |
| e | 1 | 2 | 20 |
| f | 1 | 2 | 36 |

## Castleshaw School

| | | | |
|---|---|---|---|
| 8 | 0 | 0 | 16 |

## Black Heys

| | | | |
|---|---|---|---|
| 9a | | | |
| b | 3 | 1 | 10 |
| c | 3 | 0 | 20 |
| d | 2 | 3 | 17 |
| e | 1 | 2 | 12 |
| f | 3 | 2 | 10 |
| g | 1 | 0 | 10 |
| h | 2 | 2 | 33 |

## Waters

10a, b, c, d, e, f, g, h

## Castleshaw

| | | | |
|---|---|---|---|
| 11a | 2 | 3 | 2 |
| b | 2 | 2 | 4 |
| c | 2 | 2 | 30 |
| d | 0 | 2 | 35 |
| e | 2 | 1 | 36 |
| f | 2 | 0 | 22 |
| g | 1 | 0 | 2 |
| h | 2 | 0 | 8 |

## Waters Mill

12

## Waters

13

## Castle Hill

14a, b, c, d, e, f, g, h, i, j, k, l, m, n, o, p

| | | | |
|---|---|---|---|
| q | 2 | 1 | 37 |
| 15a | 3 | 2 | 1 |
| b | | | |
| c | 2 | 3 | 4 |

## Bank

16a, b, c, d, e, f, g, h, i, j, k, l, m, n, o, p, q, r, s, t u,

## Wood Barn

17a, b, c, d, e, f

| | | | |
|---|---|---|---|
| g | 1 | 2 | 24 |
| h | 2 | 1 | 27 |

## Castle Hill

18a

## Oxhey

| | | | |
|---|---|---|---|
| 18b,c | 23 | 1 | 21 |

## Low Gate

| | | | |
|---|---|---|---|
| 19a | 1 | 2 | 20 |
| b | 1 | 2 | 21 |
| c | 1 | 1 | 16 |
| d | 1 | 1 | 30 |
| e | 0 | 1 | 17 |
| f | 1 | 1 | 26 |
| g | 2 | 2 | 26 |
| h | 2 | 3 | 34 |
| i | 2 | 2 | 4 |

## Wood

| | | | |
|---|---|---|---|
| 20a | 1 | 2 | 7 |
| b | 2 | 0 | 10 |
| c | 3 | 0 | 31 |
| d | 1 | 1 | 18 |
| e | | | |
| f | 1 | 2 | 13 |
| g | 1 | 3 | 22 |
| h | 0 | 2 | 11 |
| i | 0 | 1 | 15 |
| j | 0 | 2 | 5 |
| k | 4 | 0 | 19 |
| l | 1 | 2 | 27 |
| m | 2 | 2 | 19 |
| n | 2 | 0 | 16 |
| o | 1 | 3 | 12 |
| p | 1 | 3 | 4 |
| q | 0 | 3 | 0 |
| r | 1 | 1 | 13 |

## Moorcroft Wood

20s, t, u, v, w, x

## Millcroft

21a, b, c d, e, f, g, h, i

## Oxhey

21j, k, l, m

## Long Royd Mill

21n, o

## Oxhey

21p, q, r, s, t

| | | | |
|---|---|---|---|
| 22a | 1 | 1 | 36 |
| b | 0 | 1 | 2 |
| c | 1 | 1 | 6 |
| d | 1 | 1 | 6 |
| e | 1 | 0 | 37 |
| f | 1 | 2 | 5 |
| g | 1 | 0 | 3 |

## New Year's Bridge Mill

| | | | |
|---|---|---|---|
| 23a | 1 | 1 | 21 |
| b | 1 | 1 | 15 |
| c | 1 | 3 | 17 |
| d | | | |
| e | 1 | 1 | 19 |
| f | 1 | 2 | 22 |
| g | 2 | 1 | 28 |
| h | 0 | 3 | 0 |

## Oxhey

24a, b, c, d, e, f, g, h, i, j

## Broad Meadow

24k, l, m, n, o, p

## Upper Broadmeadow

25a, b, c d, e, f, g

## Oxhey

| | | | |
|---|---|---|---|
| 26a | 1 | 1 | 34 |
| b | 1 | 1 | 16 |
| c | 1 | 2 | 29 |
| d | 4 | 0 | 8 |
| e | 1 | 1 | 10 |
| f | 3 | 1 | 8 |
| g | 0 | 3 | 28 |
| h | 0 | 3 | 3 |

## Knowl

| | | | |
|---|---|---|---|
| 26i | 1 | 1 | 30 |
| j | 3 | 0 | 7 |
| k | 3 | 2 | 30 |
| l | 2 | 1 | 6 |
| m | 2 | 2 | 38 |

## Oxhey

| | | | |
|---|---|---|---|
| 27a | 1 | 1 | 16 |
| b | 1 | 1 | 26 |
| c | 0 | 3 | 6 |
| d | 6 | 1 | 37 |
| e | 4 | 1 | 10 |

## Crawshaw Hey

| | | | |
|---|---|---|---|
| 27ee | 82 | 1 | 9 |

## Slack Gate

27g, h, i, j, k, l, m, n

## Broadmeadow

28a, b, c,

## Hey

29a, b, c, d, e, f, g

30a, b, c, d, e

## Lower Lockwood Hey

31a, b, c, d, e

## Hey

32a, b, c, d, e

## Upper Lockwood Hey

33

## Moorcroft

34a, b, c, d, e, f, g

## Bucknam Pitts

35

## Millcroft

36a, b, c, d, e, f, g, h, j

## Upper Grange

37a, b, c, d, e, f, g

## Moorcroft

38a, b, c, d, e

39a, b

## Upper Grange

40a, b, c, d

## Grange

42a, b, c, d, e, f, g, h, i, j

43a, b

44a, b, c, d, e, f, g

45a, b, c

46b

## Upper Grange

47a, b, c, d

## Ridings

| | | | |
|---|---|---|---|
| 48a | 0 | 1 | 14 |
| b | 1 | 1 | 34 |
| c | 2 | 1 | 32 |

## Liffrey Ditch

49a, b, c, d, e

## Old Hey

50a, b

51a, b, c, d, e

## Causeway Sett

52a, b, c, d, e

53a, b

## Hull Mill

54a, b

## Delph

55a, b, c, d, e, f, g, h, i, j, k, l,

| | | | |
|---|---|---|---|
| m | 1 | 1 | ? |

n, o, p, q, r, s, t, u, v, w, x, y, y1, y2, z, A, B,

| | | | |
|---|---|---|---|
| C | 3 | 1 | 19 |
| D | 2 | 3 | 27 |

E, F, G, H, I, J, K

## Springwood

56

## Carr Coat

| | | | |
|---|---|---|---|
| 57a | 0 | 0 | 31 |
| b | 0 | 2 | 13 |
| c | 2 | 3 | 2 |
| d | | | |
| e | 1 | 1 | 31 |
| f, g | | | |

## Friar Lodge

58c, d

## Linfitts Slack

59a, b

## New Barn

60a, b, c, d, e, f, g, h, i, j, jj, k, l, m, n, o, p

## Higher Slack

60q, r, s, t, u, v, w

## Heights

61?

## Linfitts Slack

62a, b, c, d, e, f

## Well Head

63a, b, c, d, e

## Heights

64a, b

65?

66a, b

## Heights Chapel

67

## Barn

68a, b, c, d, e, f, g

## New Tame

69a, aa, b, bb, c, d, e, f, g, h, i, j

69l, m, n, nn, o, p, q, r, s, t, u, U, V, W, X, Y, Z

## Old Field

69v, w, x, y, z

## Summerhill

69A, B, C, D, E, F, G, H, I, J, K, L, M, MM, N

## Marled Earth

69O, P, Q. R. S, T

## Slack

70a, b, c, d, e, f, g

71a, b, c, d, e,

## New Barn

72a, b

| | | | |
|---|---|---|---|
| c | 6 | 0 | 11 |
| d | 2 | 0 | 0 |
| e | 2 | 2 | 38 |
| f | 2 | 3 | 32 |
| g | 2 | 1 | 16 |
| h | 1 | 2 | 12 |

| | | | |
|---|---|---|---|
| i | 2 | 2 | 34 |
| j | 2 | 3 | 16 |
| k, l | | | |
| m | 1 | 2 | 35 |
| n | | | |
| o | 3 | 1 | 36 |
| p | 1 | 1 | 39 |
| q | 1 | 1 | 34 |
| r | 2 | 2 | 11 |
| s | 1 | 1 | 32 |
| t | 1 | 2 | 24 |

## Lower Barn

73a, b, c, d, e

| | | | |
|---|---|---|---|
| f | 2 | 1 | 2 |
| g | 1 | 0 | 37 |
| h | 1 | 1 | 1 |

## Linfitts

74a, b, c, d

| | | | |
|---|---|---|---|
| e | 3 | 3 | 4 |
| f | 2 | 0 | 1 |
| g | | | |
| h | 2 | 3 | 23 |
| i, j, k | | | |
| l | 3 | 0 | 38 |
| m, n | | | |
| o | 1 | 0 | 4 |
| p | 2 | 1 | 32 |
| q | | | |
| r | 0 | 3 | 9 |
| s | 1 | 2 | 18 |
| t, u, v | | | |

75a, b

| | | | |
|---|---|---|---|
| c | 2 | 1 | 20 |
| d | 2 | 0 | 27 |

| | | | |
|---|---|---|---|
| 76a | 4 | 1 | 29 |
| b | 2 | 0 | 32 |
| c | 2 | 0 | 19 |
| d | 2 | 2 | 2 |
| e | 0 | 3 | 31 |

| | | | |
|---|---|---|---|
| 78a | 1 | 0 | 0 |
| b | 0 | 2 | 13 |
| c | 4 | 2 | 29 |
| d | 1 | 1 | 7 |
| e | 1 | 1 | 32 |
| f | | | |
| g | 0 | 3 | 20 |
| h | 1 | 0 | 28 |
| i | 1 | 0 | 16 |
| j | 0 | 2 | 32 |
| k | 1 | 2 | 11 |
| l | 6 | 2 | 16 |
| m | | | |
| n | 4 | 0 | 0 |

## Tamecroft

| | | | |
|---|---|---|---|
| 78o | 3 | 1 | 18 |
| p | 4 | 1 | 7 (with 78bb) |
| q | 1 | 0 | 20 |
| r | 0 | 3 | 32 |
| s | 0 | 3 | 7 |
| t | 2 | 1 | 7 |
| u | 2 | 0 | 21 |
| v | | | |
| w | 0 | 3 | 0 |
| x | 5 | 0 | 24 |
| y | 2 | 1 | 14 |
| z | 4 | 2 | 16 |
| aa | 5 | 0 | 28 |
| cc | | | |
| dd | 1 | 1 | 23 |

## Bank Field

| | | | |
|---|---|---|---|
| 78A | 1 | 1 | 18 |
| B | 2 | 2 | 25 |

## Birchin Bank

| | | | |
|---|---|---|---|
| 78C | 3 | 1 | 1 |
| D | 3 | 3 | 4 |
| E | 3 | 0 | 7 |
| F | 4 | 2 | 6 |
| G | 1 | 3 | 21 |
| H | 1 | 0 | 32 |
| I | 1 | 0 | 13 |
| J | 1 | 3 | 20 |

## Coatman Heights

| | | | |
|---|---|---|---|
| 78K | 1 | 1 | 14 |
| L | 1 | 2 | 29 |
| M | 1 | 1 | 22 |
| N | 1 | 3 | 2 |

## Coatmans

| | | | |
|---|---|---|---|
| 78O | 1 | 1 | 12 |
| P | 0 | 2 | 26 |
| Q | 4 | 3 | 24 |
| R | 3 | 3 | 12 |
| S | 5 | 3 | 21 |
| T | 2 | 3 | 24 |
| U | 2 | 0 | 33 |

## Grains

| | | | |
|---|---|---|---|
| 78V | 3 | 1 | 16 |
| W | 3 | 2 | 2 |
| X | 5 | 0 | 30 |
| Y | 0 | 3 | 28 |
| Z | 1 | 2 | 34 |

## Hey Barn

| | | | |
|---|---|---|---|
| 79a | 9 | 2 | 8 |
| b | 0 | 2 | 34 |
| c | 1 | 3 | 28 |
| d | 2 | 2 | 0 |
| e | 4 | 3 | 13 |
| f | 3 | 0 | 4 |
| g | 1 | 3 | 1 |

## Further Heys

| | | | |
|---|---|---|---|
| 80a | 0 | 3 | 12 |
| b | 2 | 0 | 5 |
| c, d, e | 4 | 1 | 3 |

## Lower Hill Top

| | | | |
|---|---|---|---|
| 80f | 1 | 1 | 12 |
| g | 2 | 2 | 21 |
| h | 0 | 0 | 29 |
| i | 1 | 1 | 18 |
| j | 1 | 2 | 28 |
| k | 3 | 3 | 10 |
| l | | | |
| m | 1 | 3 | 2 |
| n | 1 | 3 | 18 |
| o | 1 | 0 | 9 |
| p | 1 | 2 | 36 |
| q | 1 | 3 | 16 |

## Beswicks

| | | | |
|---|---|---|---|
| 81a | 0 | 3 | 33 |
| b | 1 | 1 | 10 |
| c | 1 | 2 | 11 |
| d | 1 | 3 | 26 |
| e | 1 | 1 | 23 |
| f | 0 | 3 | 32 |
| g | 2 | 0 | 10 |
| h | 1 | 2 | 25 |
| i | 0 | 3 | 24 |
| j | 1 | 2 | 24 |
| k | 2 | 0 | 12 |
| l | 2 | 0 | 6 |
| m | 1 | 2 | 28 |
| n, o | | | |

## Heys

| | | | |
|---|---|---|---|
| 82a | 1 | 1 | 32 |
| b | 1 | 0 | 25 |
| c | 2 | 2 | 30 |
| d | 0 | 1 | 20 |
| e | 1 | 0 | 0 |
| f | 2 | 0 | 15 |
| g | 1 | 3 | 14 |
| h | 1 | 0 | 18 |

## Garners

| | | | |
|---|---|---|---|
| 83a | 2 | 1 | 2 |
| b | 2 | 1 | 13 |
| c | 1 | 2 | 37 |
| d | 1 | 1 | 2 |
| e | 4 | 2 | 12 |
| f | 0 | 1 | 27 |
| 84a | 2 | 0 | 0 |
| b | 2 | 0 | 3 |
| c | | | |
| d | 1 | 0 | 23 |
| e | 1 | 1 | 18 |
| f | 1 | 0 | 0 |
| g | 1 | 0 | 34 |

## Heys

| | | | |
|---|---|---|---|
| 85a | 1 | 3 | 30 |
| b | 0 | 3 | 26 |
| c | 1 | 3 | 33 |
| e | 1 | 2 | 15 |
| f | 1 | 0 | 16 |
| g | 1 | 0 | 17 |

## Pingle Mill

86a, b

## Woodmans

| | | | |
|---|---|---|---|
| 87a | 2 | 3 | 28 |
| aa | 0 | 0 | 25 |
| b | 1 | 1 | 23 |
| c | 0 | 3 | 37 |
| d | 1 | 0 | 17 |
| e | 1 | 3 | 12 |
| f | 0 | 3 | 13 |
| g | 0 | 2 | 21 |
| 88a | 1 | 1 | 18 |
| b | 0 | 3 | 31 |
| c | 1 | 0 | 6 |
| d | 1 | 0 | 36 |
| e | 0 | 2 | 7 |
| f | 1 | 0 | 9 |
| g | 1 | 3 | 13 |
| i | 0 | 3 | 17 |

## Hill Top

| | | | |
|---|---|---|---|
| 89a | 4 | 3 | 20 |
| b | 1 | 0 | 24 |
| c | 1 | 0 | 3 |
| d | 0 | 2 | 9 |
| e | 1 | 1 | 5 |
| f | 1 | 1 | 5 |
| g | 0 | 3 | 29 |

## Knot Hill

| | | | |
|---|---|---|---|
| 90a | 1 | 2 | 29 |
| b | 1 | 0 | 5 |
| c | 0 | 1 | 33 |
| d | 1 | 1 | 26 |
| e | 0 | 1 | 0 |
| f | 0 | 2 | 12 |
| g | 1 | 0 | 32 |
| h | 0 | 3 | 2 |
| i | 1 | 3 | 26 |
| j | 1 | 0 | 27 |
| k | 3 | 1 | 3 |
| 91a | 0 | 2 | 0 |
| b | 1 | 1 | 2 |
| c | 2 | 0 | 26 |
| d | 0 | 1 | 16 |
| e | 1 | 1 | 16 |
| f | | | |

## Woodhouse

| | | | |
|---|---|---|---|
| 92a | 0 | 0 | 21 |
| b | 1 | 0 | 20 |
| c | 0 | 3 | 26 |
| d | | | |
| e | 0 | 3 | 16 |
| f | 1 | 1 | 16 |
| g | 0 | 2 | 4 |
| h | 1 | 1 | 13 |
| i | 0 | 3 | 27 |
| j | | | |
| k | 1 | 0 | 19 |
| l | 2 | 3 | 24 |
| m, n | | | |
| 94b | 1 | 1 | 2 |
| c | 0 | 1 | 31 |
| d | 0 | 1 | 33 |
| e | 0 | 2 | 17 |
| f | 1 | 2 | 18 |
| g | 0 | 1 | 30 |
| h | 0 | 0 | 31 |
| i | 1 | 0 | 6 |
| j | 0 | 2 | 35 |
| k | 0 | 3 | 24 |
| l | 0 | 2 | 30 |
| m | 0 | 3 | 26 |

## Hanson House

| | | | |
|---|---|---|---|
| 95a | 7 | 0 | 34 |
| b | 1 | 3 | 34 |
| c | | | |
| d | 1 | 1 | 4 |
| e | 1 | 3 | 30 |
| f | 1 | 2 | 36 |
| g | 6 | 1 | 6 |

## Hanson House

| | | | |
|---|---|---|---|
| 96a | 2 | 3 | 31 |
| b | 1 | 2 | 24 |
| c | 3 | 3 | 9 |
| d | 0 | 3 | 20 |
| e | 1 | 0 | 15 |

## Ramsclough

| | | | |
|---|---|---|---|
| 97a | 7 | 0 | 6 |
| b | 1 | 2 | 11 |
| c | 1 | 1 | 31 |
| d | 2 | 1 | 12 |
| e | 0 | 2 | 27 |
| f | 1 | 3 | 3 |
| g | 1 | 0 | 24 |
| h | 6 | 3 | 26 |

## Dodle

| | | | |
|---|---|---|---|
| 98a | 1 | 0 | 7 |
| b | 2 | 0 | 22 |
| c | 1 | 0 | 22 |
| d | 3 | 1 | 0 |

## Grains

| | | | |
|---|---|---|---|
| 99a | 2 | 0 | 12 |
| b | 2 | 1 | 28 |
| c | 4 | 0 | 18 |
| d | 2 | 1 | 16 |
| e | 4 | 0 | 9 |

## Mantley Gate

| | | | |
|---|---|---|---|
| 100a | 1 | 3 | 32 |
| b | 1 | 0 | 7 |
| c | 1 | 1 | 32 |
| d | 1 | 3 | 8 |
| e | 2 | 2 | 26 |
| f | 2 | 2 | 16 |
| g | 2 | 2 | 24 |
| h | 2 | 1 | 1 |
| i | 1 | 1 | 27 |
| j | 0 | 1 | 10 |
| 101a | 1 | 1 | 27 |

## Hethey Hill

| | | | |
|---|---|---|---|
| 102a | 3 | 0 | 5 |
| b | 2 | 1 | 5 |
| c | 1 | 1 | 2 |
| e | 1 | 1 | 24 |
| 103a | 1 | 1 | 29 |
| b | 3 | 1 | 23 |
| c, d | | | |

## Hollin Bank

| | | | |
|---|---|---|---|
| 104a | 2 | 0 | 10 |
| aa | 1 | 0 | 23 |
| b | 0 | 3 | 23 |
| c | 1 | 1 | 14 |
| d | 2 | 0 | 17 |
| e | 1 | 0 | 10 |
| f | 1 | 0 | 24 |
| g | 1 | 0 | 1 |
| h | 0 | 3 | 22 |
| i | 3 | 2 | 4 |

## Old Tame

| | | | |
|---|---|---|---|
| 105a | 2 | 3 | 13 |
| b | 4 | 1 | 6 |
| c, d, e, f, ff, g, h, i, j, k, l, m | | | |

## Horest

106a, b, c

107a, b, c, d

## Old Tame

108a, b, c, d, e

109a, b, c, d, e, f

## Stile House

110a, b, c, d, e, f

## Woodbrow
111a, b, c, d, e, f, g, h, i, j, k, l, m, n

## Calf Hey
112a, b, c, d, e

## Whitehead Mill
113a, b, c, d, e

## Brownhill Naze
114a, b, c, d, e, f

## Boothstead Edge
115a, b, c, d

## Cherry Clough
116a, b, c, d, e, f, g, h, i, j, k, l

117a, b, c, d, e, f

118a, b, c

119a, b, c, d, e, f, g

120a, b, c, d, e, f, g

121a, b, c
| d | 2 | 3 | 1 |
|---|---|---|---|

e, f, g, h

## Boothsteads
122a, b, c, d, e, f, g

## Dumfries
123a, b, c, d, e, f, g, h

## Brown Hill Naze
124a, b, c, d,

## Marsh
124e
| f | 6 | 0 | 12 |
|---|---|---|---|
| g | 3 | 0 | 34 |

## Denshaw
124h, i, j, k, l, m
| n | 2 | 2 | 17 |
|---|---|---|---|
| o | 2 | 1 | 4 |

## Back o'th Hill
| 124p | 11 | 0 | 15 |
|---|---|---|---|
| q | 4 | 0 | 21 |
| r | 2 | 0 | 20 |
| s | 1 | 1 | 31 |
| t | 7 | 0 | 20 |
| u | 4 | 0 | 0 |
| v | 2 | 1 | 19 |
| w | 1 | 2 | 27 |

## Denshaw Moor
124x

## Denshaw
125a, b
| c | 11 | 1 | 21 (with 126d) |
|---|---|---|---|
| d | 3 | 1 | 3 |
| e | 1 | 1 | 3 |
| f | 2 | 0 | 24 |

g, h, i, j, k

126a, b, c,
| d | 11 | 1 | 21 (with 125c) |
|---|---|---|---|

e, ee, ff

127a, b, c, d, dd

## Hey House
| 127e | 4 | 2 | 35 |
|---|---|---|---|
| f | 1 | 3 | 4 |
| g | 1 | 3 | 20 |
| h | 3 | 0 | 30 |
| i | 14 | 0 | 5 |
| j | 1 | 2 | 4 |
| k | 4 | 3 | 13 |

## Dorey
| 127l | 3 | 0 | 26 |
|---|---|---|---|
| m | 2 | 1 | 19 |
| n | 3 | 2 | 4 |
| o | 7 | 1 | 10 |
| p | 0 | 0 | 30 |
| q | 1 | 1 | 5 |
| r | 9 | 2 | 0 |

| 128a | 3 | 0 | 0 |
|---|---|---|---|
| b | | | |
| c | 1 | 1 | 34 |
| d | 1 | 2 | 8 |
| e | 3 | 2 | 24 |
| f | 4 | 1 | 27 |
| g | 1 | 3 | 13 |
| h | 5 | 0 | 5 |

| 129a | 3 | 2 | 3 |
|---|---|---|---|
| b | | | |
| c | 1 | 1 | 24 |
| d | 1 | 1 | 20 |
| e | 2 | 3 | 0 |
| f | 6 | 3 | 5 |
| g | 3 | 3 | 23 |
| h | 2 | 3 | 36 |

## Bowk House
130a, b
| c | 5 | 1 | 13 |
|---|---|---|---|
| d | 2 | 3 | 3 |
| e | 2 | 0 | 38 |
| f | 0 | 3 | 22 |
| g | 1 | 3 | 38 |
| h | 1 | 2 | 33 |
| i | 2 | 2 | 30 |
| j | 1 | 2 | 10 |
| k | 2 | 0 | 29 |
| l | 6 | 3 | 32 |

## Dorey
| 130m | 5 | 1 | 12 |
|---|---|---|---|
| n | 3 | 2 | 22 |
| o | 12 | 0 | 15 |
| p | 9 | 3 | 1 |
| q | 13 | 1 | 4 |
| r | 2 | 1 | 0 |
| s | 2 | 1 | 0 |

## Rough Hey
| 131a | 2 | 2 | 4 |
|---|---|---|---|
| b | | | |
| c | 5 | 3 | 35 |
| d | 2 | 2 | 23 |
| e | 3 | 1 | 15 |
| f | 1 | 1 | 10 |
| g | 1 | 3 | 32 |

## Ralphs
| 132a | 1 | 2 | 35 |
|---|---|---|---|
| b | 1 | 2 | 3 |
| c | 1 | 1 | 18 |
| d | 1 | 0 | 35 |

e, f, g, h
| i | 1 | 1 | 0 |
|---|---|---|---|

## Range
133a, b
| d | 1 | 1 | 0 |
|---|---|---|---|

## Denshaw
134a, b

## Junction
135a, b, c, d, e, f , g

## Brown Hill Naze
136a, b, c

## Rough Hey Side
| 137a | 3 | 1 | 0 |
|---|---|---|---|
| b | 0 | 0 | 28 |
| c | 0 | 1 | 11 |
| d | 1 | 1 | 3 |

| 138a | 0 | 2 | 24 |
|---|---|---|---|
| b | 1 | 1 | 4 |
| c | 1 | 2 | 0 |
| d | | | |

| e | | | |
|---|---|---|---|
| f | 2 | 1 | 8 |
| g | 2 | 2 | 1 |
| h | 4 | 1 | 12 |

## Sun Inn
| 139a | 0 | 2 | 37 |
|---|---|---|---|
| b | 2 | 1 | 2 |
| c | | | |
| d | 1 | 3 | 7 |

## Brimmy Croft
| 140a | | | |
|---|---|---|---|
| b | 12 | 3 | 17 |
| c | 3 | 2 | 27 |
| d | 2 | 3 | 15 |
| e | 10 | 0 | 33 |
| f | 8 | 2 | 35 |
| g | 0 | 1 | 9 |
| h | 8 | 0 | 0 |
| i | 1 | 3 | 21 |
| j | 3 | 3 | 22 |
| k | 8 | 1 | 31 |

## Denshaw Moor
| 140l | 21 | 2 | 32 |
|---|---|---|---|
| m | 9 | 1 | 28 |
| n | 21 | 1 | 38 |

| 141a | 3 | 3 | 12 |
|---|---|---|---|
| b | 5 | 0 | 29 |

| 142 | 13 | 0 | 28 |
|---|---|---|---|

## Rag Stones
| 143a | 2 | 3 | 11 |
|---|---|---|---|
| b | 14 | 3 | 6 |
| c | 6 | 3 | 18 |